HEADS OF FAMILIES

AT THE FIRST CENSUS OF THE UNITED STATES TAKEN IN THE YEAR 1790

VERMONT

Originally published: Government Printing Office
Washington, D.C., 1907
Reprinted: Genealogical Publishing Co., Inc.
Baltimore, 1966, 1975, 1992
Library of Congress Catalogue Card Number 75-988
International Standard Book Number 0-8063-0343-3
Made in the United States of America

HEADS OF FAMILIES AT THE FIRST CENSUS

1790

INTRODUCTION.

The First Census of the United States (1790) comprised an enumeration of the inhabitants of the present states of Connecticut, Delaware, Georgia, Kentucky, Maine, Maryland, Massachusetts, New Hampshire, New Jersey, New York, North Carolina, Pennsylvania, Rhode Island, South Carolina, Tennessee, Vermont, and Virginia. The law which authorized this enumeration appears on page 6.

A complete set of the schedules for each state, with a summary for the counties, and in many cases for towns, was filed in the State Department, but unfortunately they are not now complete, the returns for the states of Delaware, Georgia, Kentucky, New Jersey, Tennessee, and Virginia having been destroyed when the British burned the Capitol at Washington during the War of 1812.

These schedules form a unique inheritance for the Nation, since they represent for each of the states concerned a complete list of the heads of families in the United States at the time of the adoption of the Constitution. The framers were the statesmen and leaders of thought, but those whose names appear upon the schedules of the First Census were in general the plain citizens who by their conduct in war and peace made the Constitution possible and by their intelligence and self-restraint put it into successful operation.

The total population of the United States in 1790, exclusive of slaves, as derived from the schedules, was 3,231,533. The only names appearing upon the schedules, however, were those of heads of families, and as at that period the families averaged 6 persons, the total number was approximately 540,000, or slightly more than half a million. The number of names which is now lacking because of the destruction of the schedules is approximately 140,000, thus leaving schedules containing about 400,000 names.

The information contained in the published report of the First Census of the United States, a small volume of 56 pages, was not uniform for the several states and territories. For New England and one or two of the other states the population was presented by counties and towns, that of New Jersey appeared partly by counties and towns and partly by counties only; in other cases the returns were given by counties only. Thus the complete transcript of the names of heads of families, with accompanying information, would present for the first time detailed information as to the number of inhabitants—males, females, etc.—for each minor civil division in all those states for which such information was not originally published.

In response to repeated requests from patriotic societies and persons interested in genealogy, or desirous of studying the early history of the United States, Congress added to the sundry civil appropriation bill for the fiscal year 1907 the following paragraph:

> The Director of the Census is hereby authorized and directed to publish, in a permanent form, by counties and minor civil divisions, the names of the heads of families returned at the First Census of the United States in seventeen hundred and ninety; and the Director of the Census is authorized, in his discretion, to sell said publications, the proceeds thereof to be covered into the Treasury of the United States, to be deposited to the credit of miscellaneous receipts on account of "Proceeds of sales of Government property:"
>
> *Provided,* That no expense shall be incurred hereunder additional to appropriations for the Census Office for printing therefor made for the fiscal year nineteen hundred and seven; and the Director of the Census is hereby directed to report to Congress at its next session the cost incurred hereunder and the price fixed for said publications and the total received therefor.

The amount of money appropriated by Congress for the Census printing for the fiscal year mentioned was unfortunately not sufficient to meet the current requirement of the Office and to publish the transcription of the First Census, and no provision was made in the sundry civil appropriation bill for 1908 for the continuance of authority to publish these important records beyond the present fiscal year. Resources, however, are available for publishing a small section of the work, and the schedules of New Hampshire, Vermont, and Maryland have been selected. In these states the names of heads of families in 1790 were limited in number, and the records are in a condition which makes transcription comparatively easy. In the following pages all the information is presented which appears upon these schedules, and the sequence of the names is that followed by the enumerator in making his report.

It is to be hoped that Congress will again grant authority and money for the publication of the remaining schedules, in order that the entire series, so far as it exists, may be complete. For several of the states for which schedules are lacking it is probable that the Director of the Census could obtain lists which would present the names of most of the heads of families at the date of the First Census. In Virginia, for example, a state enumeration was made in 1785, of which some of the original schedules are still in existence. These would be likely to prove a reasonably satisfactory substitute for the Federal list made five years later.

THE FIRST CENSUS.

The First Census act was passed at the second session of the First Congress, and was signed by President Washington on March 1, 1790. The task of making the first enumeration of inhabitants was placed upon the President. Under this law the marshals of the several judicial districts were required to ascertain the number of inhabitants within their respective districts, omitting Indians not taxed, and distinguishing free persons (including those bound to service for a term of years); the sex and color of free persons; and the number of free males 16 years of age and over.

The object of the inquiry last mentioned was, undoubtedly, to obtain definite knowledge as to the military and industrial strength of the country. This fact possesses special interest, because the Constitution directs merely an enumeration of inhabitants. Thus the demand for increasingly extensive information, which has been so marked a characteristic of census legislation, began with the First Congress that dealt with the subject.

The method followed by the President in putting into operation the First Census law, although the object of extended investigation, is not definitely known. It is supposed that the President or the Secretary of State dispatched copies of the law, and perhaps of instructions also, to the marshals. There is, however, some ground for disputing this conclusion. At least one of the reports in the census volume of 1790 was furnished by a governor. This, together with the fact that there is no record of correspondence with the marshals on the subject of the census, but that there is a record of such correspondence with the governors, makes very strong the inference that the marshals received their instructions through the governors of the states. This inference is strengthened by the fact that in 1790 the state of Massachusetts furnished the printed blanks, and also by the fact that the law relating to the Second Census specifically charged the Secretary of State to superintend the enumeration and to communicate directly with the marshals.

By the terms of the First Census law nine months were allowed in which to complete the enumeration. The census taking was supervised by the marshals of the several judicial districts, who employed assistant marshals to act as enumerators. There were 17 marshals. The records showing the number of assistant marshals employed in 1790, 1800, and 1810 were destroyed by fire, but the number employed in 1790 has been estimated at 650.

The schedules which these officials prepared consist of lists of names of heads of families; each name appears in a stub, or first column, which is followed by five columns, giving details of the family. These columns are headed as follows:

Free white males, 16 years and upward, including heads of families.

Free white males under 16 years.

Free white females, including heads of families.

All other free persons.

Slaves.

The assistant marshals made two copies of the returns; in accordance with the law one copy was posted in the immediate neighborhood for the information of the public, and the other was transmitted to the marshal in charge, to be forwarded to the President. The schedules were turned over by the President to the Secretary of State. Little or no tabulation was required, and the report of the First Census, as also the reports of the Second, Third, and Fourth, was produced without the employment of any clerical force, the summaries being transmitted directly to the printer. The total population as returned in 1790 was 3,929,214, and the entire cost of the census was $44,377.

A summary of the results of the First Census, not including the returns for South Carolina, was transmitted to Congress by President Washington on October 27, 1791. The legal period for enumeration, nine months, had been extended, the longest time consumed being eighteen months in South Carolina. The report of October 27 was printed in full, and published in what is now a very rare little volume; afterwards the report for South Carolina was "tipped in." To contain the results of the Twelfth Census, ten large quarto volumes, comprising in all 10,400 pages, were required. No illustration of the expansion of census inquiry can be more striking.

The original schedules of the First Census are now contained in 26 bound volumes, preserved in the Census Office. For the most part the headings of the schedules were written in by hand. Indeed, up to and including 1820, the assistant marshals generally used for the schedules such paper as they happened to have, ruling it, writing in the headings, and binding the sheets together themselves. In some cases merchants' account paper was used, and now and then the schedules were bound in wall paper.

As a consequence of requiring marshals to supply their own blanks, the volumes containing the schedules vary in size from about 7 inches long, 3 inches wide, and ½ inch thick to 21 inches long, 14 inches wide, and 6 inches thick. Some of the sheets in these volumes are only 4 inches long, but a few are 3 feet in length, necessitating several folds. In some cases leaves burned at the edges have been covered with transparent silk to preserve them.

THE UNITED STATES IN 1790.

In March, 1790, the Union consisted of twelve states—Rhode Island, the last of the original thirteen to enter the Union, being admitted May 29. Vermont, the first addition, was admitted in the following year, before the results of the First Census were announced. Maine was a part of Massachusetts, Kentucky was a part of Virginia, and the present states of Alabama and Mississippi were parts of Georgia. The present states of Ohio, Indiana, Illinois, Michigan, and Wisconsin, with part of Minnesota, were known as the Northwest Territory, and the present state of Tennessee, then a part of North Carolina, was soon to be organized as the Southwest Territory.

The United States was bounded on the west by the Mississippi river, beyond which stretched that vast and unexplored wilderness belonging to the Spanish King, which was afterwards ceded to the United States by France as the Louisiana Purchase, and now comprises the great and populous states of Louisiana, Arkansas, Indian Territory, Oklahoma, Missouri, Kansas, Iowa, Nebraska, South Dakota, North Dakota, and Montana, and most of Colorado, Wyoming, and Minnesota. The Louisiana Purchase was not completed for more than a decade after the First Census was taken. On the south was another Spanish colony known as the Floridas. Texas, then a part of the colony of Mexico, belonged to Spain; and California, Utah, Arizona, and New Mexico, also the property of Spain, although penetrated here and there by venturesome explorers and missionaries, were, for the most part, an undiscovered wilderness.

The gross area of the United States was 827,844 square miles, but the settled area was only 239,935 square miles, or about 29 per cent of the total. Though the area covered by the enumeration in 1790 seems very small when compared with the present area of the United States, the difficulties which confronted the census taker were vastly greater than in 1900. In many localities there were no roads, and where these did exist they were poor and frequently impassable; bridges were almost unknown. Transportation was entirely by horseback, stage, or private coach. A journey as long as that from New York to Washington was a serious undertaking, requiring eight days under the most favorable conditions. Western New York was a wilderness, Elmira and Binghamton being but detached hamlets. The territory west of the Allegheny mountains, with the exception of a portion of Kentucky, was unsettled and scarcely penetrated. Detroit and Vincennes were too small and isolated to merit consideration. Philadelphia was the capital of the United States. Washington was a mere Government project, not even named, but known as the Federal City. Indeed, by the spring of 1793, only one wall of the White House had been constructed, and the site for the Capitol had been merely surveyed. New York city in 1790 possessed a population of only 33,131, although it was the largest city in the United States; Philadelphia was second, with 28,522; and Boston third, with 18,320. Mails were transported in very irregular fashion, and correspondence was expensive and uncertain.

There were, moreover, other difficulties which were of serious moment in 1790, but which long ago ceased to be problems in census taking. The inhabitants, having no experience with census taking, imagined that some scheme for increasing taxation was involved, and were inclined to be cautious lest they should reveal too much of their own affairs. There was also opposition to enumeration on religious grounds, a count of inhabitants being regarded by many as a cause for divine displeasure. The boundaries of towns and other minor divisions, and even those of counties, were in many cases unknown or not defined at all. The hitherto semi-independent states had been under the control of the Federal Government for so short a time that the different sections had not yet been welded into an harmonious nationality in which the Federal authority should be unquestioned and instructions promptly and fully obeyed.

AN ACT PROVIDING FOR THE ENUMERATION OF THE INHABITANTS OF THE UNITED STATES

APPROVED MARCH 1, 1790

Section 1. Be it enacted by the Senate and House of Representatives of the United States of America in Congress assembled, That the marshals of the several districts of the United States shall be, and they are hereby authorized and required to cause the number of the inhabitants within their respective districts to be taken; omitting in such enumeration Indians not taxed, and distinguishing free persons, including those bound to service for a term of years, from all others; distinguishing also the sexes and colours of free persons, and the free males of sixteen years and upwards from those under that age; for effecting which purpose the marshals shall have power to appoint as many assistants within their respective districts as to them shall appear necessary; assigning to each assistant a certain division of his district, which division shall consist of one or more counties, cities, towns, townships, hundreds or parishes, or of a territory plainly and distinctly bounded by water courses, mountains, or public roads. The marshals and their assistants shall respectively take an oath or affirmation, before some judge or justice of the peace, resident within their respective districts, previous to their entering on the discharge of the duties by this act required. The oath or affirmation of the marshal shall be, "I, A. B., Marshal of the district of ——, do solemnly swear (or affirm) that I will well and truly cause to be made a just and perfect enumeration and description of all persons resident within my district, and return the same to the President of the United States, agreeably to the directions of an act of Congress, intituled 'An act providing for the enumeration of the inhabitants of the United States,' according to the best of my ability." The oath or affirmation of an assistant shall be "I, A. B., do solemnly swear (or affirm) that I will make a just and perfect enumeration and description of all persons resident within the division assigned to me by the marshal of the district of ——, and make due return thereof to the said marshal, agreeably to the directions of an act of Congress, intituled 'An act providing for the enumeration of the inhabitants of the United States,' according to the best of my ability." The enumeration shall commence on the first Monday in August next, and shall close within nine calendar months thereafter. The several assistants shall, within the said nine months, transmit to the marshals by whom they shall be respectively appointed, accurate returns of all persons, except Indians not taxed, within their respective divisions, which returns shall be made in a schedule, distinguishing the several families by the names of their master, mistress, steward, overseer, or other principal person therein, in manner following, that is to say:

The number of persons within my division, consisting of ——, appears in a schedule hereto annexed, subscribed by me this —— day of ——, 179–. A. B. *Assistant to the marshal of* ——.

Schedule of the whole number of persons within the division allotted to A. B.

Names of heads of families.	Free white males of 16 years and upwards, including heads of families.	Free white males under 16 years.	Free white females, including heads of families.	All other free persons.	Slaves.

Section 2. And be it further enacted, That every assistant failing to make return, or making a false return of the enumeration to the marshal, within the time by this act limited, shall forfeit the sum of two hundred dollars.

Section 3. And be it further enacted, That the marshals shall file the several returns aforesaid, with the clerks of their respective district courts, who are hereby directed to receive and carefully preserve the same: And the marshals respectively shall, on or before the first day of September, one thousand seven hundred and ninety-one, transmit to the President of the United States, the aggregate amount of each description of persons within their respective districts. And every marshal failing to file the returns of his assistants, or any of them, with the clerks of their respective district courts, or failing to return the aggregate amount of each description of persons in their respective districts, as the same shall appear from said returns, to the President of the United States within the time limited by this act, shall, for every such offense, forfeit the sum of eight hundred dollars; all which forfeitures shall be recoverable in the courts of the districts where the offenses shall be committed, or in the circuit courts to be held within the same, by action of debt, information or indictment; the one-half thereof to the use of the United States, and the other half to the informer; but where the prosecution shall be first instituted on the behalf of the United States, the whole shall accrue to their use. And for the more effectual discovery of offenses, the judges of the several district courts, at their next sessions, to be held after the expiration of the time allowed for making the returns of the enumeration hereby directed, to the President of the United States, shall give this act in charge to the grand juries, in their respective courts, and shall cause the returns of the several assistants to be laid before them for their inspection.

Section 4. And be it further enacted, That every assistant shall receive at the rate of one dollar for every one hundred and fifty persons by him returned, where such persons reside in the country; and where such persons reside in a city, or town, containing more than five thousand persons, such assistants shall receive at the rate of one dollar for every three hundred persons; but where, from the dispersed situation of the inhabitants in some divisions, one dollar for every one hundred and fifty persons shall be insufficient, the marshals, with the approbation of the judges of their respective districts, may make such further allowance to the assistants in such divisions as shall be deemed an adequate compensation, provided the same does not exceed one dollar for every fifty persons by them returned. The several marshals shall receive as follows: The marshal of the district of Maine, two hundred dollars; the marshal of the district of New Hampshire, two hundred dollars; the marshal of the district of Massachusetts, three hundred dollars; the marshal of the district of Connecticut, two hundred dollars; the marshal of the district of New York, three hundred dollars; the marshal of the district of New Jersey, two hundred dollars; the marshal of the district of Pennsylvania, three hundred dollars; the marshal of the district of Delaware, one hundred dollars; the marshal of the district of Maryland, three hundred dollars; the marshal of the district of Virginia, five hundred dollars; the marshal of the district of Kentucky, two hundred and fifty dollars; the marshal of the district of North Carolina, three hundred and fifty dollars; the marshal of the district of South Carolina, three hundred dollars; the marshal of the district of Georgia, two hundred and fifty dollars. And to obviate all doubts which may arise respecting the persons to be returned, and the manner of making the returns.

SECTION 5. Be it enacted, That every person whose usual place of abode shall be in any family on the aforesaid first Monday in August next, shall be returned as of such family; the name of every person, who shall be an inhabitant of any district, but without a settled place of residence, shall be inserted in the column of the aforesaid schedule, which is allotted for the heads of families, in that division where he or she shall be on the said first Monday in August next, and every person occasionally absent at the time of the enumeration, as belonging to that place in which he usually resides in the United States.

SECTION 6. And be it further enacted, That each and every person more than 16 years of age, whether heads of families or not, belonging to any family within any division of a district made or established within the United States, shall be, and hereby is, obliged to render to such assistant of the division, a true account, if required, to the best of his or her knowledge, of all and every person belonging to such family, respectively, according to the several descriptions aforesaid, on pain of forfeiting twenty dollars, to be sued for and recovered by such assistant, the one-half for his own use, and the other half for the use of the United States.

SECTION 7. And be it further enacted, That each assistant shall, previous to making his return to the marshal, cause a correct copy, signed by himself, of the schedule containing the number of inhabitants within his division, to be set up at two of the most public places within the same, there to remain for the inspection of all concerned; for each of which copies the said assistant shall be entitled to receive two dollars, provided proof of a copy of the schedule having been so set up and suffered to remain, shall be transmitted to the marshal, with the return of the number of persons; and in case any assistant shall fail to make such proof to the marshal, he shall forfeit the compensation by this act allowed him.

Approved March 1, 1790.

Population of the United States as returned at the First Census, by states: 1790.

DISTRICT.	Free white males of 16 years and upward, including heads of families.	Free white males under 16 years.	Free white females, including heads of families.	All other free persons.	Slaves.	Total.
Vermont	22,435	22,328	40,505	255	[1] 16	[2] 85,539
New Hampshire	36,086	34,851	70,160	630	158	141,885
Maine	24,384	24,748	46,870	538	None.	96,540
Massachusetts	95,453	87,289	190,582	5,463	None.	378,787
Rhode Island	16,019	15,799	32,652	3,407	948	68,825
Connecticut	60,523	54,403	117,448	2,808	2,764	237,946
New York	83,700	78,122	152,320	4,654	21,324	340,120
New Jersey	45,251	41,416	83,287	2,762	11,423	184,139
Pennsylvania	110,788	106,948	206,363	6,537	3,737	434,373
Delaware	11,783	12,143	22,384	3,899	8,887	[3] 59,094
Maryland	55,915	51,339	101,395	8,043	103,036	319,728
Virginia	110,936	116,135	215,046	12,866	292,627	747,610
Kentucky	15,154	17,057	28,922	114	12,430	73,677
North Carolina	69,988	77,506	140,710	4,975	100,572	393,751
South Carolina	35,576	37,722	66,880	1,801	107,094	249,073
Georgia	13,103	14,044	25,739	398	29,264	82,548
Total number of inhabitants of the United States exclusive of S. Western and N. territory	807,094	791,850	1,541,263	59,150	694,280	3,893,635

	Free white males of 21 years and upward.	Free males under 21 years of age.	Free white females.	All other persons.	Slaves.	Total.
S. W. territory	6,271	10,277	15,365	361	3,417	35,691
N. "						

[1] The census of 1790, published in 1791, reports 16 slaves in Vermont. Subsequently, and up to 1860, the number is given as 17. An examination of the original manuscript returns shows that there never were any slaves in Vermont. The original error occurred in preparing the results for publication, when 16 persons, returned as "Free colored," were classified as "Slave."

[2] Corrected figures are 85,425, or 114 less than figures published in 1790, due to an error of addition in the returns for each of the towns of Fairfield, Milton, Shelburne, and Williston, in the county of Chittenden; Brookfield, Newbury, Randolph, and Strafford, in the county of Orange; Castleton, Clarendon, Hubbardton, Poultney, Rutland, Shrewsbury, and Wallingford, in the county of Rutland; Dummerston, Guilford, Halifax, and Westminster, in the county of Windham; and Woodstock, in the county of Windsor.

[3] Corrected figures are 59,096, or 2 more than figures published in 1790, due to error in addition.

Summary of population, by counties and towns: 1790.

ADDISON COUNTY.

TOWN.	Number of heads of families.	Free white males of 16 years and upward, including heads of families.	Free white males under 16 years.	Free white females, including heads of families.	All other free persons.	Slaves.	Total.
Addison	68	108	106	186	2	....	402
Bridport	79	123	122	205	....	....	450
Bristol	39	53	57	101	....	....	211
Cornwall	150	214	218	393	....	....	825
Ferrisburg	80	137	119	213	12	....	481
Hancock	9	18	11	27	....	....	56
Kingston	19	26	31	44	....	....	101
Leicester	61	94	81	169	....	....	344
Middlebury	74	125	92	176	2	....	395
Monkton	79	122	134	193	....	....	449
New Haven	133	180	218	319	....	....	717
Panton	39	57	66	97	....	....	220
Salisbury	75	122	107	215	....	....	444
Shoreham	135	198	161	337	5	....	701
Vergennes	39	73	35	79	14	....	201
Weybridge	32	48	41	84	1	....	174
Whiting	46	70	57	121	1	....	249
Total	1,157	1,768	1,656	2,959	37	....	6,420

BENNINGTON COUNTY.

TOWN.	Number of heads of families.	Free white males of 16 years and upward, including heads of families.	Free white males under 16 years.	Free white females, including heads of families.	All other free persons.	Slaves.	Total.
Arlington	170	252	252	488	....	....	992
Bennington	375	628	601	1,101	20	....	2,350
Bromley	15	21	19	31	....	....	71
Dorsett	155	240	230	487	....	....	957
Glastonbury	6	6	11	17	....	....	34
Landgrove	6	7	4	20	....	....	31
Manchester	200	338	339	596	5	....	1,278
Pownal	282	418	498	815	1	....	1,732
Reedsborough	14	16	15	32	....	....	63
Rupert	179	251	289	494	....	....	1,034
Sandgate	135	198	189	386	....	....	773
Shaftsbury	301	491	528	967	4	....	1,990
Stamford	48	69	65	137	1	....	272
Sunderland	69	113	101	199	1	....	414
Winhall	28	39	46	69	1	....	155
Woodford	14	16	18	26	....	....	60
Total	1,997	3,103	3,205	5,865	33	....	12,206

CHITTENDEN COUNTY.

TOWN.	Number of heads of families.	Free white males of 16 years and upward, including heads of families.	Free white males under 16 years.	Free white females, including heads of families.	All other free persons.	Slaves.	Total.
Alburgh	90	147	106	189	4	....	446
Bakersfield	2	4	4	5	....	....	13
Bolton	16	21	26	41	....	....	88
Burlington	60	108	68	151	3	....	330
Cambridge	62	108	84	167	....	....	359
Cambridge Gore	3	3	6	6	....	....	15
Charlotte	118	189	142	301	3	....	635
Colchester	28	42	40	55	....	....	137
Duxbury	8	9	18	12	....	....	39
Elmore	7	7	1	4	....	....	12
Essex	62	118	76	160	....	....	354
Fairfax	51	85	61	108	....	....	254
Fairfield	27	43	28	55	....	....	126
Fletcher	9	13	14	20	....	....	47
Georgia	56	105	80	155	....	....	340
Highgate	17	26	31	45	1	....	103
Hinesburgh	85	127	115	212	....	....	454
Hungerford	7	16	8	11	5	....	40
Huntsburgh	10	25	10	11	....	....	46
Hydespark	7	10	12	18	3	....	43
Isle Mott	14	18	13	16	....	....	47
Jerico	64	115	90	176	....	....	381
Johnson	21	31	16	46	....	....	93
Middlesex	13	16	19	25	....	....	60
Milton	49	90	65	128	....	....	283
Minden	2	6	6	6	....	....	18
Moretown	6	10	6	8	....	....	24
Morristown	4	6	......	4	....	....	10
New Huntington	28	34	40	62	....	....	136
New Huntington Gore	7	10	7	14	....	....	31
North Hero	31	40	25	57	3	....	125
St. Albans	44	89	61	105	1	....	256
St. George	12	14	17	26	....	....	57
Shelburne	77	108	103	176	....	....	387
Smithfield	14	28	14	28	....	....	70
South Hero	95	164	128	245	....	....	537
Starksborough	9	15	6	19	....	....	40
Swanton	14	22	25	27	....	....	74
Underhill	10	16	12	31	....	....	59
Waitsfield	13	21	16	24	....	....	61
Waterbury	16	22	27	44	....	....	93
Westford	14	23	8	32	....	....	63
Williston	93	136	120	213	....	....	469
Wolcott	5	11	7	14	....	....	32
Total	1,380	2,251	1,761	3,252	23	....	7,287

ORANGE COUNTY.

TOWN.	Number of heads of families.	Free white males of 16 years and upward, including heads of families.	Free white males under 16 years.	Free white females, including heads of families.	All other free persons.	Slaves.	Total.
Barnet	98	137	132	207	1	....	477
Barton (not inhabited)	......	......	......	......	....	....	......
Berlin	23	38	33	63	....	....	134
Billymead (not inhabited)	......	......	......	......	....	....	......
Bradford	107	158	176	313	7	....	654
Braintree	37	61	66	89	5	....	221
Brookfield	76	113	116	189	1	....	419
Brownington (not inhabited)	......	......	......	......	....	....	......
Brunswick	12	15	15	36	....	....	66
Burke (not inhabited)	......	......	......	......	....	....	......
Cabot	21	33	37	52	....	....	122
Calais	8	14	11	20	....	....	45
Caldersburgh (not inhabited)	......	......	......	......	....	....	......
Canaan	3	4	5	10	....	....	19
Chelsea	45	77	62	100	....	....	239
Concord	12	18	12	19	....	....	49
Corinth	96	147	156	275	....	....	578
Danville	101	165	139	270	....	....	574
Dewey's Gore	7	12	18	18	....	....	48
Fairley	80	132	120	210	1	....	463
Ferdinand (not inhabited)	......	......	......	......	....	....	......
Glover (not inhabited)	......	......	......	......	....	....	......
Granby (not inhabited)	......	......	......	......	....	....	......
Greensborough	5	9	4	6	....	....	19
Groton	8	15	9	21	....	....	45
Guildhall	27	55	41	62	....	....	158
Hardwick	3	3	......	......	....	....	3
Harris Gore (not inhabited)	......	......	......	......	....	....	......
Hopkins Grant (not inhabited)	......	......	......	......	....	....	......
Lemington	5	12	7	12	....	....	31
Lewis (not inhabited)	......	......	......	......	....	....	......
Littleton	11	16	14	33	....	....	63
Lunenburgh	23	30	29	60	....	....	119
Lyndon	12	29	10	20	....	....	59
Maidstone	19	34	36	55	....	....	125
Marshfield (not inhabited)	......	......	......	......	....	....	......
Minehead (not inhabited)	......	......	......	......	....	....	......
Montpelier	17	55	19	44	....	....	118
Navy (not inhabited)	......	......	......	......	....	....	......
Newark (not inhabited)	......	......	......	......	....	....	......
Newbury	144	225	222	413	12	....	872
Northfield	7	10	10	20	....	....	40
Orange (not inhabited)	......	......	......	......	....	....	......
Peachum	63	102	90	173	....	....	365
Randolph	150	227	237	429	....	....	893
Random (not inhabited)	......	......	......	......	....	....	......
Roxbury	3	6	2	6	....	....	14
Ryegate	36	46	54	87	....	....	187
St. Andrews (not inhabited)	......	......	......	......	....	....	......
St. Johnsbury	34	54	34	55	....	....	143
Sheffield (not inhabited)	......	......	......	......	....	....	......
Strafford	148	213	228	403	....	....	844
Thetford	157	211	218	419	14	....	862
Topsham	27	36	56	70	....	....	162
Tunbridge	86	121	147	219	....	....	487
Vershire	81	117	118	204	....	....	439
Victory (not inhabited)	......	......	......	......	....	....	......
Walden	2	3	3	5	....	....	11
Walden's Gore	7	9	9	14	....	....	32
Washington	17	26	13	33	....	....	72
Westmore (not inhabited)	......	......	......	......	....	....	......
Wheelock	10	14	7	12	....	....	33
Wildersburgh	16	30	16	30	....	....	76
Williamstown	31	41	34	71	....	....	146
Winlock (not inhabited)	......	......	......	......	....	....	......
Woodbury (not inhabited)	......	......	......	......	....	....	......
Total	1,875	2,873	2,765	4,847	41	....	10,526

Summary of population, by counties and towns: 1790—Continued.

RUTLAND COUNTY.

TOWN.	Number of heads of families.	Free white males of 16 years and upward, including heads of families.	Free white males under 16 years.	Free white females, including heads of families.	All other free persons.	Slaves.	Total.
Benson	129	185	182	290	1	....	658
Brandon	117	154	168	314	1	....	637
Castleton	141	210	222	376	1	....	809
Chittenden	28	38	49	72	....	....	159
Clarendon	258	343	397	740	....	....	1,480
Danby	212	276	333	589	8	....	1,206
Fair Haven	100	174	121	250	....	....	545
Harwich	28	38	49	78	....	....	165
Hubbardton	82	120	94	196	....	....	410
Ira	52	77	82	153	....	....	312
Killington	8	11	10	11	....	....	32
Middletown	122	169	172	358	....	....	699
Midway	6	7	9	18	....	....	34
Orwell	150	215	218	341	4	....	778
Pawlet	249	348	399	709	2	....	1,458
Philadelphia	9	12	9	18	....	....	39
Pittsfield	12	13	12	24	....	....	49
Pittsford	156	219	208	422	1	....	850
Poultney	190	282	292	539	7	....	1,120
Rutland	243	396	351	668	2	....	1,417
Shrewsbury	73	98	101	183	....	....	382
Sudbury	47	67	69	122	....	....	258
Tinmouth	171	247	244	442	2	....	935
Wallingford	96	142	131	262	3	....	538
Wells	115	149	176	295	....	....	620
Total	2,794	3,990	4,098	7,470	32	....	15,590

WINDHAM COUNTY.

TOWN.	Number of heads of families.	Free white males of 16 years and upward, including heads of families.	Free white males under 16 years.	Free white females, including heads of families.	All other free persons.	Slaves.	Total.
Athens	84	103	138	209	....	....	450
Brattleborough	260	381	436	758	14	....	1,589
Dummerston	274	362	394	724	10	....	1,490
Guilford	412	586	646	1,177	13	....	2,422
Hallifax	199	302	342	561	4	....	1,209
Hinsdale	76	118	142	221	1	....	482
Jamaica	49	71	66	126	....	....	263
Johnson's Gore	10	15	13	21	....	....	49
Londonderry	71	90	99	172	1	....	362
Marlborough	113	149	176	304	....	....	629
New Fane	114	163	177	320	....	....	660
Putney	291	438	492	906	12	....	1,848
Rockingham	208	327	319	587	2	....	1,235
Somerset	21	26	35	50	....	....	111
Stratton	24	27	22	46	....	....	95
Thomlinson	105	143	165	253	....	....	561
Townsend	132	192	171	315	....	....	678
Wardsborough, North District	89	128	126	229	....	....	483
Wardsborough, South District	60	72	69	129	....	....	270
Westminster	261	429	387	782	1	....	1,599
Whitingham	78	114	119	209	....	....	442
Wilmington	116	180	138	327	....	....	645
Total	3,047	4,416	4,672	8,426	58	....	17,572

WINDSOR COUNTY.

TOWN.	Number of heads of families.	Free white males of 16 years and upward, including heads of families.	Free white males under 16 years.	Free white females, including heads of families.	All other free persons.	Slaves.	Total.
Andover	47	75	74	126	....	....	275
Barnard	131	177	167	329	....	....	673
Bethel	86	126	118	229	....	....	473
Bridgwater	60	68	78	147	....	....	293
Cavendish	87	126	125	240	....	....	491
Chester	170	265	255	457	4	....	981
Hartford	168	248	250	489	1	....	988
Hartland	270	415	442	789	6	....	1,652
Ludlow	29	43	57	79	....	....	179
Norwich	181	280	322	556	....	....	1,158
Pomfret	116	177	209	319	5	....	710
Reading	137	171	211	359	6	....	747
Rochester	47	62	47	106	....	....	215
Royalton	141	195	190	363	....	....	748
Saltash	20	29	35	42	....	....	106
Sharon	102	147	147	275	....	....	569
Springfield	204	289	289	516	3	....	1,097
Stockbridge	22	32	25	43	....	....	100
Weathersfield	207	294	285	560	7	....	1,146
Windsor	240	395	406	732	9	....	1,542
Woodstock	268	390	416	787	4	....	1,597
Total	2,733	4,004	4,148	7,543	45	....	15,740

ADDISON COUNTY.[1]

NAME OF HEAD OF FAMILY.	Free white males of 16 years and upward, including heads of families.	Free white males under 16 years.	Free white females, including heads of families.	All other free persons.	Slaves.
ADDISON TOWN.					
Whitney, David	4		2		
Murray, Joseph	3		5		
Newton, John	1		1		
Newton, John, Jr	1	1	1		
Bartlet, Ichabod	1	2	4		
Picket, Ebenezer	1	3	3		
Whitney, Joshua	1	1	3		
Paine, Benjm	2		2	2	
Strong, Saml	4		3		
Case, Jonah	2	1	3		
Strong, John	1	2	3		
Case, Bessel	1		4		
Gale, John	1	2	3		
Davis, David	1		2		
Vallance, David	3	3	9		
Pangbourn, Stephen	2	1	4		
Champion, Daniel	1	3	3		
Bliss, Daniel	1	1	3		
Fountain, Joseph	1	1	1		
Martin, Francis	1	1	1		
Strong, John, Jr	1	2	1		
Dexter, Thomas	1	2	3		
Storrs, Seth	2		2		
Everest, Zadock	4	5	4		
Woodford, Timothy	2		3		
Everest, Joseph	1	5	1		
Merrills, Ebenr	2	1	3		
Pangborn, Timo	3	2	2		
Vallance, John	1		2		
Everest, Benj	1	3	1		
Belding, Titus	1	1	1		
Andrus, Theodore	1		3		
Chattock, Henry	1		1		
Ward, John	1	4	3		
Wilmot, John	1	1	3		
Wilmot, Asa	4	3	3		
Pond, Saml	3	2	3		
Hanks, Levi	1	1	2		
Low, Saml	2	1	1		
Fountain, Peter	1		2		
Kimball, Wm	1	2	2		
Pangbourn, Saml	1	3	6		
Post, Caleb	2		2		
Corey, John	1	3	2		
Smith, Simon	3	4	5		
Day, Jeremiah	1	1	3		
Spencer, Joseph	1		1		
Snell, Samuel	1	3	4		
Wright, Ebenezer	1	5	5		
Buck, Isaac	1	1	2		
Walner, Aaron	2	2	5		
Clerk, Isaiah	1	3	4		
Bills, Azariah	2	1	1		
Doran, James	1	4	4		
Squier, Daniel	3	1	5		
Bradley, Moses	1		1		
Robinson, Claghorn	1	3	4		
Reynold, Benjm	2	3	4		
Bates, James	2	1	2		
Bates, Walter	1	1	2		
Smith, Henry	1		1		
Segar, Gideon	2	1	3		
Olin, Caleb	2	5	3		
Smith, Rachel	1	3	5		
Sanford, Robert	2		1		
Molly, Kilburn	1		2		
Sacket, Joseph	1		2		
Sacket, Reuben	2	1	1		
BRIDPORT TOWN.					
Haskins, Daniel	1	1	3		
Haskins, Asahel	1		1		
Case, Gamiel	1		1		
Towner, Truman	1	1	2		
Bennet, John N	2	2	7		
Smith, Marshal	1	2	2		
Smith, Saml	1	1	1		
Doty, David	2	2	1		
Ball, Jonathan	1	3	1		
Smith, Ashur	3	1	4		
Smith, Jacob	1	1	1		
Smith, Nathan	2	1	3		
Orsbourn, Alexander	2	2	3		
Benedict, Benajah	1	2	1		
Morgan, Adam	1		2		
Case, Lummin	2	1	5		
Lewis, Leml	3	2	1		
Stone, Philip	1	3	4		
Stone, Ephraim	1	2	2		
Frost, Joel	2	2	8		
Markam, Ebenr	3		2		
Wilcox, Abner	1		4		
BRIDPORT TOWN—con.					
Mills, Timo	1	1	6		
Hunter, Jon	1		2		
Johnson, Moses	1				
Harkins, Enoch	1	2	2		
Johnson, John	1		1		
Crawford, Elijah	1	2	3		
Fitch, Jonathn	3	1	1		
Hamlin, Danl	1	1	4		
Mann, Danl	1	3	4		
Morse, Danl	1	5	1		
Baldwin, Josiah	2	2	3		
Tibbit, Edward	2	3	6		
Barrows, Saml	2	1	2		
Fitch, Zoraster	3	1	1		
Barber, John, Jr	1		1		
Barber, Joel	3	2	2		
Gray, Lamon	1	2	3		
Barber, John	1	3	3		
Barrows, Isaac	1	2	5		
Barrows, Leml	2	1	5		
Camp, Silas D	2	1	1		
Minor, Benjm	3	3	1		
Gray, Edward	3		5		
Gray, Robert B	1		2		
Barber, James	2	5	1		
Corey, David	1	4	4		
Ward, John	2	2	2		
Pratt, Caleb	4	1	4		
Howe, Solomon	1	3	2		
Hemenway, Asa	2	1	4		
Hemenway, Jacob	1		5		
Smith, Ephraim	2	1	3		
Rice, Abel	1	2	5		
Rhodes, Dier	2	4	3		
Gray, James	3	1	3		
Morse, Solomon	1	4	5		
Searls, Aaron	2	1	1		
Dorn, Joshua	1	2	5		
Searls, Enoch	1		3		
Oliver, Robert	1		1		
Southward, Benjm	1	7	1		
Buck, Saml	2		1		
Andrus, Thos	3	1	3		
Benjamin, Saml	1	5	3		
Nichols, Amos	2		2		
Crane, Amos	1	1	2		
Atwood, Ebenezer	1		1		
Patridge, Jacob	1	3	2		
Searls, Philip	1		1		
Pratt, David	1	1	1		
Williams, Joseph	1		1		
Crigger, Richard	1		1		
Crigger, Wm	1	2	2		
Crigger, James	2	2	4		
Hall, Caleb	2				
Wells, Nathl	1	2	4		
Day, Wm	1	2	2		
BRISTOL TOWN.					
Clap, Benjamin	1	2	2		
Munson, Ephraim	3		4		
Darton, Ezekiel	1	1	2		
Franklin, Joshua	2	2	5		
Rossetter, Josiah	1	1	2		
Thomas, Elijah	1	2	1		
Gilmore, Adam	1	1	1		
Ranney, Saml	1		2		
Allen, Timothy	1	2	2		
Henry, Hewey	1	1	2		
Danchey, Robert	1		1		
Bunn, John	1		5		
Arnold, John	1	4	1		
Henry, John	1		2		
Murdock, Hezekiah	1	1	4		
Bartholomew, Benjm	1	3	4		
Bride, James O	4		2		
Stewart, Saml	1	2	3		
Eastman, Oliver	1	3	1		
Eastman, Cyphrain	1	2	7		
Dudley, Simeon	1	4	2		
Eastman, Calvin	1	1	3		
Munsil, Gordon	3	3	2		
Miller, Dan	1	2	2		
Barns, Benjm	2	3	3		
Maxim, Ellis	1	1	5		
McGlanelin, Henry	1	1	1		
Brooks, Saml., Jr	1		1		
Brooks, Saml	3	3	5		
Terrill, Josiah	1		1		
Scott, Amos	2	3	5		
Sprague, Abram	2		2		
Bell, Robert	1		1		
BRISTOL TOWN—con.					
Griswold, Benjn	1	2	4		
Hull, Saml	1	1	1		
Deane, Daniel	1		1		
Covey, Nathan	2	2	2		
Bond, Seth	1	2	3		
Johnson, Eden	1	2	4		
CORNWALL TOWN.					
Foot, Stilman	3	1	2		
Foot, John	1		2		
Bell, Harvey	1	1	3		
Bently, James	1	1	2		
Donaghy, William	1	2	3		
Allen, Theophilus	2	2	3		
Blodget, Asa	2	1	3		
Place, Griffin	1	2	3		
Laurence, James	1	2	3		
Blodget, Archippus	1	4	2		
Davis, Eleazer	1	1	1		
Wright, Samuel	1		1		
Bently, Thos	1	2	5		
Nichols, Andrew	1	4	1		
Douglass, Matthew	2	1	1		
Curtis, Frederick	1		1		
Andrus, Ethan	2	1	4		
Lewis, Mathew	1	2	3		
Ingram, Saml	1	1	3		
Troop, Orange	2	1	2		
Palmer, Thaddeus	1	2	3		
Blodget, Samuel	1	4	5		
Bently, James	1	4	4		
Williamson, Moses	2	2	2		
Williamson, Wynut	1		3		
Post, Frederick	1	3	3		
Lewis, John	1		2		
Beaman, Friend	3	1	2		
Frost, Phineas	3	3	3		
Cook, Joseph	3	3	3		
Benton, Andrew	1	1	2		
Benton, Philix	1	1	2		
Samson, Eliphalet	1	1	2		
Scott, Aaron	2	6	3		
Linley, Solomon	1	1	2		
Linley, Solomon, Junr	1		3		
Johnson, Zachariah	1		4		
Linley, Oliver	1		1		
Landon, Thomas	2	6	1		
Pratt, Moses	1	3	3		
Andrus, Eldad	1	2	4		
Durphy, Jedidiah	1	1	4		
Durphy, Elijah	2	2	1		
Durphy, Joseph	1		1		
Hopkins, Nehemiah	1	1	1		
Andrus, Ephraim	1		3		
Linley, Daniel	1	2	1		
Dolph, Stephen	1	1	1		
Hancross, James	1		2		
Benedict, Zacheus	1		2		
Fisher, Isaac	1	1	3		
Kellogg, William	2	1	1		
Avery, Roger	1	1	4		
Elsworth, Anthony	2	1	2		
Elsworth, Eliphalet	1	1	2		
Hamlin, John, Jur	1	3	3		
Hamilin, Joseph, Jr	1	1	2		
Hamlin, John	1		1		
Ducher, Cornelius	1		1		
Abinathy, Jared	3	2	2		
Ford, Fredrik	2	2	2		
Linley, Simeon	1		3		
Foot, Nathan	3	2	2		
Foot, Nathan, Jur	1	2	2		
Holabut, Elisha	2	2	3		
Foot, Daniel	1	2	2		
Baker, Timothy	1	1	5		
Richard, Thomas	1		2		
Rockwel, Jeremiah	1	4	3		
Tolman, Thomas	4	2	4		
Parkill, David	1	1	1		
Holabut, Bartholomew	1	2	3		
Woodward, Asa	1	1	3		
Stebins, Ebenezer	1	2	4		
Hawley, John	1	3	3		
Bell, Jason	1	2	1		
Linley, Joel	2	2	3		
Dagget, Joseph	2	2	3		
Sperry, Levi	1	1	3		
Hall, Thos	1	3	4		
Linley, Abial	2	1	3		
Waterous, Jabesh	1		2		
Slade, William	3	2	2		
Campbell, Nathan	2	5	4		

[1] No attempt has been made in this publication to correct mistakes in spelling made by the deputy marshals, but the names have been reproduced as they appear upon the census schedules.

ADDISON COUNTY—Continued.

NAME OF HEAD OF FAMILY.	Free white males of 16 years and upward, including heads of families.	Free white males under 16 years.	Free white females, including heads of families.	All other free persons.	Slaves.
CORNWALL TOWN—con.					
Campbell, James	1	1	4		
Tomblin, Stephen	2		5		
Squier, Wait	1	1	1		
Squier, Timothy	1		3		
Hall, Benjm	1		1		
Hall, Reuben	1		2		
Gibbs, Henry	1	1	5		
Scovil, Daniel	1		2		
Douglass, Rhoda	1	1	1		
Fields, Elisha	1	1	2		
Rockwell, John	2	2	4		
Wright, Elisha	1	2	3		
Wright, Elisha	1		1		
Mead, Isaac	1		1		
Mead, Ezra	2		2		
Rockwell, John, Jr	2	2	5		
Ives, Enos	2		1		
Prat, David	1	2	1		
Ives, Enos, Jur	1	1	2		
Nutting, David	2	3	5		
Dilleno, Nathan	1	1	5		
Dilleno, Abisha	2	4	3		
Chapman, Lemuel	1	1	2		
Newell, Ebenezer	2	3	4		
Richardson, Barzill	1	3	3		
Minor, Richard	1		6		
Jarus, Israel C	3	1	1		
Ballard, John	2	1	2		
Reeves, Benjamin	2	1	6		
Newell, Riverus	1	2	6		
Sampson, Daniel	1	1	4		
Meed, Caizah	1		3		
Peck, Jacob	2	3	4		
Peck, George	4		3		
Gibbs, Nathan	1		1		
Squier, Ebenr	1	1	3		
Sampson, Wm., Jr	1	2	1		
Sampson, Wm	2	1	3		
Sperry, David	3	6	5		
Post, Roswel	1	2	5		
Bingham, Jeremiah	3	4	5		
Hull, Isaac	1	2	4		
Cogswell, Nathl	2		1		
Parker, Mathew	1		2		
Parker, James	1		1		
Sanford, Benj	2	2	2		
Bingham, Jeremiah	2		2		
Cogswell, Joseph	1	1	4		
Blanchard, Nathan	1	2	3		
Foster, Thomas	1		1		
Stickney, Lemuel	2	3			
Tomberlin, Stephen A.	1	1	1		
Chipman, Jesse	1	3	4		
Lattin, John	1	2	4		
Hatheway, Erastus	1		3		
Rockwell, Saml	1	2	2		
Seymour, David	2	2	4		
Hailey, Stephen	2	2	3		
Gilbert, Isaiah	2		3		
Ingram, Nathan	1	3	3		
Richard, Saml	1	1	4		
Dwinelle, Wm	1		1		
Brown, Warren	1	2	1		
Pratt, Ephraim	1	1	3		
Hamlin, Isaac	1		2		
Benton, Saml	3	1	3		
FERRISBURG TOWN.					
Pangbone, Samuel	1	1	4		
Pangbone, Joseph	1	1	2		
Flemmon, Bennoni	1	2	4		
Hoof, Hendrick	1		3		
Squire, Ezra	1	1	2		
Squire, Nathaniel	2		2		
Mark, Isaac	1	2	2		
Baker, Daniel	1	3	3		
Hays, Michael	1	3	3		
Munson, Jerard	1	2	1		
White, Zenos	1	2	3		
Braidy, David	2	2	3		
Burdock, Paul	2		1		
Wilson, Naham	1	1	1		
Hammon, James	1		1		
Webster, William	1	3	3		
Craddinton, Zebulon	1	1	4		
Tompson, Nathan	1	1	3		
Collinder, David	1	1	2		
Gage, Isaac	2	2	5		
Gage, William	2		3		
Holladay, Azariah	1	4	3		
Tupper, Zurul	2	2	4		
FERRISBURG TOWN—continued.					
Saxton, Jonathan	1	1	4	9	
Odle, John	1	1	5		
Hawley, Gidion	2	3	2		
Chilson, Joseph	1		1		
Burrus, Joseph	2	1	3		
Tupper, Absolum	2	2	4		
Powers, Joseph	1	3	4		
Tompson, Abel	2		4		
Drewey, Noble	1		1		
Olford, Bennedick	1	1	2		
Akins, James	1	1	1		
Barnes, Joshua	1	2	2		
Barnes, Richard	1		1		
Chase, Abraham	6	2	7		
Davies, Daniel	3	1	4		
Dakins, Timothy	1	1	1		
Dakins, Presarvid	1	4	3		
Fields, Anthoney	5	1	3		
Fuller, Ashbel	1	3	1		
Fields, John	1	3	1		
Goodridg, James	2	1	1		
Fuller, Ishem	1	4	2		
Gage, George	2	2	4		
Gage, Warler	1	5	2		
Gage, William, Ju	1	4	5		
Hoyegg, Eligah	2		2		
Hatch, Jeremiah	2		1		
Hoff, John	1	5	2		
Huntley, John	1		2		
Jacobs, Lewis	1	2	3		
Keelor, Jonathan	4	1	3		
Kellogg, William	3	1	3		
Prindle, Samuel	4		5		
Powers, Nathaniel	1	3	5		
Pourter, Noah	3	1	4		
Roggers, Timothy	2	3	5		
Robberts, Benjamin	2	2	1		
Roggers, Abraham	2		1		
Shelhaus, Martin	1	1	2	1	
Walker, Nathan	5	4	4		
Powers, Simeon	3	3	3		
Frassnor, John	6		1		
Hait, Henry	1		2		
Burt, John	3		1		
Green, Benjamin	5		6		
Saterly, Robbert	2	3	3		
Ganson, Benjamin	2	1	4		
Cronktite, Peter	1		1		
Simmons, Caleb	1	3	2		
Dakins, Timothy, Jr	1		2		
Hoyegg, John	1		2		
Odle, Abijah	1	1	1		
Case, Ephraim	1	1	1		
Higley, Nehemiah	1	1	4		
Gould, Edward	1	2	3	1	
Whippor, James	1	1	2		
Harvey, John	1		2	1	
HANCOCK TOWN.					
Bellows, John	4	2	4		
Butts, Esech	1		1		
Butts, Joseph	2	1	2		
Farnum, Eliphelet	1	2	2		
Claflin, James	3	1	7		
Cady, Noah	1		1		
Dowling, J.——	1	1	1		
Claflin, Daniel	4	3	5		
Bordman, Isaac	1	1	4		
KINGSTON TOWN.					
Lamb, Jonathan	2	1	4		
Ball, Israel	2	1	3		
Thatcher, Peter	1	3	2		
Lewis, Eli	1		4		
Brown, Adam	1	2	1		
Deane, Alexander	1	2	3		
King, Moses	3	4	3		
Farnum, Eliphalet	1		2		
Wood, Asa	2	3	1		
Rice, Joel	1		2		
Sterling, Nathan	1		1		
Wade, Timothy	1	3	4		
Lee, Phineas	1	2	2		
Converse, Jude	1	1	2		
Patrick, Joseph	1	1	2		
Beckwith, Joshua	2	2	3		
Lamb, Jonathan, Jur	2	2	1		
Parker, Joseph	1	2	3		
Lyman, Richard	1	2	1		
LEICESTER TOWN.					
Merrifield, Joseph	3	2	1		
Powers, Blanchard	1	1	4		
Mack, Robert	2	1	3		
Cook, Nathaniel	1	1	2		
Cook, Elkanah	1		3		
Sawyer, Stephen	1	1	3		
Perry, Abijah	2	1	2		
Brigham, Abner	1	1	2		
Moore, George	1		1		
Olin, Henry	2	1	6		
Swinnington, Joseph	1	1	1		
Reed, Isaac	2		2		
Whitman, Benjm	1	3	3		
Rounds, Wm	1		2		
Childs, Ebenezer	1		1		
Dagget, John	2	2	3		
Farr, Salmon	1	2	4		
Dow, James	4	1	3		
Swinnington, James	1	1	5		
Sparks, Stephen	1	3	3		
Fish, David	1	2	4		
Smith, John	2	4	1		
Chapman, Nathaniel	1		2		
Capron, Joseph	1		3		
Griswold, Moses	2	1	6		
Church, Caleb	1	2	4		
Church, Silas	1		1		
Bacon, Jacob	1	1	2		
Bacon, Asa	2	5	4		
Whitman, John	1	3	4		
Lawson, John	1	1	2		
Dow, Moses	1	5	2		
Knap, James	1		1		
Knap, Benjn	1	1	4		
Smith, Abial	2	6	3		
Woodward, Joseph	3		3		
Enos, James, Jur	1		1		
Enos, James	1	3	2		
White, Peter	1		2		
Farr, James	2	3	3		
Ripner, John	2		7		
Sawyer, Thomas	3	3	4		
Chaffey, Nathaniel	2		4		
Huntley, Samuel	3	2	5		
White, Elisha	4		4		
Brown, John	1	1	1		
Alden, Thos	4	1	2		
Cole, Allen	1		2		
Payne, Edward	1	1	2		
Moss, Jonathan	1		4		
Robins, Moses	1	1	2		
Perkins, Eliphaz	1	2	2		
Reed, Leonard	1	3	2		
Reed, Martin	1		2		
Kindall, Samuel	1	2	2		
Hosley, Joseph	3		3		
Fish, Wm	1	1	2		
Earty, Joseph	1		2		
Sabins, Nehemiah	1	1	3		
Blair, Edward	1	3	1		
Flagg, Rebekah	3	1	5		
MIDDLEBURY TOWN.					
Horton, Robert	3	1	1		
Young, Wm	2		4		
Deming, John	5	2	3		
Miller, Saml	1	1	1		
How, Uriah	1	4	4		
Painter, Gamaliel	3		1		
Keep, Saml	1		1		
Mathew, Darius	1	1	1		
——,* Freeman	1	1	3		
Stodard, Samuel	1	1	3		
Fuller, Elisha	1	1	1		
Haile, Josiah	1	2	4		
Barnard, Rufus	1	4	2		
Sumner, Wm. B	2	2	3	1	
Olmstead, Elijah	3	4	2		
Little, James	1	2	5		
Knap, Solomon	1		1		
Bulluph, Elijah	4	4	4		
Goodrich, Stephen	3		2		
Goodrich, Wm	1		2		
Kipp, Wm	1	3	2		
Wadsworth, Israel	1	1	2		
Woodworth, Hezekiah	1	4	3		
Farr, Simon	1	2	4		
Hale, Moses	2		1		
Rogers, Jabesh	4				
Kirby, Abram	2		4		
Sovereign, Saml	1		1		
Johnson, Ebenr	1	3	3		

*Illegible.

ADDISON COUNTY—Continued.

NAME OF HEAD OF FAMILY.	Free white males of 16 years and upward, including heads of families.	Free white males under 16 years.	Free white females, including heads of families.	All other free persons.	Slaves.
MIDDLEBURY TOWN—continued.					
Starkweather, Cyrus	1	1	2		
Goodrich, Leml	1	1	3		
Goodrich, Peter	2		2		
Taylor, Giles	2	1	2		
Foot, Philip	1	1	4		
Barnet, John	1	3	1		
Foot, Danl	1	1	4		
Goodrich, Bethuel	1	3	2		
Bowman, Moses	1		1		
Monger, Billey, Jr	1	2	1		
Foot, Martin	1	1	3	1	
Torrence, Robert	3		4		
Thare, Billey	1	1	1		
Thare, Calvin	1		2		
Hyde, Joshua	2	1	5		
Chandler, Simeon	2		2		
Tillotson, John	2	2	3		
Everts, Eber	2	1	5		
Washburn, Abisha	2	1	3		
Vandozer, John	1	1	1		
Chipman, John	10		5		
Chipman, Thos	1	2	2		
Smalley, Benjm	1		2		
Smalley, Imri	1	2	2		
Coller, Ebenr	1	1	1		
Hollister, Wm	1		2		
Seley, David	1	2	2		
Coudry, Saml	1	1	3		
Bentley, Abishai	2	1	2		
Bridge, Joshua	1	1	2		
Crane, James	1	1	4		
Crane, Jeremiah	1	2	1		
Norton, Lois	1	1	1		
Monger, Edmund	2	3	1		
Case, Nathan	1		2		
Monger, Nathl	2		1		
Preston, Jonathan	3	1	3		
Monger, Jonathan	1	2	3		
Monger, Reuben	1	1	1		
Gilbert, Elnathan	4	1	3		
Selick, Seymour	2		1		
Sloan, George	1	1	6		
Sage, Gideon	3	1	2		
Bordman, Amos	1		3		
Sumner, Ebenr	1	4	2		
MONKTON TOWN.					
Barnham, Samuel	3	1	2		
Day, Joseph	1	2	2		
Hotchkiss, Asahel	2	3	3		
Comstock, Abijah	3		2		
Andrus, Titus	2	3	3		
Tobias, James	2	2	2		
Height, Stephen	4		1		
Height, Benjamin	1	2	3		
Bishop, Elijah	2	1	2		
Barnum, Stephen	4	3	3		
Barnum, Ebenr	1	4	3		
Saxton, Noble	1	2			
Finney, Joel	3	3	4		
Ferriss, Alanson	1	1	3		
Ferriss, David	2		2		
Dart, George	1	5	1		
Collins, Archibal	1		3		
Carlee, John	2	2	4		
Chamberlin, Leander	1	1	1		
Holmes, Nicholas	3	2	4		
Brock, James	1	1	8		
Homes, Jonathan	1	1	2		
Smith, Daniel	3	1	4		
Duran, Joseph	1	2	1		
Pingree, Moses	1	1			
Hoag, Joseph	1	1	4		
Stearns, John	1	3	3		
Headdy, James	1	1	5		
Ferguson, Henry	1		1		
Stewart, Nathl	2	2	4		
Bemus, Silas	1	1	3		
Barnum, Richard	3	1	2		
Barnum, Jehiel	2	6	5		
Peck, Ebenezer	1	3	1		
Bordman, Josiah	1	1	4		
Ferguson, John	3	2	5		
Freddenboro, Thomas	3	2	5		
Bostwick, Austin	1		1		
Barney, Barney	2	4	2		
Atwood, Paul	1	1	1		
Finney, Rufus	1	2	1		
Page, Ephraim	1	1	3		
Laurence, Josiah	1	1	1		
Fuller, Josiah	1	1	5		
Smith, Hezekiah	1	1	2		

NAME OF HEAD OF FAMILY.	Free white males of 16 years and upward, including heads of families.	Free white males under 16 years.	Free white females, including heads of families.	All other free persons.	Slaves.
MONKTON TOWN—con.					
Willoby, Joseph	1		2		
Fuller, Stephen	2	1	4		
Willoby, Joseph	1	1	1		
Hardy, Lemuel	2	1	2		
Hardy, Silas	1	1	2		
Herrick, Daniel	2	2	4		
Smith, Hannah	2	3	2		
Stearns, Isaac	1	2	2		
Tagget, William	1	1	3		
Smith, Benjm	1	3	3		
Stearns, Ebenr	1	6	1		
Bishop, John	2		1		
Bishop, Naphthalt	1		1		
Branch, Elijah	1	3	3		
Mumford, Robinson	1	4	1		
Bishop, John, Junr	1	2	2		
Stevens, Ephraim	1	1	3		
Smith, Fredrick	1	1	2		
Rutherford, Andrew	1	1	2		
Rutherford, Thomas	1	2	3		
Tibbet, George	1	1	3		
Hodges, James	1	1	2		
Hodges, Ezekiel	1	6	3		
Ames, David	1	2	3		
Turner, Abram	3	1	1		
Smith, Thos	2	1	1		
Height, Ebenr	1		1		
Collins, Danl	4	2	2		
Nap, Isaac	1	1	1		
Buck, Jonathan	1	1	3		
Finney, Eleazer	1	2	3		
Hitchcock, Buel	2	1	2		
Deane, Ashbel	1	2	1		
Cable, Saml	1	1	2		
NEW HAVEN TOWN.					
Peck, Reuben	1		2		
Alvard, John	3	1	3		
Tobias, Joseph J	2	2	3		
Beach, Obel	1	2	2		
Peck, William	1	2	2		
Peck, Abel	1		2		
Waight, Oliver	2	2	1		
Prime, Joseph	4	3	2		
Stow, Clark	1	1	3		
Sturdivant, Justus	3	1	2		
Palmer, Jeremiah	1		1		
Fisher, Jeremiah	1	1	1		
Sturdivant, Richd	2	5	2		
Brush, Elkanah	1	4	3		
Rudd, Bezaleel	1	3	3		
Griswold, David	2	2	1		
Griswold, Nathan	1	1	2		
Brown, Phineas	1	2	4		
Wood, Robert	1	4	5		
Woodbridge, Wm	1	3	5		
West, Israel	1	2	3		
Langnothe, Joseph	2	1	3		
Turner, John	2	1	2		
Barton, Andrew, Jr	1	2	2		
Barton, Dier	1	2	2		
Barton, Andrew	2	2	4		
Evits, Luther	2		4		
Liscombe, Ezariah	1	1	4		
Rudd, Zebulon	1		1		
Dagget, John	1	5	2		
Lomis, Samuel	1		2		
Orvis, Roger	1		3		
Suard, Joseph	1		2		
Barton, David	1	3	2		
Suard, Charles	1	1	1		
Cholker, Samuel	1	1	3		
Boyenton, David	1	4	2		
Griswould, Addonijah	2	1	1		
Cook, Ichabod	1	4	5		
Treaver, Nickelas	1		2		
Hawkins, Zebulon	1		1		
Hawkins, Ebenez	2		2		
Hobbs, Isaai	2	4	3		
Wright, Johiel	1	1	4		
Hobbs, Elijah	1		1		
Rudenton, Jacob	2	1	4		
Peer, Oliver, Ju	1	2	1		
Smith, Asa	1		4		
Johnson, Buckley	2	3	3		
Barton, Anthony	1	4	1		
Trips, Augustus	1		1		
Hinman, Benjamin	1		1		
Whelon, Ashbel	2	1	4		
Bostick, John W	1	3	2		
Bird, Joseph	2	3	2		
Sarles, Benjamin B	1	2			

NAME OF HEAD OF FAMILY.	Free white males of 16 years and upward, including heads of families.	Free white males under 16 years.	Free white females, including heads of families.	All other free persons.	Slaves.
NEW HAVEN TOWN—con.					
Doud, Jiles	1	2	1		
Ashley, Enoch	1	1	3		
Doud, David	2	1	4		
Langdon, Seth	(*)	(*)	4		
White, David	1		2		
Sperry, Philo	1	2	1		
Whealon, Truman	1	1	2		
Phelps, Lemuel	1	1	1		
Norton, Isachor	1	5	1		
Norton, Appollus	1	1	1		
Cadwell, Buckley	1	1	3		
Numan, Benjamin	2	3	5		
Parker, Joseph	1	4	1		
Blancher, Asaiel	2		2		
Judd, Dan	1	1	3		
Hindman, Thomas	1	1	2		
Skull, Truman	1	6	1		
Hill, Billias	2		2		
Johnson, Ebenezr	1	2	2		
Foot, Elijah	1	5	3		
Furrall, John	1	2	3		
Wright, Ebenezr	3	4	2		
Pioc, Oliver	1	3	4		
Fields, Simon	1	1	1		
Peck, Enos	1	3	4		
Griffin, Joel	1		2		
Rabbler, Hiram	1		1		
Fields, Ebenezr	2	2	4		
Lummis, Ezra	2	1	3		
Jones, Joseph	3	1	1		
Evits, Ambrus	1	2	2		
Sherman, Amos P	1		4		
Griffin, Asa	2		1		
Spinks, Maria		1	2		
Brown, Solomon	1	4	3		
Dunning, Martin	1	3	5		
Durrom, Allen	1	2	2		
Semon, William	1	3	3		
Alhurd, Phinihas	2	2	1		
Cook, Stephen	2	2	5		
Phelps, Martha	3	1	3		
Eno, William	1	2	2		
Squires, Andrew	2	1	4		
Smith, George	1	1	2		
Smith, Allin	1	1	3		
Sprague, Esegh	1	3	2		
Grinnald, Rubin	1	3	2		
Hoyt, Seth	1	3	4		
Dailey, Gideon	1	1	3		
Hartshorn, Zapheriah	1	3	3		
Pierce, Justus	1	1	1		
Craine, Martin	1		2		
Whelor, Asa	1	2	1		
Durham, Phits	1		2		
Sprague, Gideon	1	3	3		
Jilson, Joseph	2		1		
Stebbins, David	1		3		
Peterson, Jonathan	2		3		
Lampson, William	2	1	3		
Hooker, Brainard	2	3	3		
Bradley, Miles	1	4	5		
Foot, Samuel	3		1		
Cole, Daniel	1	1	2		
Smith, Isaac	1	2	2		
Smith, Simon	1	1	3		
Nash, Samuel	1	4	2		
Ellis, Stephen					
Mils, Andrus	3	3	4		
Normen, Soloman	1		2		
Freeman, Joseph	1	1	1		
Fields, Joseph	4		2		
Fields, Rubin	1	1	3		
Phelps, Samuel	2		3		
Phelps, Joel	2		2		
Fields, Margeret			2		
Dudley, Simeon	1	5	1		
Pierc, Moses	1	1	4		
PANTON TOWN.					
Knap, Zadock	1	1	4		
Knap, Uz	1	2	3		
Knap, Dan	1		4		
Horsunton, James	1	2	4		
Horsunton, James	2		1		
Holcomb, Jedediah	1	1	2		
Spalding, Timothy	2				
Rich, Elijah	1		1		
Phelps, Giles	1	2	3		
Holcomb, Elisha	1		2		
Osgood, David	1	1	3		
Shepherd, Wm	3		3		
Shepherd, Saml	1		2		

*Illegible.

ADDISON COUNTY—Continued.

NAME OF HEAD OF FAMILY.	Free white males of 16 years and upward, including heads of families.	Free white males under 16 years.	Free white females, including heads of families.	All other free persons.	Slaves.
PANTON TOWN—con.					
Judd, Thomas	2	2	3		
Shepherd, Wm., Jr	1	2	1		
Phelps, Hezekiah	2	1	2		
Holcomb, Joseph	1	2	1		
Wilson, Joseph	1		1		
Newell, Seth	2	2	2		
Holcomb, Isaac	1	2	1		
Grandy, Elijah	2	2	3		
Spalding, Phineas	1	2	4		
Holcomb, Benja	1	5	4		
Spalding, Henry	1	1	3		
Spalding, Caleb	1	1	4		
Grandy, Edmund	1	4	4		
Kellogg, Wm	1	1	2		
Olcott, Eliphalet	1	3	4		
Ferris, Peter	1		1		
Lewis, Nathan	1	5	4		
Custer, Ephraim	3	5	2		
Holcomb, Abner	1	5	2		
Stanard, Plinny	1		1		
Phelps, Ira	1		3		
Firris, Darius	1		2		
Payne, Saml	4	2	2		
Ransom, Reuben	1	4	3		
Sacket, Joseph	4	1	4		
Bristoll, Aaron	3	5	2		
SALISBURY TOWN.					
Reed, John	1	1	4		
Parker, Jeremiah	2	1	6		
Barker, John	3	2	3		
Farnum, John	1	2	5		
Chamberlin, Elias	1	1	3		
Fife, John	1	1	4		
Chamberlin, Calvin	1	2	2		
Gaffield, Benjm	4	2	1		
Brown, Eli	1	3	2		
Adams, Saml	1	3	3		
Gaffield, Elijah	1		1		
Biggelow, Joel	1	4	5		
Kindall, Wm	1	3	6		
Graves, Joseph	2	3	2		
Severell, Solomon	1	2	3		
Olin, Stephen	1		1		
Smith, Jehul	1	5	3		
Chipman, Barnabus	1		4		
Chamberlin, Elias, Jr	1	1	4		
Scott, Isaac	2		6		
Storey, Solomon	4	3	3		
Waterous, Joseph	1		2		
Baker, James	1		1		
Buell, Jonathan	1		2		
Newton, Joel	2	2	2		
Waterous, Abey	2	1	4		
Golding, Isaiah	2	2	2		
Pratt, William	1		2		
Ives, Amasa	1	2	3		
Huntley, Asa	1	3	3		
Stevens, Thomas	1	1	3		
Dolph, Joseph	2		1		
Nichols, Amos	1	2	1		
Barnum, Joseph	1	2	(*)		
Lawrence, Asa	2		4		
Pierce, Saml	1		4		
Graves, Joshua	1		1		
Graves, Jesse	1	1	3		
Wicks, Holland	5	2	6		
Beach, Aaron L	2	1	1		
Graves, Chancey	2	1	4		
Sprague, Nathan	1	4	3		
Cudman, Peter	1	4	1		
Kelsey, Abner	1		2		
Shearman, James	1	1	1		
Stevens, Pennel	4		4		
Storey, Ephraim	1	1	2		
Graves, David	1	4	4		
Dibble, Hezekiah	1	1	4		
Hard, Stephen	1	2	4		
Hard, Abram	2		2		
Adams, Aaron	1	3	4		
Adams, Daniel	1	3	4		
Johnson, Abel	1	3	4		
Biggelow, Zenas	1		2		
Everts, Solomon	1	1	4		
Strong, Farnis	2		2		
Lyon, Ebenezer	1	2	3		
Chipman, Arni	1	3	1		
Bump, Salathiel	1		3		
Bradley, James	2	2	1		
Storey, Solomon	4		3		
Everts, Gilbert	6	2	4		
SALISBURY TOWN—con.					
Kelsey, Elias	5	1	2		
Knap, Moses	1		2		
Waterous, James	2	2	2		
Claghorn, Eleazer	1	2	3		
Hodgden, John	1	3	3		
Graves, Asa	1		6		
Ozier, Consider	2	1	3		
Moon, Martin	2	3	2		
Warner, Daniel	5		2		
Holbrook, David	1		2		
Biggilow, Solomon	1		2		
Scott, Salmon	1		4		
SHOREHAM TOWN.					
Hunter, Timothy	1		3		
Reynolds, Jared	1	1	1		
Reynolds, John	3	1	2		
Reynolds, William	1	1	3		
Nichols, Asa	1	1	1		
Smith, Eli	2	1	6		
Smith, Stephen	2	1	7		
Smith, Stephen, Jr	1		1		
Smith, Nathan	3	2	2		
Reynolds, John, Jr	1		1		
Terrill, Reber	1	2	1		
Lumidien, Henry M	1	1			
Cooper, Stephen	4	4	2		
Jenison, Levi	1	1	1		
Thomas, Jacob	1		2		
Denton, Joseph	1	2	5		
Larabee, John	2		4		
Larabee, John	1		1		
McCarty, John	2		1		
Wallace, Nehemiah	1	1	2		
Larabee, Timothy	1	1	2		
Barnum, Jabesh	1	2	3		
Tower, Samuel	3		5		
Wilson, Noah	4	2	3		
Barnum, Solomon	1		3		
Smith, Philip	1		1		
Pond, Nathaniel	1		4		
Bush, Sarah	1	2	6		
Barter, Robert	1	3	1		
Skeels, Elder	1	2	3		
Skeels, Samuel	2		1		
Brown, Jeremiah	1		2		
Cupper, Israel	1	1	2		
Rowley, Thomas, Jr	2	2	5		
Rowley, Nathan	3	1	6		
Rowley, Thomas	1		1		
Barnum, Zacheus	1		1		
Fobes, John	1	2	4		
Crigger, John	2	2	3		
Wilson, James	1	1	2		
Ramsdal, Michael	2	1	3		
Ames, Saml	1	1	1		
Wright, Elijah	2		2		
Douglas, Joseph	1	2	2		
Douglass, Domini	3	3	3		
Rich, Thos	2	2	6		
Rich, Nathaniel	4	3	3		
Atwood, Jacob	4	3	5		
Rich, Charles	1		1		
Ames, Elijah	1	4	3		
Wright, Andrew	2	2	4		
Dunbar, Saml	1	3	3		
Brookins, Philip	1		1		
Brookins, Silas	1	2	3		
Ames, Barney	1	1	2		
Goodale, Timothy	2		2		
Newton, Lemuel	2		3		
Ames, Wm	2	2	1		
Ames, Barzilla	1	1	1		
Hogel, Isaac	1	1	1		
Wright, Ebenr	1		1		
Wells, William	1	4	3		
McGinnis, Stephen	1	1	2		
Armstrong, Martin	2		1		
Armstrong, Just	2		1		
Burton, Rimmon	2	1	1		
Hagle, Cornelius	1	2	4		
Phelps, Joseph	1	2	1		
Robinson, Ralph	1		2		
Wilson, Heman	1		1		
Wright, Joseph	1	1	1		
Bailey, Joshua	4		2		
Heley, Jabez	1	2	2		
Herrington, Ammi	1		1		
Pond, Josiah	4		3		
Flagg, Isaac	3	1	3		
Moore, James	1	1	2		
SHOREHAM TOWN—con.					
McLornen, Saml	1	1	1		
Stone, Amos	2	1	3		
Fuller, James	3	1	3		
Fuller, Joseph	1	1	5		
Simons, Gardner	1		2		
Simons, Andrew	1	4	4		
Russel, David, Jr	2		2		
Culver, Eliakim	1	2	3		
Northrup, Jeremiah	2		1		
Jones, Asa	1	1	3		
Goodrich, Noah	2	1	2		
Rhodes, Obadiah	2	4	4		
Harrington, Samuel	2		1		
Jones, Noah	2	1	5		
Russell, David	3	1	4		
Smith, John	3	4	6		
Doolittle, Ephraim	1		1		
Moore, Paul	1	1	2		
Wait, Henry	(*)	(*)	1		
Wait, Barton	(*)	(*)	3		
Peck, Isaac	(*)	1	2		
Bayley, Elijah	1	3	2		
Kellogg, Elijah	1	3	4		
Pond, Wm	1	1	3		
Landers, Nathan	1	2	3		
Payne, Cull				4	
Doolittle, Ephraim, Jr	1	3	1		
Woolcot, Samuel	2		1		
Woolcot, Jesse	1	2	3		
Woolcot, Samuel, Jr	1	3	2		
Callender, Amos	(*)		2		
Newton, Liberty	2		3		
North, John	2	1	1	1	
Nichols, Allen	2	1	4		
North, Simeon	1		1		
Barnum, Stephen	(*)	4	2		
Butler, Joseph	(*)	(*)	4		
Post, Jordan	(*)		2		
Cook, Nathan	1	2	2		
Chipman, Thos	2	1	5		
Collender, Reuben	(*)	1	2		
Seger, Joseph	2	3	4		
Page, Timo	1	2	3		
Burchell, Livi	3	3	3		
Barnum, Thos	1	2	5		
Turrell, Ebenr	3	2	5		
Hemenway, Danl	1	1	1		
Martin, Solomon	1	3	1		
Chipman, Timo	1	1	3		
Lovelow, Wm	1		2		
Treet, John	(*)	1	2		
Palmer, Wm	(*)		1		
Jones, Wm	2		4		
Skeels, Belden	2	1	4		
Stone, John	1	3	1		
Wilson, Jonathn	1		1		
Holt, Barzilla	2	1	5		
Noble, Asa	2	1	2		
VERGENNES TOWN.					
Fitch, Jobe G	1	2	3	1	
Goodridg, William	3		3	1	
Brush, William	3	2	6	1	
Branch, Alexander	2	1	5		
Chipman, Samuel	2	2	1		
Lewis, John	3		3		
Lewis, Robbert	2		2	1	
Strong, Asa	2	1	1	1	
Sanner, George	1	1	2		
Spencer, Ebenezr	5	1	2		
Utley, William	4	2	3		
McIntosh, Daniel	1	3	1		
Woodbridg, Enoch	3	2	6		
Hopkins, Rosw	1	4	3		
Tompson, Isaac	2	1	2		
Dibble, James	1	1	1		
Monty, James	1	1	2		
Hackstaff, John	1		1		
Robberts, Eli	3	1	2		
Chambers, William	1		2		
Welding, James				6	
Averil, Thomas	1		2		
Korah, James	1		1		
Healy, Abner	1	1	2		
Streeter, Josiah	1		2		
Oakes, John	1		1		
Man, Ebenezr	2	1	3	1	
Huntington, Ebenzr	2	1	2	1	
Painter, Azariah	3			1	
Brush, Ruth			1		
Green, John W	1	1	2		

* Illegible.

ADDISON COUNTY—Continued.

NAME OF HEAD OF FAMILY.	Free white males of 16 years and upward, including heads of families.	Free white males under 16 years.	Free white females, including heads of families.	All other free persons.	Slaves.
VERGENNES TOWN—con.					
Stephenson, Nathaniel	1	2	3		
Brooks, Azaniah	1	3	1		
Wyman, Asa	5				
Hamlin, Isaac	1		2		
Atley, Samuel	1	1	1		
Danley, James	1		1		
Smith, George	1		4		
Booth, David	7				
WEYBRIDGE TOWN.					
Sanford, Thos	1	3	2		
Britton, Claudius	2		3		
Peck, Elisha	1		2		
Lanson, Richard	1		1		
Field, Nathl	1	2	2		
Wright, Abner	3	3	4		
Wright, Abel	1	2	1		
Dunning, Abram	2	1	3		
James, Daniel	2	5	3		
Gilbert, Joseph	3	2	6		
Lewis, John	1		1		
Jewett, Saml	3		3	1	
Laurence, Nehemiah	1	2	3		
Kellogg, Joseph	2	1	3		
Laurence, Elisha	1		1		
Kellogg, Adah		2	3		
Norton, Shadrack	1	1	4		
Laurence, Jonathan	1		1		
Jackson, John	1	2	1		
Stickney, Zilla	1	3	3		
WEYBRIDGE TOWN—con.					
Smith, Saml	1		2		
Laurence, Abel	1		3		
McGee, Joseph	2	1	3		
Jewett, Elam	3	2	3		
St. Johns, Elijah	1	1	1		
Button, Benjm	2	1	3		
Laurence, Asa	1		5		
Clark, Saml	1	4	4		
Parmele, Aaron	2	1	3		
Gilbert, Augustus	1		2		
Plumb, Joseph	3		2		
Meker, Saml	1	2	3		
WHITING TOWN.					
Wesel, Henry	2	2	4		
Haws, Asa	2		3		
Medkiff, Philemon	1	1	4		
Wilson, John	5		2		
Andrus, Benjamin	1	1	1	1	
Butler, Isaac	1	3	6		
Hull, Jehiel, Ju	1	3	2		
Hubbart, Jonas	1	1	2		
Wilcocks, Hosea	2	1	2		
Loomer, Joseph	1	1	2		
Drewry, Luther	1	1	2		
Harris, Martha		2	3		
Kirkum, Elijah	2		2		
Whelock, Ebenzr	1		2		
Connick, Jonathan	1	1	3		
Connick, John	1		4		
WHITING TOWN—con.					
Hull, Jehul	2		2		
McNeil, Thomas	2	3	1		
Day, Richard	2	1	1		
Langley, David	3	3	4		
Mongar, Jehu	2		3		
Stone, Stukely	1	1	3		
Stone, Thomas	1	2	1		
Parker, Jeremiah	1	1	2		
Brown, David	2		2		
Bush, Samuel	2		5		
Mongar, Nathaniel	1	1	3		
Bar, Alexander	1	1	3		
Needham, Joseph	2	4	3		
Moulton, Ephraim	1	1	2		
Sparlin, Philip	1	3	5		
Allen, Ezra	2	3	3		
Case, Abijah	1	1	3		
Petibone, Lumun	1		2		
Nap, Eleazer	1	1	3		
Ketchum, Elihu	1		2		
Curtis, Aaron	1	2	2		
Stone, Josias	1	2	3		
Chamberlin, Henry	1	2	5		
Washburn, Jerusha		1	4		
Foster, Joel	2	2	1		
Rust, Daniel	3		2		
Walker, Gideon	4	3	1		
Beach, John	1	2	2		
Easty, Aaron	3		1		
Winfield, Joseph	1		3		

BENNINGTON COUNTY.

NAME OF HEAD OF FAMILY.	Free white males of 16 years and upward, including heads of families.	Free white males under 16 years.	Free white females, including heads of families.	All other free persons.	Slaves.
ARLINGTON TOWN.					
Todd, Timothy	3		4		
Canfield, Nathan	3	5	4		
Stone, Luther	1	2	4		
Gifford, Wm	1	5	1		
Wright, Nathan	1	3	4		
Boice, Peter	1		1		
Blowers, Hart	3		2		
Blowers, Ephraim	1		3		
Whitney, Benjamin	1	1	3		
Boice, Hendrick	1	2	4		
Fosbury, David	1	3	2		
Bentley, Benjn	1	1	1		
Astin, Elisha	2	1	3		
Furbush, John	1	2	7		
Maddon, John	4	3	4		
Snider, Jacob	2	3	5		
Dunlap, Wm	1	2	4		
Dunlap, Seth	1	1	3		
Snider, John	1	1	2		
Sherwood, Dyah	1	1	2		
Buck, Benjamin	1	4	4		
Clarke, William	1		1		
Root, Wm	1	1	2		
Chipman, Lemuel	1	1	3		
Parks, Reuben	1	1	3		
Hawley, Mary			2		
Stodder, James	1	2	3		
Mattison, David	3	2	3		
Barber, William	1	1	1		
Himas, William	3	2	4		
Starnes, Ebenezer P	1	1	1		
Falsom, Samel	1	1	4		
Merrifield, Abraham	1	5	2		
Aylsworth, Abel	1	3	6		
Castale, Levi	2	2	4		
Rug, Mathew	1	1	6		
Coy, Daniel	2	2	8		
Daten, Caleb	2	2	4		
Hurd, Tirus	3	4	3		
Turner, Miller	1	1	1		
Crowfoot, David	1		2		
Hawley, Courtis	2	2	5		
Jones, Wm	1	5	1		
Welch, Micah	1		2		
Buck, Lemuel	2	2	4		
Horton, Elijah	1	1	4		
Darton, Joseph	1	1	2		
Warding, William	1	1	3		
Wiley, Bartholomu	1	1	4		
Austin, Jeremiah	1	1	2		
Blowers, Wm	1	2	4		
Blowers, Alice		2	2		
Blowers, Abiel	1	2	3		
Blowers, David	1	5	1		
ARLINGTON TOWN—con.					
Shays, Daniel	2	1	6		
Pettingale, Olliver	1	3	4		
Hawley, Zadock	2	1	3		
Barney, Constant	4		3		
Jones, Lucus	2		4		
Cluit, John	1		1		
McDanals, Richard	2	1	1		
Beebe, Reubin	1	1	2		
Norton, Henry	1	3	1		
Holibert, Wait	1	2	3		
Dyer, Eliab	3	1	3		
Barny, Daniel	1		2		
Wood, Moses	2	2	2		
Hard, James, Jr	1				
Parsons, David	1	2	2		
Baker, John	3	2	5		
Baker, Jonathan	1	3	3		
Main, Thomas	3	1	2		
Hall, Jeremiah	1	3	2		
Weaks, Samel	2	1	4		
Stone, Peleg	2	1	3		
Stone, Samel	2	1	2		
Stone, Elisha	1		1		
Bills, Joshua	2	1	3		
Burrit, Daniel	1	2	4		
Bennedick, Ickebod	3	2	6		
Nickols, Anna			2		
Eastman, Benjn	2	1	3		
Warters, Samel	1	2	1		
Cerm, John	1	3	3		
Buck, Ruama	1	1	1		
Buck, Robert	3	1	2		
Vandoozer, Abraham	1	2	4		
Fairchild, Jesse	2	1	4		
Clyde, Wm	1	2	5		
Washburn, Samel	1	1	6		
Jones, John	2	2	2		
Sulleven, Samel	1	2	3		
Hines, Jacob	2		1		
Burrit, Edmond	1		1		
Bostick, Mathew	4	1	5		
Daton, Daniel	1	1	1		
Mackey, John	2	3	3		
Hoick, Solomon	1	4	2		
Squires, Eli	1	1	1		
Searls, Mary	1	1	1		
Hatch, Wim	2	1	3		
Deming, Gamaleil	1	1	2		
Murwin, Elnathan	2	4	8		
Wails, Elisha	1	1	8		
Leonard, Ebenezr	1	1	2		
Leonard, Zar	1		2		
Deming, Martin	2				
Deming, Silvester	1	1	1		
ARLINGTON TOWN—con.					
Hawley, Abel	2		1		
Leonard, Benajah	1		1		
Canfield, Israel	1	4	2		
Herrman, Benjn	1	1	2		
Hawley, Andrew	2	1	2		
Butler, Solomon	3	2	2		
Berns, Susannah		1	4		
Hawley, Isaiah	1	1	3		
Sterns, Daniel	1	1	4		
Parsons, Aron	1		3		
Welman, Benjamin	1		2		
Wells, Wm	1		4		
Foot, John	1	4	3		
Elsworth, Samuel	1				
Ash, John	1	1	1		
Squires, Joseph	1	2	3		
Moffit, Zebulon	1	2	4		
Knap, Ephraim	1	2	3		
Blowers, Alixander	1		4		
Spencer, Rufus	2	1	4		
Stone, Uriah	2		1		
Wallace, Isaac H., Jur	1		4		
Wallace, Isaac H	3		3		
Whiston, John	3	2	2		
Debzin, Micah	1		2		
Williams, John	2	1	5		
Forriss, Peter	1		4		
Odel, Samel	1	1	4		
Wall, William	1		3		
Squires, Deliverance	1	1	5		
Parks, John	1	1	4		
Hawley, Josiah	3		3		
Hawley, Lemuel	2		3		
Fuller, James	1	4	1		
Pierce, Silvanus	2	1	2		
Hawkins, Benoni	1	1	2		
Hard, Philo	1	1	6		
Lince, Fredrick	1	2	2		
Ostrander, Agbert	2	4	2		
Lot, Abram	2	1	3		
Coy, Elisha	1		4		
Sharp, Uriah	1	1	1		
Gray, John	2	2	2		
Norton, David	2	2	6		
Oatman, George	1		1		
Oatman, Isaac	2	1	2		
Oatman, Daniel	3	4	3		
Oatman, Benjn	1	5	2		
Spinck, Benjn	1				
Silvester, Andrew	2	2	4		
Andrew, Thomas	2	1	3		
Oatman, George	1	3	1		
Spink, Sineca	1				
Baker, Ozi	1	3	2		

BENNINGTON COUNTY—Continued.

NAME OF HEAD OF FAMILY.	Free white males of 16 years and upward, including heads of families.	Free white males under 16 years.	Free white females, including heads of families.	All other free persons.	Slaves.
ARLINGTON TOWN—con.					
Hill, Levi	2	2	4		
Sharp, Abel	1	1	3		
Sharp, Lewis	1		3		
Hard, Zadock	2	3	3		
Weeb, Reubin	2	2	3		
Cole, Austin	3	2	5		
Cogsdill, John	1	3	3		
Boice, William	3	3	4		
BENNINGTON TOWN.					
Robinson, Moses	7	2	2		
Safford, Samel	3	1	4		
Swift, Job	3	4	6		
Walbridge, Ebenezer	3	4	6		
Tichenor, Isaac	5		2		
Smith, Noah	1	3	4	1	
Brush, Nathl	4	1	3		
Dewey, Elijah	3	1	2		
Robinson, Jonathan	1	3	3		
Butler, Eldad	2	3	1		
Robinson, David	3	3	4		
Robinson, Moses, Jr	2	2	3		
Hyde, Jacob	1		1		
Nelson, Joseph	1	1	2		
Bumford, Thomas	1	3	6		
Spencer, Nathl	1	3	3		
Hubbel, Aaron	2	2	5		
Squires, Saxton	2	4	4		
Smith, Ezekiel	1	1	3		
Wickwire, Joseph	4	1	2		
Scot, Moses	3	3	7		
Hendricks, Isaiah	3	4	5		
Haswill, Anthony	2	5		1	
Russell, David	1	1	5		
Potter, Wm	2	5	3		
Potter, Amos	1		1		
Danforth, Elhenah	2	3	4		
Jackson, Robert	1	1	2		
Robinson, John	1	3	2		
Harwood, Stephen	1	2	3		
Walbridge, Henry	2		4		
Wood, Ebenezer	2		3		
Rudd, Joseph	3	3	5		
Follit, Timothy	2		6		
Story, Benajah	1	1	6		
Griswould, Wm	3	1	3		
Hicks, Saml	2	2	2		
Norton, John	3	2	4		
Fassitt, Benjn	4	2	5		
Safford, Jacob	2	1	2		
Fairchild, Sheman	3				
House, Joseph	6	1	5		
Brown, Zacheriah	1		1		
Reed, Johua	3	1	3		
Ames, John B.	1	1	3		
Hebro, Zepheniah	2	(*)	(*)		
Meril, Jedediah	1	2	5		
Safford, Solomon	2	1	2		
Walbridge, Solomon	1	4	3		
Atkins, John	1	1	5		
Buck, Saml	1		6		
Roach, Israel	1		4		
Bliss, Luther	1	3	2		
Larrence, Nathl	1	1	4		
Scot, Phenhas	1	4	3		
Hopkins, Stephen	3	4	5		
Hurd, Moses	1	1	7		
Church, Ira	1	1	2		
Eager, William	2		2		
Rice, Silas	2	3	5		
Field, Jesse	3	2	5		
Hinsdale, Joseph	7	5	5		
Deming, Benjn	1	2	3		
Duel, Jacob	1		2		
Hubbel, Elnathan	1	3	2		
Parker, Henry	2		3		
Camp, John	1	1	4		
Larnard, Joseph	1	3	2		
Brakenidge, Daniel	1	1	2		
Wailes, John	1	3	3		
Hinemon, Ester	1		2		
Noice, Nathl	1	4	3		
Rug, Moses	1	1	1		
Rose, Elijah	1		3		
Mallery, Ephriam	1		1		
Mallery, Ephraim, Junr	1		1		
Ashley, Thomas	1	2	2		
Ashley, Zenas	1	2	1		
Brakenidge, William	1	2	3		
Hinson, John	1	3	2		
Stickney, Eliphlet	1	4	7		

NAME OF HEAD OF FAMILY.	Free white males of 16 years and upward, including heads of families.	Free white males under 16 years.	Free white females, including heads of families.	All other free persons.	Slaves.
BENNINGTON TOWN—con.					
Haynes, Aaron	3	2	9		
Haynes, David	5	2	6		
Harmon, Daniel	3	5	2		
Densemore, Eri	1	3	6		
Cason, Thomas	1	1	2		
Palmer, Timothy	1	2	2		
Car, William	1		2		
Saltar, Richard	2	2	6		
Westerfield, Robert				3	
Rude, Josua	1	2	3		
Brown, Samuel	2	1	2		
Sly, Mill	1		4		
Sly, Wim	1	2	4		
Smith, Ephraim	1	2	6		
Dolph, Sibbel			7		
Rogers, Martha		2	5		
Allen, Abiel	2	1	6		
Leonard, Williams	1				
Cleaveland, Solomon	1	2	4		
Cleaveland, Johnson	1	1	2		
Redman, Thomas	1	2	2		
Rudd, John	1	4	6		
Waters, Oliver	1	1	3		
Edy, Obediah	3	5	1		
Bushnal, James	2	1	1		
Hunt, Thomas	3	5	3		
Johnson, Geore				2	
Chase, Harverlin	1	1	1		
Mosely, Roswel	5	2	3		
Stiles, Austin	1		3		
Cristee, George	1	1	1		
Attwood, Samuel	2		2		
Smith, Champion	1	1	1		
Farnsworth, Joseph	1	3	2	1	
Blackamore, Samuel	5	2	5		
Blackamore, Saml	1		1		
Lyon, Simeon	3	4	4		
Cole, Reuben	1	2	4		
Kuzear, John	1	3	3		
Reed, John	1	3	3		
Teakles, Allixander	1	1	1		
Rug, Martha		1	2		
Clark, Nathan	1		1		
Willis, Asa	1	1	1		
Smith, Samuel	3	3	1		
Whitcomb, John	1		1		
Downs, Elisha	3	3	2		
Hall, Thomas	3		2		
Jewit, Fredrick	2	1	2		
Palmer, Samuel	1		4		
Cross, Abiel	1	3	1		
Lester, Guy	1	1	2		
Walbridge, Asa	1		4		
Colvin, Reubin	4	1	7		
Rogers, James	4	2	4		
Powers, Joseph	1	1	1		
Denio, Isreal	1				
Bordman, Elijah	6	3	6		
Wood, Job, Junr	1		2		
McEndrick, Anna			3		
Comb, Timothy	1		2		
Greenslit, James	1	3	4		
Doge, John	1	1	1		
Dewey, Eldad	4	1	8		
Chase, Ebenezer	1	2	3		
Randil, John	1	1	2		
Adow, ——				6	
Hill, Daniel	1	3	3		
Deming, James	1	2	2		
Parker, Samuel	2	5	4		
Paddock, Ichabod	1	3	4		
Paddock, Thomas	1	1	3		
Pattison, Andrew	1	3	5		
Scot, William	1	3	4		
Potter, Shradrach	1	2	3		
Luther, Martin	1	1	2		
Masasens, Francis	1	1	3		
Herington, James	1		3		
Burnit, Micajah	1	2	3		
Parsons, Aaron	2	1	2		
Blair, Robert	4	2	6		
Armstrong, Hopestil	3	4	5		
Street, Silas	2	1	2		
Cole, Peleg	3				
House, Stephen	3	1	5		
Nichols, Robert	1		1		
Willis, Stouten	2	2	3		
Yale, Aaron	1		1		
Brooks, Barnabas	1				
Smith, William	1				
White, Leonard	1				
Dyer, Silvanus	2		1		

NAME OF HEAD OF FAMILY.	Free white males of 16 years and upward, including heads of families.	Free white males under 16 years.	Free white females, including heads of families.	All other free persons.	Slaves.
BENNINGTON TOWN—con.					
Clark, Samuel	1				
Strong, Elijah	1				
Porter, David	1				
Deming, Aaron	2		5		
Hatheway, Joshua	1				
Hatheway, Simeon	2	1	2		
Hathaway, Shadrch	1	2	3		
Shephard, Ashur	1	2	3		
Fay, Joseph	3	3	2		
McCoy, Samuel	1		1		
Goreham, Stephen	1				
Johnson, Esecke	1		1		
Carpenter, Joshua	4	3	7		
Mattison, John	2	4	4		
Hyde, Asahel	1	1	3		
Newel, Normon	2	1	3		
Stout, James	1	1	3		
Fay, Elijah	3	1	5		
Hoag, Cardinal	1		1		
Billings, Bulah	2	3	5		
Harwood, Zachariah	3	5	4		
Wabbridge, Silas	1	2	4		
Grihams, Abraham	1	1	2		
Robinson, Leonard	2	2	5		
Robinson, Silas	2		3		
Robinson, Paul	1		2		
Robinson, Samel	4	2	5		
Prat, Daniel	3		2		
Follitt, Charles	1	1	2		
Abel, Thomas	2	3	4		
Staples, Joseph	1		2		
Harmon, Simeon, Junr	2	4	3		
Potter, John	2	1	6		
Larrence, John	2	2	4		
Palmer, Seth	1		2		
Nortin, Martin	2		4		
Palmer, Joseph	2	1	3		
Colefix, John	4	1	2		
Prat, Stephen	2	3	3		
McElcharan, George	2		1		
Rise, Moses	1	5	1		
Robinson, Joseph	1		1		
Peirce, David	1	3	5		
Houghton, Silas	1	3	5		
Marsh, Amos	2		2		
Fay, David	4		3		
Dewy, Loan	2	1	4		
Dewy, Elizabeth			2	1	
Nichols, Elisha	4	5	3		
Church, Samuel	1	1	2		
Wood, Job	1	5	4		
Wood, Andrew	1	1	3		
Norton, Joseph	1	3	2		
Armstrong, Hezekiah	3	1	5		
Armstrong, Reuben	1		2		
Fisk, Jonathan	2	3	3	4	
Parker, William	1		3		
Weaks, John	1	3	2		
Fisk, Jacob	1		2		
Tracy, Daniel	3		4		
Randol, Gideon	1		3		
Potter, William	1		1		
Hawks, Eleazer	3	1	2		
Biddlecome, Daniel	3	1	4		
Webster, Samuel	(*)		1		
Wood, Ephriam	3	4	2		
Fay, Jonas	4	2	3		
Green, Willard	2	1			
Bellows, Silas	2	1	6		
Godfrey, George	1	2	2		
Robinson, Joseph	2	7	2		
Hatheway, Simeon	2	1	4		
Hatheway, Levi	1	3	4		
Thomas, Joel	2	5	6		
Hubble, Lemuel	1	2	4		
Smith, Gans	1	1	3		
Wood, Joshua	1	2	2		
Rogers, Jonathan	1	1	4		
Stearns, Benjamin	1	1	3		
Rosier, Nathan	1	3	2		
Beaman, Daniel	1	2	2		
Davis, David	1	1	1		
Huntly, Elisha	1	2	2	1	
Huntley, Solomon	1	4	5		
Clark, Theophilus	3	2	3		
Sterns, Shadrach	2	2	1		
McCulloch, John	1	1	6		
Fuller, Josiah	2		2		
Webb, Benjamin	1	2	6		
Rice, Isaac	2	1	4		
Weeks, Judah	1	3	3		
Henry, John	2		1		

* Illegible.

BENNINGTON COUNTY—Continued.

NAME OF HEAD OF FAMILY.	Free white males of 16 years and upward, including heads of families.	Free white males under 16 years.	Free white females, including heads of families.	All other free persons.	Slaves.
BENNINGTON TOWN—continued.					
Finch, Joshua	1	4	4		
Hurd, Isaac	1	1	2		
Rice, Oliver	1		1		
Biddlecome, Richard	1	2	2		
Rice, Stephen	2	3	5		
Lamphier, Ezra	1	1	2		
Prindle, Sam[l]	1	4	4		
Harvey, Samuel	2	1	2		
Alixander, John	2	2	3		
Wheat, Jonathan	3	1	2		
Dorling, Joseph	1	1	2		
Cady, Cornelius	2	1	3		
Scot, Abigal	1	1	5		
Abbot, Timothy	3	1	3		
Rug, Sam[l]	1		3		
Rug, Nath[el]	2	1	2		
Rug, Joel	1		4		
Story, Daniel	4		1		
Walbridge, Gustavus	3	1	4		
Harto, John	1		3		
Lyon, Simeon	3	3	4		
Lyon, Abiel	1		1		
Stratton, Joel	1	3	1		
Raswer, Robert	1		1		
Stacia, Sam[l]	1		1		
Webster, Isaac	2	1	6		
China, William	1		4		
Herderson, Thomas	4	1	7		
Gilbert, Jonathan	1	3	4		
Geers, Joseph	2	3	4		
Parkas, Alpheus	1	2	2		
Atkins, John	1	1	6		
White, Ebenezer	2	1	1		
Wright, Eleazer	1	3	2		
Denio, Aaron	1	2	2		
Gilbert, Solomon	1	5	1		
Wright, Phinehas	1	4	3		
Barney, Rufus	2	3	6		
Burt, William	2	4	4		
Safford, Sam[l]., Jun[r]	1		1		
Davison, Peter	1	2	3		
Bolten, Richard	1				
Sheffield, Daniel	1	1	4		
Hall, Joseph	3	2	7		
Biblins, Thomas	1		1		
Hall, Edward	1		1		
Pierce, Uriah	1	3	4		
Harmon, Ezekiel	1	2	4		
Harmon, Simeon	2		2		
French, Marcy			4		
Harmon, Austin	2	1	2		
Larebe, William	1	1	1		
Wood, Nathan	2		3		
Wood, John	1	1	3		
Turner, Nath[el]	3	3	7		
Bingham, Calvin	2	5	5		
Marther, William	4	1	3		
Branch, Zepheniah, J[r]	1		4		
Phillips, Esquire	1	4	3		
Sage, Moses	3	3	6		
Alixander, John	1	1	1		
North, Asa	1		2		
Spaldin, Jacob	1	2	1		
Robins, John	2	3	5		
Larrence, Josiah	2	1	3		
Kieth, George, Jun[r]	1	2	1		
Weaks, David	2	1	4		
Dowing, David	3	2	3		
Clark, Daniel	1		1		
Whitcomb, Samuel	1	4	4		
Follit, Joseph	1	3	3		
Wood, Ebenezer, Jun[r]	1	3	3		
Marther, Stephen	1	2	2		
Sharwood, Ruth	1	1	4		
Mosyer, John		2	1		
Brown, Nath[el]	1	1	2		
Harwood, Benj[n]	2	1	3		
Clark, Joseph	1	2	1		
Tracy, Lemuel	1	2	1		
Smith, James	1	1	1		
Vaughan, Simeon	2	1	4		
Parson, Modad	1	5	4		
Parson, Jonathan	2		1		
Dibble, Benjamin	1	2	2		
Adams, William	1	3	1		
Rice, Silas	2	2	2		
Harmon, Silas	3		1		
Porter, Widow	2		1		
Kingsley, Jasan	2		1		
Wintworth, John	1		1		
Armstrong, Andrew	2				
Foskit, James	1	2	2		
Granger, Jeremiah	1	2	2		
Allen, Icabod	4	3	5		
Lomis, Jesse	1	3	4		
Beamon, Joseph	1	2	5		
Davis, Samul	1		1		
Sabins, Josiah	2	3	6		
Henry, William	4	1	5		
Davis, Josiah	1		4		
Ellit, John	1	1	2		
Armstrong, Libbeus	1		3		
Armstrong, Jacob	1		1		
Taylor, Thomas	1	2	6		
Taylor, Erastus	1	1	1		
Harwood, Peter	2	2	5		
Dickison, Nath[el]	2	3	4		
Rude, Daniel	2	4	3		
Smith, Robert	1	3	5		
Filimore, Nath[el]	2	4	4		
BROMLEY TOWN.					
Gilbert, John	1	4	3		
Dewey, Aaron	1	1	2		
Hollibert, Zacheriah	1		1		
Dewey, James	1	1			
Boland, William	1	1	1		
Molten, Joseph	1		2		
Colten, William	3		1		
Miller, Thomas	1	1	2		
Hollibert, Ebenezer	2	2	3		
Saxton, George	4		2		
Butterfield, Jonathan	1	4	4		
Cheney, Joseph	1	1	4		
Dewey, Aaron	1	1	1		
White, David	1	1	2		
Graham, David	1	2	3		
DORSETT TOWN.					
Kent, Cephu	2	1	4		
Shumway, John	2		3		
Underhil, Abraham	4	1	2		
Presson, John	1		1		
Pulford, Elisha	1		2		
Squires, Isaac	1	2	5		
Armstrong, Ebenezer	1	5	1		
Paddock, Price	1	1	1		
Chenia, Howard	1		2		
Martindil, Gershom	1	1	5		
Gray, John	2	3	6		
Gray, Isaah	1		6		
Gray, Isaac	1	4	1		
Hocumb, Noah	1	2	3		
Danton, W[m]	2	4	4		
Rider, Stephen	1	1	2		
Thomson, Amos	1	2	1		
Sykes, Silvanus	1	2	6		
Hocumb, John	1		1		
Kent, Cephus, Jun[r]	3	2	5		
Kent, Allexander	1	1	2		
Harmon, Asel	2		3		
Post, Reuben	1	1	3		
Sykes, Titus, Jun[r]	2	1	3		
Mirick, Joseph	1	3	2		
Nichols, Abraham	2	3	3		
Dimick, Ichobod	2	3	3		
Farewell, Asa	1	3	2		
Farewell, Isaac	2		2		
Farewell, John	3	1	4		
Balding, Eleazear	2	3	7		
Field, Amos	1	3	5		
Risden, Josiah	2		1		
Balding, Silas	4	2	6		
Rae, Abner	1		3		
Barns, John	1	3	3		
Lukins, John	1	2	5		
Bebe, Elisha	1	4	4		
Bonner, John	1	3	4		
More, Dudley	3	4	3		
Courtis, Zacheriah	5	3	3		
Runnals, Ephriam	1	1	2		
Allen, Henry	3	3	7		
Curtis, Joseph	1	2	3		
Curtis, Nicholus	1		5		
Clark, Nathan	1	3	4		
Gifford, Umphory	2	6	4		
Baker, Solomon	1	3	4		
Saxton, William	1	2	4		
Marsh, William	4	2	3		
More, Jedidiah	1		1		
Murrey, Mary	2	1	5		
Gilbert, Samuel	1	1	3		
DORSETT TOWN—con.					
Derga, Moses	1		2		
French, John	2	2	4		
Aylsworth, Ather	1	1	7		
Stores, Printice	1	1	3		
Basley, Price	1	2	3		
Morse, John	3		1		
Vaughn, Obediah	2	2	8		
French, Andrew	1	1	1		
Barlow, Daniel	2	1	3		
Hubbard, Thomas	2	2	2		
Morse, Noah	5	1	5		
Mattison, Amos	1		1		
Harris, Thomas	1	1	2		
Boings, Daniel	2	4	4		
Mattison, Phillip	1	3	4		
Deming, Eli	2	2	4		
Duning, Richard	2	1	5		
Burnham, Francis	1		2		
Burnham, Ashbel D	1	2	2		
Balding, Benj[n]	3	4	7		
Morse, Ebenz[r]	2	1	4		
Soper, Sam[el]	3		2		
Squires, Jonathan	1	1	2		
Mattison, Benj[n]	2	4	2		
Washbern, Tabor	1	2	3		
Barto, Sam[el]	1		2		
Barto, Francis	1		3		
Hoit, Barnabas	1	2	3		
Stores, Chipman	1	1	3		
Casson, Joshua	1		2		
Casson, Jacob	1	3	3		
Casson, Hannah		1	5		
Durge, Adeign	2		3		
Manley, George	1	2	6		
Manley, John, Ju[r]	1	2	1		
Manley, John	1		1		
Manley, Nathan	1	1	7		
Armstrong, Jonathan	1	3	5		
Warden, Jese	1	1	5		
Basil, Thomas	1		1		
Crane, David	1	2	4		
Eaton, Luther	1	1	3		
Kellog, Titus	1				
Clark, George	1	1	1		
Huggins, Zadoch	1	4	5		
Danton, Thomas	2	1	5		
Kent, John	2	1	4		
Kent, Dan	1	1	4		
Martindil, Stephen	3	3	4		
Balding, Eleazer	1	1	2		
Balding, Asa, Ju[r]	1		3		
Sykes, Israel	2		3		
Sykes, Victory	1	2	1		
Gray, Eward	3	1	3		
Gray, Sam[l]	1		2		
Hawley, Joseph	1	2	2		
Langdon, Jonathan	2	2	7		
Walton, George	1	1	1		
Balding, Asa	1	1	5		
Blackmore, Abner	1				
Manley, William	1		4		
Whelor, Nathan	1	1	1		
Rament, Joshua	1	2	2		
Hawley, Justice	1		1		
Touseley, W[m]	1	1	2		
Farnsworth, Reubin	2	4	5		
Smith, Seth	4		4		
Wells, Abraham	2	2	2		
Church, Sam[l]	1	1	3		
Grenal, Jonathan	1	3	6		
Mattison, Edward	2	2	2		
Sykes, Titus	1		4		
Cook, Shubel	1		3		
Shumway, Peter	1		1		
Colings, Abraham	1		1		
Colings, Sam[l]	2		2		
Collings, Justus	1	2	2		
Chesbro, Silvester	1	3	2		
Paddock, Anthony	3		4		
Sergents, John	3	1	4		
State, Ebenez[r]	4		6		
Kent, Moses	1	4	4		
Kingsbury, Thomas	1	2	3		
Bostick, Israel	3	1	3		
Manley, John	1		3		
Blomer, Reubin	2	1	5		
Smith, Israel	2		1		
Underhill, Isaac	1	3	2		
Underhill, W[m]	3	2	2		
Soper, Sam[l]	3		2		
Cook, John	1		2		
Allen, Seth	2		3		

BENNINGTON COUNTY—Continued.

NAME OF HEAD OF FAMILY.	Free white males of 16 years and upward, including heads of families.	Free white males under 16 years.	Free white females, including heads of families.	All other free persons.	Slaves.
DORSETT TOWN—con.					
Soper, John	2	2	2		
Sutherland, Saml	1		1		
Allen, Robert	1	2	3		
Allen, Obediah	1	2	5		
King, Joshua	1	5	4		
Sheldon, Joseph	1	3	4		
Collins, Charles	1	3	4		
Scoffield, Seth	1		2		
Munson, Erastus	1	2	1		
Weaver, Fredrick	1		1		
GLASTONBURY TOWN.					
Tibbets, George	1		4		
Wood, Coffin	1	3	4		
Clark, Jonathan	1	3	2		
Clark, Asa	1	1	1		
Fuller, Mathew	1	2	4		
Sly, Henry	1	2	2		
LANDGROVE TOWN.					
Utley, Asa	1	2	6		
Utley, Oliver	1		2		
Utley, Pebody	1		2		
Richardson, Daniel	1	1	4		
Carpender, David	2		4		
Tuttle, Daniel	1	1	2		
MANCHESTER TOWN.					
Ormsby, Gideon	8	1	5		
Roberts, Christopher	2	4	3		
Munson, Jarud	4	1	4		
Biggelow, Ezra	1	1	4		
Taylor, Moses	1		3		
Smith, Pirez	1	2	4		
Brevoort, Isaac	4	3	4	1	
Ells, Warterman	2	2	1		
Mindus, Wilhelmus	2		1		
Hicks, Daniel	1	1	2		
Hicks, Benjn	1	1	4		
Mackintire, Benjn	3	1	6		
Smith, Noah	2		3		
Barber, Daniel	1	3	4		
Gould, William	1	1			
Weller, Asa	3	3	3		
Danks, Shadrack	2		2		
Powel, Martin	1	1	3	1	
Brunson, Eli	3	1	5		
Lummis, Fredum	2				
Hitchcock, Ebenezer	1		2		
Hoit, Meriam		2	4		
Giffin, James	2	3	2		
Sheldon, Josiah	2	3	2		
Field, George	1	3	2		
Pettibone, Saml	3	2	5		
Rose, Joel	2	6	3		
Curtis, Caleb	1				
Curtis, David	1		1		
Soper, Stephen	3	1	4		
Anderson, David	3	1	3		
Purdey, Benjn	2		2		
Purdey, Daniel	3	2	5		
Hawley, Jabez	3	4	3		
Hollistor, Gurdin	2	1	3		
Brown, Timothy	5	1	6		
Munson, Rufus	1	1	1		
Allin, Abel	2	1	2	2	
Richardson, Amos	1	2	3		
Richardson, Nathan	2		1		
Richardson, John	1	2	4		
Richardson, Andrew	2	2	5		
Sabin, John	1	3	2		
Mackentire, Richard	2	2	1		
Whitman, George	1	1	2		
Washburn, Stephen	3	1	3		
Collins, Soloman	1	1	5		
Collins, Nathaniel	2	2	7		
Ormsby, Jonathan	3		5		
Purdey, Benja., Jr.	4	4	4		
Jones, Daniel	3	2	4		
Bullis, Charles	1		1		
Bullis, Henry	1	6	3		
Curtis, Elias	2	2	6		
French, David	1	2	4		
Luis, James	1	4	3		
Obriant, Timothy	1		2		
Robert, John	1	2	4		
Curtis, John	1		3		
Purdy, Reuben	3	2	5		
Gates, William	1	1	3		

NAME OF HEAD OF FAMILY.	Free white males of 16 years and upward, including heads of families.	Free white males under 16 years.	Free white females, including heads of families.	All other free persons.	Slaves.
MANCHESTER TOWN—con.					
Hilliard, Daniel	1	1	3		
Roberts, John	1		1		
Hilliard, Joshua	1	2	3		
Richardson, Nathan, Jr.	1	2	3		
Meed, Timothy	4	1	4		
Meed, Truman	1	4	2		
Soper, Timothy	1		4		
Anderson, James	1	1	3		
Spencer, Stephen	1	2	2		
Meed, Jacob	1	3	2		
Kinney, Jesse	1	1	1		
Whelpley, Jeremiah	3	4	1		
Vanderlap, John	1	3	1		
Gideons, Job	2	3	6		
Anderson, Robert	1	1	2		
Sperey, Moses	4	1	3		
Saxton, George	1	3	5		
Wood, Berzeliel	1	4	3		
Stephens, Daniel	1	3	3		
Boorn, Nathaniel	1		1		
Boorn, Amos	1		2		
Soper, Moses	2		2		
Hennise, Richard	2	1	3		
Straight, Saml	3	3	5		
Peck, Simeon	1	3	2		
Boorn, Jarod	1	1	2		
Smith, Joseph	1		1		
Pettibone, Abel	1		4		
Chipman, Wm	1	2	2		
Corey, Jacob	1	1	6		
Colvin, Richard	2	3	5		
Wood, Edmond	1		5		
Wood, Nickalus	1		3		
Lord, John	1	1	1		
Thomas, Charles	1		1		
French, Saml	2		2		
Odel, Jeremiah	1		2		
Woodword, Ebenezer	1	5	3		
Benadicts, Ezra	1	1	2		
Duning, Eliakim	1		3		
Blackesly, Ezra	1	1	1		
Sidway, James	1	2	1		
Bennedict, Saml	1	4	1		
Hyde, Clarke	1	2	4		
Cowel, Saml	1		2		
Benedict, Jonathan	2	1	3		
Holt, James	1	1	2		
Hyde, Nehemiah	2	1	3		
Akins, Jonathan	2	2	2		
Jemison, Jeames	3	1	4		
Jemison, William	1		1		
Loggins, Robert	3	2	2		
Loggins, Hugh	1		2		
Wait, Jeremiah	3	3	3		
Cornwell, Joseph	3	2	2		
Berkit, Danil	3		3		
Beedle, John	1		2		
Henderson, Edward	1	3	2		
Cornwill, Reubin	1		1		
French, Samuel	1		2		
French, Joshua	1				
Lee, David	2	1	3		
Bullice, Jarman	2	5	1		
Beedle, William	2	4	6		
Bristol, Abel	2	3	4		
Bates, Zadock	1	2	3		
Serjents, John	2	1	3		
Odil, Jacob	4		5		
French, Joseph	2	2	5		
French, Elijah	1	1	6		
Sutherland, Saml	5	5	7		
Johns, Daniel	1	1	3		
Day, Dudley	1	1	1		
Vaughn, James	1	3	4		
Saxton, Aron,	2	2	3		
Soper, Elizabeth		2	6		
Dye, Wm	2		5		
Runalds, Phillip	2	3	4		
Jones, John	1	3	4		
Squire, Isaac	1		2		
Robbet, Peter	4	4	2		
Sterge, Christopher	2		1		
Collens, Christopher	2	3	4		
Sunderland, Wallis	1	2	3		
Prindle, Gideon	1	2	5		
Bull, Thomas, Junr	1		2		
Harmond, Daniel	1		1		
Holmes, Edward	1	1	6		
Harmond, Benjn	1		2		
Mason, Aron	1	4	5		
Smith, Fredrick	1	1	1		
Bull, Thomas	4		6		

NAME OF HEAD OF FAMILY.	Free white males of 16 years and upward, including heads of families.	Free white males under 16 years.	Free white females, including heads of families.	All other free persons.	Slaves.
MANCHESTER TOWN—con.					
Sunderland, Peleg	2	1	2		
Smith, John	2	4	6		
Chipman, Deborah		1	5		
Beers, Benjn	1	3	6		
Palmer, Noah	2	2	4		
Dickson, Joseph	2	5	3		
Burton, Elijah	1	3	3		
Brintnal, George	2	1	3		
Andres, Elijah	2	4	1		
Soper, Stephen	1		1		
Soper, Thomas	1		5		
Dun, Dunkin	1	3	2		
Coery, Jonathan	2	3	3		
Smith, Nathan	2	3	3		
Bracket, Christopher	2	2	4		
Basley, Daniel	2		1		
Austin, John	1	3	3		
Kyle, Wm	1	4	2		
Kyle, Ephraim	1	4	5		
Boiden, Edmond	1		2		
Glazier, David	2	1	4		
Walton, Perez	1	1	2		
Wakelin, Benjn	1				
Boiden, Jonathan	1		5		
Hogobone, John	2	4	4		
Andres, Nathl	2	1	1		
Edmons, Joseph	1	4	3		
Bishop, Benony	1	1	4		
Boorn, Nathl., Junr	1	3	2		
Boorn, Barned	1	2	3		
Allen, William	4	1	2		
Pettibone, Seth	1	4	2		
Pettibone, Eli	1		1		
Burton, Josiah	3	2	2		
Burton, Isaac	1		1		
Hollister, Elijah	3	3	2	1	
Nickerson, Constant	1	6	1		
Hurd, Abijah	2		1		
Stodder, Stephen	5		5		
Lockwood, Josiah	1	2	3		
Canfield, Silas	1	5	4		
Coley, Levi	1	1	4		
Taylor, Jonathan	1	2	5		
Ferrey, Josiah	1	2	2		
Meed, Timothy, Junr	2	4	4		
Meed, Phillip	2	4	5		
Purday, David	2	1	4		
POWNAL TOWN.					
Jewet, Thomas	1	2	4		
Wright, Charles	1		1		
Wright, Solomon	2	4	2		
Prat, Daniel	1	3	2		
Hungerford, Amasa	1	6	5		
Bowdish, Joseph	1	1	1		
Carpender, Barned	1	2	3		
Doby, Benjamin	1		3		
Allen, Christopher	1	3	7		
Reynolds, Robert	2		1		
Page, Elijah	1	2	2		
Nobles, Eli	3	4	3		
Towsley, Gideon	1	4	2		
Mash, Nathan	1	2	2		
Mash, Eleazer, Jur	2	1	1		
Moon, Asa	2	1	3		
Noble, John	1		1		
Aylsworth, Judiah	4	1	3		
Fay, Isaac	1	1	2		
Ladd, James	1	2	4		
Blood, John	2	3	5		
Larabee, Eleazer	4		5		
Mash, Eleazer	3		2		
Demick, Abel	3	4	5		
Lovit, John	2	1	2		
Jinks, Levi	1	3	1		
Rud, John	1		2		
Larabee, Joseph	1		1		
Downer, John	3	2	6		
Wallace, Isaac	1		1		
Eaton, Benjamin	4	5	5		
Morgin, Benjamin	1	1	5		
Barber, Joseph	2	4	4		
Clark, Nathaniel	1		3		
Tharp, Benjn	2	1	2		
Wallace, Nathl	3		2		
Carter, Fredrick	2	2	3		
Carpender, Gardner	1	1	1		
Barber, Joseph, Junr	1	1	1		
Bates, Francis	1		2		
Bates, Stephen	1	1	1		
Bates, Daniel	1	1	2		

BENNINGTON COUNTY—Continued.

NAME OF HEAD OF FAMILY.	Free white males of 16 years and upward, including heads of families.	Free white males under 16 years.	Free white females, including heads of families.	All other free persons.	Slaves.
POWNAL TOWN—con.					
Jewet, Benj[n]	2	2	1		
Munson, Timothy	2	1	2		
Scanton, Joshua	2		1		
Scanton, William	1		2		
Mattison, Joshua	1	4	4		
Perkins, John	1	3	3		
Bushnal, Ephriam	1	2	3		
Page, David	3	3	4		
Shermon, Andrew	1	4	3		
Myas, Hezekiah	1	3	5		
Clarke, Ithamer	1	3	3		
Gardiner, George, Ju[r]	2	1	5		
Gardner, Oliver	1	1	3		
Gib, Caleb	2	2	3		
Hovey, Zacheus	2		1		
Gardner, Abraham	2	1	6		
Gardner, George	1		1		
Borns, Samuel	1	1	3		
Green, Timothy	1	3	2		
Burrit, Peter	3	3	5		
Duning, Josiah	1	5	3		
Shermon, John	2	3	3		
Kittle, Elias	1	1	2		
Duning, Michil	2	1	3		
Hunt, John	1	1	2		
Lille, Reubin	2	1	4		
Rusil, Asa	2	1	4		
Timothy, Daniel	2	2	6	(*)	
Taylor, John	1	3	3		
Prat, William	1	2	2		
Prat, Silas	1	4	1		
Burt, Aaron	2		1		
Blood, Jared	1	1	3		
Tulley, John	1	3	3		
Youngs, John	1	3	2		
Youngs, Abraham	1	1	2		
Moon, Robert	2				
Brown, Richard	4	5	3		
Prosen, John	1	7	2		
Angel, Eseck	1	4	3		
Westinghousen, John H	2	1	4		
Lord, Jonathan	1	4	3		
Hall, William & Guardner	5	2	5		
Printice, Ichabod	3		1		
Stannard, David	1	1	2		
Deal, Bostion	1	1	2	1	
Deal, Peter	1		3		
Phillips, Syrel	1		2		
Wagaer, John	1	2	4		
Voshbough, Abraham	3	4	5		
Lewis, Mathew	2	1	2		
Thomson, Nathan	1	1	3		
Drake, Josiah	1	2	1		
Phillips, Elijha	1	1	2		
Aylsworth, Wanton	4	1	2		
Buchland, Isaac	2	2	4		
Weeb, Jeremiah	1	2	4		
Akins, David	2		1		
Page, Virgil	2	1	2		
Roberts, Samuel	2	1	3		
Sherman, Jacob	1	1	2		
Wright, Josiah	3	3	4		
Aylsworth, Judiah	1	1	3		
Carley, Joseph, Jun[r]	2	3	2		
Green, Samuel	1	3	2		
Samson, Isaac	3		3		
Brigs, Enos	1	1	2		
Fowler, Joseph	1	1	3		
Case, Nath[l]	3	2	4		
Welch, Samuel	2	2	3		
Welch, John	1	2	3		
Jackson, Lyman	1	4	2		
Hall, Benjamin	1		1		
Ovit, William	2	3	5		
Turner, John	2		2		
Cartwright, Christopher	1	2	4		
Smith, Derrick	2	3	4		
Prat, Elijah	1		1		
Morey, Daniel	1	1	2		
Welch, Elijah	1		2		
Welch, Daniel	1	1	1		
Hurd, Ebenezer	1	1	3		
Phillips, Job	4	1	3		
Phillips, Daniel	1	1	5		
Lewis, Abisha	2	1	4		
Aldin, John	1	1	1		
Lewis, Abisha, Jun[r]	1	2	3		
Lewis, Daniel	1		1		
Thomson, Benoni	1	4	4		
Houghton, Joseph	3	1	3		
Thomson, Levi	3	1	7		
Cook, John	1		2		
Tuffs, Henry	1	2	1		
Witham, Malica	1	1	4		
Morgin, Anna	1		2		
Hendricks, Unice			2		
Pembleton, Benajah	1		3		
Nobles, Josiah	1	2	6		
Courtis, James	1	5	5		
Hindricks, W[m]	2	1	4		
Powers, Larrence	1	2	4		
Rusil, Jonathan	1	1	3		
Andrew, Noel	1		9		
Niles, John	1		1		
Parker, Moses	1	3	1		
Mattison, Henry	2		3		
Niles, John, Jun[r]	2	3	2		
Myas, Joseph	1		1		
Mattison, James	1		2		
Moffit, John	2	1	4		
Kies, Samuel	3	2	3		
Witham, Witherly, Jun[r]	1	1	2		
Dunham, Obediah	1	1	2		
Smith, David	1	2	1		
Fairchild, Levi	1	2	2		
White, Thomas	1		1		
White, Perez	1	1	2		
Phillips, Seyral	1	2	1		
Stephen, Thomas	1	1	2		
Potter, John	3	5	4		
Fuller, Jedediah	1	1	2		
Goff, David	2	4	4		
Aylswoth, Phillips	2	2	3		
Hosford, Stephen	1	3	1		
Mattison, Richard	1	1	5		
Aylsworth, John	1	1	2		
Cole, Peleg	1	1	5		
Case, James	1		8		
Gardner, Joseph	2	6	3		
Hosford, Joseph	2		1		
Gardner, Paul	1	4	5		
Aylsworth, John	1	2	2		
Guardner, Benj[n] 3rd	1	3	5		
Browning, Thomas	1	5	2		
Parker, Abel	4	3	5		
Weaver, Rufus	1		5		
Williams, Israel	1	6	4		
Williams, Isaah	1	1	3		
Bates, Francis, Jun[r]	1	4	1		
Sweet, Mical	1	3	4		
Mattison, Francis	1	1	2		
Card, Daniel	1	1	5		
Gardner, David	2	5	4		
Gardner, Daniel	3	2	5		
Angel, Abiather	4	3	5		
Watson, Oliver	1		1		
Woolrodoriger, John	1		1		
Potter, James	1	3	2		
Potter, Abell	1	1	3		
Runnals, Benj[n]	3	2	4		
Aylesworth, William	1	2	5		
Webb, Jeremiah	1	2	4		
Frost, Benj[n]	3	4	3		
Frost, Elijah	1	3	2		
Moon, Robert	2	3	4		
Alsbro, Martin	1	3	2		
Roberts, Peter	1		1		
Roberts, Sam[l]	1	3	8		
Veets, Hezekiah	1	4	2		
Dorling, Jedediah	1	4	3		
Fuller, Ickebod	1	3	5		
Wakelin, John	2	1	3		
Comings, Joseph	3		1		
Cumings, William	1	2	4		
Cumings, Abraham	1		1		
Arnold, David	3	1	3		
Aylesworth, Henry	1	5	4		
Hunt, Amony	2	5	3		
Potter, Amos	3	1	3		
Mattison, Abell	1	2	5		
Barber, Sam[l]	2	1	4		
Bowdish, John	1	2	3		
Barber, William	1	4	4		
Straight, Job	1	1	3		
Phillips, Elisha	1	1	3		
Warrin, Moses	1	6	3		
Orsburn, Isral	1	2	2		
Brown, John	1	1	2		
Brown, William	1	4	4		
Page, Stephen	1	2	5		
Brown, Presila		3	2		
Turner, John	1	2	2		
Mattison, Thomas	1	2	3		
Orns, Benj[n]	2	2	3		
Herrington, Stephen	1		2		
Aylesworth, Mary			2		
Eldrige, Job	2	4	5		
Burlison, John	1	1	4		
Watson, Freburn	1	3	1		
Stanton, John	2	5	5		
Cole, David	1		3		
Cole, Pelig	1		1		
Baker, George	1	2	3		
Briggs, Joseph	1	2	7		
Herington, James	1		3		
Eldrige, Nathan	4	2	4		
Watson, Silas	3	1	4		
Potter, Abell	1	1	2		
Cole, Job	2		1		
Burnet, Caleb	1	1	4		
Burlison, John, Jun[r]	1		1		
Banister, Thomas	1		2		
Sheldin, Jonathan	1		3		
Berlison, Job	1	4	1		
Nichols, Nathan	1	1	8		
Eldrige, Daniel	3	2	4		
Potter, Zerubable	1	1	2		
Dowds, Daniel	1		5		
Nickols, Caleb	1	2	3		
Scile, Ebenezer	2	1	3		
Gardner, Benj[n]	2	3	4		
Bates, Francis	1	4	1		
Browning, Blacamone	1	2	5		
Card, Jonathan	3		3		
Bates, Josiah	1	1	3		
Williams, Joseph	1	3	3		
Williams, Joseph	1		2		
Baker, William	2	2	1		
Mattison, James	1	1	1		
Cory, John	2	5	3		
Myas, Gideon	1	3	3		
Clarke, Caleb	1	2	3		
Jackson, Robert	1	1	2		
Welch, Sam[l]	1	3	2		
Hamenly, John	1	2	3		
Welch, Ebenezer	1		1		
Cooly, Thomas	1	4	2		
Strait, Asa	1		1		
Blood, Jared	1	1	3		
Harvey, Jasen	1		1		
Phillips, Daniel	1		3		
Phillips, Job	1	1	3		
Kittle, Elias	1	2	2		
Hougton, Joseph	3	2	5		
Saxton, Ebenezer	2	2	4		
Prat, Stephen	1	2	3		
Stearns, Reuben	1		3		
Niles, Ama	1	2	2		
Thirbur, Jonathan	1	3	1		
REEDSBOROUGH TOWN.					
Root, John	1	1	1		
Chapman, Thoop	1	3	4		
Davison, Daniel	2		2		
Thomson, Eleazer	1	1	3		
Thair, Sam[l]	1		3		
Their, Simion	1		2		
Buck, Frances	1	3	2		
Myas, Simeon	1		3		
Hartwill, Joseph	2	4	6		
Vollentine, Robert	1		1		
White, Robert	1	1	3		
Brown, John	1	2	2		
Keys, Ezra	1				
Hayword, Abijah	1				
RUPERT TOWN.					
Robinson, Moses	3	3	2		
Harmon, Enos	2	2	6		
Hodge, Abel	2		2		
Stanord, Lemuel	2		3		
Reed, Daniel	4	1	3		
Sykes, Asbel	1	5	2		
Church, Jonathan	1	2	3		
Moore, James	1	1	5		
Touseley, David	1	1	3		
Maloon, John	1	1	2		
Touseley, Thomas	1		3		
Southwell, John	3		3		
Seamour, Limon	3	1	2		
Harmon, Caleb	1	1	7		
Greenman, Preserved	1		1		
Touseley, Hezekiah	1	3	6		
Touseley, William	1	1	2		
Southwel, Asel	1	2	3		

* Illegible.

BENNINGTON COUNTY—Continued.

NAME OF HEAD OF FAMILY.	Free white males of 16 years and upward, including heads of families.	Free white males under 16 years.	Free white females, including heads of families.	All other free persons.	Slaves.
RUPERT TOWN—con.					
Harmon, Nehemiah, Junr	1	2	4	....	....
Scott, David	1	2	7	....	....
Harmon, Nehemiah	1	1	1	....	....
Harmon, Alpheas	1	....	5	....	....
Harmon, Selee	1	1	3	....	....
Dewey, Sirenus	1	2	5	....	....
Gookins, Saml., Jn	2	....	2	....	....
Gookins, Saml	1	....	4	....	....
Stiles, Jonas	1	2	2	....	....
Memsel, Solomon	1	1	2	....	....
Johnson, Seth	1	2	1	....	....
Moore, Jabez	1	1	1	....	....
Smith, Ebenezer	1	5	5	....	....
Harmon, Martin	2	....	4	....	....
Nelson, Paul	1	7	2	....	....
Hays, Anna	2	5	4	....	....
Clark, Timothy	1	....	1	....	....
Fraker, Phillip	1	3	4	....	....
Draper, Nathaniel	1	....	1	....	....
Weavour, Jacob	3	....	1	....	....
Slouter, John	2	1	4	....	....
Clark, Andrew	1	....	3	....	....
Nelson, Younglove	2	....	3	....	....
Graves, Simon	1	5	3	....	....
Ransom, Jonathan	2	2	3	....	....
Graves, Elisha	1	....	1	....	....
Moore, James	2	2	1	....	....
Crain, Addanijah	3	3	4	....	....
Bentley, Thomas	1	2	4	....	....
Baley, Richard	1	3	4	....	....
Baley, William	2	3	2	....	....
Scott, Hezekiah	1	....	2	....	....
Googins, William	1	....	3	....	....
Spencer, Phinehas	2	2	4	....	....
Crain, Addenijah, Jn	1	2	4	....	....
Thomson, Joseph	1	3	1	....	....
Graves, Josiah	2	....	3	....	....
Shelden, Isaac	2	2	2	....	....
King, Palletire	1	3	5	....	....
Sheldon, Ezra	2	1	4	....	....
Speers, Nathaniel	1	2	2	....	....
Nelson, Moses	1	2	1	....	....
Blakeley, John	1	2	1	....	....
Sheldon, David	1	8	2	....	....
Smith, Stephen	2	2	2	....	....
Stodder, Reubin	3	3	4	....	....
Spencer, John	1	1	3	....	....
Graves, Syras	1	2	2	....	....
Kinney, Aseph	2	2	3	....	....
Johnson, Levi	1	2	5	....	....
Jones, Ephaim	1	....	1	....	....
Jones, Olive	....	2	1	....	....
Trumble, Alixander	2	1	1	....	....
Nelson, Daniel	2	....	4	....	....
Farrow, Jonathan	3	1	2	....	....
Levit, Samel	2	1	4	....	....
Phillips, Samel	1	4	1	....	....
Trumble, Judah	1	3	2	....	....
Graves, Jonathan	1	4	3	....	....
Sheldon, Aseph	3	....	3	....	....
Smith, Enoch	1	3	1	....	....
Backe, Elisha	1	1	3	....	....
Sheldon, Phinehas	4	....	5	....	....
Stannard, Libbeus	1	4	3	....	....
Hobbern, John	1	3	5	....	....
Diking, Martin	1	1	3	....	....
Curtis, Amos	3	4	2	....	....
Curtis, Amos, Junr	1	....	1	....	....
Sheldon, Joel	1	6	3	....	....
Loggins, John	1	....	2	....	....
Colten, David	1	3	3	....	....
Heriman, Nathl	1	2	5	....	....
McClanathan, Josiah	1	1	1	....	....
Frarey, David	1	3	4	....	....
Weed, John	1	3	3	....	....
Weed, Ichial	1	....	3	....	....
Weed, Ichial, Junr	1	1	3	....	....
Brown, John	1	....	1	....	....
Burt, William	3	2	4	....	....
Harman, Benjn	1	....	2	....	....
Whitney, Isaac	1	1	2	....	....
Brandy, Peter	3	....	1	....	....
Parker, John	1	2	4	....	....
Parker, James	1	2	2	....	....
Terrel, Arid	2	2	4	....	....
Hopkins, Samuel, 2d	2	3	4	....	....
Hopkins, Samel	1	1	4	....	....
Stone, Moses	1	2	3	....	....
Graves, Incrase	1	....	9	....	....
Kent, Abel	1	1	2	....	....

NAME OF HEAD OF FAMILY.	Free white males of 16 years and upward, including heads of families.	Free white males under 16 years.	Free white females, including heads of families.	All other free persons.	Slaves.
RUPERT TOWN—con.					
Huston, Wm	1	1	2	....	....
Levit, Joseph	1	3	3	....	....
Hubbert, Lutions	1	1	2	....	....
Hayes, Israel	1	4	2	....	....
Harmon, Amos	2	1	1	....	....
Hopkins, Marcey	....	5	2	....	....
Robinson, Stephen	1	1	3	....	....
Rising, Simeon	1	....	1	....	....
Rising, Aron	3	....	2	....	....
Hopkins, Samel	1	1	3	....	....
Norton, Nathl	2	2	2	....	....
Sheldin, Seth	1	....	....	....	....
Norton, Zadack	1	....	....	....	....
Harmon, Seth	1	4	2	....	....
Taylor, Joel	1	....	3	....	....
Sheldon, John	3	3	4	....	....
Elwil, Jese	1	3	2	....	....
McClenethan, Wm	1	....	1	....	....
Oles, Stephen	1	2	1	....	....
Hastings, Jonathan	1	....	1	....	....
Bennington, Thomas	1	1	1	....	....
Baley, Henry	2	....	2	....	....
Phillips, Elihu	1	2	4	....	....
Hunt, Samel	2	2	4	....	....
Rising, James	1	....	....	....	....
Rising, Jonah	1	....	....	....	....
Hopkins, Daniel	2	1	6	....	....
Bording, Samel	1	1	3	....	....
Mansfield, Amos	1	3	3	....	....
Rising, Aron	1	1	1	....	....
Noble, Ephraim	2	1	4	....	....
Yale, Amesa	1	1	2	....	....
Dones, Levi	2	4	5	....	....
Gray, Isaac	1	1	2	....	....
McClere, Wm	1	1	5	....	....
Mac, John	1	....	2	....	....
Harrace, Thaddeus	1	1	4	....	....
Hough, Justin	2	1	3	....	....
Noble, Reubin	1	....	3	....	....
Noble, Luke	1	1	4	....	....
Noble, Reubin	1	....	....	....	....
Tucker, Samel	1	1	3	....	....
Loggins, Daniel	1	....	3	....	....
Risden, Ornisemis	1	4	4	....	....
Coley, William	1	3	2	....	....
Smith, Israel	3	1	3	....	....
Allen, Moses	2	1	3	....	....
Turner, Roswell	1	1	3	....	....
Porter, James	1	1	2	....	....
Towsley, Nathel	2	4	3	....	....
Courtis, Josiah	1	1	5	....	....
Shelden, Moses	3	4	3	....	....
Stedman, John	1	3	3	....	....
Stedman, Robert	2	....	3	....	....
Albro, Samuel	1	1	1	....	....
Harmon, Ruibin	3	2	8	....	....
Harmon, Oliver	1	2	3	....	....
Smith, Joseph	2	2	3	....	....
Barto, Thomas	1	1	1	....	....
Barto, William	2	4	3	....	....
Eastman, Stephen	1	3	2	....	....
Tousley, Mathew	1	1	2	....	....
Eastman, Jonathan	1	....	3	....	....
Eastman, Enoch	2	6	3	....	....
Moore, Grove	1	1	2	....	....
Blacmore, Eseck	1	1	1	....	....
Ingrom, Jarit	1	....	1	....	....
Lin, James	1	1	2	....	....
Barnes, Lemuel	1	1	4	....	....
Malone, John	1	1	2	....	....
Eastman, Jonathan	1	....	2	....	....
SANDGATE TOWN.					
Hoit, David	4	2	7	....	....
Curtiss, Hull	1	3	2	....	....
Woodward, Alpheus	3	2	4	....	....
Woodward, Noah	2	2	4	....	....
Lewis, Daniel	2	1	4	....	....
Lewis, Samel	1	1	4	....	....
Curtis, Caleb	1	3	2	....	....
Curtis, Jonathan	1	....	1	....	....
Conkey, Richard	1	3	3	....	....
Hurd, Reubin	2	2	4	....	....
Hurd, Jedediah	1	....	4	....	....
Hurd, Daniel	2	....	4	....	....
Hurd, Isaac	1	....	3	....	....
Schels, Simeon	1	1	1	....	....
Thomas, Reubin	2	1	4	....	....
Squires, Hemon	1	....	1	....	....
Hurd, Timothy	1	1	3	....	....
Squres, Gideon	2	....	2	....	....

NAME OF HEAD OF FAMILY.	Free white males of 16 years and upward, including heads of families.	Free white males under 16 years.	Free white females, including heads of families.	All other free persons.	Slaves.
SANDGATE TOWN—con.					
Hurd, Eleazer	1	1	3	....	....
Hurd, Wines	1	1	1	....	....
Bristole, Samel	4	4	7	....	....
Blackman, Isaac	2	2	5	....	....
Basset, Enoch	1	3	3	....	....
Prindle, Nathan	2	2	1	....	....
Kimsberlly, Abel	1	1	1	....	....
Nichols, James	2	1	1	....	....
West, John	1	1	4	....	....
Peck, Aron	2	....	3	....	....
Burts, Joshua	1	1	3	....	....
Burts, Wait	1	1	3	....	....
Burt, William	1	....	2	....	....
Lakins, Robert	1	1	1	....	....
Walden, James	1	2	2	....	....
Burril, Jessee	1	1	5	....	....
Rug, Oliver	2	1	2	....	....
Hopkins, Robert	2	2	3	....	....
Tarrence, Thomas	2	2	6	....	....
Buck, Abel	1	1	3	....	....
Hurd, Ned	2	2	3	....	....
Cotgrieve, John	1	....	1	....	....
Bristol, Elnathan	1	4	4	....	....
Stilson, Luther	1	....	2	....	....
Stilson, Comfort	1	1	3	....	....
Stilson, Abel	1	....	2	....	....
Buckingham, Andrew	1	....	4	....	....
Murdock, James	1	1	6	....	....
Jones, Nathel	1	....	1	....	....
Hurd, Abner	1	5	3	....	....
Hurd, Cooly	1	2	1	....	....
Norton, Wm	1	3	4	....	....
Sherman, Samel	1	....	1	....	....
Sceely, Benjm	1	2	2	....	....
Gould, Chester	1	1	1	....	....
Rood, Simion	1	1	4	....	....
Hurd, John	2	....	6	....	....
Pick, Joshua	1	3	3	....	....
Bristol, Job	1	3	4	....	....
Perry, Ezekiel	1	....	2	....	....
Hurd, Luis	2	1	3	....	....
Both, Andrew	1	1	4	....	....
Torrence, Wm	3	3	2	....	....
Lamb, Benjm	1	2	2	....	....
Hambleton, Thomas	3	2	4	....	....
Johnson, Mathew	2	2	2	....	....
Warner, Eliphas	3	1	4	....	....
Hurd, Daniel, 2nd	3	....	5	....	....
Hambleton, James, Jr	3	3	4	....	....
Hurd, Adam	1	2	3	....	....
Hurd, Elijah	2	2	4	....	....
Pebbles, Saml	1	....	3	....	....
Sanford, Simeon	2	1	2	....	....
Hurd, Simeon	3	1	2	....	....
Peet, Elijah	1	1	3	....	....
Hurd, Richard	2	3	3	....	....
Clarke, Eliphlet	1	....	1	....	....
Wilson, Gilbert	1	1	1	....	....
Sanford, Ephraim	1	1	4	....	....
Sanford, David	2	1	2	....	....
Hurd, Samel	2	....	2	....	....
Hurd, Simeon	1	....	1	....	....
Hurd, Lovil	1	3	1	....	....
Baker, Eldad	2	4	2	....	....
Thomas, Jacob	1	....	4	....	....
Baker, Silas	1	....	2	....	....
Haselton, Simeon	2	1	1	....	....
Lacy, Ebenezr	1	3	4	....	....
Youngs, Ebenezer	1	4	2	....	....
Duning, Amos	2	2	3	....	....
Burril, Jesse	1	2	4	....	....
Lake, James	1	2	3	....	....
Hurd, Fredrick	1	1	2	....	....
Burt, Richard	1	1	2	....	....
Burnit, Silas	1	1	2	....	....
Tucker, Daniel	2	2	5	....	....
Prindle, Salmon	1	3	1	....	....
Burnit, Charles	2	1	3	....	....
Shepherd, Abel	1	....	1	....	....
Hakness, Wm	1	3	2	....	....
Stutson, John	3	....	5	....	....
Stutson, Tnomas	1	....	1	....	....
Sylvester, Stephen	1	3	3	....	....
Hulit, Nehemiah	1	....	....	....	....
Gray, Edward	1	....	2	....	....
Bisbuy, Benjm	3	1	4	....	....
Parkins, Wm	2	2	5	....	....
Herrington, Richard	1	2	4	....	....
Burch, Ezra	2	1	3	....	....
Burch, Nehemiah	1	4	3	....	....
Morehouse, Ephraim	2	1	3	....	....

BENNINGTON COUNTY—Continued.

NAME OF HEAD OF FAMILY.	Free white males of 16 years and upward, including heads of families.	Free white males under 16 years.	Free white females, including heads of families.	All other free persons.	Slaves.
SANDGATE TOWN—con.					
Sherman, Enoch	1	2	1	....	....
Rood, Jonah	2	2	4	....	....
Bristole, Abraham, Jr	1	......	3	....	....
Bristole, Daniel	1	2	2	....	....
Hurd, Simeon, Jr	1	1	3	....	....
Burt, Josiah	2	1	3	....	....
Cogswill, Joseph	1	......	1	....	....
Cogswill, Faris	1	......	4	....	....
Cogswill, Asa	1	......	3	....	....
Bristol, Gideon	2	1	2	....	....
Bristol, Nathel	1	1	7	....	....
Bradley, James	1	1	1	....	....
Bradley, James, Junr	1	1	4	....	....
Rug, David	1	1	3	....	....
Washburn, Samel	3	......	......	....	....
Johnson, John	1	2	3	....	....
Hambleton, John	1	1	1	....	....
Morehouse, Nathan	1	2	2	....	....
Tattle, Amos	3	......	2	....	....
Bristol, James	2	2	5	....	....
Sidmore, Daniel	1	1	4	....	....
Hard, Theophelus	2	1	5	....	....
Sidmore, James	1	2	2	....	....
Park, George	1	4	3	....	....
Andrup, Elihu	1	4	5	....	....
Brown, Daniel	1	4	4	....	....
SHAFTSBURY TOWN.					
Olin, Gideon	3	2	7	....	....
Galusha, Jonas	2	4	6	1	....
Galusha, David	5	1	8	....	....
Howlit, Mary	......	1	2	....	....
Goss, Jonathan	1	1	2	....	....
House, Jonathan	1	4	4	....	....
Mattison, Abraham, Junr	1	3	4	....	....
Martin, Masha	3	......	3	....	....
Martin, Simeon	1	3	1	....	....
Martin, Amaziah	3	1	3	....	....
Martin, Nathan	1	1	1	....	....
Black, David	1	1	3	....	....
Pierce, John	1	4	3	....	....
Ward, William	3	3	4	....	....
Mathews, David	3	1	7	2	....
Wheeler, Nathan	2	2	4	....	....
Larrence, Petter	1	1	3	....	....
Perry, Josiah	2	2	10	....	....
Harace, Ebenezer	2	2	3	....	....
Burnit, Jedediah	1	3	3	....	....
Cross, Elisha	3	2	3	....	....
Rogers, Ebenezer	2	......	2	....	....
Cole, David	2	2	3	....	....
Brown, Constent	2	1	1	....	....
Larrence, Rufus	1	......	1	....	....
Ward, Stephen	2	1	7	....	....
Burnham, Samel	2	......	2	....	....
Millins, William	1	......	3	....	....
Smith, Roger	1	2	2	....	....
Howlit, Parley	2	5	4	....	....
Slocumb, Jonas	2	1	4	....	....
Holmes, William	1	1	2	....	....
Brigs, John	1	2	2	....	....
Perry, Winslow	1	1	6	....	....
Larrence, Bigelow	5	4	6	....	....
Leonard, Nathan	2	5	3	....	....
Burnit, Thomas	2	1	3	....	....
Burnit, James	1	......	1	....	....
House, Samel	2	2	5	....	....
Huntington, Amos	5	1	3	....	....
Burows, Amos	4	2	2	....	....
Burnham, William	4	2	5	....	....
Montauge, Nathl	2	......	2	....	....
Rice, Abner	1	3	4	....	....
Burnham, Asa	2	2	6	....	....
Stevens, Henry	1	2	2	....	....
Bottom, Simeon	3	2	4	....	....
Huntington, Nathan	3	1	4	....	....
Huntington, John	1	......	3	....	....
Wright, Isaiah	2	1	4	....	....
Bakon, Daniel	1	4	3	....	....
Spencer, Charles	2	3	5	....	....
Adams, Henrey	1	2	4	....	....
Hunt, Seth	1	1	3	....	....
Justin, Gershom	1	1	2	....	....
Whitford, Peleg	1	1	5	....	....
Herrington, Squire	1	1	1	....	....
Herrington, Levi	1	2	2	....	....
Fisk, Jeremiah	1	......	1	....	....
Fisk, Jeremiah, Junr	1	......	1	....	....
Salsbury, Martin	......	......	......	....	....
Herrington, Abraham	1	2	1	....	....
Herrington, Paul	3	1	3	....	....

NAME OF HEAD OF FAMILY.	Free white males of 16 years and upward, including heads of families.	Free white males under 16 years.	Free white females, including heads of families.	All other free persons.	Slaves.
SHAFTSBURY TOWN—con.					
Herrington, William	1	1	1	....	....
Burlington, William	1	2	2	....	....
Doge, Alexander	1	......	2	....	....
West, Thomas	3	1	3	....	....
Pierce, Cleather	2	......	3	....	....
Boings, Obediah	2	2	2	....	....
Millinton, Solomon	4	2	3	....	....
Simons, Josiah	1	2	5	....	....
Luther, Samel	3	1	2	....	....
Salsbury, Daniel	1	4	4	....	....
Salesbury, Nathan	1	......	1	....	....
Cole, Parker	5	3	6	1	....
Cole, Robert	2	3	4	....	....
Munro, Joshua	2	1	2	....	....
Martin, Samel	1	......	2	....	....
Cole, Benjm	2	2	6	....	....
Draper, Nathan	2	......	4	....	....
Faning, Thomas	1	2	1	....	....
Hibberd, Elijah	1	1	7	....	....
Rice, Artemas	1	......	2	....	....
Dunlap, Robert	1	4	6	....	....
Lincoln, John	1	1	4	....	....
Kilburn, Aruna	1	1	2	....	....
West, Barnitt	1	1	3	....	....
Daniels, John	1	2	4	....	....
Millington, Solomon	1	......	2	....	....
Brigs, Josias	1	2	4	....	....
Weaver, Thomas	1	2	1	....	....
Olin, John	2	2	3	....	....
Green, Asa	1	......	2	....	....
Hulin, John	1	......	1	....	....
Beamon, Josiah	1	......	1	....	....
Ginning, Lemuel	1	1	3	....	....
Olin, Giles	3	5	2	....	....
Hulin, Allixander	3	5	1	....	....
Watson, John	3	3	2	....	....
Galusha, Jonas	2	......	2	....	....
Galusha, David, 2d	1	2	2	....	....
Lemgotha, Robert	3	3	3	....	....
Herrington, James, Jn	1	2	4	....	....
Draper, Gideon	1	3	1	....	....
Slocumb, Samel	1	3	4	....	....
Hawley, Rana	......	1	2	....	....
Putnam, Fredrick	1	......	1	....	....
Mattison, David	1	3	1	....	....
Burk, John	1	......	1	....	....
Burk, Levi	1	1	3	....	....
Weavor, Nickolus	1	2	5	....	....
Weavor, Benjn	1	3	4	....	....
Stone, Alexander	1	1	7	....	....
Carpender, Timothy	5	......	4	....	....
Spencer, Isaac	1	1	1	....	....
Galusha, Amos	2	2	3	....	....
Dickson, Moses	1	2	1	....	....
Mattison, Peleg	3	6	3	....	....
Warrin, Thomas	2	......	4	....	....
Bottum, Palletire	1	......	3	....	....
Smith, John	3	......	1	....	....
Hatch, Asa	3	2	6	....	....
Carpender, Isaah	3	2	3	....	....
Blood, Caleb	2	1	4	....	....
Pike, John	2	2	6	....	....
Hambleton, John	1	2	3	....	....
Trial, Daniel	1	......	1	....	....
Abba, Johnathan	2	......	1	....	....
Barrackman, John	1	3	2	....	....
Huntington, Samel	3	4	7	....	....
Colegro, Jeremiah	1	5	3	....	....
Clark, Daniel	1	1	2	....	....
Galusha, Jacob	2	2	7	....	....
Waldow, Miatha	4	......	4	....	....
Glass, James	2	4	2	....	....
Holmes, William	1	2	2	....	....
Cole, Bethuel	2	3	4	....	....
Lummis, Russill	1	1	3	....	....
Welmath, Ephaim	1	2	5	....	....
Andrews, Isaac	3	3	3	....	....
Andrews, Isaac, Jur	1	3	1	....	....
Daniels, John	1	3	6	....	....
Harriss, William	1	2	2	....	....
Mathews, Isaac	2	1	3	....	....
Welch, Ebenezer	1	1	3	....	....
Basley, Levi	1	......	2	....	....
Willoughby, Bliss	1	1	2	....	....
Dewey, Samel	2	......	1	....	....
Tibbets, Jonathan	3	2	4	....	....
Spencer, Andra	......	......	3	....	....
Wordin, Ickebod	1	3	2	....	....
Downer, John	2	4	9	....	....
Whipple, Elijah	1	3	7	....	....
Cliff, Joseph	1	3	3	....	....
Alden, Seth	1	......	4	....	....

NAME OF HEAD OF FAMILY.	Free white males of 16 years and upward, including heads of families.	Free white males under 16 years.	Free white females, including heads of families.	All other free persons.	Slaves.
SHAFTSBURY TOWN—con.					
Corey, David	2	......	4	....	....
Rogers, Ishmeil	1	2	2	....	....
Buril, Fredrick	1	1	2	....	....
Hibberd, Ahimas	1	3	4	....	....
Hibberd, Elijah	1	1	4	....	....
Doolittle, John	3	2	4	....	....
Whitman, Volentine	1	4	3	....	....
Bates, Arvin	1	1	1	....	....
Goff, Caleb	2	4	4	....	....
Benton, Gardner	1	......	2	....	....
Harriss, William	1	1	3	....	....
Corey, David	1	2	3	....	....
Cole, Job	1	1	3	....	....
Hadlock, Jonathan	1	2	6	....	....
Olin, Jonathan	1	1	1	....	....
Olin, Jonathan, Jur	1	2	3	....	....
Rouss, James	1	2	3	....	....
Meed, Levi	1	2	2	....	....
Meed, Israel	1	4	2	....	....
Day, Joseph	1	2	2	....	....
Kibbe, Joseph	1	......	2	....	....
Hawley, John	3	4	4	....	....
Mattison, Henry	1	5	4	....	....
Kilburn, Asa	1	1	1	....	....
Jonnson, Freburn	1	......	1	....	....
Mattison, Petter	2	2	5	....	....
Corkins, John	1	2	2	....	....
Burk, John, Jur	1	3	3	....	....
Mattison, Samel, Jur	1	2	2	....	....
Smith, Ebenezer	1	2	2	....	....
Smith, Benjn	1	1	3	....	....
Smith, Benjn, Jur	1	1	1	....	....
Smith, Daniel	3	3	3	....	....
Herrington, James	1	1	2	....	....
Stone, Nathan	1	3	5	....	....
Mattison, Samel	2	......	4	....	....
Wording, Rufus	2	1	2	....	....
Whaley, Samel	2	5	6	....	....
Babbit, John	1	2	2	....	....
Mattison, Richard	1	3	2	....	....
Wording, Juder	1	3	3	....	....
Mattison, Francis	2	1	5	....	....
Brigs, Joseph	1	......	2	....	....
Mattison, Asa	1	......	1	....	....
Mattison, Calvin	1	......	2	....	....
King, Samel	1	2	3	....	....
Andrew, Thomas	3	1	3	....	....
Lucus, Aaron	1	......	5	....	....
Walker, Hezekiah	2	2	3	....	....
Stanley, John	2	6	5	....	....
Singer, Peter	2	3	3	....	....
Millington, Samel	1	3	8	....	....
Runnals, Robert	1	......	2	....	....
Bennit, Joseph	1	......	1	....	....
Antisle, Simon	3	1	6	....	....
Dimmick, Solomon	1	1	1	....	....
Beckit, David	1	3	4	....	....
White, Perigreen	1	2	3	....	....
Dimmick, Mahitabel	......	......	4	....	....
Edwords, Daniel	3	2	5	....	....
Runnals, Constant	1	......	5	....	....
Stanley, John	1	1	2	....	....
Morse, Davis	2	2	5	....	....
Trewwan, Reubin	1	4	5	....	....
Cob, William	2	2	5	....	....
Dyer, Benja	1	2	3	....	....
Moswer, Daniel	1	4	3	....	....
Clark, Salmon	1	......	2	....	....
Starkweather, Daniel	2	......	2	....	....
Brown, James	1	1	2	....	....
Dwinals, Stephen	3	4	4	....	....
Bates, Nathan	2	2	3	....	....
Corey, Benja	1	......	3	....	....
Allin, David	2	1	4	....	....
Colvin, David	1	1	1	....	....
Blancher, John	1	2	1	....	....
Rothbone, Amos	1	......	2	....	....
Jarow, Ama	1	......	4	....	....
Niles, George	2	4	8	....	....
Draper, James	3	2	3	....	....
Draper, Jonathan	2	......	1	....	....
Millington, John	2	2	8	....	....
Reasoner, David	1	......	1	....	....
Clark, Jeremiah, Jur	2	1	5	....	....
Clark, Jeremiah	4	1	5	....	....
Clark, James	2	......	4	....	....
Pattison, Stephen	1	1	2	....	....
Eldrige, Nathan	2	......	3	....	....
Woodale, James	1	2	2	....	....
Carr, James	1	2	2	....	....
Judd, Aruna	1	3	5	....	....
Gun, Moses	2	4	1	....	....

BENNINGTON COUNTY—Continued.

NAME OF HEAD OF FAMILY.	Free white males of 16 years and upward, including heads of families.	Free white males under 16 years.	Free white females, including heads of families.	All other free persons.	Slaves.
SHAFTSBURY TOWN—con.					
Doge, Noah	3	1	4		
Bran, Daniel	2	5	6		
Warner, Israel	2		5		
Colins, Zerubbabel	3	1	3		
Blancher, Achabel	1	1	1		
Cross, Ickebod	3	1	3		
Barnon, Timothy	3	4	5		
Fuller, Hosea	1	1	7		
Turner, John	2	2	6		
Peck, David	1	2	2		
Printice, James	1	4	3		
Chase, Jeremiah	1	1	2		
Fuller, Elijah	1		1		
Fuller, John	2	2	2		
Thomson, Joseph	1	3	6		
Ingorson, Ebenezer	1	2	2		
Dyer, Charls	3	4	6		
Cob, Matthias	3	1	5		
Millington, John	3	3	3		
Corey, Jacob	1	1	4		
Tuvey, John	2		4		
Blakesley, John	1		3		
Sage, Jonathan	4	4	3		
Bates, Joshua	1	1	3		
Olin, Justin	3	1	8		
Mattison, William	1	2	2		
Mattison, Zerubabel	3	3	4		
Mattison, Thomas	3	3	3		
Sly, Mill	2	2	5		
Sly, Gedeon	2	2	3		
Hardin, James	1	2	2		
Younglove, Samel	1	3	1		
Trumble, John	1	1	2		
Niles, John	3		5		
Ellice, Reubin	2	2	5		
Ellice, Moses	1	3	3		
Trumble, Simeon	1	3	2		
Ellice, Reubin, Jn.	1	2	6		
Cartwright, Nickolus	1	3	3		
Niles, Elisha	1	1	2		
Fuller, Solomon	1	2	3		
Dyer, Henry	1	1	3		
Bennit, Jedediah	1	3	3		
Wright, Peter	2	3	4		
Newton, Nathaniel	3	2	4		
Bruster, Joseph	1	4	1		
Hawley, William	1	4	3		
Sweet, James	1	1	3		
Wright, Samel	1		1		
Huntington, Jeremiah	2	3	2		
Ames, Joseph	3	2	4		
Smith, Gideon	1	3	3		
Wing, Daniel	1	3	3		
Hoskins, Anthoney	3	4	2		
STAMFORD TOWN.					
Deen, Perez	2	3	4		
Langdon, Barnebus	1		1		
Langdon, John	2	1	7		
Miller, Squire	3	2	3		
Bates, Stephen	2	3	4		
Bates, William	1	1	3		
Baker, Sergent	1		2		
Baker, Mathew	1		1		
Annis, James	2	4	2		
Phettiplace, Resolved	2	1	4		
Slocum, Peleg	1		1		
Razer, Benjn	1	2	4		
Brown, Samel., Jur	1	1	2		
Coy, Mary	1		3		
Tupper, Benjn	3	4	3		
Rayment, Elisha	1	4	4		
Shaw, Stephen	1		2		
Tucker, Nathan	3	1	2		
STAMFORD TOWN—con.					
Edgeton, Roswell	1		2		
Ryne, Edword	2	3	2	1	
Cook, Timothy	1	1	2		
Mattison, Benajiah	1	5	1		
Bell, William	1		1		
Linn, Andrew	1	3	3		
Rament, Josiah	1		1		
Brown, Samel	2		1		
Seldin, Andrew	1	1	1		
Finney, Bethuel	1	1	4		
Mony, Jonathan	2		2		
Smith, Oliver	2	3	8		
Phillips, Zabudy	1	1	2		
Meed, Israil	1	1	4		
Harriss, James	1		4		
Clark, Moses	3	1	5		
Buckman, Samel	1	1	2		
Smith, Elisha	2	1	3		
Smith, Timothy	1	2	3		
Seldin, Thomas	1		3		
Seldin, Thomas, Jur	2		4		
Gilmore, Robert	1	2	4		
Richard, John	1	2	1		
Porter, Ebenezer	2		2		
Gardner, John	1	1	3		
Whitney, Isaac	1	2	4		
Ball, Zembebel	1	2	3		
Mallery, Neram	1		3		
Jones, Enos	2	1	3		
Whiple, John	1	4	4		
SUNDERLAND TOWN.					
Smith, Daniel	1		3		
Farman, Joseph	1	2	4		
Hicks, Simeon	1	4	3		
Parker, Charles	1		6		
Parker, Reubin	1	1	5		
Allen, Joseph	1	5	2		
Hoit, Samel	4	3	3		
King, Caleb	1	3	3		
King, John	1	3	2		
Borman, Sherman	2	1	2		
Lee, Elisabeth		2	2		
Waldo, Loice		2	1		
Parsons, John	3	2	4		
Juston, Michal	2	1	1		
Warren, Stephen	3	1	3		
Warren, Luman	1		3		
Bakon, Amos	1	2	2		
Lewis, Timothy	1	2	4		
Catling, Roswel	1		4		
Lewis, Timothy, Junr	1	3	2		
Avery, Robert	1	2	4		
Wilman, Gideon	1	1	3		
Welman, Benjn	1		2		
Lewis, Edward	1	6	1		
Bradley, Azariah	1	1	4		
Sherwin, Jacob	3	1	1		
Bradley, John	1	1	1		
Lewis, Benjm	2	2	3		
Bradley, Stephen	2	2	2		
Bartlit, Samel	2	3	4		
Kenney, Benjamin	1		2		
Everts, Edward	1	2	3		
Everts, Abner	1	1	2		
Bacon, Benjamin	1		2		
Everts, Charles	1	2	3		
Smith, Amos	1	2	3		
Bradley, John	6	1	3		
Lewis, Jonathan	1				
Fuller, Daniel	1	2	3		
Griffen, Benjn	2	2	4		
Comstock, Jason	2	1	1		
Wood, James	3	1	4		
SUNDERLAND TOWN—continued.					
Whipple, Ezra	3	2	4		
Hill, Abnah	2	3	1		
Hoit, Joseph	1		2		
Bingham, Hanah	1		3		
Lee, Chancey	1	1	2		
Oens, Leonard	4	1	5		
Bradley, Gilbert	4	1	6		
Howel, John	2		2		
Chipman, Amos	2	3	5		
Wooward, Noble	1		1		
Bishop, Lemuel	1	2	5		
Lamphier, Samel	1	3	6		
Wallace, Nathaniel	1	2	3		
Vanderider, Andara	1		3		
Meggs, Benjm	1	2	1		
Seamons, Richard	2		3	1	
Brunson, Gideon	4		5		
Bruson, Isaac	1	2	3		
Field, Francies	2	2	5		
Buckley, Asa	2				
Bradley, Lemuel	3	1	6		
Coffin, Eleazer	1	2	2		
Graves, Edmond	3		2		
West, Obediah	2				
Brunson, Timothy	2	3	4		
Herrison, Edward	1	1	2		
Bentley, Elisha	1		4		
WINHALL TOWN.					
Beebe, Asa	1	4	3		
Beebe, Asa, Ju	1		1		
Wheelor, Moses	1	1	3		
Wheelor, Beriah	1	1	3		
Williams, Isaac	2	2	2		
Taylor, Moses	1		2		
Brooks, John	1	1	4		
Fuller, Shubil	2	1	1		
Whitney, Ephaim	1	1	2		
Rose, Nathaniel	1		2		
Rose, Joseph	2	1	4		
Rose, Benjn	2	2	2		
Taylor, Jonathan	1	2	5		
Eaton, Ebenezer	1	3	1		
Eaton, Nathan	1	2	5		
Day, Russel	1	1	5		
Taylor, Seth	3		2		
Whitney, Ebenezer	1	2	1		
Barnard, John	2	1			
Foot, Addenijah	1	3	3		
Sprage, Jonathan	2	2	1		
Day, Oliver	1	2	2		
Brown, Nathaniel	3	2	3		
Day, Ephaim	2	3	2		
Barrit, Benjn	1	2	2		
Wheelor, Aaron	1	4	4		
Williams, James	1	2	3	1	
Whitney, Elisha	1	1	1		
WOODFORD TOWN.					
Scott, Mathew	1	2	2		
Scott, Noah	1		2		
Scott, Zerish	1	1	2		
Wilson, Joseph	2		1		
Forgeson, Hezekiah	1	2	5		
Hunt, Joseph	1	2	4		
Reed, Benjn	1	3	2		
Moore, Caleb	2	4	1		
Peirce, Zadock	1				
Peirce, Eli	1				
Grover, Benjn	1		2		
Biggelow, Noah, Ju	1	2	1		
Bigelow, Noah	1	1	3		
Dant, Samel	1	1	1		

CHITTENDEN COUNTY.

NAME OF HEAD OF FAMILY.	Free white males of 16 years and upward, including heads of families.	Free white males under 16 years.	Free white females, including heads of families.	All other free persons.	Slaves.
ALBURGH TOWN.					
Dolong, Ezekiel	1	1	4		
Covey, Samuel	3	2	3		
Kickle, Frederick	1	2	2		
Kelly, Thomas	1	1	1		
Legard, John	1	1	4		
Taylor, Reuben	2				
Grigs, Abraham	2		3	2	
Able, Henry	1	1	2		
Marvin, Benjamin	2	2	4		
Miller, Henry	1		2		
ALBURGH TOWN—con.					
Maning, Gabriel	1	3	4		
Maning, Joshua	1	4	2		
Garlick, Reuben	2	6	1		
Duel, Michael	2	3	3		
Tar, George	1	3	1		
Frier, Samuel	1	1	1		
Martin, Jacobus	1	1	5		
Vanblete, John	1	1	2		
Weeks, Joseph	1	1	1		
Mott, Jacob	1	1	3		
ALBURGH TOWN—con.					
Mott, Joseph	3				
Soal, William	5	1	2		
Mott, Samuel	4	5	1		
Grigs, John	3	2	5		
Andrew, Thomas	3	1	4		
Honsinger, Michael	3		2		
Fisher, James	2		2		
Mott, Joseph, Junr	1	1	2		
Mott, Richard	2		3		
Conroy, Patrick	2	1	3	1	

CHITTENDEN COUNTY—Continued.

NAME OF HEAD OF FAMILY.	Free white males of 16 years and upward, including heads of families.	Free white males under 16 years.	Free white females, including heads of families.	All other free persons.	Slaves.
ALBURGH TOWN—con.					
Clarke, Titus	1	2	2		
Lado, John	2	1	1		
Gilfinning, James	2				
McGregor, Duncan	1	3	3		
Young, James	2				
Wait, Nathanl	1	1	3		
Savage, John	2		6		
Holbrook, Abraham	1	1	2		
Holbrook, Nathaniel	1		1		
Caragan, Peter	3		1		
Burget, Coonrod	1	1	1		
Deniah, Eli	1	2	2		
Clarke, Daniel	2		3		
Harvey, David	1	2	1		
Dorrow, James	2				
Truman, Peter	1	1	2		
Concklin, Abraham	1	1	3		
Coók, Philip	1	1	2		
Cook, Jacob	3		2		
Waggoner, Francis	2	1	2		
Haydon, Joseph	1		2		
Munro, Elijah	1		4		
Hogan, Edward	1				
Williston, Mr	1		1		
Miars, William	1	2	2		
Hammon, Benjamin	2	3	2		
Wood, Hezekiah	1		1		
Miller, John	2	2	2		
Smith, Humphry	1	1	3		
McLane, Hugh	1	1	4		
Smith, Daniel	3	4	2		
Brandige, William	1	2	1		
Pickle, John	1	1	1		
Beagle, Daniel	1	2	3		
Smith, John	3		2		
Cnilton, John	1	2	3		
Reynolds, Thomas	1	2	2		
Niles, Nathan	1	2	2		
Reynolds, Elisha	1	1	2		
Pickle, Jacob	1		1		
Pickle, Christopher	2		1		
Sole, Timothy	1	1	2		
Sole, Joseph	1	1	1		
Garner, George	3				
Gibson, John	1	1	3		
Chambers, John	1	2	2		
Miller, Samuel	2	1	3		
Helms, Samuel	1	1	1		
Sweat, James	2		2		
Por, Moses	2	1	1		
Logan, David	1	1			
Sweat, Stephen	1		2		
Brewer, Jeremiah	3	2	3		
Wilson, George	2	1	3		
Wilson, George, Junr	1		3		
Montle, Francis	3		3		
Montle, Francis, Junr	1	1	1		
Honie, John	1	3	4		
Baer, Coonrod	1	2	3		
Risgate, Jeremiah	5	1	2	1	
BAKERSFIELD TOWN.					
Baker, Joseph	3	2	3		
Maynard, Stephen	1	2	2		
BOLTON TOWN.					
Butler, Asaph	1		1		
Palmer, Thomas	2	2	4		
Warren, Aaron	1	3	1		
Kenedy, John	2	2	3		
Blair, James	1		3		
Kenedy, Robert	1	2	4		
Stinson, Robert	1	3	3		
Mores, James	2		4		
Bell, Samuel	1	3	3		
Joinor, William	1		1		
Joinor, Francis	2	3	3		
Dewey, Charless	1	4	2		
More, John	1	1	4		
Vanornam, John	1		1		
Dewey, Noah	2	2	3		
Dewey, Ezra	1	1	1		
BURLINGTON TOWN.					
Keys, Col. Stephen	4	3	4	1	
Boyington, Cap. Job	2	5	3		
Hitchcock, Col. Samuel	5	1	4		
Loomis, Phineas	5	2	8	1	
King, Gideon	4		1		

NAME OF HEAD OF FAMILY.	Free white males of 16 years and upward, including heads of families.	Free white males under 16 years.	Free white females, including heads of families.	All other free persons.	Slaves.
BURLINGTON TOWN—con.					
Collins, John	4		2		
Saxton, Col. Fredrick	1	2	4	1	
Hawley, James	2	1	6		
Grant, John	1				
Peasley, Zacheus	2				
Ames, Charless	3	1	3		
Ames, Thomas	2		1		
Judson, Eli	2	1	2		
Lawrence, Stephen	3	1	2		
Lane, Samuel, Esqr	2		4		
Lane, Elisha	1	3	4		
Staunton, David	1	3	4		
Chapman, Timothy	1		7		
Barney, Capt. Thomas	3	3	7		
Bottom, Lemuel	3		2		
Shearsvoes, John A	1	1	1		
Spear, Barnabas	1	1	1		
Spear, Dearing	1	2	3		
Spear, Barzilla	2	2	3		
Pitcher, Isaac	1	2	4		
Castle, Daniel	2	2	5		
Averill, Josiah	1		4		
Castle, Asher	1	1	2		
Jarems, Mr	1		1		
Marvin, Sirus	2	2	4		
Davidson, Alexander	1				
Howe, Aaron	1		2		
Smith, Nathan	1		4		
Lowry, Joel	1	1	3		
Vansickling, John	1	2	2		
Barns, Joshua	2	3	2		
Thatcher, Mr	3	6	1		
Thatcher, John	1		1		
Benedict, Peter	1	3	3		
Tylor, Nathan	2				
Doxey, John	1	2	3		
Allen, Samuel	1	3	3		
Ferris, Benjamin	1				
Brown, Ebenezer	1				
French, Isaac	2				
French, Jeremiah	3		2		
Smith, Samuel	1	2	5		
Stearns, Pierce	1				
Lawrence, Noah	1		3		
Blanchard, Moses	2	1	1		
Ward, William	5	2	3		
Saxton, Nehemiah	1	1	1		
Webb, Isaac	1	2	3		
Holibart, Daniel	3	1	4		
Coit, William	1		3		
Knickerbacor, John, Esqr	1				
Hartt, Jonathan	1		2		
Adams, Benjamin	1				
Hocum, Richard	1				
Hartt, Zachariah	1		4		
CAMBRIDGE TOWN.					
Fassett, John	6	1	4		
Montague, Samuel	4	3	4		
Spafford, John	1	1	5		
Cady, Walter	1		5		
Thustin, Joseph	1	1	2		
Kingman, Alexander	1		3		
Campbell, William	3	1	4		
Eaton, Samuel	1	1	2		
Davis, Elijah	1		4		
McLaghlin, James	2	2	1		
Mudget, Ezra	5	3	2		
Billings, Moses	1		1		
Kingsley, Stephen	3	3	4		
Hatch, Caleb	1		1		
Billings, Lt. Silas	2	1	2		
Page, Thomas	2		3		
Hall, John	1	2	1		
Spafford, Capt. David	1	7	5		
Kingsley, Daniel	1		1		
Warren, Ichabod	1	3	3		
Hopkins, Frederick	1		3		
Cochran, Col. Robert	3	5	4		
Pomeray, Docr. John	2	2	3		
Brewster, Jonah	1	4	4		
Taylor, Joseph	1	2	3		
Hastings, Robert	1	1	2		
Prior, William	1	2	3		
Fassett, Amos, Esqr	5	3	7		
Billings, Nathan	3		6		
Mudget, William	1	1	2		
Melven, Nathan	3	1	3		
Fassett, David	1	2	3		
Hastings, John	1	1	1		
Hubbel, Bildad	2	1	3		

NAME OF HEAD OF FAMILY.	Free white males of 16 years and upward, including heads of families.	Free white males under 16 years.	Free white females, including heads of families.	All other free persons.	Slaves.
CAMBRIDGE TOWN—con.					
Cady, Amos	1	2	1		
Tiffaner, Christopher	1		5		
Cochran, Samuel	1	1	4		
Kingsley, Daniel, Junr	1		2		
Fassett, Docr. Nathan	3	2	4		
Holmes, Samuel	1	2	4		
Hopkins, Henry	1	1	1		
Follett, Martin D	2		1		
Cochran, Thomas	1		1		
Baker, Zebulon	1	3	4		
Wickwire, Joseph	2	1	2		
Robison, Robert	1	1	2		
Horner, James	3	1	1		
Goodwin, Daniel	1		1		
Kingsley, Nathan	3	1	3		
Gilmore, James	3	1	4		
Powel, Truman	1	5	2		
Page, Parker	2	1	2		
Palmerly, Giles	3		5		
Dewey, Archibald	1	1	1		
Wood, John	2	2	2		
Millard, Calvin	2				
Page, James	1	1	2		
Robison, Isaac	1		3		
Dickison, John	1		2		
Reynolds, William	1	1	1		
Keeler, Aaron	1	1	2		
McLaghlin, William	1	2	1		
CAMBRIDGE GORE.					
Page, Amos	2	4	1		
Church, Anna		1	3		
Horner, Thomas	1	1	2		
CHARLOTTE TOWN.					
McNeile, John, Esqr	4	4	3	1	
Place, Thomas	1		2		
Mosure, Jesse	1	2	4		
Gibbs, Abel	1	2	2	1	
Place, Samuel	1		1		
Place, Simon	1		3		
Barns, Daniel	1		2		
Hosford, Roger	1	3	2		
Dorman, Eben	1	2	1		
Wilcott, Joseph	1	3	2		
Baker, Eliab	1	1	2		
Beach, Joseph	1	4	2		
Castle, Thaddeus	1	1	4		
Atwood, David	1				
Lawrence, Nathan	1				
Castle, William	1	1	2		
Holibard, Abiram	1	1	3		
Yale, Stephen	2				
Bull, Michael	1	2	3		
Dorman, Samuel	1	1	1		
Holibard, Elisha	1	1	2		
Barns, Hezekiah	3	2	4		
Rich, Samuel	1		1		
Cutler, Dewsbury	1	2	4		
Keeler, Ebenezer	1	1	1		
Chandler, Abner	1		2		
Chandler, Hill	1		1		
Squire, Heber	2	2	5		
Martin, Wait	1	2	4		
Williams, William	2	2	3		
Cogswell, Isaac	2	1	6		
Blanchard, Rial	3	4	4		
Shapley, William	2		5		
Painfield, Samuel, Junr	1		1		
Calagan, Patrick	2		2		
Wirm, Jacob	1	4	5		
Sprague, Joseph	3		3		
Ramington, Jonathan	1	2	1		
Curtis, Zara	1	1	3		
Reed, Benjamin	1	1	2		
Martin, Reuben	2	5	2		
Frisby, Elisha	2		3		
Palmer, John	1	3	3		
Hovey, Ebenezer	3	4	3		
Abbot, Abial	1	4	1		
Rich, David	1		4		
Newel, Abel	5		2		
Powel, William	2	2	3		
Ufford, Benjamin	3		2		
Clarke, Clement	1	1	4		
Cook, Ebenezer	1	1	2		
Sheldon, Israel	1	3	3		
Crane, Miles	1				
Narmore, Asa	1		2		
Perkins, Philo	1				

CHITTENDEN COUNTY—Continued.

NAME OF HEAD OF FAMILY.	Free white males of 16 years and upward, including heads of families.	Free white males under 16 years.	Free white females, including heads of families.	All other free persons.	Slaves.
CHARLOTTE TOWN—con.					
Wood, William	1	1	3		
Butterfield, James, Junr.	1	1	1		
Brooks, Jabez	2				
Brakeridge, Francis	3		2		
Grant, Charless	4	1	4		
Tharp, John	3		1		
Stone, Jacob	1	1	4		
Furman, Jebediah	1		1		
Squire, Solomon	2	1	4		
Cumings, Zedadiah	1	2	2		
Butterfield, James	2	1	5		
Dolittle, Ebenezer	1		2		
Rose, John	1		3		
Sawyer, Jonathan	1	1	3		
Seamons, Joseph	1	2	2		
Reed, William	1	2	4		
Jentle, Andrew	2		2		
Donnon, Ezra	2		1		
Bartlett, Elisha	2		2		
Hill, John	3	2	3		
Yale, Moses	3	1	4		
McNeile, Capt. Charless	2	2	5		
Towner, Erasmus	1		1		
Catlin, Amos	1	2	2		
Tupper, Darius	1	2	5	1	
Barns, Asa, Junr	1		2		
Penfield, Samuel	4	1	6		
Taylor, Ebenezer	2		4		
Long, Boardman	1		1		
Hill, Zimry	1	2	3		
Rasford, Isaac	4	2	2		
Hoffard, Daniel	2	1	1		
Hoffard, Daniel, Junr	2	1	4		
Hill, James	1	1	5		
Prindle, Gideon	2		1		
Chamberlain, Ebenezer	1	3	4		
Brakenidge, Jonathan	2	1	4		
Rowley, Reuben	1	3	3		
Farnam, Josiah	2	3	1		
Olford, Alexander	1	3	2		
Barns, Asa	3	1	2		
Keeler, Elijah	1	1	2		
Holibard, Thaddeus	1		4		
Hall, Joseph	1		3		
Holibard, Solomon	1		1		
Holibard, Isaiah	1	1	2		
Woolcot, Elijah	2		2		
Allen, John	1	3	4		
Lappum, Asa	2	2	3		
Howard, Joseph	1	3	1		
Atwood, Jonathan	2		1		
Story, James	2	1	4		
Huff, Daniel	2	2	3		
Wheeler, Preserved	3		1		
Marble, Nathan	1		3		
Hubbel, David	2	1	2		
Holibard, Samuel	2	2	2		
Worcester, Ephraim	1	1	3		
Strong, Asahel	3		5		
Fuller, Ammi	1	1	2		
Penfield, Samuel	3	1	6		
Pechard, Abisha	1	1	2		
Adset, Samuel	1	3	2		
COLCHESTER TOWN.					
Allen, Genl Ira	5	2	5		
Allen, Elisha	1	2	7		
Austin, Samuel	2	2	2		
Austin, Paul	1	2	1		
Staunton, Joshua	5	1	2		
Plumb, Joseph	1	2	4		
Boardman, Benjamin	1	1	2		
Mallet, Robert	1		1		
Law, John	1				
Maxfield, David	2	4	1		
McLane, Duncan	1	4	3		
Chase, Samuel	1	3	3		
Hill, Thomas	1	3	4		
Henderson, Caleb	1	3	3		
Lake, Collins	1	1	1		
Lake, Ephraim	2	1	1		
Stevens, John, Esqr	1	1	6		
Downing, Dennis	1	1	1		
Downing, John	1				
Winters, John	1				
Winters, Hawley	1				
Baker, Simon	1				
Bean, John	2	2	3		
Right, Isaac	1	1	4		
Charlton, Henry	1				
Manson, William	1				
COLCHESTER TOWN—con.					
Hill, David	1				
Johnson, Jacob	3	4	1		
DUXBURY TOWN.					
Avery, Walter	2	2	3		
Parker, Daniel	1	2	2		
Morse, John	1	6	2		
Morse, Daniel	1	3	3		
Briant, Jeremiah	1	1	1		
Page, Samuel	1	4	1		
Crage, James	1				
Shepherd, George	1				
ELMORE TOWN.					
Olmstead, James	1	1	3		
Olmstead, Seth	1		1		
Elmore, Jesse	1				
Elmore, Martin	1				
Gibbs, Job	1				
Leach, Joseph	1				
Gibbs, Silvester	1				
ESSEX TOWN.					
Chipman, Jonathan	1		2		
Chipman, Joseph	1		2		
Miller, Calvin	1		2		
Monross, Jesse	2	1	2		
Staunton, Solomon	1	1	4		
Slaughter, Henry	1	3	1		
Baker, Ezra	2	1	2		
Reed, Ebenezer	3	2	3		
Yeoman, Elisha	2	1	4		
Nash, Asahel	1	2	2		
Tyler, David	2				
Reed, Stephen	3		3		
Tubbs, Simon	2	2	3		
Kellog, David	2	2	3		
Reevel, Samuel	2		4		
Gallard, Jonathan	2	1	2		
Morgan, Daniel	4		2		
Morgan, Daniel, Junr	1	1	4		
Nelson, Samuel	1		4		
Nobles, Stephen	2	1	2		
Nobles, Morgan	3	2	2		
Castle, Abel	1	5	2		
Winchel, Jonathan	2	4	2		
Bingham, Abner	1	1	3		
Andrews, Isaac	3		3		
Hall, David	2	2	5		
Bradley, Capt. Samuel	2	1	5		
Day, David	1	2	2		
Bixby, Joel	1	1	1		
Lawrence, John	1		2		
Sinclear, John	2	1	1		
Sinclear, Samuel	1		2		
Castle, Nathan	1	2	2		
Castle, David, Junr	1	3	2		
Thomson, James	1	2	5		
Hicks, Levi	1	2	2		
Thomson, William	1	2	4		
Smith, Samuel	2	2	1		
Messinger, Lemuel	1	1	4		
Evens, Stephen	1	1	2		
McNall, Joseph	2		3		
Major, George	2	3	3		
Woodworth, Joel, Esqr.	9	1	5		
Thompson, David	2	1	1		
Bliss, Timothy, Esqr	4	3	3		
Stevens, Cap. Abraham	4	1	3		
Dunham, Gideon	1		2		
Day, David	4	1	3		
Mitchell, Ensign	1	2	2		
Curtis, Gideon	2		1		
Taft, Moses	2	2	7		
Collins, Nathaniel	1	2	4		
Skinner, Thomas	4		1		
Willard, Dubartis	3	4	2		
Spoor, John	1		4		
Evans, Barnabas	2		2		
Smith, Orange	2	2	1		
Norton, William	1		2		
Castle, David	2		1		
Sinclear, Jeremiah	1	2	2		
Harvey, Joel	1		2		
Spoor, William	2		3		
FAIRFAX TOWN.					
Farewell, John	2		2		
Parker, Thomas	2	2	4		
FAIRFAX TOWN—con.					
Farewell, Oliver	1		2		
Farewell, David	1				
Chadock, William	1	1	1		
Fullington, Francis	2	3	6		
Spafford, Broadstreet	2	1	2		
Spafford, Nathan	1	1	4		
Spafford, Asa	1	2	3		
Bornet, Robert	1	1	3		
Bornet, Robert, Junr	1	1	2		
Maxfield, William	1	3	2		
Grosvenor, Licester, Junr	1		2		
Richards, Capt. Thomas	2	2	4		
Squiers, Lieut. Silas	1	1	2		
Crissey, John, Junr	1	2	6		
Spafford, Josiah	4	3	1		
Andress, Levi	1	2	5		
Andress, John	1	1	2		
Churchwell, William	3	3	4		
Maxfield, David	1	1	2		
Crissey, John	5		1		
Hartt, John	2	2	1		
Farnsworth, Oliver	1	1	2		
Farnsworth, Levi	1	3	2		
Bowen, Roswell	1		1		
Farnsworth, James	2		2		
Farnsworth, Joseph	1		1		
Wilson, Joes	2				
Russell, Thomas, Esqr	2		3		
Clarke, Daniel	3		1		
French, John	1	1	1		
Strong, Arial	1		1		
Lothrop, Elkanah	1	4	1		
Orton, Gideon	1		2		
Burton, Nathaniel	2	1	1		
Strong, Jacob	3	2	2		
Story, Francis	1	4	1		
Beeman, Joseph	5	2	3		
Lovegrove, Paul H	2	2	1		
Barnet, Jose	1	1	2		
Kingsley, Roger	1	1	2		
Porter, Asahel	2		2		
Safford, Erastus	1		2		
Orton, Ichabod	1	3	4		
Grosvenor, Cap. Leuester	2		1		
Newbury, John	1	1	1		
Buck, Joseph	2		3		
Buck, Gold	2	2	1		
Buck, George	2		2		
Hateley, Abijah	2	1	2		
FAIRFIELD TOWN.					
Roberts, Lemuel	1	2	5		
Saul, Joseph	2	2	2		
Brown, Barzilla	1		3		
Wheeler, Joseph	1	1	5		
Wheeler, Zalmon	1	1	2		
Hoit, David	1		2		
Lobdin, Ebenezer	5	2	1		
Whitney, Sherad	1		2		
Squier, Asa	1	2	2		
Baker, David	1		2		
Taund, Edmund	1	2	1		
Wheaton, Joseph	1		1		
Luse, Isaac	1		2		
Lockwood, John	1	1	1		
Leach, John	3	4	4		
Bradley, Andrew	4	2	6		
Smith, Johiel	2	3	1		
Gregory, Ralph K	2	1	2		
Wakeman, Levi	2		3		
Gregory, Levi	1	1	1		
Gregory, Keeler	2	1	1		
Barsley, Whitmore	1				
Barsley, Nathaniel	1	2	2		
Northrop, Thomas	1		4		
Pangbowen, Jesse	2				
Hawley, James	2				
Smith, Daniel	1	1			
FLETCHER TOWN.					
Scott, Lemuel	3	2	1		
Palmer, Elisha	1	1	2		
Kingsley, John	1		3		
Chadock, Samuel	1		2		
Daley, Elijah	2	1	2		
Woodworth, Elisha	2	4	5		
Thustin, Peter	1	3	2		
Flood, Moses	1	1	2		
Goodwin, Asa	1	2	1		

CHITTENDEN COUNTY—Continued.

GEORGIA TOWN.

NAME OF HEAD OF FAMILY.	Free white males of 16 years and upward, including heads of families.	Free white males under 16 years.	Free white females, including heads of families.	All other free persons.	Slaves.
Allen, Asa S.	2		1		
Blodget, Sardius	2	2	3		
Bliss, Frederick	2		1		
Chadsey, James	1	1	2		
Chadsey, Benjamin	1		2		
Davis, Stephen	6	1	5		
Davis, Francis	2	1	5		
Dodge, Brewer	1	2	5		
Dee, Elijah	3	4	4		
Everts, James, Esqr	3	1	4		
Ferrend, William	1	4	4		
Fairchild, Stephen	3		2		
Fairchild, Stephen, Junr	2		3		
Fairchild, Joel	1	2	2		
Goodrich, Solomon	2				
Van Gilder, Andrew	5	2	5		
Hurlbut, Widow	1	1	1		
Hill, Elizabeth			2		
Hill, Jonathan	2	4	2		
Holmes, Benjamin	3	1	5		
Holmes, Stephen	2	1	4		
Hubbel, Abijah	1	1	1		
Hathaway, Abraham	5	1	4		
Loomis, Noah	2	4	5		
Loomis, Elijah	1	1	6		
Laflin, James	1		2		
Laflin, Samuel	1	3	1		
Laflin, Abraham	1	2	1		
Lamb, Edmond	2	2	1		
Naramore, Docr. Nathl.	2	1	3		
Perry, Nathl	2	1	3		
Prat, Paul	2		2		
Pearce, Abel	1	1	2		
Stannard, Daniel, Esqr.	1	3	2		
Silvester, Richard	1	2	5		
White, John, Esqr	2		4		
Wood, Nathanl	2	1	5		
Torrance, Thomas	2	2	3		
Farewel, Elisha	1	5	2		
Graves, Nathan	1		1		
Griswold, Joseph	2	2	2		
Philips, Mr	2	3	4		
Cadwell, Charless	1		2		
Wood, Jonathan	1	3	2		
Perrigo, David	2	2	2		
Ward, Liman	2	1	5		
Alvord, Benedict	1	2	3		
Willis, John	2	1	1		
Giffin, Edward	2	1	5		
Maxfield, Isaac	2				
Nichols, Nathan	4		2		
Barker, Elijah	3	3	5		
Winchel, Hezekiah	1	1	3		
Hubbell, John	1		1		
Bliss, Abner	2	3	1		
Farewell, Isaac	1	1	2		
HIGHGATE TOWN.					
Waggoner, John	2		2		
Sat, John	3	6	2		
Galor, Baunt	1	1	1		
Shidler, John	1	1	3		
Claw, John	2	1	4		
Willeen, Cornelius	1	1	1		
Steenhawer, George	1	4	4		
Scisco, Henry F	1	2	3		
Pangman, Peter	1	4	3		
Fitchout, Jacob	3	2	4		
Scrior, Nicholas	1	3	4		
Wilson, George	1	1	2		
Lampman, Michael	4		2	1	
Lampman, Abraham	1		3		
Butterfield, Jonathan	1	1	2		
Frazer, Daniel	1	1	2		
Hiliker, John	1	3	3		
HINESBURGH TOWN.					
Spafford, Job	1	1	3		
Smalley, Olford	1		2		
Stewart, William	1	1	6		
Ferrend, Joseph, Junr	1	1	3		
Ferrend, Joseph	5		5		
Sweet, Abraham	1	1	1		
Tanner, John	2				
Meacham, Jacob	1	3	3		
Wheeler, Nathan	1	3	6		
Green, Jonathan	1		6		
Wade, John	1	1	2		
Wade, Hezekiah	1	1	1		
Taylor, Amos	1				

HINESBURGH TOWN—con.

NAME OF HEAD OF FAMILY.	Free white males of 16 years and upward, including heads of families.	Free white males under 16 years.	Free white females, including heads of families.	All other free persons.	Slaves.
Hine, William	1		3		
Hine, Simeon	2	2	4		
Barto, Benjamin	3	1	2		
Bostwick, Lemuel, Esqr	1		3		
Mash, Docr. William B.	1				
Wilson, John	1	1	6		
Wilson, John, Junr	1	1	2		
Weller, David	3	1	2		
Bassett, Seth	1	2	6		
McCune, Robert	1	2	2		
McCune, George	1	4	1		
Andres, Amos	2	2	1		
Stowel, Abel	1		2		
Hurlbut, Elijah	1				
Weller, Jonathan	1	1	1		
Butler, Thomas	1	3	5		
Sherman, Prince	1	4	2		
Collins, Elisha	2	1	3		
Burrit, Andrew	2	1	2		
Barbar, Elisha, Esqr	3	3	4		
Barbar, Horice	1				
Bostwick, Gashum	1	2	3		
Bostwick, Ebenezer	1	3	4		
Bostwick, Doctor	1	2	2		
Billings, Elkanah	1	3	2		
Cummings, James	2	3	1		
Clarke, Zadock	2	3	3		
Congor, Asher	1	2	2		
Derwine, Samuel	1	2	4		
Derwine, Amasa	2		2		
Farland, Thomas	3	1	4		
Gates, James	1		4		
Holibard, Cornelius	1	1	1		
Horskins, Enoch	3	1	3		
Hinsdale, Aaron	1		1		
Lassel, Joshua	1	2	2		
Marshal, Silas	1				
Lawrence, Isaac	1	3	3		
Lawrence, Elijah	1	1	2		
Lawrence, Samuel	1	1	1		
Lawrence, Isaac, Junr	1		2		
Leavensworth, Cap. Nathan	3	1	2		
Munson, Thaddeus	2	3	3		
Meach, Elisha	2	4	2		
Mead, Lockwood	1	1	2		
Mead, Alpheus	1	1	3		
Marshal, Jonathan	1	2	3		
Nobles, Esbon	1	2	3		
Bostwick, Edmund	3	1	2		
Place, Thomas	3	2	2		
Pariner, Azariah	3	1	4		
Parker, William	1	1	2		
Palmer, George	1		5		
Stewart, Nathan	1		1		
Stewart, Thaddeus	2	1	1		
Spencer, Daniel	1	1	2		
Steele, Eliphes	3	1	3		
Tuttle, Hezekiah	1	1	2		
Peck, Elijah	2	2	3		
Boynton, Justis	1	1	2		
Barnum, Daniel	2		1		
Stone, Ebenezer	3	2	2		
Gates, David	1	2	5		
Sprague, Eleazar	1		2		
Roberts, David	1		3		
Beach, David	1	2	4		
Beach, Robert	1	3	2		
Palmerly, Reuben	1	1	3		
Parish, Asa	1	3	1		
Smith, Benjamin	3	2	3		
Spencer, Noah	1	2	3		
Smedley, Moses	2	1	1		
HUNGERFORD TOWN.					
Sheldon, Col. Elisha	6	1	1	4	
Hawley, James	1	3	3		
Sheldon, George	1		2		
Deming, Selah	2	1	1		
Sheldon, Elisha, Junr	4	1	1	1	
Basteel, John	1	2	3		
Dutcher, Ruluf	1				
HUNTSBURGH TOWN.					
Webster, Mr	3	2	2		
Hubbard, Samuel	3		1		
Rice, Stephen	7	1	2		
Allen, Aaron	2	3	3		
Stone, John	2	3	1		
Horskins, Seth	1		2		

HUNTSBURGH TOWN—con.

NAME OF HEAD OF FAMILY.	Free white males of 16 years and upward, including heads of families.	Free white males under 16 years.	Free white females, including heads of families.	All other free persons.	Slaves.
Cobourn, Amasa	1				
Bridgeman, John	2	1			
Peckham, Cap. Samuel	3				
Gates, Paul	1				
HYDESPARK TOWN.					
Garvin, Ephraim	1	1	6		
Martin, Peter	2	4	3		
Dick, Anthony				3	
McDaniel, John	1	1	2		
Taylor, Gamaliel	1		2		
Hyde, Jedadiah	1	6	3		
Fitch, Jabez	4		2		
ISLE MOTT TOWN.					
Wales, Nathaniel	3	1	1		
Blanchard, William	1	3	2		
Fisk, Ichabod E	2	3	1		
Eton, Noah	1				
Knap, Abraham	2	1	3		
Knap, Abraham, Junr.	1	1	2		
Rasey, Joseph	1				
Hall, Enoch	1		3		
Wait, Gardiner	1	4	1		
Howcomp, Jesse	1		1		
Mitchel, George	1				
Hall, Nathaniel	1				
Hall, Elihu	1				
Corion, Charless	1		2		
JERICO TOWN.					
Chittenden, Noah, Esqr.	5	2	4		
Castle, Jonathan, Esqr.	1	1	2		
Lane, Jedadiah	3	3	3		
Lane, Roger	2		2		
Morgan, Joshua	1	2	4		
Lowrey, Thomas	2	2	3		
Bostwick, Nathaniel	1	3	4		
Fay, Salmon	3		5		
Fay, Edward	2	1	2		
Whitmash, David	3	1	1		
Lee, Lucy	2	1	3		
Lee, Reuben	1		4		
More, Nathan	2		4		
Messinger, Roderick	2	4	5		
Bartlett, Ebenezer	3		1		
Bartlett, Benjamin	1	1	6		
Brown, Timothy	1	1	5		
Brown, Joseph, Junr	1	1	1		
Brown, Charless	1	1	2		
Clarke, Guy	1	5	2		
Hutchinson, Daniel	2	3	4		
Bostwick, Arthur	1	1	1		
Brown, Joseph	2		1		
Stone, Dudley	1	3	2		
Catlin, Wait	2	1	3		
Butler, Reuben	1		1		
Burns, Andrew	1	2	1		
Butler, Asaph	1		2		
Burchard, Elisha	1	2	3		
Bills, Daniel	1	1	2		
Chapin, Lewis	4		6		
Closson, Jonathan	2	3	4		
Cole, Docr Matthew	2		2		
Farnsworth, Benjamin	3	1	5		
Gott, Samuel	3		2		
Hodges, Leonard	2	3	1		
Holembeck, John	2	1	5		
Hall, Joseph	1	3	4		
Hyde, Ephraim	1		1		
Lee, Elon	2	1	1		
Lyman, John	2	1	3		
Kilbourn, Joel	2	3	4		
Lee, Azariah	2	2	2		
McArthur, Lieut. Peter	3	3	5		
Martin, Ebenezer	3		7		
McFarling, Jesse	1		3		
Manuel, Peter	2	2	3		
Rood, Azariah	2	1	2		
Rood, Thomas	2	1	3		
Rouse, Oliver	1	2	1		
Russell, Capt. John	3	4	3		
Smith, William	1	2	3		
Thomson, John	2	1	3		
Wilson, Joseph	3	3	4		
Lyman, Noah	1	3	2		
Reed, Peter	3		2		
Sinclear, John	1	1	6		
Bixby, Jonathan	1	5	2		

CHITTENDEN COUNTY—Continued.

NAME OF HEAD OF FAMILY.	Free white males of 16 years and upward, including heads of families.	Free white males under 16 years.	Free white females, including heads of families.	All other free persons.	Slaves.
JERICO TOWN—con.					
Spafford, Jacob	1		1		
Dilts, Peter	1	1	1		
Barsley, Joshua	2				
Johnson, John	1				
Henry, Enoch T.	1	1	2		
Chittenden, Martin, Esqr	1				
JOHNSON TOWN.					
Erwin, David	1	3	4		
Mills, Daniel	1	2	5		
Eaton, Samuel	2	1	3		
Seamons, John	1				
Rogers, William	2	1	2		
McConnel, Thomas	5	1	4		
McConnel, Moses	1				
Grag, Isaac	1		3		
Chamberlain, Thomas	1	1	2		
Davis, Moses	1	2	3		
Smith, Aaron	1	2	1		
Grag, George	1	1	2		
McConnel, John	1		1		
McConnel, John, Junr	1		2		
Grag, Thomas	2		2		
Saunders, Joshua	3				
McLanel, Jeremiah	2		1		
Hastings, Theophilus	1		1		
Hemkins, John	1	1	4		
Miller, Samuel	1		4		
Barnet, Nehemiah	1	1	2		
MIDDLESEX TOWN.					
Putnam, Seth, Esqr	1	2	4		
Putnam, Ebenezer	1	3	5		
Warren, Lovewell	1		2		
Harrington, Jonah	4	3	4		
Tucker, Joseph	1				
Harriss, Samuel	1	1	1		
Martin, George	1	2	4		
Mud, Thomas	1	5	2		
Putnam, Levi	1	2	1		
Benton, Nathan	1		1		
Hodley, Daniel	1	1	1		
Holden, Edmund	1				
Putnam, Jacob	1				
MILTON TOWN.					
Mansfield, Amos	8	1	3		
Rood, Silas	3	1	1		
Joslin, Benjamin	3		3		
Smith, Nehemiah	2	1	2		
Waters, Abel	3	1	3		
Taylor, Absalom	3	2	4		
Smith, Ebenezer	1		1		
Story, Stephen	3	3	3		
Jackson, Solomon	2		2		
Mansfield, Theophilus	4	1	1		
Stackhouse, Joseph	1	2	4		
Irish, William	2	4	3		
Soper, Mordaica	2	3	4		
Woodworth, Wier	2		3		
Logings, Samuel	1		2		
Logings, Samuel, Junr	1		2		
Hull, Samuel	1	1	6		
Owen, Elijah	4	2	2		
Owen, Elijah, Junr	1	1	1		
Castle, Solomon	2	1	3		
Blasdel, Nathaniel	2	1	3		
Owen, John	2		5		
Malary, Luther	1	1	2		
Bull, Gideon	1	2	1		
Day, Enos	1				
Newel, Medal	4	1	5		
Chance, Evens	1	2	3		
Church, Amaziah	1	1	3		
Cooley, Solomon	1	2	5		
Blackman, Ephraim	1	4	3		
Hartt, William	1		1		
Matthews, Aaron, Esqr	2	2	3		
Church, Ephraim	1		1		
Church, Samuel	2	1	6		
Gifford, Gideon	2		1		
Gage, Robert	1	3	2		
Irish, Stephen	1	2	1		
Bachelder, Abel	1	1	3		
Leat, Miles	1	1	1		
Ashley, Enoch	1	3	4		
Ashley, Elisha	2	3	4		
Dewey, Thomas	1	2	2		
Hancey, Gideon	3		3		
MILTON TOWN—con.					
Hill, Calvin	2		1		
Austin, Job	1	1	1		
Austin, Joseph	1				
Austin, David	1	5	4		
Gilder, Jacob	1		6		
Winchel, Hezekiah	1	3	1		
MINDEN TOWN.					
Crafts, Colonel	4	3	4		
Cutler, Mr	2	3	2		
MORETOWN TOWN.					
Heaton, John	3	3	2		
Achison, Seth	1	1	2		
Sherman, Abner	3	2	4		
Haseltine, Joseph	1				
Haseltine, Ebenezer	1				
Tucker, Ephraim	1				
MORRISTOWN TOWN.					
Norton, Mr	1		2		
Walker, William	2		1		
Walker, Jacob	1		1		
Herd, Aaron	2				
NEW HUNTINGTON TOWN.					
Stevens, David	1	1	3		
Fargo, Samuel	1	1	2		
Raiment, John	3	5	4		
Johns, Johiel, Esqr	1	3	2		
Martin, John	1		2		
Ambler, Ebenezer	1	1	1		
Cook, Archibald	1	1	3		
Allen, Joseph	1		2		
Russell, Silvester	2		2		
Brewster, Ozem	3	4	6		
Barton, Solomon	1	3	2		
Gillet, Asa	1	1	1		
Robins, Daniel	1	1	2		
Stevens, Orange	1		2		
Harriss, Leban	1	1	1		
Starr, Comfort	1	1	3		
Alger, Asa	1	2	1		
Starr, Pearly	1				
Joslin, Zebediah	1	3	3		
Alger, Nathaniel	1	3	2		
Brownson, Amos	2		2		
Anderson, John	1	2	2		
Hall, James	1	2	5		
McFarson, Joseph	1	2	4		
Saunders, Jonathan	1		1		
Everts, Jesse, Junr	1		2		
Thesber, Squire	1				
Williams, Rufus	1	3	2		
NEW HUNTINGTON GORE.					
Turner, Abel	4	1	5		
Turner, Samuel	1	2	3		
Fairman, Jacob	1	3	2		
Shepherd, Elisha	1	1	2		
Turner, John	1		1		
Benham, Enos	1		1		
Allen, Edward	1				
NORTH HERO TOWN.					
Minard, Henry	1		1		
More, John	2		1		
Martin, John	2	1	1		
Pelott, Simon	3		3	1	
Brownson, John	1	4	2		
Trunumbal, Asahal	1	1	2		
Stone, Ephraim	1	1	6		
Ball, Jacob	2	2	1		
Wales, George	1	1	2		
Ayres, Ebenezer	1				
Hutchins, Nathan	1		2		
Hutchins, Nathan, Junr	1				
Hutchins, Asahel	1		1		
Hazen, Nathan	1	3	6		
Butler, Benjamin	2	3	2		
Knight, John	1	3	6	2	
Paine, Roger	1		1		
Herrick, John	1		3		
Wood, Solomon	1	1	2		
NORTH HERO TOWN—con.					
Ladd, Jedadiah	2		3		
Wood, Enos	1	3	2		
Hanes, Samuel	1		2		
Hazen, Andrew	1		2		
Hanes, Jonathan	1				
Hanes, William	1				
Hazen, Joseph	3	2	2		
Hazen, Azahel	1				
Brownson, Reuben	1		2		
Townd, Silas	1		1		
Brownson, Liman	1				
Strong, William	1		1		
ST. ALBANS TOWN.					
Hoit, Winthrop	1	3	4		
Campbell, David	2	2	2		
Vandozer, Abraham	1	2	2		
Hathaway, Silas, Esqr	8	1	4	1	
Hathaway, Ralph	3	2	4		
Meigs, Daniel	4	2	2		
Bradley, Benjamin	4	2	2		
Hoit, Jonathan	2	4	3		
Brooks, Azariah	1	2	2		
Sawyer, Noahdiah	1		5		
Potter, Freeborn	3		3		
Potter, Noel	2	2	4		
Jenkins, Valentine	1	3	4		
Powers, David	6		5		
Edmond, Eliphalet	1	1	2		
Greene, Job	1	1	2		
Greene, Nathan	1		1		
Winters, Timothy	2	2	4		
Colkins, Samuel	3	3	4		
Kellog, Joseph	1	2	3		
Griffin, William	1	1	3		
Weldon, Jesse	5	1	2		
Weldon, David	2		1		
Rood, Elijah	2	1	3		
Spoor, Abraham	1	3	2		
Davis, Allen	2		1		
Horton, Samuel	1	1	1		
West, Samuel	1		2		
Odle, David	2		6		
Hartt, Jonathan	1	1	2		
Hines, Solomon	1		2		
Hines, Joseph	1		1		
Dutcher, Christopher	1	2	1		
Tupper, Hazel	2		1		
Soal, Rowland	1				
Potter, Andrew	2	4	3		
Clarke, Ebenezer	1	2	3		
Gibbs, Thomas	1	3	1		
Gibbs, Isaac	4	1			
Gibbs, Joshua	1	2	2		
Brooks, Adonijah	2	2	1		
Howard, John	2	3	3		
Howard, Elisha	3				
Warren, Asa	1		2		
ST. GEORGE TOWN.					
Ferris, Joseph	1				
Sutton, James	1	1	1		
Sutton, Benjamin	1	5	2		
Lockwood, Reuben	1				
Lockwood, Nathan	1	1	2		
Isham, Johiel	1	3	2		
Isham, Joseph	1				
Isham, Daniel	1	2	1		
Isham, Joshua	3		5		
Isham, Jaira	1	1	5		
Higby, Elnathan	1	2	3		
Higby, Wheeler	1	2	5		
SHELBURNE TOWN.					
Vernornom, Isaac	1	3	3		
Pierson, William	1	3	1		
Pierson, Moses	3		1		
Pierson, Usnel	1	1	1		
Pierson, Ziba	1	2	1		
Post, Jared	1	3	3		
Kip, Samuel	1		2		
Andrews, Moses	1	1	1		
Smith, Zadock	1	1	6		
Rowley, Cap. Aaron	3	3	3		
Powers, Joseph	1		3		
Vanner, Richard	1	1	1		
Taber, John	1		2		
Smith, Caleb	1		1		
Stockwell, Levi	1	1	4		

CHITTENDEN COUNTY—Continued.

NAME OF HEAD OF FAMILY.	Free white males of 16 years and upward, including heads of families.	Free white males under 16 years.	Free white females, including heads of families.	All other free persons.	Slaves.
SHELBURNE TOWN—con.					
Barbar, Daniel	3	2	4		
Comstock, Daniel	4	1	5		
Henderson, Jesse	1		2		
Hurlbut, Timothy, Esqr.	1	3	3		
McCivers, James	1	2	4		
Smith, William	3	1	2		
Hall, Thomas	3	1	6		
Smith, Caleb	3	1	3		
Harrington, William C., Esqr.	1	1	1		
Stevens, Josias	1		3		
Deming, Asahel	3		3		
Meach, Frederick	2		1		
Trowbridge, Keeler	2	1	5		
Hatch, Lasel	1				
Clark, Lemuel	1	1	3		
Robison, Joseph	1	1	2		
Sutherland, Adam	1	1			
Thair, Dan	2		3		
Gregory, Salmon	1	1	1		
Clark, Samuel, Junr.	1		2		
Hatch, Barnabas	1	3	4		
Cole, Rufus	1	1	3		
Leonard, Robert	1				
Ismond, James	1		1		
Bitgood, Ramington	2		3		
Whitley, John	1		1		
Cook, Ezekiel	2	2	4		
Collins, Alexander	1				
Hall, Phineas	1	2	3		
Mills, Samuel	1	2	1		
Morehouse, Elisha	2	3	3		
Reed, Joshua	1	1	2		
Parish, William	1	2	2		
Seely, Benjamin	1	4	3		
Slocum, Asa	1				
Holibard, Asahel	1	2	3		
Holabard, Consider	1		2		
Nichols, David	2	4	3		
Lyon, Gashum	1	4	4		
Lyon, Abel	1		2		
Seamons, James	1	1	1		
Morehouse, Sturgens	1	4	4		
David, John	1	1	2		
Drew, Peter	1	2	3		
Holabird, Abel	1	1	3		
Ferris, Zebulon	1	2	1		
Heacocks, Elihu	1	1	1		
Lyon, Robert	2	1	3		
Lyon, Jane (widow)			3		
Besto, Ebenezer	1	2	2		
Lyon, William	1	1	1		
Fairchild, Daniel	3	1	1		
Hamilton, Charless	2	2	2		
Hamilton, Dudley, Junr	1	1	1		
Hamilton, Joseph	1	1	1		
Lyon, Asa	1	4	3		
Brown, Abraham	1	2	3		
Lawrence, John	2	2	3		
Hammond, Isaiah	1	2	4		
Burrett, Israel	3	3	3		
Shead, Daniel	2	3	1		
McMullin, Neile	1				
SMITHFIELD TOWN.					
Sherwood, Gabriel	1	1	1		
Barlow, Hubbart, Esqr.	6	1	2		
Noble, Asahel	2	1	3		
Barlow, Diamond	3	1	1		
Hall, Lewis	4	2	3		
Leach, John	2	1	3		
Burr, Jabez	2	1	1		
Beaton, William	1	2	2		
Sunderland, John	1		2		
Mitchel, John	1	2	3		
Holister, Samuel	1				
Jewet, Elnathan	1				
Burlington, Clark	2	2	7		
McNamar, John	1				
SOUTH HERO TOWN.					
Pearl, Col. Stephen	2		3		
Phelps, Abel	6		4		
Landon, Benjamin	2	2	4		
Phelps, Joseph	2	3	4		
Smith, Majr Jacob	1	5	2		
Janes, Humphrey	2	1	1		
Campbell, William	2	1	2		
Stewart, William	1	4	3		
Fairchild, Jesse	2	2	1		
SOUTH HERO TOWN—con.					
Loyd, Thos. P., Esqr.	4				
Burnel, Solomon	2		4		
Welch, Nathaniel	3		3		
Morison, David	1	1	3		
Pearl, Timothy	1	3	6		
Duel, Ephraim	3		7		
Griffin, Jonathan	1		1		
Hacket, Allen	4	2	3		
Griffin, David	1	5	3		
Pelton, James	1	1	2		
Pixley, Asa	1	3	4		
Martin, Eleazar	2	4	5		
Peters, Ebenezer	2	2	3		
Blanchard, John	1	1	1		
Allen, Col. Ebenezer	4		5		
Allen, Cap. Timothy	2		2		
Johnson, Samuel	1	2	2		
Birdich, James	3	3	3		
Lawrence, Horman	2		1		
Hall, Alpheus	1	2	4		
Janes, Herman	1	2	2		
Peter, Valentine	1				
McNall, Uriah	1				
Laslin, Matthew	1				
Laslin, Charles	1				
Dennis, Jesse	1	2	4		
Hide, William	1	1	3		
Eldridge, Amos	1	4	4		
Davidson, John	4	1	3		
Sawyer, Col. Ephraim	4		3		
Sawyer, Ephraim, Junr.	1	2	4		
Martin, Jonah	2		4		
Fletcher, Isi	1				
Cady, William	1		4		
Welch, Amos	1	2	1		
Drake, Festus	2	3	2		
Adams, Isaac	1	2	2		
Fletcher, Samuel	3	2	3		
Winters, Obadiah	4	3	3		
Wonen, Bishop	1	2	4		
Mincley, Barnabas	1	2	2		
Slawson, Eleazar	4	2	2		
Fisk, John	1	1	3		
Ventine, Abraham	1	1	3		
Jones, Joel	2		1		
Hazen, Levi	1		3		
Mincley, John	4		3		
Barns, Robert	1		1		
Rosmond, Colrod	1	3	2		
Reynolds, Grinnel	2	1	1		
Dody, Obadiah	1	2	6		
Burns, Samuel	3	3	4		
Gibson, John	1	2	1		
Linsey, James	2	1	2		
Williams, Amariah	1				
Hazens, William	2	1	3		
Clarke, Ozial	2		3		
Fulson, John	1		8		
Farnsworth, William	1	3	1		
Norton, John	2	2	2		
Hyde, Jedadiah, Junr.	1	4	1		
Butler, William	1	2	2		
Campbell, William, Junr	1	2	1		
Hyde, Elijah	3	2	3		
Adams, Joseph	1				
Gordon, Alexander	6		3		
Closs, Reuben	1	1	5		
Parker, Dennis	1	1	2		
Oldridge, John	1	3	1		
Wiley, Joseph	1	1	3		
Hazen, Andrew	1		2		
Coonley, David	1	1	3		
Lent, Roswell	1				
Moffet, William	1				
McBurgh, Wilson	1	3	2		
Starks, Joseph	1	1	4		
Hoig, Daniel	1		5		
Stark, Benajah	2		8		
Lawrence, Susanna	1	1	3		
Mincley, Kelcon	1	1	3		
Graham, Aaron	1	1	3		
Starks, Samuel	1	2	1		
Allen, Lambertson	4	1	3		
Graham, Hugh	1	2	1		
Sampson, Daniel	1				
Mincley, John, Junr	1	2	3		
STARKSBOROUGH TOWN.					
Darrow, Samuel, Esqr.	4	1	5		
Ketch, James	1		2		
Bostwick, Austin	1		1		
STARKSBOROUGH TOWN—continued.					
Tupper, John	1		2		
Bostwick, Joseph	2	1	3		
Bidwell, George	1	2	2		
Pierce, Warner	3				
Shatock, Jonas	1	2	4		
Northrop, Mr	1				
SWANTON TOWN.					
Lampman, Stephen	1		3		
Butterfield, Capt. Thomas	3	3	2		
Hitchcock, Luke	1	3	3		
Tanner, Joseph	1	2	3		
Aslestine, Isaac	1	1	1		
Lampman, Henry	1	1	1		
Noke, John	2	5	3		
Clarke, Thomas	1	3	2		
Lewis, Asa	1				
Aslestine, Coonrod	3	3	3		
Abels, Asahel	1				
Heath, Phineas	1	3	4		
Robison, Israel	2		1		
Greene, William	3	1	1		
UNDERHILL TOWN.					
Benedict, Elijah	2		3		
Hurlbut, Adam	4	2	4		
Post, Darius	2	1	4		
Post, Darius, Junr	1		2		
Eaton, Abner	1	1	7		
Dixon, Jared	1	2	2		
Dixon, Alexander	2	1	1		
Butler, Benjamin	1	2	4		
Smith, Ezekiel	1	3	2		
Sheldon, Caleb	1		2		
WAITSFIELD TOWN.					
Wait, Gen. Benjamin	5	4	3		
Wait, Ezra	1	1	4		
Sherman, Thomas	2	2	3		
Wait, Jeduthan	1		1		
Sherman, Beriah	1	2	3		
Dena, Francis	3	2	2		
Bartlett, William	1	3	3		
Rider, Phineas	2		3		
Palmater, Isaac	1	2	2		
Rider, Salma	1				
Seamonds, David	1				
Chase, Mr	1				
Peke, Mr	1				
WATERBURY TOWN.					
Kenedy, Jason	1	5	5		
Munson, Caleb	3	1	1		
Knap, Paul	1	2	3		
Holden, Richard	1	2	2		
Wilson, Isaac	3	1	2		
Wells, Reuben	1	1	11		
Mash, Elias	1		1		
Bartlett, Philip	1	4	1		
Butler, Ezra	2	1	2		
Right, Jonathan	1	1	2		
Smith, Thomas	1	2	2		
Parcher, Robert	2		2		
Waters, Amos	1		4		
Jones, Stephen	1				
Sherman, Stiles	1	4	3		
Cragne, John	1	3	3		
WESTFORD TOWN.					
Crandol, David	2	2	3		
Crandol, David, Junr.	2		2		
Burdick, Joseph	2	1	1		
Austin, Jeremiah	5	1	1		
Balch, Silas	1	1	3		
Wilmouth, James	2		1		
Woodworth, Shubal	1		4		
Noles, David	1		1		
Barlow, Warren	1		4		
Northaway, Francis	1	1	3		
Seeley, John	2				
Palmerly, Hezekiah	1	1	6		
Johnsom, Stephen	1	1	3		
Cobourn, David	1				
WILLISTON TOWN.					
Chittenden, His Excly Thoms, Esqr.	7		4		
Spafford, Jonathan, Esqr.	4	2	2		

CHITTENDEN COUNTY—Continued.

NAME OF HEAD OF FAMILY.	Free white males of 16 years and upward, including heads of families.	Free white males under 16 years.	Free white females, including heads of families.	All other free persons.	Slaves.
WILLISTON TOWN—con.					
Brownson, Amos, Esqr.	2	1	3		
Chamberlain, John	3		2		
Brownson, Joel, Esqr.	2	2	3		
Chamberlain, Joshua	2	2	4		
Taylor, John	1		4		
Shaw, Daniel	2	2	3		
Taylor, Eldad	2	1	2		
Chittenden, Giles	2		2		
Harrington, Timothy	1	1	4		
Ferrend, Jared	1	1	2		
Donaly, Robert	1	2	4		
Wade, Joshua	1		1		
Barnett, Samuel	2	1	1		
Hallock, Stephen	4	2	6		
Hallock, Stephen, Junr.	1	2	1		
Hallock, Content	2				
Rogers, Thomas	1	2	4		
Walden, Abiathar	1		4		
Tomlinson, Eliphalet	1				
Barbar, Martin	1	1	2		
Andress, Benoni	1	1	1		
Flemming, Asa	1	3	2		
Squire, Benjamin	1				
Everts, Jesse	1	3	1		
Stevens, James	2	2	7		
Stevens, James, Junr.	1	1			
Taylor, Abraham	1	2	2		
Bishop, Daniel, Junr.	1		3		
Bishop, Daniel	2	1	3		
Welden, Benjamin	1	1	1		
Porter John	1	3	1		
Auger, Lt. Felix	1	1	2		
Whitcomb, Robert	2	2	2		

NAME OF HEAD OF FAMILY.	Free white males of 16 years and upward, including heads of families.	Free white males under 16 years.	Free white females, including heads of families.	All other free persons.	Slaves.
WILLISTON TOWN—con.					
Brownson, Asa	2	3	4		
Jones, Josiah	1	1	2		
Fay, Nathan	1	2	2		
Arnold, James	4		3		
Arnold, Levi	1		2		
Betty, James	1				
Graves, William	1		2		
Graves, Thaddeus	1	3	3		
Beach, John	1	3	1		
Murray, Kesiah	4	5	3		
Joslin, Jacob	1		6		
Hulburd, David	3	4	5		
Bradley, Elisha	1	2	3		
Trowbridge, Stephen	1	3	3		
Bradley, Stilman	1	1	2		
Bradley, Eber	1	2	2		
Cook, John	1				
Tolcott, David	4		3		
Tolcott, Parker	1	2	1		
Gray, Zalmon	2		1		
Dodge, Stephen	1	1	3		
Holmes, George	1	1	2		
Parker, Cardy	1		2		
Lee, Timothy	1	1	4		
Devorex, John	1	1	4		
Winslow, Nathaniel	1	1	4		
Tolcott, David, Junr.	2	1	1		
Miller, Solomon, Esqr.	2	2	3		
Beach, Silas	1	1	5		
Winslow, Lemuel	1	1	2		
Adams, John	1	3	2		
Trowbridge, Seth	1	3	1		
Bates David	2				

NAME OF HEAD OF FAMILY.	Free white males of 16 years and upward, including heads of families.	Free white males under 16 years.	Free white females, including heads of families.	All other free persons.	Slaves.
WILLISTON TOWN—con.					
Allen, Nathan	2	1	1		
Bradley, James	1		2		
Bradley, Joseph	1	3	2		
Chamberlain, Samuel	1	2	2		
Tuttle, Timothy	1	4	1		
Murray, Curtis	1		1		
Ames, Ezra	1	1	4		
Allen, Elihu	2	1	1		
Russel, Oliver	1				
Close, Stephen	1				
Snider, Jacob	1	1	6		
Squiers, Stephen	1	3	1		
Jones, John	1		1		
Center, Jeremiah	1	3	4		
Leonard, Joel	1	2	2		
Judson, Enoch	1		1		
Hawley, Philo	1		4		
Taylor, Eldad, Junr.	1	3	4		
Meigs, Simon	1		1		
Puckings, Andrew	1	2	3		
Lowrey, Gad	1				
Cook, John	1				
Smith, Abraham	1	4	4		
Crane, James	1				
Crane, Peter	1	1	4		
WOLCOTT TOWN.					
Whitney, Hezekiah	3	2	3		
Taylor, Thomas	3	4	2		
Hubbel, Zeth	1		7		
Guyer, Luke	2				
Taylor Robert	2	1	2		

ORANGE COUNTY.

NAME OF HEAD OF FAMILY.	Free white males of 16 years and upward, including heads of families.	Free white males under 16 years.	Free white females, including heads of families.	All other free persons.	Slaves.
BARNET TOWN.					
Abbot, Job	2	3	1		
Aikins, Samuel	2	1	4		
Blair, Robert	1	3	2		
Bonnett, Joseph	1	1	2		
Brock, Robert	1	4	3		
Brock, Walter	3	3	6		
Brown, Isaac	1	1	4		
Brown, James	1	3	2		
Buchannan, John	3	1	4		
Calder, James	1	3	3		
Cross, James	1	2	3		
Cross, Moses	1	1	2		
Chamberlin, Raiment	1		2		
Evens, Joseph	2	1	1		
Fowler, Jonathan	2	1	2		
Garland, George	1	1	5	1	
Gibbrith, John	2				
Gibson, George	1	4	1		
Gilchrist, James	2	1	1		
Gilchriston, John	3	2	3		
Gilfellon, William	2	1	1		
Gilfellon, William	1	1	1		
Goddard, John	1	2	2		
Goodewille, David	2		1		
Hadley, Parrit	2	2	4		
Hadley, Samuel	1				
Hall, Jacob	1		1		
Hall, Levi	1	1	1		
Hazeltine, Thomas	2		2		
Hazeltine, Timothy	1		1		
Herriman, John	1	1	1		
Hervey, Alexander	2	4	5		
Hervey, Archibald	1				
Hinman, John	2	3	3		
Holladay, Noah	1	4	4		
Hustin, Samuel	1	3	2		
Johnson, Obediah	1				
Keyes, John	2	2	4		
King, Elijah	1		3		
Kinley, James	1				
Lachy, Andrew	1	1	2		
Lard, Robert	1	2	4		
Lofferty, James	1		6		
Long, Alexander	2	1	1		
Long, Andrew	1				
McCallum, John	1				
McClerran, James	2	2	2		
McClarren, John	1	2	2		
McFarling, Daniel	1	3	3		
McFarling, John	1				
McNabb, John	1	2	2		
McNadoe, John	2	2	2		
Manchester, Ezekiel	1		1		

NAME OF HEAD OF FAMILY.	Free white males of 16 years and upward, including heads of families.	Free white males under 16 years.	Free white females, including heads of families.	All other free persons.	Slaves.
BARNET TOWN—con.					
Mann, James	1	5	2		
Maxfield, William	1		2		
Oar, James	1	1			
Pierce, Esther		1	2		
Pierce, Samuel	1	3	1		
Pierce, Simon	1	2	3		
Pollard, Edward	1				
Rankin, Andrew	1	1	1		
Rankin, John	2		2		
Rider, William	1	1	3		
Rider, Stevens	2	1	3		
Robinson John	1	1	2		
Ross, Hugh	1	3	2		
Ross, John	1	2	3		
Shaw, John	3	2	2		
Shaw, William	2	2	3		
Smith, Thomas	1	1	4		
Sommer, Bartholomu	1	2	6		
Sommer, Robet	3	2	2		
Shearer, William	2	1	3		
Stevens, Enos	5	1	1		
Stevens, John	1				
Stevens, Oliver	1	2	1		
Stevens, Phinehas	2	2	3		
Stiles, Caleb	1	1	1		
Stevens, Samuel	1	4	3		
Stiles, Caleb	1	1	2		
Stimson, William	1				
Stewart, Archibald	1	1	1		
Stewart, Clood	3		1		
Stewart, James	1	2	2		
Stewart, Walter	1				
Sylvester, Levi	1	1	1		
Tace, William	1	1	5		
Thomson, Alexander	1	4	3		
Thurston, Phinehas	1		1		
Twaddle, Robert	1		2		
Waddle, John	2		4		
Warden, William	3	1	3		
Watson, Peliliah	1		3		
Wesson, Aron	1		3		
Wolcott, Emerson	1	2	2		
Wood, Stephen	1	2	2		
Youngman, Thomas	1		4		
Youngman, John	1	1	1		
BARTON TOWN.					
Not inhabited.					
BERLIN TOWN.					
Ayers, Jonathan	3				
Baily, Joshua	1	2	5		

NAME OF HEAD OF FAMILY.	Free white males of 16 years and upward, including heads of families.	Free white males under 16 years.	Free white females, including heads of families.	All other free persons.	Slaves.
BERLIN TOWN—con.					
Black, Jacob	1	1	4		
Collens, Cornelius	3	1	1		
Ellis, Jabez	1		2		
Emerson, Jonathan	1	1	4		
Flay, William	2	2	3		
Fowler, Jacob	2	2	4		
Hubbard, Eleazer	1		5		
Hubbard, James	3	2	2		
Ingham, Micajah	1	2	1		
Martin, Daniel	1		2		
Martin, Daniel	1	2	2		
Nye, David	2	1	3		
Nye, Elijah	1	2	1		
Perley, John	1	1	4		
Perrin, Zachariah	2	2	4		
Sawyer, John	3		3		
Silloway, Aaron	1	2	2		
Silloway, Hezekiah	2	4	3		
Smith, Joseph	1	1	2		
Strong, Aaron	1		2		
Taplin, John	3	5	4		
BILLYMEAD TOWN.					
Not inhabited.					
BRADFORD TOWN					
Aldrich, Silas	1	3	4		
Amesbury, Thomas	1		1		
Andros, Bildad	3	1	2		
Aspenwall, Samul	1		1		
Baldwin, Benjamin	4	3	3		
Baker, Theodore	1	1	3		
Barnet, Benjamin	1	2	4		
Barron, John	2	1	6		
Barron, Joshua	1	3	5		
Baron, Michal	2	1	2		
Benfield, George	1	5	3		
Bliss, Ellis	4	1	4		
Bliss, John	1	1	1		
Brown, Edmond	1	3	3		
Carter, Benjamin	3		2		
Chamberlin, Ashur	3	4	3		
Cheney, Elias	1		1		
Clark, John	1	1	1		
Clark, John	3		3		
Clark, Joseph	2	4	6		
Colby, Simon	1	3	2		
Collins, Daniel	1	3	5		
Collins, Ichabod	1	5	3		
Collins, Levi	1	1	3		
Collins, Timothy	1	2	2		

ORANGE COUNTY—Continued.

NAME OF HEAD OF FAMILY.	Free white males of 16 years and upward, including heads of families.	Free white males under 16 years.	Free white females, including heads of families.	All other free persons.	Slaves.
BRADFORD TOWN—con.					
Cook, Silas	1	2	2		
Cox, Mathew	1	2	3		
Darling, William	2	3	2		
Davis, Benjamin	1	3	5		
Davis, David	2	2	7		
Davis, Obediah	1	4	1		
Davis, Samuel	1	1	4		
Eaton, Jonathan	1		2		
Eastman, Josiah, mov'd to the Lake					
Fenton, Francis	2		3		
Fifield, Daniel	1	1	2		
Fifield, Samuel	3		2		
Follet, Francis	1		3		
Follet, Giles	1	2	2		
Foster, Reubin	3	2	3		
Frizzle, Benjamin	1		2		
Fuller, Lemuel	2	1	4		
Garey, Joshua	2		4		
Glines, John	2	2	5		
Greenwood, John	1	3	2		
Heath, Isaac	1	6	3		
Hidden, James	1	2	3		
Hinkson, Samuel	2	3	2		
Hobbes, Caleb	1	1	4		
Horner, James	1		1		
Horner, John	1	1	2		
Hunkins, Robert	3	5	4		
Jacob, John	1	1	5		
Jenkins, Elijah	1	1	2		
Jenkins, Joseph	1	1	1		
Jenkins, Stephens	2	3	3		
Keeler, James	2	2	3		
Kenedy, David	2	2	4		
Leach, James	2	1	4		
Martin, Ephraim	1	1	2		
Martin, Ephraim	1	1	4		
Martin, John	1	1	3		
Martin, John	1	1	2		
Martin, Jonathan	1	3	2		
Martin, Nathaniel	1	4	1		
Marten, Reuben	2	2	4		
Martin, Samuel	2	1	3		
McConnel, Stephen	2	3	4		
Miller, Hugh	3		3		
Miller, James	1	1	2		
Miller, Robert	1	2	5		
Moore, Daniel	3	2	4		
Moore, Samuel	1	2	4		
Newell, Elisha	1	1	2		
Nothey, David	1	1	3		
Olmstead, Ebenezer	3	3	3		
Osborn, Lemuel	1		3		
Page, Caleb	1	4	4		
Parker, Silas	1	1	2		
Pecket, Giles	2		3		
Pecket, John	1	1	1		
Perkins, Peter	1	2	1		
Peters, Andrew B	2		2		
Pillsbury, Thomas	1	1	3		
Preston, John	2	2	4		
Rhody, Frederick	1	1	2		
Rogers, Elizabeth	1		2		
Rogers, Perley	1	1	2		
Rolling, Stephen	2	3	4		
Rowell, Thomas	4		2		
Sanders, Obededom	1	1	5		
Sharp, Jepther			1	7	
Smith, James	1	1	4		
Smith, John	1	2	3		
Smith, Joseph	1		2		
Stearns, Elias	1	5	3		
Stebbins, Arad	1		3		
Stevens, Nicholas	1		4		
Stimson, Abijah	1	1	1		
Taylor, Benjamin	1	3	2		
Underwood, John	1		2		
Underwood, Phinehas	1	2	3		
Phillip, Verbeck	1	1	3		
Welton, Peter	2	4	2		
White, John	2	1	3		
White, Nathaniel	1	2	5		
White, Nicholas	1	1	5		
Woodworth, John	1	2	4		
BRAINTREE TOWN.					
Bass, Edward	3		1		
Bass, Samuel	3	3	4		
Bracket, Henry	2	1	2		
Copeland, David	3	2	2		
Curtis, Nehemiah	2	3	2		
Dolbe, Exeter				3	

NAME OF HEAD OF FAMILY.	Free white males of 16 years and upward, including heads of families.	Free white males under 16 years.	Free white females, including heads of families.	All other free persons.	Slaves.
BRAINTREE TOWN—con.					
Dolbe, Peter				2	
Dyre, Ichabod	1	4	2		
Fitts, Samuel	2	4	4		
Flint, Asahel	3		1		
Flint, Silas	3		1		
Ford, William	4	4	2		
French, Elijah	1	3	3		
Fuller, Stephen	1	3	4		
Gleson, Beza	1	1	3		
Gooch, Joseph	1	1	4		
Gooch, Joseph	2		1		
Harwood, Samuel	4	4	4		
Hutchinson, Nathan	1	1	1		
Kinney, Thomas	1	3	2		
Nichols, Benjamin	1	3	7		
Nichols, Isaac	4	2	1		
Nichols, Samson	1	2	2		
Parmile, Eleazer	1	2	1		
Parmile, Jehiel	1	1	5		
Patridge, Reuben	2	4	4		
Pratt, Mathew	1	2	3		
Scott, Wiliam	1	2	1		
Spear, Elijah	1	2	3		
Spear, Jacob	2	3	3		
Spear, Jacob	1	2	4		
Spear, Nathaniel	1	4	2		
Spear, Samuel	1		6		
Trash, Silas	1		2		
Veasy, Benjamin	2		2		
Wait, Daniel	1				
White, Ebenezer	1				
BROOKFIELD TOWN.					
Adams, Reuben	2	2	1		
Ainsworth, Ebenezer	1		3		
Ainsworth, Edward	1	3	2		
Ellis, Elisha	2	2	4		
Ames, Edmond	1	1	2		
Bailey, Samuel	3	4	3		
Bigelow, Amasa	1	2	2		
Bigelow, David	1		2		
Bigelow, Ely	1	3	3		
Bigelow, Josiah	1	1	3		
Bigelow, Timothy	2	3	2		
Burnham, Elijah	1	3	4		
Burton, Levi	1		2		
Carly, Ichabod	1		2		
Carly, William	1		1		
Coult, Benjamin	2	1	2		
Cowles, Timothy	1	6	1		
Cushman, Nathaniel	4		2		
Davison, Paul	1	3	4		
Durkee, Oliver	4	1	1		
Fisk, Experience	1	1	3		
Freeman, Samuel	1	3	1		
Gaylord, Hezekiah	3	3	4		
Groover, Amaziah	[illegible]	2	3		
Hand, Ira	1	1	3		
Hamlin, Oliver	1	3	4		
Herrington, John	1	2	2		
Hopkins, Stephen	1	1	2		
Howard, Benjamin	1		1		
Howard, Charles	1		1		
Howard, John	2	1	3		
Howard, Jonas	1	1	1		
Hubbard, Moses	1	1	5	1	
Humphrey, Amos	1	2	1		
Humphrey, James	1	4	5		
Humphrey, Nathaniel	1		4		
Humphrey, Nathaniel	1		3		
Huntington, Asa	1		4		
Hutchinson, Jerom	1		3		
Hyde, Abraham	1		1		
Hyde, Amasa	1	3	2		
Hyde, Benjamin	2	2	6		
Hyde, Ichabod	3	2	7		
Ingraham, Phillip	2	3	4		
Kellogg, Phinehas	1	2	2		
Kingsbury, Daniel	3	3	2		
Lord, Ichabod	1	1	3		
Lyman, Abel	3	5	3		
Lyman, Elijah	1		2		
Lyman, John	3		1		
Martin, Walker	1		2		
McKnight, Theophilius	1		1		
Olverd, John	1		1		
Olverd, Nathan	2		2		
Olverd, Selah	1		1		
Payne, John	1		2		
Payne, Noah	1		1		
Pierce, John	1	3	3		
Pride, Abner	3	4	3		

NAME OF HEAD OF FAMILY.	Free white males of 16 years and upward, including heads of families.	Free white males under 16 years.	Free white females, including heads of families.	All other free persons.	Slaves.
BROOKFIELD TOWN—con.					
Reed, Jonathan	1	3	4		
Rood, Simeon	1	3	4		
Sebree, Benjamin	1	3	3		
Skiff, Saunders	1		2		
Smith, Josiah	1	3	2		
Smith, Josiah	2		2		
Smith, Venus	1	1	1		
Sticknor, Lemuel	2	1	2		
Stratton, Ebenezer	1	2	3		
Thatcher, Samuel	1		1		
Thompson, Francis	1	2	2		
Tyler, Phinehas	3	2	3		
Wakefield, Elijah	1	1	3		
Wakefield, William	3	1	1		
Waterman, John O	1	2	2		
West, Francis	1	1	2		
Wheatley, Nathaniel	4	3	4		
BROWNINGTON TOWN.					
Not inhabited.					
BRUNSWICK TOWN.					
Grapes, Phillip	1	2	3		
Hyde, David	3	1	2		
Lamkins, Joshua	2	1	3		
Merrill, John	1	3	3		
Rich, Hervey	1		4		
Smith, Gideon	1	5	2		
Smith, Jonathan	1	1	8		
Smith, Philo	1		1		
Tuttle, Reuben	1		1		
Wait, Joseph	1	1	5		
Wait, Nathaniel	1	1	3		
Wait, Robert	1		1		
BURKE TOWN.					
Not inhabited.					
CABOT TOWN.					
Batchelor, Thomas	1	1	2		
Blanchard, James	1	3	6		
Blanchard, David	1	2	6		
Carr, Joseph	1	2	4		
Chapman, Edmond	3	2	1		
Darforth, Samuel	3	2	2		
Durgin, Abraham	1	1	3		
Heath, Jonathan	1	3	3		
Hill, Isaac & Moses	2				
Hitchcock, Lyman	2	1	1		
Keezer, Reuben	1	6	2		
Liferd, Fifield	1		2		
Liferd, Thomas	3	1	4		
Marsh, Ephraim	3				
Morse, James	2	2	2		
Samburn, Simon	1	4	3		
Varnam, Benjamin	1	3	4		
Webster, Benjamin	2		2		
Webster, Nathaniel	1	2	4		
Whittier, John	2	2	1		
CALAIS TOWN.					
Haskel, Moses	1		3		
Jennings, James	3		1		
Short, Shubael	1	3	3		
Twiss, Samuel	1	1	1		
West, Francis	1	1	2		
Wheelock, Abijah	1	1	3		
Wheelock, Asa	4	3	2		
Wheelock, Peter	2	2	5		
CALDERSBURGH TOWN.					
Not inhabited.					
CANAAN TOWN.					
Bradley, David	1	1	5		
Hugh, John	2		3		
Spencer, Hubbard	1	4	2		
CHELSEA TOWN.					
Allen, Sleuman	1	1	4		
Badger, Samuel	1		1		

ORANGE COUNTY—Continued.

NAME OF HEAD OF FAMILY.	Free white males of 16 years and upward, including heads of families.	Free white males under 16 years.	Free white females, including heads of families.	All other free persons.	Slaves.
CHELSEA TOWN—con.					
Barns, Daniel	1	1	1		
Bixby, Ichabod	1	4	2		
Bond, Asa	1	3	2		
Brigham, Abraham	1	3	2		
Buckannan, Stephen	1	2	2		
Church, Asa	1	1	1		
Dinsmore, Abel	2	1	1		
Douglas, Caleb	1	2	2		
Douglas, Ivory	1	2	4		
Dunbar, Seth	2		2		
Field, Patrick	2	2	4		
Flint, Nathan	1		3		
Fox, Nehemiah	1		2		
Franklin, Ichabod	1	2	1		
Gordon, John	3	2	2		
Griswold, Jedediah	2		1		
Hatch, Michael	3	3	4		
Huntington, Samuel	2	1	3		
Huntington, Theophilus	4	1	3		
Jewit, David	1		2		
Lane, Jonathan	4		2		
Lathrop, Elisha	1		1		
Lathrop, Joshua	2	1	2		
Lathrop, Rufus	3		2		
Lincoln, Samuel	2	2	3		
Lincoln, Samuel	3	2	3		
McDowl, John	3		2		
Moore, Samuel	1	2	3		
Moore, Thomas	1	3	3		
Moore, Thomas	1		1		
Norris, Jacob	2	1	1		
Nutt, John	1	1	2		
Oak, Nathaniel	1	3	5		
Perkins, Jacob	3	1	2		
Randol, Joseph	1	3	1		
Smith, Enos	1	2	1		
Smith, William	4		3		
Spaldin, Elisha	1	1	1		
Wales, Roger	1	2	2		
Willis, John	1		1		
Willis, John	4	1	4		
Willis, Jonathan	1	2	4		
Wright, Benjamin	1	4	2		
CONCORD TOWN.					
Badcock, Stephen	1	1	2		
Ball, Joseph	2	1	1		
Hoit, Samuel	1	3	2		
Hudson, Samuel	2		2		
Hutchinson, Jonathan	3	3	3		
Knight, Joseph	1	3	2		
Lewis, Jonathan	1	1	2		
Moore, Joseph	2		2		
Scott, Andrew	2				
Streater, Benjamin	1				
Streater, Beononi	1		1		
Underwood, Amos	1		2		
CORINTH TOWN.					
Armon, John	1	1	4		
Avery, Andrew	1		3		
Ayers, Richard	2		2		
Bailey, James	3	1	2		
Balkum, Elijah	1	3	1		
Bennet, William	1	3	3		
Berrey, Simon	4	1	2		
Bixby, Ebenezer	1		1		
Bowen, Peter	4	3	3		
Brown, Benjamin	3		1		
Cluff, Zacheus	1	1	4		
Colby, Ezekiel	1	3	1		
Colby, John	2	3	3		
Cullier, Thomas	3	2	1		
Cootbath, Winthrop	2	3	2		
Cotton, William	1	5	3		
Crook, Charles	1	2	2		
Crook, Reuben	1		1		
Crook, Thomas	1	2	3		
Currier, Joseph	1	3	4		
Currier, Samuel	1	1	1		
Darbarn, Nathaniel	1	1	3		
Davis, Joshua	1	3	2		
Davis, Simeon	2		3		
Drue, Clark	1	2	3		
Drue, Daniel	1	1	5		
Drue, Jonathan	1	2	1		
Dustin, Jonathan	2		3		
Eastman, Edmond	2	5	5		
Fellows, Joseph	2		1		
Fellows, William	1	1	4		
CORINTH TOWN—con.					
Fowler, Abner	2	1	4		
French, Simon	1	4	2		
Greely, Jonathan	1	3	1		
Hadley, Jonathan	2	2	5		
Hale, Joshua	3				
Hazeltine, Samuel	2	1	5		
Heath, Abel	2		1		
Humphrey, Ebenezer	1	1	1		
Ingalls, Israel	2	1	4		
Jackman, Abel	1	1	1		
Johnson, Simeon	1	2	4		
Kent, Thomas	2		1		
Learned, Isaac	2		2		
Loverin, Simeon	1	2	4		
Lovewell, John	1	1	2		
Lovewell, Nehemiah	5		2		
Lucus, James	1	2	4		
Lunn, Noah	2	1	3		
McCurtis, Robert	3	1	6		
McFarling, Moses	2	1	2		
McKeen, David	2	5	6		
Martin, Benjamin	1	2	6		
Merrill, Elias	1				
Merrill, Peter	2	3	5		
Miller, Mathew	2	4	3		
Mills, John	1	3	8		
Moore, John	1	1	1		
Moulton, David	2	1	2		
Muzzy, Benjamin	3	1	4		
Norris, Benjamin	2	4	2		
Norris, Benjamin	1	1	2		
Norris, Moses	3		2		
Norris, Samuel	3	2	1		
Nerthing, John	1	3	7		
Orr, Robert	1	3	3		
Page, Reuben	1	3	2		
Richardson, Caleb	1	2	4		
Richardson, Samuel	1	3	3		
Ring, Elijah	3	1	5		
Robic, Edward W	1		2		
Rolin, Richard	2	2	3		
Rowe, Robert	1	3	2		
Samburn, Benjamin		1	2		
Sanborn, Moses	1		1		
Sanborn, Reuben	1	2	3		
Skinner, Benjamin	1	3	2		
Sluman, Peter	1	3	2		
Sleeper, Jacob	2	1	4		
Smith, Alexander	1	1	3		
Stevens, Daniel	1	1	3		
Swan, Joshua	1	2	4		
Swan, Joshua	1	1	1		
Taplin, Benjamin	1		2		
Taplin, Elisha	1	2	2		
Taplin, John	1	1	1		
Taplin, Johnson	2	1	2		
Taplin, Mansfield	1	2	7		
Taplin, Nathan	1		4		
Taplin, William	1	2	5		
Towl, Brackett	1	2	6		
Ward, Charles	1	3	3		
Webster, Samuel	1	1	5		
Wells, Jacob	1	2	5		
Whillier, David	1		1		
Wood, Daniel	1	2	3		
DANVILLE TOWN.					
Babbet, Uri	1	1	1		
Bailey, Richard	1	1	2		
Barns, George	2	3	3		
Barker, Zebediah	2	2	5		
Batchelor, Daniel	1	3	5		
Batchelor, Timothy	2	2	1		
Blanchard, Peter	3		4		
Blunt, Ephraim	1	4	4		
Blunt, Jeremiah	2	3	3		
Bowers, Jerathmel	1		1		
Boyes, Samuel	2		1		
Bracket, Simeon	1	1	1		
Brainard, Israel	2	3	6		
Carr, Timothy	3		4		
Chesley, Nathaniel	2	2	3		
Clark, Samuel	2	2	1		
Clemons, William	1	2	3		
Cook, Paul	1		2		
Cross, Daniel	2	2	3		
Curtiss, John	1		1		
Daniels, John	2		3		
Daniels, Samuels	1	2	2		
Daniels, Solomon	2	2	4		
Devanport, ——	1	1	1		
DANVILLE TOWN—con.					
Dean, Francis	1	4	1		
Demerit, James	1				
Dowe, Thomas	1		1		
Dowe, Thomas	3		4		
Dunbar, David	2	1	2		
Eastman, Theodore	1	1	1		
Elliot, Nathaniel	3		2		
Ely, Samuel	2		6		
Emerson, Jonathan	1		2		
Farly, Benjamin	1	1	1		
Farly, Samuel	4	2	6		
Fry, Reuben	1		1		
Fuller, Samuel	2	1	3		
Garden, Thomas	1	1	2		
Gilman, Joseph	1		1		
Gilman, Nathaniel	1		1		
Goodwin, Jacob	1	3	3		
Gourding, Joseph	2	1	2		
Hardy, Daniel	2	3	3		
Harris, Timothy	3	2	4		
Hartshorn, Aaron	1	4	4		
Haverland, Benjamin	1	3	2		
Hayward, Ephraim	2		4		
Hill, Samuel	4		2		
Hill, Thomas	1	1	1		
Hull, Joseph	1		1		
Kilsey, James	2	2	2		
Ketteridge, James	2		2		
Ketteredge, James	1		1		
Kiniston, Isaac	1				
Kiniston, David	1		1		
Leavensworth, Jesse	5	2	4		
Linsey, John	1	4	3		
Lovejoy, Jeremiah	1	2	3		
Magoon, Alexander	2		2		
Magoon, Ephraim	3	2	2		
Magoon, Joseph	1	1	4		
Meers, Oliver	2	1	1		
Merrill, Abel	2		1		
Merrill, Abner	3		3		
Morrill, Abraham	2		4		
Morrill, Isaac	1	2	5		
Morrill, Jeremiah	1	2	2		
Morrill, Joseph	1	2	4		
Morrill, Paul	3	2	4		
Morrill, Seargent	2	1	3		
Nevins, John	1	2	4		
Page, Ebenezer	2	2	5		
Page, Edward	1		2		
Pell, James	1		3		
Phillips, Nehemiah	2	1	3		
Pinkam, Samuel	1	1	5		
Pope, Eleazer	2	3	3		
Pope, Joseph	1	1	2		
Preston, Benjamin	1	1	3		
Rendols, Israel	1	5	3		
Rendols, Israel	1		1		
Rogers, Joseph	1	3	4		
Runnells, Enoch	1	2	2		
Russell, Jethro	2	1	1		
Sawyer, Ebenezer	1	2	3		
Shoot, John	3	2	2		
Sias, Charles	3	3	3		
Sias, Solomon	1		2		
Stevens, Joshua	1	1	1		
Stevens, Samuel	3		1		
Sweat, Luke	2		8		
Trussell, Jacob	2	5	4		
Webster, Moses	2	1	3		
Wheeler, Daniel	1	3	4		
Wells, Paul	1	4	4		
West, Noah	1	1	2		
Whittier, Abner	1	2	3		
Whittier, David	2	2	5		
Whittier, Joseph	1		1		
Whittier, Seargents	1	4	7		
Youngman, Peter	1		1		
DEWEY'S GORE.					
Hunt, Joshua	1	6	3		
Leavenworth, Jesse	1		1		
Norris, Benjamin	1	1	1		
Norris, David	2	5	3		
Page, Peter	1	1	2		
Peasly, Jedediah	1	3	4		
Woodward, Nathaniel	5	2	4		
FAIRLEY TOWN.					
Ames, David	2	1	2		
Ames, Thaddeus	1	2	2		

ORANGE COUNTY—Continued.

NAME OF HEAD OF FAMILY.	Free white males of 16 years and upward, including heads of families.	Free white males under 16 years.	Free white females, including heads of families.	All other free persons.	Slaves.
FAIRLEY TOWN—con.					
Annis, Jesse	3	2	5		
Avery, Nathan	1	3	3		
Baldwin, Ebenezer	2	3	3		
Barron, Moses	1	1	4		
Bassett, Elnathan	2	5	5		
Basset, Oliver	1		1		
Batchelor, James	1	1	2		
Batchelor, John	1		2		
Bliss, Samuel	2		2		
Bliss, Samuel	2		1		
Blood, Elijah	2		6		
Cady, Barnabas	2		1		
Capin, Ebenezer	1	2	1		
Carpenter, Ephraim	1		3		
Carpenter, Rufus	1		1		
Chapin, Ithamar	2	2	1		
Child, Cephas	1		4		
Child, Phinehas	1		3		
Churchill, Francis	2	3	1		
Coburn, Lemuel	1	1	1		
Coburn, Samuel	1	1	1		
Cotton, George	1		4		
Cotton, John	1	1	3		
Cotton, John	2		1		
Cook, Ebenezer	2	3	3		
Curtis, Hiram	1	1	1		
Dickinson, Elijah	1	1	2		
Dickeson, Reuben	2		2		
Dickeson, Reuben	1	3	2		
Dodge, Samuel	1	2	1		
Dogget, Joseph	1		2		
Follet, Benjaman	2		3		
Freeman, Daniel	3	1	2		
Houghton, Samuel	1	1	3		
House, Francis	2	4	4		
Ives, John	1	1	3		
Jaquis, John	3	2	3		
Lamb, Asa	1	1	3		
Marston, John	1	2	3		
Marston, Peter	3	2	4		
Marston, William	1	1	5		
May, Asa	1				
May, Stephen	1	3	2		
May, Thomas	2	1	3		
Moor, John	1	2	1		
Morey, Israel	11	2	4		
Morey, Israel	1	1	2		
Morey, Solomon	1	4	3		
Morse, Amos	1		1		
Morse, Calvin	1	3	3		
Niles, Nathaniel	6	1	4		
Niles, Sands	1	3	3		
Omsbeck, Ichabod	3		3		
Omsbeck, Joseph	2	2	3		
Pierce, James	2	3	4		
Pierce, Oliver	2	2	3		
Putnam, John	1	1	4		
Richardson, James	1	2	2		
Robinson, Samuel	3		2		
Ralph, Ephraim	1	5	2		
Russ, Jonathan	2	1	2		
Sessions, David	1		3		
Simons, John	1	4	2		
Smith, Samuel	1	3	3		
Southward, Asa	1	3	2		
Southward, Lemuel	1	3	2		
Southward, Ralph	2		1		
Stratton, Benjamin	2		6		
Swift, Joshua	1	3	7		
Trusdal, Thomas	1	1	1		
Walker, Eliakim	1	2	4		
West, Jonathan	1	3	6		
Wiggins, Joshua	3	3	2		
Wiggins, William	1	1	2		
Woodworth, Amasa	3	1	2		
Wild, Elisha	1	1	2	1	
Wild, Randol	1		4		
Wright, Thomas	1	3	1		
FERDINAND TOWN.					
Not inhabited.					
GLOVER TOWN.					
Not inhabited.					
GRANBY TOWN.					
Not inhabited.					
GREENSBOROUGH TOWN.					
Davison, Paul	1		1		
Shepard, Aron	2	3	1		

NAME OF HEAD OF FAMILY.	Free white males of 16 years and upward, including heads of families.	Free white males under 16 years.	Free white females, including heads of families.	All other free persons.	Slaves.
GREENSBOROUGH TOWN—continued.					
Shepard, Ashbel	3	1	1		
Shepard, Horace	1		3		
Stanly, Timothy	2				
GROTON TOWN.					
Abbot, James	2	3	1		
Bailey, Israel	1		3		
Darling, John	4	2	5		
Hermon, Aaron	2	1			
James, Jonathan	1	1	4		
Morse, Edmond	2	1	2		
Townshend, Timothy	1		2		
Darling, Robert	2	1	4		
GUILDHALL TOWN.					
Benjamin, John	1	1	1		
Burnes, Edmond	1	1	2		
Cheney, Benjamin	1	2	2		
Cook, Benjamin	4	1	3		
Crafford, Eleazer	2	2	1		
Crafford, John	1		1		
Cram, Jonathan	4	2	2		
Curtiss, Abner	2		2		
Curtiss, Clark	1	1	2		
Cutler, Benoni	4	3	4		
Cutler, Charles	1		2		
Farnham, Nathaniel	1	3	3		
Hartshorn, Ebenezer	1	3	6		
Hopkinson, David	2	5	2		
How, Samuel	2		1		
How, Simon	2				
Ives, Joel	1				
Judd, Eben W	5		1		
Linsy, John	3	1	2		
Nash, Samuel	1	1	6		
Roberts, Joseph	2	1	1		
Rosbrooks, Eleazer	3	5	4		
Rosbrooks, James	1	1	1		
Rosbrooks, John	4	1	3		
Rosbrooks, William	1	2	4		
St. John, James	1	2	2		
Wheeler, George	3	3	4		
HARDWICK TOWN.					
Norris & Sabins	2				
Norris, Mark	1				
HARRIS GORE.					
Not inhabited.					
HOPKINS GRANT.					
Not inhabited.					
LEMINGTON TOWN.					
Bailey, Orsamus	1	1	3		
Baley, Ward	4	4	4		
Cook, Jared	2				
D'Forest, Mills	3	2	1		
Luther, James	2		4		
LEWIS TOWN.					
Not inhabited.					
LITTLETON TOWN.					
Adams, James	2		1		
Brown, James	1		2		
Felton, Joseph	1	2	2		
Hamlet, William	1	1	6		
Knoulton, Thomas	1	2	1		
Morgan, Cornelius	2	2	4		
Pike, Nathan	3		3		
Potter, Barnabas	2	2	3		
Sylvester, Peter	1	1	2		
Wood, John	1	4	3		
Wood, Joseph	1		6		
LUNENBURGH TOWN.					
Buckman, Abner	1		2		
Buckman, Joseph	2		4		
Bruce, Ezekiel	1		3		
Cross, Uriah	1	4	4		
Currier, Joseph	1		4		
Dodge, Phinehas	1		3		

NAME OF HEAD OF FAMILY.	Free white males of 16 years and upward, including heads of families.	Free white males under 16 years.	Free white females, including heads of families.	All other free persons.	Slaves.
LUNENBURGH TOWN—continued.					
Eames, Aaron	1		1		
Emerson, Jacob	1				
Everitt, Penuel	1	1	4		
Gates, Samuel	3	2	2		
Grout, Amaza	3	2	1		
Gustin, Elisha	1	4	4		
Hope, Joseph	2		1		
Lamson, Reuben	1	3	2		
Parker, Josiah	1	3	3		
Phelps, Samuel	1	3	1		
Quimby, Moses	1	2	5		
Saunders, Jonathan	2	1	2		
Smith, Christopher	1	1	3		
Spafford, Elijah	1	1	2		
Watson, Alexander	1	1	4		
Williams, Abraham	1	1	2		
Wheeler, Jason	1		3		
LYNDON TOWN.					
Cahoon, Daniel	5		2		
Davis, Jonathan	1		1		
Hacket, Stilson	1	2	2		
Hall, Daniel	2	2	4		
Hervey, Daniel	2				
Hines, Nathan	4	1	1		
McGaffy, Andrew	4	1	3		
Reneff, Daniel	1	1	2		
Robert, Charles	2				
Spooner, James	3	2	3		
Sprague, Jonah	2	1	2		
Thurston, Thomas	2				
MAIDSTONE TOWN.					
Amy, John	1	1	1		
Amy, Michal	3	1	2		
Amy, William	1		4		
Byram, Benjamin	2	2	3		
French, Hains	1	2	2		
Gaskill, David	2	4	3		
Gibb, John Taylor	1	3	5		
Gilds, Abraham	1	2	6		
Hawkens, Reuben	2		3		
Hugh, John	3	1	4		
Lounsbury, Jarus	2	2	3		
Lucas, James	3	3	2		
Rich, John	4	3	3		
Sampson, Aaron	1	2	1		
Schoff, Daniel	2	1	2		
Schoff, Isaac	1	1	1		
Schoff, Jacob	1	1	1		
Stevens, Isaac	1	5	3		
Williams, Willian	2	2	6		
MARSHFIELD TOWN.					
Not inhabited.					
MINEHEAD TOWN.					
Not inhabited.					
MONTPELIER TOWN.					
Brooks, Theophilus	3	1	3		
Carpenter, Allen	1	2	4		
Cutler, Jonathan	5	3	2		
Davis Jacob	12		5		
Davis, Perley	2				
Dodge, Solomon	3	2	2		
Frizzle, Joel	1		1		
Hawkins, James	2	3	3		
Hurlbutt, Josiah	2	2	3		
Morey, James	1		5		
Peck, Nathaniel	2				
Putnam, Ebenezer	1	2	4		
Snow, Jonathan	3		1		
Stevens, Prince	8	1	4		
Templeton, John	3	2	3		
Wheeler, Jerathmel	4	1	4		
Woodworth, Ziba	2				
NAVY TOWN.					
Not inhabited.					
NEWARK TOWN.					
Not inhabited.					
NEWBURY TOWN.					
Abbot, Bencroft	1	2	1		
Abbot, Ezra	1	1	2		

ORANGE COUNTY—Continued.

NAME OF HEAD OF FAMILY.	Free white males of 16 years and upward, including heads of families.	Free white males under 16 years.	Free white females, including heads of families.	All other free persons.	Slaves.
NEWBURY TOWN—con.					
Abbot, James	1		1		
Aikens, Benjamin	1	3	2		
Aikens, James	1	2	4		
Bailey, Charles	2	2	3		
Bailey, Charles	2		1		
Bailey, Fry	2	3	5		
Bailey, Isaac	2		5		
Bailey, Jacob	2	4	3		
Bailey, Jacob	2	1	3		
Bailey, John G	4	5	6	1	
Bailey, John	4		4		
Bailey, Joshua	1	5	4		
Bailey, Webster	1	2	6		
Barnard, Job	1	1	2		
Barnet, Samuel	3		2		
Bigelow, Jabez	1	1	2		
Bliss, Peletiah	1	3	5		
Boyes, William	4	2	4		
Bricket, Abraham	1	1	1		
Brock, Robert	1	1	1		
Brown, John	1	3	3		
Brock, Thomas	1	7	6		
Burroughs, Thomas	1	1	1		
Butterfield, Jonathan	3		2		
Carlton, Dudley	2	2	6	1	
Carter, Andrew	1	1	2		
Carter, Andrew	1		1		
Carter, William	1	1	2		
Cawley, Timothy	1		2		
Chamberlin, Abigail	1		3		
Chamberlin, Blanchard	1		2		
Chamberlin, Elanah	2	2	4		
Chamberlin, Err	2	3	5		
Chamberlin, Joseph	1	4	5		
Chamberlin, Moses	1	3	4		
Chamberlin, Nathaniel	3	4	5		
Chamberlin, Remembrance	3	4	5		
Chamberlin, Silas	1	5	3		
Chamberlin, Thomas	1	1	3		
Chamberlin, Uriah	1	2	4		
Chapman, Jonah	1	2	6		
Chase, Stephen	1	2	3		
Clark, Timothy	1	1	2		
Clark, John	2	2	3		
Colby, Joseph	1	2	3		
Colby, Nicholas	1	3	7		
Crown, John	3	5	3		
Dodge, James	1	1	1		
Doe, Reuben	1	1	1		
Doe, William	2	2	2		
Dorrah, Arthur	1	5	3		
Downer, Andrew	3	1	5		
Downer, Moses W	1	2	4		
Emery, John	1	1	1		
Fellows, Samuel	1	1	3		
Ford, Paul	1	1	2		
Forster, John	1	1	3		
Fowler, Jacob	1	2	4		
Gale, Samuel	1	1	2		
Gale, Thaddeus	1	1	2		
Gates, Ezra	1		5		
Gates, Jonathan	1		1		
Goodwin, Jonathan	4	1	3		
Goodwin, Nathaniel	1	1	2		
Hadley, Samuel	1	4	2		
Hale, Joshua	5	1	3		
Hazeltine, David	2	2	1		
Hazeltine, John	2	1	4		
Heath, Azuba	1	4	6		
Heath, James	1		1		
Herriman, Joseph	1	2	2		
Hibbard, Jacob	2	2	3		
Hibbard, Thomas	1	2	3		
Hill, Samuel	1	1			
Hovey, Simeon	1	2	3		
Johston, James	1	1	1		
Johnson, John	1		1		
Johnson, John	2	2	2		
Johnson, Moses	2		1		
Johnson, Robert	2	3	9		
Johnson, Thomas	4	4	5		
Johnson, William	1		2		
Jones, Samuel	1	1	1		
Kenedy, William	1				
Kenedy, Patrick	1	3	1		
Kent, Jacob	5		3		
Kent, Joseph	1		3		
Kimball, Asa	2				
Kunningham, David	1	1	2		
Kunningham, James	1	1	2		
Lee, Samuel	1		2		

NAME OF HEAD OF FAMILY.	Free white males of 16 years and upward, including heads of families.	Free white males under 16 years.	Free white females, including heads of families.	All other free persons.	Slaves.
NEWBURY TOWN—con.					
Linsey, Benjamin	1	4	1		
Linsey, Samuel	1	1	3		
Lovewell, Nehemiah	1	1	2		
Lovewell, Robert	1	1	3		
Mann, Solomon	2		1		
McCutchin, Hugh	1	1	6		
McDuffee, Worcester				3	
McKetch, Thomas	1	1	6		
Mellon, Thomas	1	3	3		
Mills, John	3	3	3		
Mills, Nathaniel	1	2	2		
Moor, George	1	2	5		
Munroe, Samuel	1	2	3		
Page, Jacob	2	2	7		
Peach, William	1	4	4		
Powers, Stephen	1	1	2		
Pratt, Josiah	1	2	2		
Putnam, Asa	1				
Putnam, Israel	1		4		
Putnam, Torrent	1	2	3		
Randols, Samuel	4	1	4		
Ricker, Benjamin	2		2		
Ricker, Joshua	1	2	3		
Rogers, Daniel	1		3		
Saunders, John	2	1	4		
Sawyer, John	2		2		
Scagel, Jacob	2		1		
Scott, John	2	3	3		
Sleeper, Joseph	1	1	3		
Smith, Gideon	2	1	2		
Smith, James	1	1	3		
Spear, James	2	2	3		
Stevens, Levi	1		2		
Stevens, Simon	1	2	2		
Stevens, Otho	1	1	4		
Stevens, Samuel	1	1	3		
Straw, Moses	1	1	3		
Sylvester, Levi	3		2		
Sylvester, Levi	1		2		
Tenney, Asa	3		1		
Thompson, Samuel	1	1	2		
Teuxbury, Phillip	1		1		
Tucker, Samuel	3	2	4		
Vance, James	1	1	2		
Vance, John	1	1	4		
Vance, John	1	3	6		
Virginia, Jeremiah				7	
Wallace, William	7	3	5		
White, Ebenezer	3	3	3		
White, Samuel	2	1	3		
White, Timothy	2		2		
NORTHFIELD TOWN.					
Ashcraft, William	2	3	4		
Jones, Aquila	1	2	4		
Nicholas, Nathaniel	1				
Richardson, Stanton	2	3	1		
Robinson, Amos	2	1	4		
Robinson, Nathaniel	1		4		
Shipman, Eliphas	1	1	3		
ORANGE TOWN.					
Not inhabited.					
PEACHUM TOWN.					
Abbot, Jeremiah	1	2	2		
Ambrose, Benjamin	2		2		
Bailey, Abijah	1	4	4		
Bailey, Benjamin	1	1	4		
Bailey, Cyrus	1	1	1		
Bailey, James	2	3	3		
Bailey, James	3		3		
Bailey, Luther	2	2	4		
Bailey, Moses	2		1		
Bailey, Moses	2		4		
Baker, Samuel	1	1	2		
Blanchard, Abel	2	3	3		
Blanchard, Abel	2	2	2		
Blanchard, Joel	2	3	3		
Blanchard, Reuben	1		2		
Brown, Joseph	2	4	5		
Buel, Abraham	2		2		
Carr, Robert	1	1			
Carter, Levi	1	2	8		
Chamberlin, William	2	1	5		
Currier, David	6		5		
Drue, Enoch	1	2	1		
Eaton, Solomon	1	1	1		
Elkins, Jonathan	5	1	2		

NAME OF HEAD OF FAMILY.	Free white males of 16 years and upward, including heads of families.	Free white males under 16 years.	Free white females, including heads of families.	All other free persons.	Slaves.
PEACHUM TOWN—con.					
Elkins, Jonathan	1	1	2		
Elkins, Moses	1	2	2		
Foster, Ephraim	4	1	3		
Gibson, William	1	2	3		
Gilman, Ezekel	1	3	1		
Guy, Jacob	1	2	6		
Guy, James	3	3	5		
Hall, Timothy	2	1	4		
Hinman, Seth	1	1	5		
Johnson, Dole	1	4	4		
Kelley, William	1	1	2		
Knox, William	1	2	4		
Linsey, James	2		1		
Martin, Andrew	1	2	5		
Ashbel, Martin	2		1		
Martin, Samuel	1				
Massey, John	1	1	2		
Mathews, Hugh	2		4		
McLaughlin, Archibald	3	3	4		
Merril, Jesse	1	2	1		
Miner, Abner	1		2		
Miner, James	1	2	3		
Miner, Reuben	2	2	4		
Miner, Samuel	1		1		
Morse, Moody	2	1	5		
Perry & Bevins	2				
Pettingal, Jonathan	1		1		
Redington, Isaac	5		2		
Scott, William	1		1		
Skeels, John	1	3	4		
Sumner, C. Edward	1	1	2		
Thayer, Benoni	1	3	3		
Varnham, Abraham	1		1		
Vernam, William	1	2	5		
Walker, Joseph	1	2	1		
Walker, Simeon	1	3	3		
Welch, Benjamin	1	3	5		
Wesson, John	1	3	2		
RANDOLPH TOWN.					
Adams, Robert	1	4	2		
Adams, Silas	1		1		
Allyn, Wolcott	1	1	3		
Amesdown, Jonathan	1	2	2		
Anesworth, Amasiah	1		1		
Anesworth, Lemuel	1		1		
Bacon, John	1	2	6		
Bales, David	1	1	3		
Bates, Edward	1	1	7		
Bates, Eliphalet	1		1		
Bates, Jonathan	2	3	4		
Bates, Moses	1	1	2		
Bates, Oliver	1	2	2		
Bates, Samuel	2		3		
Bates, Solomon	1	1			
Belknap, David	1		1		
Belknap, Moses	1	1	7		
Belknap, Simeon	1	3	2		
Bissel, Daniel	3		2		
Bissel, Daniel	2		1		
Bissel, Elias	2	1	3		
Bloget, Benjamin	1	6	1		
Bloget, Caleb	2	3	4		
Bloget, James	2		3		
Bloget, James	1	2	3		
Bloget, John	1	1	2		
Bloget, Joshua	2	3	2		
Bloget, Henry	1	1	2		
Blodget, Salmon	1	2	1		
Blodget, Sylvanus	1	1	2		
Bond, Stephen	1	3	4		
Boylus, Timothy	1		3		
Brainard, Ely	1		3		
Call, Joseph	1	2	3		
Carpenter, David	1	2	3		
Carpenter, Jacob	1		3		
Carpenter, John	3	4	4		
Carpenter, Jonathan	1	1	3		
Carpenter, Joseph	2		2		
Carpenter, Nathan	1	2	1		
Chase, Seth	3	4	3		
Cobb, Jacob	1	1	6		
Coggsdill, Jesse	1	1	1		
Convass, Israel	4	3	7		
Darby, John	1	2	5		
Davis, Experience	2	1	2		
Davis, Nathan	1	3	2		
Eddy, James	1		3		
Edgerton, Asa	2	4	2		
Edgerton, Ezra	3		1		
Edgerton, Oliver	1	1	1		

ORANGE COUNTY—Continued.

NAME OF HEAD OF FAMILY.	Free white males of 16 years and upward, including heads of families.	Free white males under 16 years.	Free white females, including heads of families.	All other free persons.	Slaves.
RANDOLPH TOWN—con.					
Edgerton, William	1	1	2		
Edson, Josiah	3	3	3		
Edson, Samuel	1		2		
Edson, Timothy	2	4	2		
Ellis, Elijah	1	1	3		
English, John	1	2	1		
Evins, Edward	2	3	5		
Evins, John	2	5	2		
Evins, William	2	2	4		
Farnham, John	1	2	3		
Fisk, Stephen	1		2		
Flint, Samuel	2	2	6		
Gillet, Abner	1	1	3		
Goodale, Elisha	1		2		
Green, David	1	2	4		
Griswold, Joseph	4		3		
Handy, Joshua	2	3	6		
Hedges, David	4	4	5		
Hibbard, Zebulon	3	3	2		
Hide, Azariah	2		1		
Huntington, Christopher	3	1	3		
Huntington, James	2		1		
Joiner, William	1	3	3		
Kibbee, Israel	1	1	2		
Kibbee, Josiah	2		1		
Kibbee, Reuben	1		1		
Lamb, Joseph	1		4		
Lamb, Nathan	1	2	1		
Lamson, Amos	2		2		
Lamson, Jonathan	1	2	4		
Lamson, Samuel	1	1	1		
Lamson, Thomas	1	1	4		
Lard, John	1	1	5		
Lee, Asa	1		3		
Lilley, Elisha	2	1	2		
Martin, Gideon	2	3	2		
Maxwell, John	1	2	2		
Miles, Hannah	2	2	2		
Miles, Timothy	2	3	5		
Molton, Phinehas	3	4	3		
Morgin, Justin	2	1	4		
Morris, James	1	2	3		
Neff, Thomas	1	2	5		
Newton, Isaac	2	3	1		
Nye, Nathan	1		2		
Oalds, John	1	3	2		
Orcutt, Jacob	1	1	1		
Orcutt, Lemuel	1	1	3		
Paine, Lemuel	1	2	3		
Palmer, Isaac	1	2	3		
Parker, Daniel	1	1	5		
Parrish, Jacob	2		4		
Parsons, Moses	1	2	2		
Peckham, Jonathan	2	1	3		
Peckham, Nye	1		1		
Peckham, Pardon	1	1	3		
Peckham, Philip	1		1		
Pember, Samuel	1		5		
Pember, Stephen	2	1	3		
Perry, Asahel	1	2	2		
Pinnee, Oliver	1	3	3		
Richardson, Sam[n]	2	1	7		
Riddle, John	1	1	3		
Rood, Moses	1	4	3		
Smalley, Daniel	1	3	2		
Smalley, Jonathan	1	3	3		
Smith, Aaron	2	2	3		
Smith, Parker	1	3	3		
Smith, William	1		3		
Sprague, Jonath[n]	2	2	5		
Sprague, William	1	2	2		
Sprought, Michel	1	4	3		
Steel, Andrew	1	2	2		
Steel, James	2	3	3		
Steel, Samuel	1	1	2		
Steel, Zadock	1	2	3		
Story, Asa	1	4	5		
Stoors, Hurdins	1	1	4		
Townshend, John	3		3		
Tucker, Ashbel	1	4	5		
Tucker, Benjamin	5		2		
Tucker, Woodword	2	1	2		
Turner, David	3	3	4		
Vaughn, Jabez	1		4		
Walbridge, Eleazer	2	4	6		
Walbridge, Oliver	1		3		
Walbridge, Henry	2	2	3		
Washburn, Abner	1	2	3		
Washburn, Jonah	2	2	3		
Washburn, Jonah	2		2		
Washburn, Josiah	2	3	3		
RANDOLPH TOWN—con.					
Weston, Abner	2	1	2		
Wilcox, Elisha	1	2	3		
Woodward, Asahel	2		4		
Woodward, David	1		1		
Woodward, Eleazer	1	2	4		
Woodward, Jehiel	2	1	4		
York, Joseph	2	3	2		
York, Garshom	2		3		
RANDOM TOWN.					
Not inhabited.					
ROXBURY TOWN.					
Dudley, Ezra	1	1	1		
Huntington, Christopher	4	1	4		
Lewis, Isaac	1		1		
RYEGATE TOWN.					
Brock, Andrew	4	1	4		
Chamberlin, Nicholas	1		3		
Crague, William	2	2	5		
Gardner, Hugh	1		1		
Goodwin, Wiloby	1	4	1		
Gray, John	1	5	3		
Heath, Ebenezer	1	1	2		
Heath, Jesse	1	4	2		
Heath, Simon	1	3	1		
Hervey, William	1				
Hunderson, James	1	4	3		
Hunt, Joshua	1		1		
Hunt, Joshua	1		3		
Johnson, Elihu	2	1	1		
Johnson, William	1	4	6		
Miller, Alexander	1	2	4		
Nelson, James	1	2	3		
Nelson, William	3	3	3		
Oar, John	1	1	1		
Page, Barker	1	1	2		
Page, Jonathan	1		3		
Page, Josiah	2	3	4		
Pattee, John	1	2	7		
Reed, David	1		1		
Remach, John	1		1		
Ritchie, John	1		1		
Johnson, Samuel	1	3	1		
Runnels, George	1		2		
Russell, John	1		1		
Simm, Camel	1	1	3		
Steward, Allen	1	2	3		
Swithier, Joseph	1		2		
Taylor, John	1	2	2		
Wallis, John	2	1	2		
Whitlaw, James	2	2	3		
Wright, Benjamin	1		2		
ST. ANDREWS TOWN.					
Not inhabited.					
ST. JOHNSBURY TOWN.					
Adams, Jonathan	4	2	2		
Adams, Martin	1	2	3		
Arnold, Jonathan	7		5		
Ayer, John	1	1	2		
Ayer, Samuel	1				
Barnabas, Barker	1		1		
Barker, John	1		1		
Barker, John	2		1		
Clifford, Jonathan	1				
Colby, Ezekel	1		2		
Cole, Simeon	3	4	2		
Doolittle, David	1		2		
Edson, Nathaniel	1	1	2		
Hall, Moses	1	4	3		
Hervey, Ira	1				
Ladd, John	2	2	3		
Lord, Joseph	3	2	1		
McGaffy, John	1	1	1		
Noyes, Moses	1	1	1		
Parkard, Daniel	1				
Parkard, Richard	1	1	2		
Richards, Bradley	2	3	4		
Richards, Jonathan	1		1		
Ripley, William	1				
Roberts, Joel	1	2	1		
Robinson, Jonathan	1	1	3		
Sawyer, Eleazer	2	1	2		
ST. JOHNSBURY TOWN—continued.					
Stiles, George	1		2		
Stiles, Samuel	1	1	1		
Thrubur, James	1				
Todd, Thomas	3	3	2		
Trescott, Jon[a]	1	1	2		
Trescott, William	1	1	2		
Wheeler, Gardiner	2		1		
SHEFFIELD TOWN.					
Not inhabited.					
STRAFFORD TOWN.					
Alger, Jared	1	2	2		
Alger, John	1	1	4		
Alger, Silas	4	2	7		
Badcock, Jesse	1		4		
Badcock, Richard	1		1		
Baker, Benjamin	1		1		
Baldwis, Isaac	1		1		
Barrows, David	1	4	3		
Bartlett, Moses	1		2		
Batchelor, Jethro	1	1	5		
Beeman, Elijah	2	2	4		
Blake, Elijah	1	1	2		
Blake, Sanburn	1	2	1		
Blake, Timothy	3	2	6		
Bliss, John	1		1		
Brisco, William	1		1		
Brown, Heman	3	1	5		
Brown, Absolom	2	1	6		
Brown, Josiah	1	4	5		
Brown, Moses	2	6	1		
Brown, Nathaniel	2	1	2		
Brown, William	1		2		
Bullock, John	1	2	4		
Buffum, Stephen	1	2	2		
Cambo, John H	1		4		
Carpenter, Elias	2		1		
Carrier, Isaac	1	3	3		
Chamberlin, Amasa	1	4	4		
Chamberlin, Asahel	3	1	3		
Chamberlin, Elias	1	3	3		
Chamberlin, Isaac	2	1	2		
Chandler, Andrew	1	2	2		
Comstock, John	1		2		
Corey, Phillip	1		1		
Deming, Ebenezer	1				
Denison, William	2	3	6		
Dillingham, Thomas	2	2	3		
Everist, Israel	1		5		
Flanders, Zebulon	1	1	2		
Foster, Thomas	2	3	3		
Fray, John	1	1	1		
Frary, Jonathan	1	1	1		
George, Benjamin	2	2	4		
George, Isaac	1	2	3		
Gilbert, Ezra	1	1	3		
Gilbert, Heber	1	3	1		
Gile, John	1	1	1		
Gilman, Daniel	2	1	3		
Green, Elijah	2	2	2		
Greer, James	1	1	2		
Griffin, David	2				
Hacket, Moses	1	4	4		
Hall, Elihu	1	3	4		
Hall, William	1	2	1		
Hardy, Bela	1	2	4		
Harris, John	3		2		
Harris, John, Jun[r]	1	1	1		
Harskel, Zurel	1	1	4		
Haze, Eleazer	1		2		
Haze, Robert	1	1	2		
Hide, Asa	2	4	4		
Hide, James	1	1	1		
Homes, Chandler	2		3		
Hopkins, Asa	1	2	1		
Hopkins, John	2		2		
Hunt, Solomon	1	3	5		
Hurlburt, Elijah	2	2	1		
Johnson, Willis	1	3	4		
Judd, Phillip	1	2	3		
Judd, William	2		2		
Kimball, Caleb	1	2	4		
Ladd, Ashbel	1	2	4		
Ladd, Oliver	1	1	2		
Leny, John	2		2		
Lilly, Benjamin	2	1	1		
Lucus, Thomas	1		3		
Man, Zadock	1	3	3		
Marvin, Jonathan	1		2		

ORANGE COUNTY—Continued.

NAME OF HEAD OF FAMILY.	Free white males of 16 years and upward, including heads of families.	Free white males under 16 years.	Free white females, including heads of families.	All other free persons.	Slaves.
STRAFFORD TOWN—con.					
May, Hezekiah	2		3		
Merriman, Joseph	1		2		
Miller, James	1	2	5		
Miller, William	1	5	2		
Moody, Clement	1	3	4		
Moody, Elisha	2	2	6		
Morey, Moses	2	3	5		
Morey, Zenos	3	1	3		
Morey, Zenos	1	2	3		
Muncil, Benjamin	1	1	2		
Newell, Asa	1	2	1		
Newman, Ebenezer	1	1	2		
Newman, William	3	3	5		
Norton, Elihu	1	2	1		
Norton, Elihu	1	1	2		
Norton, Elisha	1		4		
Norton, Joseph	1	2	4		
Norton, Nathan	1	2	2		
Norton, Zerah	1	2	1		
Osmore, Eleazer	1	4	2		
Packard, Zachariah	1	1	2		
Paine, Jesse	1	2	2		
Palmer, Amos	1	2	5		
Parish, Mary		2	1		
Parseval, Asahel	1		2		
Pinnock, Aaron	1		5		
Pinnock, Alexander	1	3	3		
Pinnock, Ira	1	2	1		
Pinnock, Isaac	1		2		
Pinnock, James	1		1		
Pinnock, Joseph	1	2	1		
Pinnock, Haman	2	1	3		
Pinnock, Oliver	1	1	4		
Pinnock, Peter	2	3	2		
Post, Daniel	1		2		
Powell, Calvin	1	1	1		
Powell, Elisha	1	1	5		
Powell, Daniel	2	2	4		
Preston, Alexander	1		2		
Preston, Benjamin	1	1	4		
Preston, Robert	2	2	1		
Preston, William	3		1		
Rich, David	1	4	1		
Rich, Jonathan	4	1	3		
Rich, Solomon	2	1	3		
Robinson, Abraham	1	1	4		
Robinson, Daniel	4	2	5		
Roberts, Eliphalet	3	2	1		
Root, Daniel	1	1	1		
Root, Levi	3	3	2		
Root, Oliver	2	1	1		
Root, Solomon	1		3		
Root, William	1	1	5		
Rowel, Jonathan	1	1	4		
Samburn, Moses	1	3	3		
Seekins, Aaron	3	4	1		
Shepard, Elisha	1	2	2		
Shepard, Thomas	1	1	4		
Smith, Frederick	2	3	5		
Stevenson, James	1	1	4		
Trusdall, Aaron	1	1	4		
Tucker, Benjamin	1		1		
Vaughn, William	2		2		
Wedge, John	2	2	5		
Wells, David	1	3	4		
West, Daniel	3	4	3		
West, Gilman	2	4	4		
White, Ebenezer	1		1		
White, Joel	1	2	4		
Williams, Asa	3	4	2		
THETFORD TOWN.					
Abbot, Walter	1	5	4		
Annes, Ezra	1		1		
Annis, Jacob	1	2	1		
Annis, Jacob	2		1		
Annis, John	1	2	4		
Baker, John	1	3	4		
Bartlett, Samuel	1	1	2		
Bartholomew, Timothy	1	2	5		
Baxter, Nichard	2	1	4		
Bennet, James	1	2	1		
Blanchard, Daniel	1	1	5		
Bliss, James	1		2		
Bliss, John	1	2	2		
Bliss, John	1		2		
Brown, John	1	4	6		
Buckingham, Jedediah P	2	1	2		
Burges, Benjamin	1	4	5		
Burgoine, Augustus H.	1	1	5		
THETFORD TOWN—con.					
Burnham, William	3	4	6		
Burnham, Thomas	1	2	1		
Burroughs, John	1	1	3		
Burton, Asa	2		3		
Bush, Eleazer	1	1	1		
Cadwell, Aaron	1	1	1		
Cadwell, Moses	1		2		
Cadwell, Moses	1	1	2		
Chamberlin, Abner	1	1	2		
Chamberlin, Amos	2	4	5		
Chamberlin, Benjam^{n}	5	3	2		
Chamberlin, Charles	2	1	7		
Chamberlin, Joel	1	2	3		
Chamberlin, John	1		1		
Chamberlin, John	1	2	1		
Chamberlln, Joseph	1	1	4		
Chappel, Joseph	1		1		
Clark, David	1		2		
Clark, Elijah	2	1	4		
Clark, Joseph	1	1	2		
Childs, Jonathan	1		3		
Childs, William	1	3	4		
Crandall, Richman	1		2		
Cross, Nero				5	
Cushman, Eleazer	1	3	4		
Cushman, William	2		2		
Davis, Isaac	2	3	2		
Divine, Thomas	1	2	2		
Downer, Cushman	1	1	2		
Downer, James	1	1	1		
Downer, Joseph	1	1	5		
Doyne, Francis	1	1	1		
Earnest, Frederick	1	1	2		
Eaton, Orange	1	1	1		
Eaton, William	3	1	4		
Faunce, Joseph	1	2	2		
Fellows, Adolphus	1		2		
Fellows, Gustavus	1	2	1		
Fisk, William	1	2	6		
Fisk, Isaac	1		1		
Fletcher, Leonard	1		3		
Fowler, Phillip	1	1	1		
Francis, Jacob	1	2	2		
Freeman, William	1	1	5		
Frizzel, John	2		2		
Gahisha, Samuel	1	2	2		
Gillet, Adonijah	1	1	2		
Gillet, Simon	1	2	3		
Green, Joseph	2	2	3		
Hammon, Elijah	1		2		
Hanks, Asa	2	3	3		
Hardy, Daniel	1	2	2		
Hinkley, Orimel	2		3	1	
Hinkley, Garshom	1	1	3		
Hogins, Daniel	1	3	2		
Horsford, Aaron	3	1	3		
Horsford, Elihu	1	2	4		
Horsford, Joseph	2	2	5		
Horsford, Obediah	1	2	2		
Howard, Abijah	1	2	5		
Howard, Abner	1	1	3		
Howard, Elijah	1		1		
Howard, Elijah	1	2	1		
Howard, Jonathan	1	2	3		
Howard, Zebedee	1		2		
Hubbard, Josiah	2	2	2		
Hunt, Samuel	1		1		
Inglish, David	3	2	3		
Keyes, Joseph	1		1		
Kinney, David	1	1	2		
Knox, George				4	
Lawrence, Levi	2	3	2		
Lock, James	7	1	5		
Loomis, Beriah	1	5	6		
Lord, Joseph	1		4		
Mann, Frederick	1	1	2		
Mann, Nathan	2	2	3		
Merrill, Isaac	1		3		
Moors, James	1	2	1		
Moors, Thomas	1		2		
Moors, William	2	1	5		
Nelson, Charles	1		2		
Newcomb, Justus	1		1		
Newcomb, Simon	2	1	6		
Nichols, Jonathan	1				
Osmore, Aaron	1	1	1		
Osborn, John	1	1	2		
Page, Abraham	1		3		
Paine, John	3		2		
Paine, Thomas	2		3		
Parker, Levi	1	2	3		
Pettegrew, Stephen	1		4		
THETFORD TOWN—con.					
Pettingill, Peter	2		1		
Phillips, Alpheus	1		3		
Pinneo, James	3	1	1		
Post, Eldad	3	2	2		
Post, Aaron	2	2	3		
Post, John	1	3	3		
Preston, Tirus	2	3	5		
Rice, John	1	2	3		
Rogers, John	2	1	3		
Rogers, Samuel	1	5	5		
Sacket, William	2	2	4		
Saxton, Daniel	1	1	1		
Sukins, Martin	2		5		
Sheldon, Selah	1	2	2		
Sawyer, James	2	2	2		
Snow, Jonathan	1	2	5		
Smith, Israel	2	1	1		
Stephens, Abiel	1	5	3		
Steward, John	1	3	2		
Strong, Elisha	1	1	5		
Strong, David	1		1		
Strong, Ezekiel	1	2	3		
Strong, Joel	1	2	7		
Strong, Solomon	1		4		
Sweetland, Noah	1	2	5		
Swift, Ebenezer	1		1		
Swift, Ebenezer	1	1	1		
Swift, Judah	1	2	1		
Thayerd, Joseph	1	2	6		
Thomas, Peter				4	
Tyler, Jeremiah	1				
Tyler, Joshua	1	2	6		
Wallis, Richard	1	4	5		
Waltch, John	1	1	1		
Waterman, Levi	1	2	2		
Way, John	1	2	1		
Wheaton, Jonathan	1	3	2		
Wheeler, Amos	1	1	3		
White, James	3	4	4		
Wire, Joseph	1	3	4		
Wadkins, Nathan	1		2		
Wood, Abiel	2		1		
Wood, Israel	2	2	2		
Wood, Israel	1	2	1		
Woodworth, Levi	1		1		
Wright, Abel	2	3	3		
Wright, John	1		1		
TOPSHAM TOWN.					
Bagley, Aaron	1	2	2		
Brown, Timothy	2	3	2		
Burroughs, Josiah	1	3	3		
Caldwell, James	1	2	2		
Carter, Samuel	1	6	3		
Chillis, William	1		1		
Crown, Samuel	1		2		
Diamond, Reuben	1	3	4		
Dicky, Adam	2	3	4		
Emery, Richardson	1	3	2		
Fifield, John	1				
Graves, Thaddeus	1		4		
Hood, William	1	2	5		
Kent, Jacob	1	3	4		
Kunningham, James	1	1	2		
Loverin, John	2	2	4		
Mann, Nathan	1	2	2		
Mann, Robert	2	1	3		
Neasmith, John	1	1	2		
Petty, William	1	4	3		
Putnam, Porter	1	3	1		
Robinson, John	1	1			
Sawyer, Sylvanus	1	1	2		
Smith, Johnson	4	1	2		
Taber, Lemuel	3	4	5		
Thompson, Samuel	1	1	3		
Wilson, James	1	4	3		
TUNBRIDGE TOWN.					
Alexander, William	1	2	1		
Allyn, Amos	1	2	4		
Andrus, James	1	1	3		
Anesworth, Ephrain	3	3	2		
Austin, Seth	4	4	5		
Barret, Thomas	1	2	2		
Bloget, David	3		2		
Branch, Peter	2	1	5		
Burroughs, Almer	1	2	1		
Burroughs, Zebulon	2	2	2		
Button, Louis		2	1		
Camp, Abel, Junr	1	4	3		

ORANGE COUNTY—Continued.

NAME OF HEAD OF FAMILY.	Free white males of 16 years and upward, including heads of families.	Free white males under 16 years.	Free white females, including heads of families.	All other free persons.	Slaves.
TUNBRIDGE TOWN—con.					
Camp, Gould	2		3		
Camp, William	1	1	2		
Chapman, Becket	2	1	1		
Cheney, Eliphalet	1	2	3		
Cheney, John	1		2		
Clemons, William	3	3	7		
Cheney, Thomas	1	2	3		
Chambers, William	2	5	3		
Colburn, Abiah	1	1			
Cresey, Daniel	1	1	3		
Cowelery, James	1	1	4		
Currin, Hubbard	1	2	2		
Curtis, Elias	2	5	4		
Curtis, Simeon	2	3	2		
Curtis, Solomon	1		3		
Cushman, Solomon	2	2	3		
Davis, Dudley	1	2	1		
Deane, Asa	1	2	2		
Dean, Levi	1	2	1		
Dewey, Timothy	1	2	2		
Durkee, Solomon	1		4		
Eastman, Ebenezer	1	1	4		
Eaton, Samuel	1	2	2		
Eaton, Daniel	1	1	1		
Flanders, Josiah	1	2	2		
Folensbee, Moses	1	3	4		
Forest, Robert	1		4		
Gifford, Ziba	1		3		
Gray, James		2	2		
Green, Jonathan	2		2		
Grow, David	1	1	2		
Grow, Edward	1	2	2		
Grow, Peter	1	1	2		
Hale, John	1	1	2		
Hatch, Reuben	2	4	3		
Hayse, John	1	2	2		
Hazen, Frederick	1	1	2		
Hutchinson, Abijah	1	1	1		
Hutchinson, Elisha	2	1	4		
Hutchinson, Hezekiah	1	3	3		
Hutchins, John	1	2	2		
Kilsey, James	1		3		
Kingsbury, Lemuel	1	1	2		
Kingsbury, Nathaniel	1		1		
Kire, William	1	1	3		
Knox, David	1	4	5		
Lasdal, John	2	1	4		
Lilley, John	2				
Lyon, James	1	6	1		
Mastin, Thomas	2		1		
Moody, John	3	1	4		
Nichols, Humphrey	1	3	2		
Noyes, Aaron	2	2	5		
Ordway, Michael	1		2		
Ordway, Moses	1	6	7		
Ordway, Sewell	1		1		
Otis, Edward	1	1	2		
Pratt, Daniel	1		2		
Pratt, Levi	1	2	1		
Pudray, James	2	1	2		
Riddle, John	1	2	2		
Roberts, Jonathan	1	4	2		
Ross, Lemuel	1	3	2		
Smith, Obediah	1	3	3		
Stanley, Mathew	1	1	4		
Stedman, Alexander	4	4	4		
Thompson, Nathan	4	2	1		
Tracy, Elijah	1	2	3		
Tracy, Cyrus	1	2	1		
White, Henry	2	1	2		
White, Simeon	1	1	1		
White, William	2		3		
Whitney, Peter	3	1	6		
Wright, William	1		2		
VERSHIRE TOWN.					
Avery, Charles	1	1	4		
Ayers, Joseph	1	1	2		
Ayers, Nathaniel	1	1	4		
Baldwin, Asa	1		4		
Baldwin, Jabez	1	2	2		
Baldwin, Stephen	3		3		
Barrett, Benjamin	1	1	2		
Barrett, Luke	1	2	1		
Barrett, Thaddeus	2	1	2		
Bartholomew, Moses	1	3	2		
Bartholomew, Oliver	2	2	4		
Blake, Nicholas	1	2	2		
Bliss, Simeon	1		1		
Cadwell, Jonathan	1		1		
Carr, John	1	1	1		

NAME OF HEAD OF FAMILY.	Free white males of 16 years and upward, including heads of families.	Free white males under 16 years.	Free white females, including heads of families.	All other free persons.	Slaves.
VERSHIRE TOWN—con.					
Carrier, John	2	1	2		
Child, Samuel	3	2	3		
Cotton, Enoch	3	1	2		
Cotton, George	1		2		
Cotton, Julius	1	2	1		
Comestock, Michael	2		1		
Comestock, Samuel	2		3		
Dake, Joseph	1	4	2		
Daniels, Joseph	1	2	1		
Drake, Ebenezer	1		1		
Durgin, Samuel	1				
Blish, Joseph	1	2	2		
Fuller, Nathan	1	1	3		
Fuller, Stephen	1	2	2		
Godfrey, James	1		3		
Godfrey, Moses	3	1	1		
Godfrey, Simon	1	2	2		
Griswold, Shubal	1		1		
Horham, Jonathan	1	3	1		
Jones, Nathaniel	1	2	3		
Langdon, James	3	2	1		
Langdon, John	2	1	5		
Loveland, Amos	1	2	3		
Maltbie, Jonathan	4	3	7		
Maltbie, William	1	5	5		
Marshall, Joseph	1		4		
Matteson, Amos	3	1	4		
Matteson, John	2	2	3		
Mattoon, Nathaniel	1	1	1		
Miner, Anderson	1	1	5		
Morey, Charles	1	2	4		
Morey, Simon	2	2	3		
Night, Isaac	2		3		
Peters, Andrew	1	3	2		
Porter, Caleb	1	1	1		
Porter, Elijah	3	5	4		
Porter, Thomas	1	1	3		
Post, Daniel	1		2		
Prescott, William	4	4	6		
Runnels, Stephen	1	2	5		
Slaton, Phinehas	1		1		
Sacket, Philo	1		1		
Skinner, Daniel	1	2	1		
Smith, Asa	2	3	5		
Taft, Aaron	1	1	2		
Taft, Eleazer	1	3	2		
Thompson, Seth	1	3	2		
Titus, Ephraim	1		1		
Titus, Lenox	2	2	3		
Titus, Michael	3	3	5		
Town, Asa	2	5	4		
Walker, Elijah	1	1			
Walker, Joel	2	3	3		
Warriner, Reuben	1	1	4		
West, Ebenezer	1	1	1		
West, Ebenezer	2		1		
West, John	1	1	1		
West, John	1		4		
West, Jonathan	1	2	4		
West, Joseph	1	2	1		
West, Samuel	1	2	2		
White, Hugh	1		2		
White, Samuel	1	1	3		
Woodward, John	1		1		
Woodward, Thaddeus	1		2		
Yates, Barzilla	1	2	6		
VICTORY TOWN.					
Not inhabited.					
WALDEN TOWN.					
Perkins, Nathaniel	2	2	2		
Samburn, Samuel	1	1	3		
WALDEN'S GORE.					
Barker, John	1				
Davis, Dudley	2	3	4		
Ketteredge, Samuel	2	2	4		
Magoon, Jonathan	1	3	1		
Magoon, Saunders	1	1	2		
Saunders, Oliver	1		3		
Varnam, Ebenezer	1				
WASHINGTON TOWN.					
Baker, Asaal	4	2	5		
Baker, Isaiah	1	1	1		
Bartholomew, Eleazer	3		1		
Blakesley, Eber	2		2		

NAME OF HEAD OF FAMILY.	Free white males of 16 years and upward, including heads of families.	Free white males under 16 years.	Free white females, including heads of families.	All other free persons.	Slaves.
WASHINGTON TOWN—continued.					
Bliss, Samuel	1	2	1		
Burton, Amos	1		2		
Burton, Jacob	1	1	2		
Ingraham, Robert	2		2		
Powers, Stephen	1		1		
Ray, Gideon	1	1	2		
Smith, Elisha	1		1		
Strong, Stephen	1		2		
Tracy, Bela	1		3		
Tracy, Elias	1		3		
Waite, Nathaniel	3	4	2		
White, Thaddeus	1	2	3		
Williams, Joseph	1				
WESTMORE TOWN.					
Not inhabited.					
WHEELOCK TOWN.					
Bracket & Fisk	2				
Dowe & Glines	2				
Harris, Joseph	1				
Niles, Ephraim	2	4	4		
Page, Joss	1		1		
Porter, Peter	1				
Swezey, Dudley	4	2	3		
Venen, Joseph	1	1	4		
WILDERSBURGH TOWN.					
Adams, Job	1	2	1		
Blanchard, Asa	1	1	1		
Carpenter, Reuben	4		2		
Dodge, John	1		1		
Goldesbury, John	4		3		
Gould, John	3	1	1		
Gould, John	3	1	3		
Hale, Apollos	1	3	2		
Harrington, Nathan	1	2	2		
Nichols, Joseph	1	2	4		
Rogers, Samuel	1	2	4		
Scott, Samuel	3	1	2		
Sherman, Asaph	2		1		
Sherman, Jonathan	1	1	2		
Stacy, Malum	2				
Thompson, Stevens	1		1		
WILLIAMSTOWN TOWN.					
Baker, Edmond	1		2		
Buck, Isaac	1	1	3		
Chaffee, John	2				
Cheney, Joseph	1	2	2		
Clark, Abijah	1	2	2		
Clark, Benjamin	1	2	3		
Coburn, Hezekiah	2	2	4		
Colman, Eliphalet	1	4	3		
Crane, Joseph	1	3	4		
Franklin, Samuel	1		4		
Gould, Waterman	1		1		
How, Perley	1	2	4		
How, Samson	1		1		
Huling, Alexander		1	1		
Jeffords, Jacob	2		1		
Jeffords, Moses	2		1		
Johnson, Henry	1	1	1		
Luce, Ephraim	1	2	2		
Lyman, Josiah	1	2	4		
Lynde, Cornelius	2	2	3		
Morse, Moses	1				
Payne, Elijah	2		3		
Paul, James	1		2		
Robinson, Ezekiel	1	1	2		
Rust, Joseph	1	1	3		
Smith, James	2	1	2		
Smith, Levi	1				
Smith, Sylvester	1	1	2		
Thwing, James	1	3	5		
Walcott, Elijah	3		2		
Wise, Abner	3	1	4		
WINLOCK TOWN.					
Not inhabited.					
WOODBURY TOWN.					
Not inhabited.					

RUTLAND COUNTY.

NAME OF HEAD OF FAMILY.	Free white males of 16 years and upward, including heads of families.	Free white males under 16 years.	Free white females, including heads of families.	All other free persons.	Slaves.
BENSON TOWN.					
Austin, Pervius	4	1	4		
Abbot, Jonas	1	1	2		
Bisbie, Robert	1	2	1		
Barber, Simeon	1	2	3		
Barber, Joseph	1		3		
Barber, Margeret	1	2	5		
Barber, Levi	1	1	2		
Barber, Robert	1	1	3		
Barber, John	1				
Bassett, Rufus	1	3	4		
Barker, Oliver	1	2	2		
Belden, Levi	1	4	3		
Barnes, Esther	2	2	1		
Belden, Charles	1	3	1		
Belden, Elisha	1	3	4		
Belden, Phinehas	2	1	2		
Belden, Phinehas, Jr.	1	1	1		
Belden, Abraham	1		2		
Barnes, John	1	1	2		
Barber, Daniel	2	1	5		
Benson, John	1	2	2		
Briggs, Simeon	2				
Bugby, Peletiah	1	4	3		
Branch, Mason	3	5	2		
Branch, Luther	1		1		
Branch, Isaac	2	1	1		
Barks, Seth	2	3	3		
Chittenden, Solomon	1	1	3		
Carter, Jabez	2	3	5		
Carter, John	1	1	1		
Clark, Joseph	1	4	1		
Cooly, Hezekiah	1	2	2		
Cheeseman, Amos	1	3	5		
Calkins, Samuel	2	1	1		
Crowfoot, Stephen	2		1		
Crowfoot, Stephen, Jr.	1		2		
Dunning, John	1		1		
Dunning, Stephen	1	3	2		
Dunning, Enoch	1		1		
Durfee, Peleg	1		1		
Davis, Samuel	1		1		
Durfee, Walker	1		1		
Danforth, Jonathan	3	2	3		
Flagg, Barzillai	1	1	2		
Flagg, Elijah	1	2	3		
Ford, William	1	3	4		
Fisher, John	2		1		
Farnam, Asa	2	2	3		
Foredom, Gideon	2	5	2		
Gibbs, Darius	1	3	2		
Gibbs, Friend	1	3	2		
Goodrich, Allen	1	2	3		
Goodrich, Josiah	1	2	2		
Goodrich, Simeon	2	3	2		
Gleason, Jacob	2	3	3		
Goodrich, Caleb	1				
Goodrich, Thoms.	3	1	3		
Gleason, Benoni	1	1	2	1	
Hocomb, Amos	2	1	1		
Higgins, Saml.	2	3	3		
Hotskiss, James	3	1	3		
Hotchkiss, David	1	1	2		
Hennise, William	3				
Harrison, Lemuel	1	1	4		
How, Asa	1		3		
Hinman, Abijah	1		3		
Holbert, Abijah	1				
Haywood, Saml.	1	1	3		
Haywood, James	1	2	2		
Holton, Benjamn.	1		1		
Haywood, Benjn.	2	3	2		
Hinman, Daniel	2	3	5		
Jones, William	2	4	3		
Jones, Jonathan	1				
Johnson, Ozias	1	1	2		
Luddington, Wm.	1		2		
Lewis, Ebenezer	2	2	1		
Leet, Allen	1	2	2		
Maynard, Shube.	1	2	3		
Merrit, Barthol w.	1	1	2		
Martin, David	1	1	3		
Manly, Calvin	1		1		
Meecham, Willm.	1	2	4		
Marsh, Reuben	2		4		
Munro, John	1	1	2		
Meecham, Jonan.	6		5		
Miller, Charles	2		1		
Miller, Charles, Jr.	1		2		
Noble, James	2	3	3		
Noble, John	1		2		
Noble, Ithamar	2	1	3		
Olmstead, Stephen	2		2		

NAME OF HEAD OF FAMILY.	Free white males of 16 years and upward, including heads of families.	Free white males under 16 years.	Free white females, including heads of families.	All other free persons.	Slaves.
BENSON TOWN—con.					
Olmstead, Stepn., Jur.	3	1	3		
Olmstead, Jesse	1	2	1		
Parkill, James	1	4	6		
Parsons, Reuben	1	1	1		
Payne, Sparrow	1	1	2		
Parker, Prince	1	1	4		
Peters, Comfort	1	1	3		
Roots, Stephen	2	2	1		
Roots, Oliver	2		2		
Risden, John	1		1		
Roots, Amos	1	2	2		
Shaw, Joseph	1		1		
Shaw, John	1	1	4		
Shaw, Benjamin	1		1		
Smith, Asahel	1	1	1		
Smith, Asahel, Jr.	1	1	2		
Smith, Chauncey	1	1	3		
Strong, Russell	1		2		
Standish, Lemuel	2	2	2		
Stoddard, Jonathan	1	6	2		
Smith, Ella	1	2	1		
Stacy, Joseph	1	1	3		
Southwick, David	2	3	3		
Stacy, Benjamin	1		2		
Spicer, Elijah	1	2	2		
Shelden, Elijah	1		3		
Stiles, Israel	1	3	2		
Stiles, Silas	1	1	2		
Tyler, Jonathan	1	1	3		
Warden, James	1		1		
Winters, William	1		2		
Wilkinson, Lewis	2	3	4		
Wilcox, Elijah	3	3	2		
Wallace, Heman	1		4		
Woodward, Jonathn.	4		2		
Walch, Nathaniel	1	3	1		
Ufford, Shoers	2		3		
BRANDON TOWN.					
Ambler, James	1	2	3		
Avery, Daniel	2		2		
Avery, Simeon	2	3	1		
Buttols, John	1				
Barnes, Vinten	1	1	2		
Burnet, Samuel	1	2	5		
Beebe, Alexander	1	2	3		
Barnard, Joel	1	1	3		
Bigelow, Simeon	1	4	2		
Buckland, Timothy	1	2	1		
Buckland, David	5	2	6		
Bacon, Nathaniel	3	1	2		
Bacon, Nathl., Jur.	1		1		
Bacon, Philip	1	2	4		
Blake, Obadiah	1		2		
Barker, Joseph	1	4	5		
Barnes, Moses	1		4		
Clark, John	2	1	5		
Cutler, Amos	1	1	4		
Cheney, Edward	3	3	5		
Crooks, John	1	1	4		
Cross, Daniel	1	2	2		
Collins, Thaddeus	1	1	2		
Childs, Parly	1		2		
Cook, Samuel	1				
Darling, Samuel	1	2	3		
Dodge, Jonathan	1	3	1		
Darby, Roger	1		1		
Darby, Asa	1				
Dodge, William	3	2	4		
Duyee, Stephen	2	2	4		
Daniels, Nathan	1	3	4		
Dixon, William	1				
Darby, Shadrach	1	1	1		
Finny, David	2	2	3		
Flint, Nathan, Jr.	1	1	1		
Flint, Ephraim	1	1	1		
Fisk, Nathaniel	4	5	5		
Fisk, Eben	1		1		
Flint, Nathan	2	1	3		
Fields, Joshua	2	4	2		
Farrington, Jacob	3		3		
Gilbert, Moses, Jr.	1	3	3		
Gilbert, Moses	1		1		
Gilbert, Abraham	1	2	2		
Goodenough, Asa	1	1	2		
Goodenough, Sarah	1	1	5		
Goodenough, Elijah	1	1	2		
Grandy, Reuben	1	1	5		
Goss, Joshua	1	4	5		
Holbert, Benja.	1	5	3		
Hill, John	2		1		

NAME OF HEAD OF FAMILY.	Free white males of 16 years and upward, including heads of families.	Free white males under 16 years.	Free white females, including heads of families.	All other free persons.	Slaves.
BRANDON TOWN—con.					
Holt, Silas	1	1	3		
Hall, Stephen	2	1	3		
Hawly, Joseph	1	3	1		
Hawley, David	1		1		
Howlet, William	1	2	1		
Horton, Gideon	2		1	1	
Horton, Hiram, Jr.	1		5		
Horton, Gideon, Jr.	1	2	2		
Jones, Philip	1	3	2		
Jacobs, David	2	1	2		
Jones, John	1				
June, David	4	1	5		
King, Simeon	1	1	7		
King, Simeon, Jr.	1		3		
Kelsy, Samuel	1	4	2		
Keep, Samuel	1		1		
Lyon, Jabez	1	2	6		
Larkin, Joseph	1	2	3		
Larkin, Lorain	1	3	3		
Lull, John	1	1	2		
Mott, John	1	3	4		
McCollom, John	2	3	3		
Mott, Gideon	1		3		
Mott, Samuel	1	2	3		
Merritt, Noah	1	1	5		
Merriam, David	1	3	2		
Olds, George	1	3	3		
Cobb, Justus	1				
Polly, Amasiah	1	1	5		
Patch, Ephraim	1	1	5		
Steward, Abraham	2	3	4		
Scovill, S. Saml.	1	1	3		
Scovill, Eunice	1		2		
Simonds, Jacob	1		1		
Squire, Ebenezer	1		5		
Strong, Noah	2	4	5		
Strong, Ephraim	1	1	2		
Stiles, John	1	1	2		
Strong, Reuben	1	3	1		
Strong, Isaac	1	1	2		
Sutton, Willard	1	6	3		
Sutton, John	2	3	1		
Starkweather, Elisha	1	1	4		
Starkweather, Roger	1		3		
Simonds, Jacob	1		5		
Soper, Prince	1	2	3		
Soper, Solomon	2	2	5		
Stiles, Daniel	1	1	2		
Sheldon, Nathl.	1	1	2		
Tuttle, Othniel	1	1	1		
Tuttle, Solomon	1	4	2		
Tuttle, Thomas	2	1	1		
Tuttle, John	1	2	2		
Tracy, Solomon	1	1	3		
Welch, Nathaniel	1	1	4		
Whaland, John	1		4		
Worster, Ebenezer	1		3		
White, Jabez	1	1	2		
Whaland, James	1		2		
Whaland, Peter	1	1	2		
Webb, Isaac	1	1	4		
Wood, Charles	1	1	4		
Wood, Christopher	1				
Winslow, Calvin	1		2		
Winslow, Jedediah	3		1		
CASTLETON TOWN.					
Ackly, Benjamin	1	3	2		
Arvin, David	5		1		
Belknap, Jesse	1	2	5		
Brownson, Abijah	2	4	2		
Branch, Joseph	1		1		
Bond, Moses	1	2	3		
Brown, Jeremiah	2	5	4		
Brush, Josiah	1	4	4		
Brockway, Timothy	1	1	3		
Bord, D. Cornelius	1	1	1		
Brownson, Benja.	1	4	1		
Branch, Darius	1	1	1		
Branch, Rufus	2	2	3		
Bliss, Daniel	4	4	2		
Bordin, Ezekiel	1		5		
Blanchard, Asahel	1		2		
Brau, Eleazer	1	6	3		
Bradley, Thomas	1	1	2		
Bordin, Elisha	1		1		
Calkins, Simeon	2	1	2		
Cushman, William	2	3	3		
Cogswell, Peter	1		2		
Clark, Robert	1	1	5		
Carter, Lorenzo	1	1	1		

RUTLAND COUNTY—Continued.

NAME OF HEAD OF FAMILY.	Free white males of 16 years and upward, including heads of families.	Free white males under 16 years.	Free white females, including heads of families.	All other free persons.	Slaves.
CASTLETON TOWN—con.					
Clark, Beldad	1	2	3		
Clark, David	1	2	3		
Carier, Revd Matthias	3	1	3		
Clark, Genl Isaac	4	4	6	1	
Cogswell, Eli, Esq	3	1	6		
Carver, Benjamin	3	1	3		
Carver, Ralph	1	1	2		
Culver, Joel	1		2		
Culver, Francis	2	2	3		
Carter, David	1	1	1		
Dudly, Ephraim	1		1		
Darby, Oliver	1	1	1		
Donnihue, Jeffery	3		1		
Davis, Noah	2		1		
Dunning, Andrew	2	1	4		
Dyer, William	1	3	3		
Dart, Joshua	1	3	3		
Drake, Joel	2		2		
Drake, Eli	1	3	1		
Eaton, Daniel	1	2	3		
Eaton, Enoch	1		2		
Eaton, Rebenah		1	3		
Eaton, John	3	1	7		
Evitts, Timothy	1	1	6		
Foot, George	3	5	6		
Fisher, Peter	1		3		
Fox, Aaron	1	1	1		
Fisher, Abijah	1		1		
Graves, William	1	4	1		
Gates, Cyrus	1	2	4		
Griswold, Azariah	1	5	1		
Gilmore, James	4		2		
Gill, William	1	2	4		
Garnsy, Wido Sarah	2	1	4		
Hartwell, Ebenezer	3	5	5		
Hall, Ebenezer	1		2		
Huit, Asa	1		5		
Hollibert, Israel	2	1	2		
Hollibert, Curtiss	1		1		
Hall, Elias	1	1	5		
Hall, Silas	1	1	5		
Hammon, Nathan	1	4	1		
Hunt, Elnathan	1		2		
Hunt, Jonathan	1		1		
Hodgis, Lewis	2	3	2		
Hoit, Noah	2	2	2		
Hawley, Ezekiel	1		1		
Hyly, Brewster	3		6		
Hyde, Aruna	1		1		
Hawkins, Gaylor	1	2	5		
Hawkins, Joseph	1	1	2		
Hawkins, Moses	1	2	3		
Hoit, Noah	2	1	4		
Hyly, Brewster, Jr	2	3	4		
Johnson, Adam	1	3	3		
Jones, Asahel	1	1	2		
Kellog, Preserver	1	2	4		
Kilburn, James	2	3	5		
Kilburn, Roswell	1	2	3		
Kilburn, Abraham	1	2	1		
Lee, Noah	2	3	4		
Lincoln, Charles	2	2	3		
Lincoln, Sylvester	1	3	3		
Lake, Gershom	1	2	5		
Lusk, Samuel	1	4	2		
Long, Alexander	1	1	3		
Long, Zachariah	1	3	3		
Moulton, Rueben	3	4	5		
McKinstor, Amos	1		4		
McKinstor, John	1				
Moulton, Gershom	2		4		
Moulton, Freeman	1	1	1		
Mason, John	1	2	2		
Mason, Robert	1	3	4		
McIntosh, Duncan	5	3	1		
Moulton, Wid. Hipsy	2	1	2		
Merrills, Enos	2	1	2		
Mason, Wid. Anna	1	1	2		
Nothrop, Nathaniel	1	4	3		
Norton, Josiah	1	4	4		
Olford, Amos	1	2	3		
Pike, John	1		2		
Porter, Seth	1		2		
Porter, John	1	5	2		
Pond, Benjamin	1	2	2		
Pond, Josiah	2	1	2		
Parmer, Jared	2	1	2		
Polly, Joseph	1	2	3		
Phelps, David	1	2	2		
Phelps, Truman	1	1	2		
Parmer, James	1	1	1		

NAME OF HEAD OF FAMILY.	Free white males of 16 years and upward, including heads of families.	Free white males under 16 years.	Free white females, including heads of families.	All other free persons.	Slaves.
CASTLETON TOWN—con.					
Roberts, William	1	3	3		
Rogers, Joseph	1	2	2		
Robinson, Isaiah	1	5	4		
Redfield, Reuben	2	1	2		
Remington, Zadock	4	3	2		
Robinson, Ebenezer	1	1	2		
Southwic, Isaac	1	3	3		
Stanton, Robert	2		3		
Stacy, Cornelius	1	1	1		
Simmons, James	1	1	3		
Scovel, Daniel	1		2		
Shaw, Samuel	1	1	3		
Sturdevant, Perry	1		4		
Stevens, Asahel	1		1		
Stevens, Luke	2		2		
Sever, Robert	1		1		
Sanford, David	2	1	2		
Tucker, Isaac	1		2		
Turner, Reuben	1		2		
Turner, Henry	1		4		
Wolcott, William	1		3		
Woodward, Joseph	1		1		
Whipple, James	2		1		
Whitlock, John	4	2	3		
Whitlock, Zalmon	1		3		
Woodward, Arunah	2	3	4		
CHITTENDEN TOWN.					
Averill, Wyman	1	1	1		
Beech, Gersham	2	1	6		
Barnard, Dan	1		1		
Barnard, Andrew	1	2	1		
Bancroft, John	3		3		
Baldwin, Josiah	1	3	3		
Bogue, Samuel	1	2	2		
Bogue, Jeffery	1	2	2		
Bogue, Oliver	1	3	4		
Broom, Noah	1	2	1		
Cowe, James	3	1	5		
Cowe, John	1	1	1		
Dyke, Jonathan	2	3	5		
Egleston, Freeman	1	1	1		
Fish, Joseph	1	2	4		
Green, Zebediah	1	2	3		
Harrison, Samuel	1	3	3		
Keelor, Thomas	1	2	2		
Ladd, Nathl, Esqr	2	3	5		
Nelson, Nathan	3		2		
Olmsted, Jabez	1	3	2		
Parsons, Josiah	1	3	3		
Stearns, John	1	1	1		
Taylor, Solomon	1	1	2		
Thomas, Joseph	2	2	3		
Thomas, Joseph, Junr	1	1	2		
Thomas, Eber	1	1	1		
Woodward, Amos	1	3	3		
CLARENDON TOWN.					
Allen, Joseph	1	2	1		
Arnold, Stephen	2	1	5		
Arnold, Oliver	3	4	5		
Angel, Nedebijah	1	1	8		
Adjutant, John	1	3	5		
Adams, John	2	4	4		
Baker, Docr Elisha	3	2	4		
Baker, Jonathan	1	3	3		
Bigelow, Nathan	3	6	3		
Bell, Benjamin	1	3	2		
Bowman, John	3	1	5		
Brown, Purchase	1	1	4		
Bordman, Elisha	1	1	2		
Brigs, Daniel	3		4		
Brigs, Philip	1	1	3		
Button, Frederick	1	2	2		
Button, Joseph	2	3	5		
Beels, Red Isaac	2	1	3		
Robinson, Stephen	1	1	4		
Beech, George	1	1	3		
Blanchard, Caleb	1	2	3		
Blanchard, Rubin	1	2	1		
Beech, Moses	1		1		
Blanchard, Joseph	1		1		
Blanchard, John	2		3		
Blanchard, Clerk	1		2		
Boland, William	2	1	5		
Burlingham, Solomon	1	2	3		
Curtis, Thaddeus, Esq	3	1	3		
Clark, William	1	3	3		
Crossman, William	2	3	3		

NAME OF HEAD OF FAMILY.	Free white males of 16 years and upward, including heads of families.	Free white males under 16 years.	Free white females, including heads of families.	All other free persons.	Slaves.
CLARENDON TOWN—con.					
Condon, Caleb	1		4		
Crary, Nathaniel	1	1	2		
Crary, Ezra, Esqr	1		4		
Crary, Nathan	1	2	2		
Carpenter, William	3	1	2		
Clark, Jedediah	1		2		
Clark, Jedediah, Junr	2	1	3		
Cobb, John	1		1		
Cobb, John, Junr	1	2	1		
Condon, John	1		3		
Crocker, Andrew	1	4	3		
Condon, Joseph	1		1		
Condon, Jobe	1	4	2		
Capwell, Stephen	1	1	2		
Clark, Ezekiel	2	1	3		
Carley, Ebenezer	1	2	4		
Chatman, William	2	1	3		
Cooper, Abel, Esqr	2	4	3		
Colvin, Daniel	1	3	2		
Colvin, Levi	2	1	2		
Colvin, Jeremiah	1	1	2		
Chapman, Obadiah	1	2	4		
Cary, Samuel	1		1		
Chatsy, Richard	1		1		
Chaffee, Comfort	1	3	2		
Dantforth, John	2		1		
Davis, Obadr	1		1		
Dean, David	1		3		
Davis, John	2	2	1		
Davis, John, Junr	1	1	3		
Dean, Henry	1		3		
Eddy, Thomas	1	3	4		
Eddy, James	1	1	3		
Eddy, Jonathan	2	1	3		
Eddy, Peter	1		2		
Eddy, Peleg	1		1		
Eastman, Deliverance	1	2	2		
Eastman, Ely	1	1	4		
Edmunds, James	1	1	5		
Edmunds, William	1	2	1		
Edmunds, James, Jun	1	2	3		
Foster, Whitefield	3	1	3		
Foster, George	1	1	3		
Fuller, Samuel	1	1	2		
Foster, Benjamin	2	2	4		
Franklin, Nathan	1		1		
French, Ziba	1	2	3		
Fairfield, John	1	2	2		
Fasset, Joshua	1	2	1		
Graves, William	1		3		
Gould, Henry	1	2	3		
Graves, Barny	1		2		
Gould, Jacob	3		3		
Gould, Jacob, Junr	1		2		
Green, Ezekiel	1	3	2		
Green, Philip	1	1	5		
Gould, Benjamin	1	1	2		
Gould, Benjamin, Junr	1		3		
Goodridge, Wido Mary		3	4		
Goff, Daniel	1	2	4		
Green, Peleg	2	1	5		
Green, Jobe	1	1	2		
Gilcrease, William	2	7	2		
Hancock, Oliver	1	1	3		
Hunt, W. Henry	1	2	5		
Huit, Gideon	1	3	4		
Huit, Gideon, Junr	1	1	1		
Horry, Ichabod	1	2	1		
Hammond, Asa	2	1	2		
Harrington, William	1	2	2		
Howland, Caleb	1	4	2		
Hutchins, Thomas	1	2	3		
Heywood, Christopher	2	3	6		
Heywood, Isaac	1	2	1		
Harrington, Theophilus	1		2		
Harrington, Caleb	1	2	4		
Hadges, Doctr Silas	1	5	4		
Hill, John	2	1	1		
Hastings, Aron	1		4		
Hall, George	1	4	2		
Hill, John	1	1	4		
Johnson, Moses	1	1	2		
Jinks, James	3	3	5		
Jewn, David	1		4		
Jonas, Ezekiel	1		3		
Ide, Squire	2	1	6		
Johnson, Elihue	1	1	1		
Johnson, Zachariah	1		3		
Ingolls, Caleb	1		5		
Kindall, Silas	1	1	3		

RUTLAND COUNTY—Continued.

NAME OF HEAD OF FAMILY.	Free white males of 16 years and upward, including heads of families.	Free white males under 16 years.	Free white females, including heads of families.	All other free persons.	Slaves.
CLARENDON TOWN—con.					
Kimball, Joseph	1	1	2		
Kinny, Peabody	1	2	6		
King, Jonathan	2	3	2		
Luther, Elisha	1	2	1		
Lalkee, Isaac	1	4	4		
Lacy, David	1	2	3		
Lantford, Daniel	1	1	4		
Loomis, Epaphros	1	2	4		
Moore, Abner	1	2	4		
Miller, Daniel	1		1		
Merrill, Nathaniel	1		1		
Marsh, Daniel	2	5	4		
McCoy, David	1	2	5		
Mosely, Increase	1		1		
Matterson, Francis	2	2	4		
Olds, Jasper	1		1		
Pitcher, Ebenezer	1		1		
Pitcher, Ebenezer, Jur.	2	3	2		
Parker, Jonathan	1	1	2		
Parker, Jonathan, Jun.	4	2	4		
Parker, Benjamin	1	4	1		
Pittingill, Joseph	4		3		
Parmerly, Timothy	1		1		
Parmerly, Mark	1	1	2		
Pratt, Edmund	1	1	5		
Platt, Jehu	2	1	1		
Parker, Ephraim	1		2		
Powers, Jonathan	1		1		
Place, Nathan	1		5		
Platt, Daniel	1	1	2		
Parmer, David	2	1	3		
Perkins, Ebenezer	1		3		
Perrigo, John	1	1	2		
Perrigo, Brownson	1	1	1		
Perrigo, Elijah	1		1		
Parker, Philip	1		2		
Parker, Peter	1	1	2		
Pratt, Abijah	1	1	1		
Pearl, John	2		2		
Potter, Noel	2	2	2		
Parker, David	1		2		
Pill, Thomas	1		5		
Priest, Joshua	2	3	7		
Potter, David	1	1	6		
Peck, Lewis	1	2	1		
Parker, Matthew	1	3	2		
Priest, Samuel	1	3	3		
Rose, John	1	3	3		
Rice, Thomas	2	1	6		
Rice, Randall	1		1		
Russell, Isaac	1	2	2		
Remington, Jotham	1				
Rice, Nathan	2	3	5		
Richards, Nathanl.	1		5		
Robinson, Amos	2	2	4		
Robinson, Stephen, Jur.	1	1	4		
Rounds, George	3	5	5		
Robinson, Stephen	1	2	3		
Robinson, Amos	1	2	4		
Rice, Jonathan	2	1	3		
Rice, Amos	1		2		
Randall, Jonas	1	2	3		
Rounds, James	1	2	7		
Reynolds, Jeremiah	1	2	3		
Roberts, Collins	1	3	1		
Smiley, John	2	2	4		
Smith, Asa	4		4		
Smith, John	1	2	1		
Smith, Colo. Elihu	2	2	5		
Smith, Johnson	1	1	1		
Spencer, Abel	2	1	4		
Spafford, Col. Solomon	1	4	2		
Steward, William	1	3	4		
Steward, Joshua	1	4	4		
Steward, Oliver	1	4	4		
Spencer, Piercee	2	1	2		
Scott, George	1		1		
Spencer, John	2	1	6		
Scovill, Matthew	1		2		
Sawyer, Jacob	1	2	3		
Stratton, Isaac	1	2	2		
Sprague, Jesse	3	1	2		
Sprague, Abraham	1	1	1		
Salisbury, Abraham	2	3	1		
Smith, Joseph	1	1	3		
Smith, Daniel	1	2	2		
Simmons, John	2		4		
Simmons, Charles	1	1	3		
Simmons, John, Junr.	1	2	6		
Smith, Ozial	2	4	4		
Sherman, Joshua	1	6	3		

NAME OF HEAD OF FAMILY.	Free white males of 16 years and upward, including heads of families.	Free white males under 16 years.	Free white females, including heads of families.	All other free persons.	Slaves.
CLARENDON TOWN—con.					
Sherman, William	4	3	4		
Smith, Silas	1		1		
Skul, Elijah	1	3	4		
Scovil, Abijah	1	2	2		
Stratton, Betsy		1	1		
Salisbury, Gardiner	1	2	1		
Stowre, David	1	3	3		
Tutler, Reuben	3	4	4		
Townsend, Jacob	1		5		
Titus, Robert	1	2	4		
Train, John	1				
Train, Robert	1	2	3		
Train, William	1		2		
Titus, Abel	1		2		
Tripp, Abial	1	2	3		
Tripp, Parmer	1	2	4		
Torrence, John	1		3		
Thornton, Stutely	1	1	2		
Toms, John	1	2	4		
Warner, David	1		4		
Wells, James	1	2	2		
Washer, Solomon	1	2	2		
Whitney, Silas	2	2	6		
Whitney, Silas, Junr.	1		2		
Whitney, Oliver	1	2	2		
Whitney, Bart	1		1		
Weeks, John	2	3	5		
Wench, Abijah	1		2		
Wheeler, Daniel	1	2	3		
White, Abner	1	5	3		
Walker, Ichabod	3	4	4		
Wheeler, Wilder	2	1	3		
Warner, Omri	1		4		
Wily, James	1	2	3		
Weaver, Capt. Jabez	1	2	3		
Walker, Lewis	2	1	5		
Walker, Lewis, Junr.	1		2		
Whitney, David	1	4	3		
Weaver, Richard	1	2	5		
Wescot, George	1	1	3		
Wescot, Oliver	2	1	2		
Wescot, Jobe	1	1	1		
Wescott, Thomas	1	1	2		
Whitney, Elijah	1		3		
Wescott, James	1	5	2		
Yaw, Tempy		3	2		
DANBY TOWN.					
Allen, John	1		4		
Allen, Prince	1	2	2		
Allen, Zoath	1		1		
Allen, John	1		1		
Abbee, Eleazer	1	1	3		
Aldridge, Stephen	1		1		
Adams, Plyn	2		3		
Antony, Abraham	1		7		
Andrus, Elisha	2	1	2		
Andrus, Elisha, Jur.	1		1		
Abbe, Salathiel	1		1		
Barnum, Gideon	2	1	5		
Bull, Wido. Abijah		3	3		
Brown, Jeremiah	1	2	5		
Buxton, John	1	4	3		
Brown, Amos	2	2	3		
Barnes, Daniel	1		2		
Bromly, William	1	2	3		
Browning, Benjamin	1	5	2		
Blackman, Abner	1		2		
Bull, Williamson	1	4	5		
Bollard, Ezekiel	2	1	2		
Bollard, Isaac	1	2	4		
Barnes, Bradford	2	3	2		
Bullist, William	1	1	2		
Bromley, William	2		2		
Burt, John	2	3	4		
Barret, Alexander	1	1	2		
Broomly, Bethuel	1	3	2		
Broomly, Daniel	2	2	4		
Broomly, Boston	1	1	2		
Broomly, William	1		1		
Beebe, Ammon	2	2	2		
Barlow, John	1		1		
Burlingham, Gideon	1		1		
Beebe, Timothy	2		2		
Bull, Joseph	1	1	9		
Bull, Timothy	1		2		
Clark, Henry	4	3	3		
Calvin, Isaac	2	3	2		
Calvin, Amos	3	4	3		
Calvin, Titus	1	3	5		

NAME OF HEAD OF FAMILY.	Free white males of 16 years and upward, including heads of families.	Free white males under 16 years.	Free white females, including heads of families.	All other free persons.	Slaves.
DANBY TOWN—con.					
Comstock, Jeremiah	1		1		
Comstock, David	1	1	1		
Colvin, Luther	2	1	6		
Colvin, Stephen	1	3	2		
Cook, Daniel	1		1		
Cook, Daniel, 2nd	1		3		
Calkins, Richard	1	4	1		
Cook, Seth	2	1	3		
Calkins, Stephen	1	1	1		
Conger, Gershom	1	2	3		
Conger, John	1		1		
Crandle, Caleb	1	1	1		
Chase, Henry	1	2	5		
Conger, Enoch	1	2	4		
Conger, Jobe	1	5	3		
Conger, Pricilla	2		2		
Davis, Josiah	1	1	2		
Dyke, Peter	1	3	4		
Day, Joseph	2		1		
Day, James	1		1		
Douglas, Peleg	1	5	4		
Eddy, Jacob	2	2	7		
Edmunds, William	1	6	4		
Edmunds, Obadiah	2	2	4		
Eddy, Amos	1	1	4		
Fay, John	1	2	3		
Fish, Reuben	1	1	2		
Fish, Benoni	2		3		
Fowler, Benjamin	2	1	4	2	
Fish, Elisha	1	2	3		
Foster, William	1	3	2		
Green, Caleb	3		3		
Grippen, Lemuel	3	1	2		
Griffith, James	1		3		
Griffith, David	1	1	1		
Griffith, George	1	2	1		
Griffith, Bethiah			1		
Griffith, Philip	2		2		
Holmes, Perkins	1	1	4		
Harrington, Israel	1	2	2		
Harrington, Peter	1	3	1		
Harrington, John	1	1	1		
Harrington, Gardner	1	1	1		
Herrick, Henry	1	2	4		
Harrington, Oliver	1	2	2		
Harrington, Thomas	1	3	3		
Herrick, Henry	1	1	2		
Harrington, Thomas, Jr.	1	2	4		
Horton, Abel	1	1	4		
Howlet, Daniel	1	3	5		
Harrington, Elisha	1		1		
Harrington, Thomas	1		1		
Harrington, Lott	1		1		
Harrington, Samson	1	1	3		
Harrington, Mercy	2		4		
Hopkins, Abel	1	3	4		
Hilyard, John	1	1	1		
Hilyard, Minor	1	1	1		
Holmes, Samuel	1	1	1		
Hatheway, James	1	2	5		
Harris, Jason	1		2		
Hill, Aaron	1	2	5		
Huntley, Durill	1	1	3		
Holmes, Ozial	1	4	3		
Hill, Bela	1	1	3		
Hill, William	1		1		
Irish, Jonathan	1		1		
Irish, Jesse	3	3	1		
Irish, Gideon	1	1	3		
Irish, David, Jur.	1		1		
Irish, Jonathan	1	5	6		
Irish, Joseph	1	1	5		
Irish, David	2		3		
Irish, Abel	1	3	6		
Irish, Jesse	1		1		
Johnson, John	1	1	1		
Johnson, Adam	1		3		
King, Jobe	2	1	5		
Kelsy, Benjamin	2	2	7		
Kelly, Daniel	1	1	1		
Kempfield, Dennis	1	1	3		
Ketchum, Jonathan	1		1		
Lobden, Darius	1	1	1		
Lobden, Jared	1		2		
Lewis, Jacob	1	1	1		
Lobden, Darius	1	2	3		
Lattin, Richard	1	1	5		
Lake, William	1	2	2		
Lewis, Peter	2	2	5		
Lapham, Nathan	2	4	6		
Lowings, William	2	3	5		

RUTLAND COUNTY—Continued.

NAME OF HEAD OF FAMILY.	Free white males of 16 years and upward, including heads of families.	Free white males under 16 years.	Free white females, including heads of families.	All other free persons.	Slaves.
DANBY TOWN—con.					
Langdon, Richard				6	
Morey, Ebenezer	3	4	4		
Matterson, David	1	1	3		
Morrice, Lottie		2	2		
Morey, Caleb	1		3		
Mory, Warton	1		2		
Nichols, Ebenezer	1		3		
Nichols, David	1	2	4		
Nichols, James	1				
Nichols, Antony	2	3	3		
Nichols, Charles	2	4	3		
Nichols, Thomas	1				
Olcut, Thomas	2		1		
Perkins, Holmes	1	1	4		
Philips, Caleb	1	2	3		
Philips, Chad	1		1		
Parks, Benjamin	1	2	2		
Philips, Israel	1		1		
Parish, Daniel	2		2		
Parmer, James	4	3	4		
Parmer, Gilbert	1	4	6		
Parmer, Elias	1	4	3		
Parmer, Ichiel	1	3	4		
Rogers, Wing	2	2	4		
Randall, Snow	2	2	2		
Rogers, Stephen	6	3	6		
Rogers, Deliverance	2		2		
Ross, Joseph	1	2	3		
Ross, Joseph, Junr	1	1	1		
Randall, Matthew	2		2		
Russell, William	1	4	2		
Ross, Eleazer	1	2	1		
Remington, Joshua	1	3	6		
Sherman, Levi	1	2	5		
Sherman, Elihu	1	2	4		
Salisbury, Nathan	2	6	2		
Sprague, Joseph	1		1		
Sall, John	1	3	2		
Signor, John	1	1	3		
Signor, Henny	1	1	1		
Smith, Ezekiel	2	4	4		
Sutton, Benjamin	4	2	3		
Sutton, Benja, Junr	1		1		
Seely, John	1	1	2		
Sairy, Stephen	1	1	2		
Seely, Jonathan	2	3	3		
Sole, James	1	1	2		
Stafford, John	1	3	2		
Sherman, Philip	1	2	3		
Stafford, Rowland	1	1	6		
Shippy, Jacob	1	1	3		
Sherman, Daniel	1	3	5		
Smith, Ebenezer	1	1	5		
Smith, Caleb	1	2	2		
Smith, Nathan	1	1	3		
Seeley, Israel	1	6	2		
Smith, Zebulun	1	3	3		
Stephen, Theodore	1	1	3		
Thayer, Oliver	1	1	2		
Taft, Levi	1	2	4		
Tanner, Benjn	1	3	5		
Tabor, Walter	2	1	3		
Terry, Jonathan	1	1	2		
Taft, Phinehas	2	4	4		
Willer, Nathan	1	1	3		
Woodin, Peter	1		3		
White, Andrew	1	5	3		
White, Peter	1	1	2		
Wing, Matthew	1	2	1		
Wing, Matthew, Jur	1		1		
White, Edward	1	1	4		
Williams, S'phen	3	3	3		
Willer, Isaac	1	3	4		
Willer, Henry	1	2	4		
Willer, William	1		1		
Winnow, Jacob	1		7		
Veal, Moses	1	3	4		
Veal, Constant	1	1	3		
Veal, Edward	2	4	2		
FAIR HAVEN TOWN.					
Arvin, David		4	3		
Austin, Shubail	2		2		
Braynard, Timy	1	3	3		
Biddell, Richard	1	2	2		
Ballard, Joseph	1		1		
Ballard, M. John	1		1		
Buell, William	4	1	2		
Boyle, Charles	3				
Barlow, Nathan	2	1	1		

NAME OF HEAD OF FAMILY.	Free white males of 16 years and upward, including heads of families.	Free white males under 16 years.	Free white females, including heads of families.	All other free persons.	Slaves.
FAIR HAVEN TOWN—con.					
Cleveland, Josiah	1	1	3		
Cleveland, Oliver	2	1	4		
Chilson, Elihu	1	1			
Clark, Ashbel	3		3		
Chamberlain, Josh	1	4	1		
Cuttin, Isaac	4	2	1		
Carter, Elijah	2				
Cushman, Danl	1	2	3		
Cranmer, Henry	3		2		
Cranmer, Henry, Jr	1		4		
Cole, Samuel	1		1		
Cranmer, John	1	1	2		
Cook, H. Ebenr	1		1		
Cone, Asabel	1	3	2		
Church, Oliver	1				
Debile, Thomas	1	2	3		
Doghasty, Cornelius	1		5		
Darrar, Jeremiah	1	1	5		
Dixon, Thomas	2	1	5		
Everetts, Eli	2		4		
Freleigh, John	2		2		
Goodrich, Timothy	1	3	1		
Gibbs, Shelden	1	1	1		
Holmes, Moses	1	1	4		
Holt, Stephen	1	1	5		
Hill, Frederick	1	4	2		
Handy, James	1		3		
Calkins, Charles	3	2	2		
Hambleton, Ezra	1		1		
Hambleton, Joel	1	1	1		
Hows, John	2		3		
Hyde, Lemuel	2	3	5		
Horton, Jesse	1		4		
Hurlburt, William	1	5	2		
Hinman, Josiah	1	3	4		
Jones, Horace	1		1		
Jones, Ezekiel	4		5		
Kilsy, Curtiss	5	1	4		
Leonard, Gamaliel	1	3	2		
Lee, John	2	1	3		
Lyon, Matthew	5	2	9		
Lay, Amos	2		2		
McCarter, James	1	1	3		
Mitchell, Ichabod	2	2	6		
Merrit, Michael	6	1	5		
McCarter, Alexr	1		2		
Malcolm, Israel	2	2	1		
Munger, David	1	1	1		
McLuiry, James	1	1	3		
McCarthy, Charles	3	4	1		
McCarthy, Danl	2	3	4		
Meecham, John	1	5	5		
Newton, Jonathan	3	2	3		
Newland, Jabez	1		3		
Orms, Jonathan	2		1		
Orton, Elisaba	1	1	4		
Priest, Noah	1		2		
Petty, Benjamin	2	1	2		
Priest, Philip	2	2	7		
Phippany, Benjn	1	1	1		
Richard, William	1	2	2		
Rogers, Stephen	4		2		
Rice, Charles	1	2	2		
Querry, Simeon	2	2	3		
Skinner, Thomas	1		1		
Spooner, John	2	3	2		
Safford, Silas	2	1	5		
Snow, Joseph	1		3		
Sharpe, James	1	1	3		
Stephens, Nathan	1		1		
Stannard, Saml	2	2	3		
Smith, Simeon	6	1	3		
Smith, Dan	5	2	5		
Smith, Russell	2	1	1		
Strong, Worham	2		4		
Sanford, David	1		2		
Smith, Joseph	1		1		
Tryon, Elijah	1	1	2		
Taft, Gideon	1				
Trowbridge, Levi	1	3	2		
Trowbridge, Israel	1		3		
Taylor, Elijah	2	1	1		
Weller, Benjamin	1		1		
Weller, Cooley	1	2	1		
Wetherell, James	3	1	1		
Wilkes, Thomas	2	2	2		
Whipple, Ethan	1	1	3		
Utler, Abraham	2	1	1		
Keeler, Hezekiah	1	2	1		
Brownson, Cornelius	2	1	2		
Quevy, David	1	1	3		

NAME OF HEAD OF FAMILY.	Free white males of 16 years and upward, including heads of families.	Free white males under 16 years.	Free white females, including heads of families.	All other free persons.	Slaves.
HARWICH TOWN.					
Allen, Elihu	1	4	3		
Baker, Gideon	4	3	1		
Baker, Reuben	1	1	1		
Brock, John	1	1	4		
Carr, Joseph	1	1	6		
Carpenter, Beloved	1		3		
Cornwel, Benjamin	1	1	3		
Gerry, Elijah	1	3	3		
Gilman, Daniel	2	2	3		
Garret, William	2	3	2		
Gilman, Saml	1	1	1		
Hill, Stephen	3	4	3		
Harris, Asel	1	1	3		
Jenkins, John	1	3	5		
Mann, John	1		2		
Stafford, John	3	5	7		
Stafford, Stuckely	1	3	3		
Sherman, Danl	1	3	3		
Stafford, Parmer	1	3	4		
Stafford, Thomas	1		1		
Sherman, Abraham	1		1		
Stafford, Rowland, Jr	1	2	3		
Tallman, David	1		1		
Taber, Gideon	1	1	3		
Wood, Jonathan	1	1	4		
Wilber, Jacob	1	1	2		
White, Jacob	2		1		
Wheeler, John	1	2	2		
HUBBARDTON TOWN.					
Ackley, Champion	1	1	4		
Ashley, Abner	3	1	7		
Dewey, Elijah	1	1	1		
Davis, David	1	2	4		
Dewey, Israel	2	2	6		
Debro, Samuel	1		2		
Dodge, Nehemiah	1				
Doud, Peleg	3		4		
Doud, Peleg, Jr	1		2		
Forest, William	1	1	4		
Flag, Thophelus	1	1	2		
Foster, Chandler	1	2	1		
Gregory, Ithamar	1	4	4		
Gilbert, Thaddeus	2	2	3		
Gilbert, Thomas	3		2		
Gillet, Benjamin	1		1		
Churchill, Jenna	1	2	6		
Culver, Nathan	1	2	7		
Churchill, Josiah	2	1	1		
Churchill, Joseph	2	3	5		
Churchill, Saml	1		2		
Churchill, Ezekl	2	2	2		
Churchill, Jesse	1	1	2		
Churchill, John	1	2	2		
Churchill, Silas	1		1		
Churchill, William	2	1	2		
Churchill, Saml., Jr	1	3	2		
Handy, Joshua	1				
Hubbard, Amos	1	1	2		
Hubbard, Saml	2	2	6		
Hollebert, John	2				
Hamlin, Eleaser	1	1	1		
Hoit, Nathan	1	3	4		
How, Isaac	2		1		
Hicock, Mathew	1	1	2		
Hicock, Benjamin	2	1	3		
Hicock, Uriah	4	1	3		
Hicock, David	1	5	3		
Jennings, Joseph	1		3		
Keeler, Uri	1	3	2		
Lewis, Ebenezer	1	2	2		
Lawrence, Joab	2		3		
Lawrence, Bigelow	2	1	5		
Meed, James	1				
Nicherson, John	1				
Osgood, Josiah	1		4		
Pierce, Nathan	1				
Parson, Samuel	1				
Payne, Daniel	1				
Spalding, Wm., Jur	1	2	2		
Stanton, Jonathan	2		2		
Spalding, William	2		2		
Sellick, John	3	1	3		
Sellick, Benjamin	1	1	2		
Squire, Jesse	1	1	1		
Saint John, John	1	2			
Sabins, Isaac	1		2		
Saint John, Nehemh	2		2		
Rumsey, Isaac	3	1	3		
Rumsey, Hezekiah	1	1	4		

RUTLAND COUNTY—Continued.

NAME OF HEAD OF FAMILY.	Free white males of 16 years and upward, including heads of families.	Free white males under 16 years.	Free white females, including heads of families.	All other free persons.	Slaves.
HUBBARDTON TOWN—continued.					
Rumsey, John, S	2	1	1		
Rumsey, John, 2d	3		1		
Ray, Gilbert	1	3	1		
Rumsey, Noah	1				
Rumsey, Nathan	2	1	4		
Rumsey, William	1	3	3		
Rumsey, Joseph	5	4	3		
Rumsey, Danl	1	2	6		
Trowbridge, William	1	3	3		
Willard, Ebenezer	3	3	4		
Whitlocke, David	1		1		
Whitlocke, Sarah		2	3		
Wood, Lamuel	2	1	3		
Wright, Asahael	1	5	2		
Woolwic, Duresher	1		3		
Willard, Ephraim	1		2		
Whelply, James	2	1	4		
Walker, Elisha	1		2		
Webster, Abdili			2		
Warren, Simeon	1	1	2		
Willard, Joseph	1				
Lewis, Ebenezer	1				
IRA TOWN.					
Allen, Benjamin	1	4	3		
Adams, Daniel	1	1	1		
Andresen, Matthew	1	2	1		
Andresen, John	1	3	4		
Baley, Benjamin	1	1	3		
Baley, Benjamin, Junr.	3		1		
Bates, Reuphus	1	4	2		
Baley, Edward	1	2	5		
Baier, John	1	2	3		
Brown, Deacn	2	1	7		
Baier, Isaac	1	1	1		
Burlingham, John	3	1	4		
Carr, Daniel	2	2	3		
Carr, Hezekiah	1	1	3		
Car, Benjamin	1	5	1		
Carpenter, Cephas	2	2	5		
Collins, Nathan	1		3		
Collins, Thomas	2	1	2		
Collins, Benoni	4	3	6		
Colvin, Jeremiah	1	1	1		
Collins, John	1	3	5		
Cleft, Hezekiah	1	1	2		
Colvin, Reuphus	1	1	4		
Davis, Benjamin	1	1	1		
Egbert, John	1		1		
Gilman, Jonathan	5	3	5		
Hunter, Daniel	3	1	4		
Hicks, Asa	1	1	2		
Joiner, Asel	5	2	3		
Masen, Nathaniel	1	3	2		
McLouth, Lawrence	1	2	3		
Morton, James	1	2	2		
Morin, Edward	1	1	3		
Moulton, John	1	2	6		
Newton, Samuel	2	1	2		
Newton, Jason	1	1	4		
Owen, Samuel	1	1	4		
Owen, Joseph	2	1	3		
Obrien, Thomas	1	1	6		
Parks, William	1		2		
Roberts, David	1	2	2		
Roberts, Penrihase	1	1	1		
Shays, David	1	1	1		
Sherman, George, Jr	1	3	5		
Sherman, George	1		1		
Towers, Joseph	3	1	5		
Tiffany, Hezekiah	1	2	2		
Tower, Nathaniel	1	2	6		
Taylor, Matthew	1		1		
Wescot, Ziba	1	2	2		
Wood, Barnard	1	2	2		
Wood, Houn. Henry	1	1	2		
KILLINGTON TOWN.					
Briggs, Asa	1	3	3		
Edy, Nathan	4	1	2		
Easterbrooks, Thos	1				
Easterbrooks, Richd	1				
Fuller, Amasa	1				
Mason, Benja	1				
Nawson, Simeon	1	1	2		
Washburn, Isaiah	1	5	4		
MIDDLETOWN TOWN.					
Ashur, Dyer	2	2	2		
Beardly, Ichiel	2	1	4		
Beardly, Cyrus	1	1	4		
Bateman, Joseph	1	1	6		

NAME OF HEAD OF FAMILY.	Free white males of 16 years and upward, including heads of families.	Free white males under 16 years.	Free white females, including heads of families.	All other free persons.	Slaves.
MIDDLETOWN TOWN—continued.					
Bateman, Eleaser	1	1	5		
Baldwin, Frederic	1	1	5		
Burnham, John	8	2	7		
Burnham, Jacob	1		1		
Buckingham, Wm	1		1		
Blunt, Ashur	1	4	3		
Bull, Gideon	1	2	1		
Bushnell, Asa	1	2	2		
Brewster, Jona	5	2	4		
Bigelow, Edmund	1		5		
Butler, Benjamin	2	1	4		
Clark, David	2	3	2		
Campbell, Robert	1		1		
Clark, Thophilus	1	1	2		
Clark, Ezra	1		1		
Clark, Elisha	1	2	3		
Colegrove, Nathan	1		3		
Clark, Jonas	2		3		
Clark, Enos.	1		1		
Crowell, John	1	1	3		
Carr, Ephraim	3	1	4		
Clark, Rufus	1	4	2		
Clark, Roswell	1		2		
Cleveland, Stephen	1	2	3		
Coy, Benjamin	1	3	5		
Corbin, Edward	2	1	6		
Corbin, Eastman	1	1	2		
Caswell, Beal	3	1	5		
Cluff, Phinehas	1		3		
Colegrove, Nathl., Jr.	2	1	3		
Cluff, Joseph	1	1	4		
Caswell, Josiah	1		3		
Day, Amos	1	6	3		
Day, Robert	1	4	5		
Downey, William	2	1	3		
Davidson, Thomas	2		2		
Davidson, Thos., 2nd	1		1		
Downing, Thos	1	2	3		
Farr, Salmon	1	3	3		
Frisbie, William	2		5		
Filman, Luther	2	3	4		
Frisbie, Jonathan	1	2	4		
Ford, Daniel	1	3	3		
Ford, Nathan	1		4		
Frisbie, Joel	1	3	3		
French, Thomas	1	3	1		
Gardner, Asa	1		2		
Griswold, David	2	1	4		
Griswold, Jona	1	1	4		
Green, David	2	1	3		
Hubbard, Jesse	2	2	3		
Hubbard, Selah	1		1		
Hubbard, Abel	1	1	4		
Hamlin, Simn	2		4		
Hamlin, Simn., 2d	2		1		
Handy, Prisilla	2	2	3		
Haskins, Richd	1	2	2		
Hazon, Nehemh	1	2	3		
Hurd, Bethuel	1	3	4		
Haynes, Jona	1	2	5		
Hollister, Danl	1	1	4		
Hall, Saml	1	1	1		
Haskins, Benja	1	2	4		
Johnson, Isaiah	1		3		
King, Theodore	1	1	2		
Loomis, Reuben	1	2	2		
Lusk, Moses	1		4		
Minor, Lewis	1	1	2		
McLure, James	1	3	4		
McLure, John	1	3	1		
McLure, Thomas	1	1	2		
Matterson, Dyer	1	3	2		
Minor, Gideon	4	1	3		
Mahurin, Jona	1	1	2		
Morgan, Thomas	2	1	2		
Mahurin, John	1		1		
Mahurin, Hezekiah	2	1	3		
Mallory, Silas	1	4	2		
Parker, Abel	1		2		
Pratt, Samuel, Jr	1		1		
Perry, Ezekiel	1	1	5		
Perry, Azar	1	2	4		
Pratt, Samuel	1	3	1		
Perkins, Francis	1	3	2		
Record, Nathan	1	1	3		
Rochare, Joseph	1	1	2		
Rochure, Solomon	1	1	1		
Reed, Increase	1	1	4		
Richardson, Stepn	1		1		
Ruggles, Silas	1	3	4		
Reed, Baruch	1		1		
Record, Rial	2		2		

NAME OF HEAD OF FAMILY.	Free white males of 16 years and upward, including heads of families.	Free white males under 16 years.	Free white females, including heads of families.	All other free persons	Slaves.
MIDDLETOWN TOWN—continued.					
Spalden, Joseph	1		1		
Smith, James	1	1	6		
Smith, Caleb	1	3	3		
Shipperson, Anselon	1	3	2		
Stoddard, Samuel	1	1	6		
Sunderland, John	2	1	8		
Sunderland, Saml	1	6	4		
Smith, Timothy	1	1	4		
Torrington, Levi	2	2	3		
Tracy, Stephen	3		3		
Western, James	1	4	1		
Wood, John	1		2		
Wood, Nathaniel	2		1		
Wood, Nathl., Jur	1		2		
Wood, Philemon	2	1	4		
Wood, Levi	1		2		
White, Caleb	1	1	2		
Wood, Jacob	1	1	4		
White, Abraham	1	3	1		
White, Nicholas	2		3		
Walton, John	1	2	1		
Walton, Henry	1	2	1		
Woodward, Rufus	1	3	2		
Walton, Nathan	2	1	3		
Waldo, Gamaliel	1	2	6		
Wood, Ephraim	2	3	4		
MIDWAY TOWN.					
Farmer, Benjamin	1		1		
Farmer, Benja., Jur	2	2	3		
Bettys, Andrew	1	2	5		
Butler, Isaiah	1	2	1		
Emerson, Jonathan	1	3	6		
McKee, John	1		2		
ORWELL TOWN.					
Allen, William	1		1		
Allen, William, Jur	1	2	2		
Abel, Isaiah	1	1	2		
Abel, Asa	1	1	2		
Austin, Apollos	1				
Ames, Abner	2	3	4		
Babecock, John	2	1	3		
Bridge, Jesse	1		2		
Bottom, Jesse	1	1	2		
Bacon, Nathaniel	2	2	2		
Blyn, Bella	3	1	1		
Blyn, Simeon	1	1	1		
Brewer, Samuel	1		1		
Brewer, Archibald	1	2	2		
Blyn, Jonathan	2		1	1	
Brown, Samuel	1		4		
Benson, Ellis	2	3	2		
Basum, Joseph	4				
Bush, Joseph	1		2		
Brown, Luther	1		5		
Bush, Stephen	3	3	6		
Babcock, Ebenezer	1	2	7		
Benedict, James	2	1	1		
Bennet, Elijah	1	2	3		
Benedict, Peter	1				
Bottom, Roswell	2				
Cartwright, Edward	1	1	3		
Cook, Samuel	2	3	1		
Crouch, Richard	1	1	2		
Clarke, Smith	1	3	4		
Chote, Story	1				
Chote, Arpheus	1				
Chote, William	1				
Chapin, Sylvanus	2				
Clark, Cyrus	1	4	3		
Clark, Josiah	1	2	4		
Cook, Joab	1		1		
Cook, Ivory	1		3		
Cuttin, Elijah	1	1	1		
Cuttin, David	2	2	3		
Cole, Adny	1	2	4		
Culver, Esther	2	2	3		
Chasler, John	3	4	1		
Clark, Lemuel	1	4	5		
Darby, William	1		2		
Dickerson, John	1				
Davenport, Thos	1		5		
Egleston, Thomas	2	5	3		
Fuller, William	1	2	1		
Flagg, Ebenezer	1	2	1		
Fisher, Ephraim	2	3	5		
Fisher, William	3	1	3		
Fuller, Jacob	2		1		
Foster, Ichabod	4	3	3		

RUTLAND COUNTY—Continued.

NAME OF HEAD OF FAMILY.	Free white males of 16 years and upward, including heads of families.	Free white males under 16 years.	Free white females, including heads of families.	All other free persons.	Slaves.
ORWELL TOWN—con.					
Gay, John	1	4	2		
Griswold, Ebenezer	1	4	3		
Griswold, Sam[l]	1	4	1		
Griffiths, Thomas	1	1	3		
Gleason, Ebenezer	1		2		
Green, Ebenezer	1		1		
Griffith, Ebenezer	1	2	1		
Griswold, Simeon	2	1	5		
Hibbard, Jared	1	4	3		
Hill, Peter	1	3	2		
Hollinback, Will[m]	3	1	2		
Hulbert, Ebenezer	4	3	9		
Hollinback, Ab[m]	1	2	1		
Hinman, Adoniram	1	2	2		
Harris, Josiah	1				
Hibbard Uriah	1	3	2		
Hibbard, Timothy	1		2		
Hall, Gershom	1	1	2		
Hall, Gershom, J[r]	2	1	2		
Hall, John	2		2		
Jenks, Antony	2	2	1		
Knap, William	1	3	3		
Kelsy, Isaac	1	3	2		
Leonard, David	3	3	5		
Lyon, Andrew	2		2		
Morton, Samuel	1	4	4		
Marston, Martin	2	2	3		
Morton, William	1		1		
Mallery, Zaccheus	1		1		
Masters, Wheeler	2	1	1		
M[c]Coster, Peter	1	2	2		
Murray, Ebenezer	2	3	4		
McMannors, John				3	
Minor, Shrove	1		1		
More, Seth	1		1		
Nichols, Sam[l]	1	1	1		
Noble, James	3		3		
Owen, Frederick	1	3	5		
Oliver, Robert	2	1	1		
Oliver, Andrew	1		1		
Peters, Abimilech	1	1	2		
Parks, Asahel	2	4	2		
Perkins, Westly	2	3	5		
Parks, Jesse	2		4		
Parmer, Amos	1	1	4		
Parmer, Azariah	1		1		
Phelps, Elnathan	1	1	2		
Parmer, Abel	1	4	4		
Stearns, Alden	1	1	1		
Stearns, Thomas	1				
Spencer, Ebenezer	1	2	3		
Smith, Sims	1	1	2		
Smith, Reuben	1	1	1		
Smith, Abijah	1		1		
Spencer, Nath[l]	1				
Smith, Joel	1				
Stephens, Beriah	1				
Scovell, Daniel	1				
Scovell, Nathaniel	1				
Scovell, Thomas	2	4	5		
Swan, Abraham	1	1	3		
Spalding, Stephen	3	2	4		
Spalding, Simeon	1	2	3		
Spalding, Samson	2	2	4		
Smith, Ichiel	1	4	2		
Smith, Reuben	1	3	5		
Smith, Plinny	1	2	2		
Sanford, Joseph	3	1	4		
Spafford, Amos	4		3		
Tuttle, Jesse	1		3		
Torry, Samuel	1	1	2		
Thomson, John	1	1	2		
Thomson, Jonathan	1				
Ward, Ruggles	1	1	4		
Warren, Jabez	1	3	4		
Winchest, James	1	1	2		
Warren, David	2	4	4		
White, Ruloff	4	2	2		
Wilson, Ebenezer	4	3	5		
Wilson, Michael	2	1	2		
White, Lorenzo	1	2	3		
Woodward, James	1	6	3		
Wilson, Elias	1	1	5		
Weaver, William	1				
Rice, Nehemiah	1	2	2		
Remmerly, John	1	3	1		
Rice, Jonas	1	2	4		
Root, Eli	1		2		
Ranny, Daniel	1	2	2		
Rice, Jacob	1	1	2		
Wentworth, Elijah	1	2	4		
Lord, Samuel	1	1	1		

NAME OF HEAD OF FAMILY.	Free white males of 16 years and upward, including heads of families.	Free white males under 16 years.	Free white females, including heads of families.	All other free persons.	Slaves.
ORWELL TOWN—con.					
Keeler, Ezra	1	1	5		
Burk, Joseph	1	1	1		
Osborn, Joseph	1				
Younz, Simeon	1	2	2		
PAWLET TOWN.					
Allen, Caleb	1	3	3		
Allen, Timothy	1	1	1		
Adams, Asal	1	1	1		
Atwater, Simeon	1	1	2		
Abbot, John, Jun.	1	4	3		
Abbot, John	1		1		
Abbot, Daniel	1		4		
Agar, Cabel	1	1	3		
Agar, John	1		1		
Adams, David	2	1	5		
Adams, Levi	3	2	5		
Adams, Gideon	1	1	3		
Andrus, Asa	2		4		
Andrews, Robert	1	1	1		
Andrews, Zebulun	2	3	3		
Aspinwell, Eleaser	1	2	4		
Averill, Moses	1	2	3		
Averill, Elisha	3	1	5		
Adams, John	2	2	1		
Armstrong, Joseph	1	3	5		
Adams, Jesse	1	3	3		
Averill, Daniel	1	2	3		
Andrus, Amos	1	1	4		
Adams, Asa	1		2		
Bennet, Isaac	1		2		
Blossom, Seth	2	1	1		
Brown, Silas	3	1	3		
Baley, Daniel	1		2		
Blossom, Isaac	1		3		
Belts, Sealey	1		2		
Barr, Samuel	1	1	3		
Brassell, William	1	4	2		
Brassell, Gabriel	1		3		
Baldridge, John	3	1	6		
Bennet, James	1		2		
Bennet, Samuel	2		2		
Bennet, Aaron	1		1		
Brownson, Eldad	1	4	5		
Bennet, Cromwel	1	3	2		
Beebe, Rev[d] Lewis	1	1	5		
Bushnell, Benajah	1	1	6		
Brewster, Nathaniel	1	2	3		
Blackman, Simeon	1		1		
Bowman, Ezra	1		2		
Bushnell, Ichiel	1	1	2		
Bennet, Roswell	1	1	1		
Baker, Elijah	1		1		
Baker, Ebenezer	1	1	2		
Baker, Ichabod	1		2		
Boyle, Nathaniel	1		2		
Brewster, Love	1	3	2		
Branch, Daniel	4	2	5		
Blakely, David	2	1	7		
Butts, Samuel	3	1	5		
Butts, Samuel, Jur.	1		1		
Brewster, Timothy	1	2	6		
Baker, Rufus	1	4	6		
Bennet, Nathan	1	3	6		
Bushnell, Abisha	2	2	4		
Buxton, Simeon	1		1		
Baker, Reuben	2	3	4		
Bebe, Ephraim	3	4	4		
Curtiss, Moses	1		3		
Curtiss, Eldad	1	2	2		
Crocker, Josiah	1	1	1		
Carver, Nath[n]	1	1	3		
Crouch, David	1	1	2		
Carver, David	1	2	3		
Carver, Ezra	1	1	1		
Cook, Joseph	1	3	1		
Crouch, John	1	4	2		
Crouch, Benjamin	1	3	3		
Chapman, Daniel	1	2	2		
Capron, Joseph	1		2		
Cobb, Joshua	4		5		
Cobb, Ebenezer	2	3	5		
Cobb, John	2	4	3		
Cobb, Gideon	1		1		
Chipman, Cyrus	4	1	4		
Coburn, Ebenezer	1	4	4		
Chipman, Lemuel, Esq.	2	3	4		
Clark, Asa	1		2		
Cox, Robert	1		3		
Clark, Ozias	2	2	3		
Clark, Daniel	1	1	2		

NAME OF HEAD OF FAMILY.	Free white males of 16 years and upward, including heads of families.	Free white males under 16 years.	Free white females, including heads of families.	All other free persons.	Slaves.
PAWLET TOWN—con.					
Chaply, Hannah			4		
Cleveland, Moses	2	1	2		
Cleveland, Calvin	1		1		
Cleveland, Tracy	1	2	6		
Cook, Samuel	2	1	4		
Cole, David	2		3		
Cobb, Elkanah	4	5	4		
Darro, Samuel	1		1		
Dennison, Daniel	2	3	4		
Dutton, Calvin	1				
Elsworth, Hezekiah	1		1		
Edgerton, Jedediah	2	4	3		
Edgerton, Simeon	2	2	7		
Edgerton, Jacob	2	1	2		
Evins, Abiather	1	1	1		
Fitch, John	4	1	5		
Fitch, Daniel	1	1	3		
Fitch, Elisha	1	6	4		
Fitch, Rufus	1	2	3		
Fuller, John	1	1	5		
French, Nathan	1	4	2		
French, John	1		1		
Fields, Asa	1	1	5		
Fuller, Minor	1		2		
Fitch, Daniel	2	6	5		
Fitch, Lemuel	2	1	4		
Fitch, Joseph	3	2	1		
Fitch, Ephraim	1	2			
Fitch, Benjamin	1	1	1		
Gilder, Nicholas	1		2		
Gray, Widow Elisabeth			3		
Grandy, Asa	1	2	2		
Grant, John	1	3	3		
Giers, Israel	1	2	3		
Gilmore, David	2	4	4		
Gilmore, Sylvanus	3	1	2		
Hollister, Enoch	1	3	2		
Hollister, Ashbell	1	2	2		
Hollister, Elijah	1	2	3	1	
Harkel, Joseph	2	5	3		
Hatch, Doct[r]. Erastus	3	2	2		
Hanks, William	2	1	2		
Hanks, Arunah	1		1		
Hatch, Timothy	1		2		
Hatch, Timothy, Jun.	1	1	4		
Hopkins, James	1	1	5		
Herrick, Simeon	1	4	2		
Harman, Joel	2	1	7		
Harman, Thaddeus	1	2	3		
Harman, Ezekiel	2	3	6		
Haskins, Eliphalet	1	1	1		
How, Hezekiah	1	4	1		
Hull, Stephen	1	1	2		
Hix, John	1	1	1		
Hunt, Samuel	2	3	2		
Harman, Nathaniel	2	1	6		
Jones, Silas	1	2	2		
Jones, Joseph	1	1	2		
Kellog, Joseph	2	3	3		
Kingsley, Ebenezer	1	2	2		
Kellog, Aaron	1	1	1		
Lee, David	1	3	2		
Lake, William	1	2	1		
Leech, James	1	2	3		
Lewis, Samuel	1	1	1		
Loomis, Oliver	1	1	3		
Lewis, David	1	1	3		
Leppinwell, Ebenezer	1	2	3		
Loomis, Roswell	1		2		
M[c]Intire, Peter	1	2	1		
M[c]Knight. Friendly	2	1	3		
M[c]Knight, Daniel	1	1	2		
Mott, John	1	2	5		
Meecham, Abraham	1	3	2		
Moffet, Joel	3	2	4		
Menroe, Josiah	1	1	2		
Mars, Charles	1	1	1		
Maxfields, John	1		2		
Meecham, Isaac	1	4	2		
Montague, Adonijah	1	1	3		
Mosely, Abisha	2		4		
Noble, David	1	1	5		
Peck, Sperry	1	1	1		
Peck, Daniel	1		1		
Pepper, Simon	1	2	3		
Page, Achilles	2	2	4		
Patterson, Thankfull		1	3		
Porter, Moses	2	4	5		
Page, Jonathan	1		2		
Potter, William	2	5	5		
Porter, Samuel	1	2	5		
Pelly, Edmund	1	1	2		

RUTLAND COUNTY—Continued.

NAME OF HEAD OF FAMILY.	Free white males of 16 years and upward, including heads of families.	Free white males under 16 years.	Free white females, including heads of families.	All other free persons.	Slaves.
PAWLET TOWN—con.					
Perkins, Jacob	2	2	2		
Rockwell, Seth	1	1	1		
Rockwell, Timothy	1	2	2		
Robinson, Richard	1	1	3		
Reed, Philip	3	3	2	1	
Rood, Abijah	3	2	4		
Reed, Simon	1	7	2		
Rush, Jacob	1	2	1		
Rush, Jacob, Junr	1		1		
Rush, Apollos	1		1		
Riley, John	1		3		
Reed, Jedediah	1	3	3		
Robertson, Richard	1	1	3		
Robertson, Abel	1	2	2		
Robertson, Ephraim	1	1	2		
Rose, Samuel	4		2		
Stratton, Samuel	1	1	3		
Seeres, Samuel	1	2	3		
Smith, Martin	3	1	2		
Steel, Eldad	2		2		
Smith, Josiah	2	1	3		
Sterns, Isaac	2		1		
Stoddard, John	1	3	2		
Stark, John	1	1	8		
Spicer, Jacob		3	2		
Smith, Benoni	3	4	6		
Stark, John	1	2	3		
Story, Asa	1		1		
Seers, Simeon	2	3	5		
Sykes, Jacob	1	2	3		
Smith, Nathaniel	2	5	4		
Smith, Eliphalet	1		3		
Sitchwell, Belcher	1	2	2		
Strong, Return	2	4	3		
Shelden, Seth	2	3	4		
Starkweather, Stephen	2		2		
Skinner, Ashbell	1	1	4		
Simonds, Joel	4	4	8		
Todd, Doctr Elias	3	2	6		
Tracy, Nathaniel	1	1	2		
Turner, Lemuel	1		2		
Tracy, Hezekiah	3	4	7		
Taylor, Stephen	2	1	1		
Thomson, John	1	2	5		
Tubbs, Clement	1	1	2		
Toby, Josiah	1	1	2		
Tryon, Jesse	3	2	2		
Uran, James	1		1		
Upham, Joseph	1		1		
Wales, John	1	4	3		
Williams, Nathan	1	1	2		
Wood, Jonathan	1	2	2		
Wheeler, Edmund	1		5		
Wheeton, Anselm	1	2	1		
Whitman, Samuel	2	3	2		
Worster, Henry	1	2	5		
Willard, Jonathan	1		1		
Willard, Widow Sarah		4	3		
Willard, Jonathan, Jur	1		1		
Willard, Joseph	1	1	4		
Warner, Gad	1	2	2		
Watkins, Bodwell	1	3	3		
Wylly, Asa	1	3	5		
Willard, John	1	1	2		
Winchester, Andrew	1	2	5		
Welch, Daniel	2	2	5		
Willard, Jonathan	2		1		
Williams, Edward	1	2	1		
Wilcox, John	1	2	4		
Warner, Reuben	1	1	1		
Wright, Samuel	2	2	6		
Williams, Abel	1	1	3		
PHILADELPHIA TOWN.					
Churchel, John	1				
Churchel, Caleb	1	1	2		
Churchel, Michael	1				
Churchel, Isaac	2	2	4		
Extel, Ezra	1	2	1		
Hawly, Nathan	1	1	2		
Keelor, Seth	3	2	6		
Keelor, Jesse	1		1		
Bullest, John	1	1	2		
PITTSFIELD TOWN.					
Bow, Daniel	1	1	1		
Bow, Jacob	1	2	2		
Dutton, Joseph	1	1	4		
Davis, William	1	1	2		
Holt, Stephen	1	3	3		

NAME OF HEAD OF FAMILY.	Free white males of 16 years and upward, including heads of families.	Free white males under 16 years.	Free white females, including heads of families.	All other free persons.	Slaves.
PITTSFIELD TOWN—con.					
Hotchkiss, Thomas	1	1	4		
Gaine, John	1				
Martin, George	1	2	2		
Warner, Israel	1		3		
Warner, David	1		1		
Warner, Joseph	2	1	2		
Whitcomb, Antony	1				
PITTSFORD TOWN.					
Adams, Elijah	1	1	3		
Adams, Richard	1	2	2		
Adams, Saxton	1		2		
Adams, Elisha	3	1	3		
Burjis, Dennis	1	5	4		
Barns, John	3	2	1		
Barns, Ithiel	1		5		
Bachelor, John	1	4	3		
Burnet, Benjamin	1	2	6		
Bradford, Elisha	1	2	2		
Brown, Elijah	1	1	5		
Bates, James	1	1	3		
Barnard, Roger	1	2	1		
Brooks, Ichabod	1	1	2		
Brown, Elijah	5		1		
Brewster, Justin	1				
Cooley, Gideon, Jur	3	2	3		
Cooley, Gideon	2		5		
Cooley, Jacob	2	1	3		
Cropton, Ozias	1	1	1		
Cross, Joel	2	2	3		
Childs, David	3	1	1		
Chandler, Joseph	1	1	3		
Crippin, Darius	1	1	4		
Cooley, Benjamin	2	3	5		
Cross, Uriah	1	3	5		
Cole, Levi	1	3	3		
Coply, Samuel	1	2	5		
Coleman, Antony	1		4		
Cox, William	1	2	2		
Drury, Ebenezer	3	4	2		
Drury, Abraham	2		1		
Drury, Calvin	1		1		
Dunton, Thomas	1	3	3		
Doolittle, Moses	1	2	4		
Ewings, James	2	3	4		
Fin, John	2	2	1		
Fairfield, Nathanl	1	1	1		
Fairfield, Samuel	1	2	4		
Freeman, Ezra	1	2	6		
Fenny, David	1		1		
Gibbs, Ebenezer	5	1	4		
Griswold, Miles	2		3		
Gitchell, David	1	2	4		
Gorham, John	1	2	2		
Hall, Elias	1	4	5		
Hitchcock, John, Jr	1	1	1		
Hopkins, Ashbell	1		1		
Hopkins, Nehemiah	2		1		
Hopkins, Martin	1		2		
Harwood, Eleazer	1	2	3		
Hill, C. George	1	1	2		
Hopkins, Elias	1	3	3		
Hopkins, John	1		4		
Hopkins, Noah	1		2		
Hopkins, Stephen	2	1	2		
Hopkins, James	3				
Handy, Richard	2	4	3		
Harris, Peter	1		2		
Hammond, Thomas	2		6		
Handy, Caleb	2	3	4		
Handy, Caleb, Jur	1		2		
Hall, David	1				
Hitchcock, John	5		2		
Hopkins, John	1		4		
Herrick, Elijah	1	1	3		
Harwood, Simeon	1		3		
Ives, Reuben	1	2	4		
Jenning, Joseph	1	2	4		
Jenner, Stephen	1	5	2		
Jackson, Jonathan	1		5		
Jackson, Samuel	1				
Jackson, David	1	3	2		
June, Joshua	1	3	3		
Kellog, Amos	2		3		
Kingsly, Nathn	1	1	7		
Kellog, Joseph	1		2		
Kneedom, Jeremiah	1				
Ladd, Amasa	2	1	2		
Lawrence, Amos	2	1	2		
Lathrop, A. John	1		1		
Lampson, Roger	1	1	2		

NAME OF HEAD OF FAMILY.	Free white males of 16 years and upward, including heads of families.	Free white males under 16 years.	Free white females, including heads of families.	All other free persons.	Slaves.
PITTSFORD TOWN—con.					
Lee, Jedediah	2	1	2		
Lake, Israel	1	1	2		
Lyman, Ebenezer	1	2	6		
Moss, Joshua	1	1	3		
Marble, Ephraim	1	2	4		
Meed, Stephen	3	1	2		
Moshier, Joseph	1	1	3		
Morgan, Israel	3	2	6		
Millard, Abiathar	1	3	5		
Maatson, Isaac	3		3		
Montague, Rufus	1	1	2		
Mossman Jimy	1		2		
Mossman, Joshua	1	1	2		
Olcutt, William	1				
Olmstead, Gideon	1	2	2		
Olver, Abraham	1	3	2		
Olmstead, Moses	1	4	4		
Powers, Jeremiah	1		2		
Osburn, Isaac	1	2	3		
Patterson, John	2	1	2		
Philips, Antony	2	1	5		
Patterson, James	1		1		
Powers, Peter	1	1	1		
Patterson, Alexander	1	3	4		
Pamerly, Simeon	2	3	5		
Rice, Peter	1	3	3		
Right, Wait	1	3	2		
Rich, Elisha	1	1	3		
Rowley, Jonathan	2	3	3		
Rowley, Hopkins	1		2		
Rowley, Joseph	1	1	1		
Ripley, Phinehas	2	1	6		
Russell, Ebenezer	1	1	1		
Stanton, Abraham	2		1		
Stephens, Roger	2		3		
Stephens, Abel	1	4	4		
Stevens, Benjamin	2	2	2		
Stevens, Simeon	1	1	2		
Sweet, Amos	1	1	2		
Stephens, Benjamin, Jr	2	1	2		
Stephens, James	1	1	3		
Smith, Ephraim	1	1	3		
Stephens, Jonathan	1	1	3		
Strickland, Roger	1	1	2		
Shelden, Samuel	1	1	2		
Sweet, Samuel	1	3	3		
Stephens, Asa	1		2		
Sweet, Robert	1		3		
Sweet, Jonathan	1	1	1		
Shelden, Gideon	1	1	4		
Spencer, William	1	2	4		
Start, David	1	2	2		
Tupper, Simeon	3		3		
Thompson, Robert	1	2	2		
Titus, John	1	2	2		
Warner, Jonathan	1	2	4		
Webster, Nathan	3	2	3		
Webster, Amos	1	1	1		
Wood, Jeremiah	1	2	2	1	
Williams, Thomas	2		2		
Woodruff, Elisha	2	4	4		
West, Asa	1	2	3		
Whipple, Abner	1		2		
Waters, Samuel	2		3		
Warner, Eleazer	1	1	4		
Wiswell, Benjamin	1	3	4		
Wetherly, Nathan	1	1	1		
Weed, Jacob	2	1	2		
Weed, Amos	1	1	1		
Wait, Ruth			3		
Warner, Suel	1		2		
Woodward, John	1		3		
Wicker, Frederick	1	1	1		
Wicker, Luther	1	2	3		
POULTNEY TOWN.					
Ashley, Stephen	1		2		
Ashley, John	1	2	4		
Ashley, William	1	3	3		
Allen, Samuel	1				
Ashley, Thomas	3	1	6		
Ashley, Zebulun	1	1	1		
Athen, Thomas	1	3	2		
Adams, Jeremiah	1	1	1		
Adams, Benjamin	1	1	2		
Adams, Elijah	1		4		
Armstrong, Jeremh	1	1	3		
Adams, Abner	1	5	3		
Buckland, Samuel	2		1		
Buhas, Timothy	1	2	3		
Brookings, James	2	3	4		

RUTLAND COUNTY—Continued.

NAME OF HEAD OF FAMILY.	Free white males of 16 years and upward, including heads of families.	Free white males under 16 years.	Free white females, including heads of families.	All other free persons.	Slaves.
POULTNEY TOWN—con.					
Brookings, Cyrus	2	1	3		
Bates, James	1		1		
Brookings, Ithamer	2	3	3		
Brookings, Boaz	2		1		
Brookings, Philip	2		1		
Bran, Jeffery				5	
Bucker, Calvin	1		4		
Birje, David	1	4	3		
Bateman, Eleazer	1	1	2		
Bateman, Zadock	1		1		
Buckland, William	4		3		
Cole, Nathaniel	1	4	2		
Craw, Seth	2		5		
Crittenden, Timothy	2		2		
Crittenden, Seymour	1	2	3		
Cady, Ephraim, Jur.	1	3	3		
Campfield, Ebenr.	5	1	6		
Cady, Ephraim	1		1		
Crosby, William	1	2	2		
Cooper, William	1		1		
Chub, John	1		2		
Church, David	2	4	2		
Clark, Samuel	1	1	5		
Coleman, John	2	1	3		
Dixon, David	1	1	1		
Demoranville, Stephen	2	4	5		
Dixon, Archibald	2	1	2	1	
Dewey, Zebediah	2	1	4		
Dewey, Zebediah, Jur.	1		1		
Dewey, John	1	1	2		
Darby, Phinehas	2	3	4		
French, Jonathan	1		1		
Farnum, Barzilla	1	1	5		
Fellows, Nathan	1	1	5		
Fennell, Edward	1	3	2		
Frisbie, James	1	2	2		
Frisbie, Ebenezer	2	1	3		
Goodwin, Thomas	1	2	2		
Goodwin, Elijah	1	1	2		
Gorham, James	1	1	2		
Green, Robert	1		3		
Grant, Josiah	4	2	9		
Grant, John	3	2	1		
Gerrard, John	1	1	3		
Gorham, Jared	1		2		
Gorham, Seth, 1st	1	1	2		
Gorham, Seth, 2nd	1	2	2		
Huff, Wido. Ruth		1	1		
Hooker, James	1	3	3		
Hooker, Samuel	1		1		
Horford, Reuben	2	2	3		
Hickock, Simeon	2	1	2		
Hickock, Thaddeus	1	1	2		
Hyde, James	3	2	6		
Herrick, Rufus	1	1	2		
Herrick, Ephraim	1	2	2		
Hyde, Thatcher	2	2	5		
Hollibert, David	1		3		
Hibbard, Ithamar	2	3	5		
Hooker, James	1	1	3		
How, John	1	3	1		
Howker, Thomas	1	2	3		
Howland, Joseph	1		2		
Holbrook, Peletiah	2	5	1		
How, Peter	1		8		
Huggins, William	1	1	2		
Hyde, Henry	2	5	3		
How, Jacob	2		3		
How, Silas	2	1	2		
Hosford, Aaron	2	3	2		
Hill, Solomon	1		4		
Herrick, Edward	1	1	2		
Jordon, Samuel	1	2	3		
Joslin, Lindsey	2	2	4		
Joslin, Jabez	1	3	4		
Kellog, Samuel	1		1		
Kellog, Samuel, Junr.	1	1	3		
Keys, David	1	3	2		
Lewis, Josiah	2				
Lewis, John	1	2	3		
Lee, William	4		2		
Lee, Samuel	1	2	5		
Lincoln, Benja.	1	4	4		
Lampson, Edmund	2	1	1		
Lee, Abijah	1	3	1		
Loggin, Hezekiah	2	1	1		
Leed, Ephraim	1	2	1		
Martin, John	3	3	3		
Marsh, Josiah	1	2	5		
Marshall, Joseph	2	2	2		
Marshall, Ichabod	3	3	7		

NAME OF HEAD OF FAMILY.	Free white males of 16 years and upward, including heads of families.	Free white males under 16 years.	Free white females, including heads of families.	All other free persons.	Slaves.
POULTNEY TOWN—con.					
Manning, Dan	1	3	4		
Miles, Simeon	2		4		
Mallory, Calvin	1	1	2		
Mallory, James	2	1	1		
Marker, Joseph	1	1	2		
Morgan, Jonathan	1	1	2		
Mosely, Prince	1	1	4		
Moss, Joseph	3	1	4		
Moss, Solomon	1	1	3		
Morgan, Caleb	1	2	3		
Meers, John	2	2	1		
Norton, Solomon	2	3	6		
Newton, William	3		6		
Olds, Aaron	4	3	4		
Otis, L. Barnabas	1	3	1		
Pember, Eli	1		3		
Pember, Andrew	2	4	2		
Pipkin, Stephen	1	2	2		
Preston, John	1	4	5		
Phelps, John	1	3	2		
Pond, Abel	1	2	4		
Parker, Isaac	1	2	4		
Parmer, Zenas	1		3		
Paddin, Robert	1		2		
Pierce, John	1	4	3		
Parker, Abel	4		4		
Pierce, Phinehas	1	4	4		
Parker, William	1		2		
Pond, Mabel	2		2		
Pond, Samuel	4	1	4		
Pond, Samuel, Jr.	1	2	2		
Parmer, Joseph	1	2	2		
Rusco, Stephen	4	1	2		
Rusco, Simeon	1		4		
Reed, Josiah	1	2	3		
Richards, Danl.	2	3	7		
Richards, John	3	2	3		
Richards, Zebulun	1	1	2		
Ranson, John	2	2	1		
Richard, Barnibas	1	5	4		
Rand, Joseph	1	2	5		
Rice, Jason	1	3	3		
Rose, Russell	1	1	4		
Rogers, Joseph	2		4		
Rice, Levi	1	1	2		
Rice, Nathan	1				
Robertson, Eleab	1	3	3		
Squire, Thomas	1	1	4		
Sanford, Oliver	1		1		
Smith, Ebenezer	1		3		
Smith, James	2	2	1		
Smith, Sarah		1	2		
Stephens, Zebulun	1	1	4		
Stockings, Jonathan	3	1	2		
Safford, Jonas	1	3	2		
Smith, Nathaniel	1	1	5		
Strong, Darius	1	1	3		
Soper, Gilbert	1	2	2		
Strong, Oliver	3	3	6		
Scribner, Peter	2		2		
Smiley, Aaron	1	1	2		
Seeley, Stephen	1		2		
Stephens, Reuben	2		4		
Stephens, Cyrus	1	3	1		
Smith, Joel	1	4	2		
Smith, Peter	1	1	8		
Thatcher, Amasa	3		3		
Thompson, Daniel	3		5	1	
Thomas, Revd. James	2		2		
Talmage, William	1		1		
Talmage, Henry	3	1	3		
Turner, Moses	3	1	3		
Taylor, Richard	1		1		
Tilden, John	1	3	5		
Trumbull, John	1	2	2		
Wood, Thomas	1	4	4		
Woodman, Samuel	1	3	3		
Whitney, Solomon	1	1	3		
Ward, William	1	4	4		
Webb, John	1	2	1		
Ward, Barnard	1	2	2		
Walson, Titus	1	4	4		
Woodman, Saml.	1	3	3		
Yeoman, Nathan	1	1	4		
RUTLAND TOWN.					
Andrews, John	3	2	3		
Andrews, Ebenezer	2	1	2		
Andrews, Ahial	2		2		
Ames, Matthias	1	1	2		

NAME OF HEAD OF FAMILY.	Free white males of 16 years and upward, including heads of families.	Free white males under 16 years.	Free white females, including heads of families.	All other free persons.	Slaves.
RUTLAND TOWN—con.					
Beebe, Solomon	1	1	3		
Barr, William	3	1	4		
Buell, Elias	5	1	4		
Buell, Solomon	1	1	1		
Brigham, John	1		2		
Beech, Gershom	1	2	4		
Barnes, William	1		6		
Brundage, Joseph	1	1	1		
Bowker, Elias	2		2		
Bowker, Nathaniel	1	1	1		
Boardman, Timothy	1	2	2		
Bridge, John	2		2		
Blanchard, Benjamin	3		4		
Bates, Christopher	1	2	4		
Bates, Jonathan	1	1	3		
Bates, Daniel	1		1		
Briggs, William	1	1	4		
Butts, Francis	1		1		
Blanchard, Ebenezer	4	2	3		
Butler, James	2				
Butler, ——	1		2		
Bingham, Orias	1		3		
Beebe, Ezekiel	1		1		
Beebe, Ezekiel, Junr.	1	2	3		
Beebe, Allen	1	3	3		
Bissell, John	2	3	3		
Baldwin, Miles	1	3	2		
Beeman, Nathaniel	1	4	3		
Chipman, Nathl., Esq.	4	2	4		
Claghon, Colo. James	2	1	4		
Cook, Ashbell	3	3	2		
Cook, John	1	1	3		
Campbell, Daniel	2		2		
Calvin, Sanford	1		2		
Caruth, Josiah	1	3	3		
Cushman, Ethel	1		1		
Cheney, Ephraim	1	1	4		
Carpenter, Jabez	2	3	3		
Clark, Joseph	1	4	3		
Campbell, Samuel	2		4		
Campbell, Saml., Junr.	1	2	3		
Campbell, David	1		3		
Clark, Nathan	2	1	3		
Cornish, Gabriel	1		1		
Cornish, Benja.	1	2	2		
Carpenter, Abram.	1	1	3		
Johnson, Cook	1		4		
Cunningham, John	2	1	4		
Carr, Samuel	1		3		
Cheney, Timothy	3	5	2		
Chatterton, Isaac	1	2	3		
Chatterton, Wait	2	2	3		
Cobin, Zebediah	2	1	2		
Cobin, Nathaniel	1	2	3		
Capron, Benjamin	1	5	2		
Cushman, Frederic	2	2	4		
Coleburn, John	1	1	2		
Dewey, Jeremiah	3	2	5		
Dewey, Barzillai	2	2	1		
Dewey, Jeremiah, Jr.	1	2	2		
Daniels, Nathl.	3	1	3	1	
De Land, Rufus	1	2	2		
Eddy, Josiah	2	2	1		
Fuller, Asa	1	5	4		
Fenton, John	2	1	5		
Fenton, Matthew	1	2	2		
Fin, John	1	3	2		
Fin, David	2		4		
Fitch, John	1	3	5		
Gray, Samuel	1	3	3		
Gove, Nathanael	4	1	2		
Graham, A. John	3		2	1	
Greene, Daniel	2	6	1		
Graves, Asa	4		4		
Gates, Nehamiah	4	2	6		
Grinold, Noah	1	2	1		
Graham, Robert	1	2	3		
Giddons, Dan	1	1	4		
Goodridge, Amos	1	2	5		
Gill, Obadiah	1				
Harmon, Oliver	1	2	3		
Heywood, Ebenezer	2	2	2		
Harman, Reuben	1		1		
Hart, Josiah	2	2	1		
Harris, Israel	3	4	7		
Harred, Clark	1	1	2		
Hicock, Aaron	4	3	4		
Hymes, Amos	3	3	5		
Hale, Thomas	2	2	5		
Hulett, John	1	2	4		
Hobbs, Jacob	3	1	4		

RUTLAND COUNTY—Continued.

NAME OF HEAD OF FAMILY.	Free white males of 16 years and upward, including heads of families.	Free white males under 16 years.	Free white females, including heads of families.	All other free persons.	Slaves.
RUTLAND TOWN—con.					
Hendrick, Asa	2	1	2		
Hibbard, Ebenezer	1	1	2		
Hibbard, Augustin	1	6	2		
Hale, William	1				
Hale, Asa	2		5		
Humphrey, Willis	1	2	4		
How, John	1	2	1		
How, Amasa	1	1	1		
Hanes, Lemuel	2	1	5		
Johnson, Libbeus	1	4	2		
Johnson, John	1	3	2		
Johnson, Silas	1		2		
Johnson, Benjamin	2	5	3		
Kitcham, John	2	2	6		
Keeler, Jesse	2		2		
Keeler, Lott	2		2		
Keeler, Joseph	3	1	3		
Humphrey, Amherst	1	1	2		
Keeler, Ely	2	1	1		
Kingsly, Phinehas	2	2	7		
Ladd, Henry	1	1	2		
Ladd, Harman	1		1		
Lister, Simon	2	1	1		
Lilly, Turner	1	2	3		
Lilly, Richard	1	1	3		
Lee, Thomas	2		1		
Lee, Ashbell	1	1	2		
Long, Levi	1	3	1		
Long, Jesse	1		1		
Lewis, Abner	1	1	1		
McConnell, Saml	3		3		
Molthrop, Jude	1	2	2		
Moon, Thomas	1	5	3		
Meeds, James	3	1	2		
Meeds, Abner	1	4	3		
Moses, Asa	1	2	3		
Moses, Ezekiel	1		2		
Moses, Shubael	1		2		
Moses, Zebulun	1		1		
Moses, Zebulun, Jur	1	4	3		
Moses, Jonah	2	1	3		
Miller, Aaron	2		5		
Moses, Elnathan	1	4	5		
Murdock, Saml	1	1	3		
Meed, Zebulun	3	1	3		
Meed, Henry	1		2		
Meed, Silas	2	2	6		
Meed, Zebulun, Jur	1		5		
Meed, Stephen	1	2	2		
Moses, John	2		2		
Morey, Philemon	1	1	3		
Moses, John, Jur	1	1	3		
Northerway, George	1	1	4		
Norton, Benjamin	1	3	4		
Nichols, Asaph	1	2	4		
Osgood, Nathan, Esq.	1	2	3		
Olvord, Oliver	1	1	2		
Patterson, Andrew	1	2	4		
Porter, Asa	2		2		
Prentice, John	6	1	4		
Perry, Daniel	1	3	2		
Post, Roswell	1	2	3		
Post, Elias	1	1	2		
Post, William	8	1	1		
Post, Noah	1	1	1		
Parsons, Bartholomew	3		1		
Purdy, Solomon	2	3	2		
Pratt, Ebenezer	1	1	3		
Pratt, Silas	2		2		
Pratt, Joshua	1		3		
Porter, Ezekiel	1	2	2		
Preston, Levi	1	1	1		
Perry, Joshua	1	3	4		
Phelps, Amos	1	4	3		
Pratt, Nathan	1	1	5		
Post, Simeon	1	1	3		
Partridge, Jonathan	2		2		
Roberts, Joel	1	1	2		
Reynolds, Joshua	3	4	4		
Reed, Issachar	1	1	3		
Ramsdale, John	4	1	3		
Roots, Guernsey	2	1	3		
Roots, Wd, Elisabeth	2	1	5		
Roberts, William	1		3		
Ratz, Wido, Jerusha		1	3		
Reed, Aaron	2	1	4		
Reynolds, Jonathan	3	4	3		
Reed, Daniel	1		2		
Staples, Asa	1	1	4		
Serjeants, Moses	1		2		
Strong, Henry	1	3	4		
RUTLAND TOWN—con.					
Steward, James	1		2		
Shaw, Luther	1	1	1		
Squire, Daniel	1		1		
Shaw, John	1		1		
Shaw, William	1		2		
Stratton, Jabez	2	2	5		
Stratton, John	1	2	3		
Smith, Solomon	3	4	3		
Smith, Samuel	1		3		
Smith, John	2		2		
Smith, Elijah	1	1	4		
Smith, John, Jur	1	4	6		
Smith, Joel	2		5		
Stowers, Nathan	2	2	2		
Southerland, Peter	5	2	5		
Southerland, James	1		5		
Southerland, John	4		4		
Strong, David	4	2	3		
Seward, Stephen	1	2	2		
Smith, John, 3rd	2	1	1		
Stowers, Joseph	1	5	5		
Stratton, Ichabod	1		1		
Tuttle, David	2	3	5		
Tuttle, Ichabod	1		1		
Tuttle, Primus	1	2	2		
Tuttle, Nathaniel	1	1	1		
Thrall, Aaron	3	1	2		
Thrall, Samuel	2		3		
Thrall, Eliphas	2		2		
Taft, Alphus	1	3	2		
Williams, Honl Sam	5	2	4		
Wheelock, Eleaser	1	1	3		
Williams, Dcctr Sam	2	2	2		
Warner, Elisha	1		1		
Whitney, Micah	1		1		
Whatney, Nathaniel	1		3		
Wyllis, Abraham	1	1	1		
Wyllys, Adam	2		3		
Wetherly, George	1	1	2		
Walker, Jedediah	4	1	3		
Williams, Stephen	1	2	2		
Whitman, Jeremiah	1	3	2		
White, Henry	1	3	3		
Whitman, Zolva	1	1	1		
Ward, Jabez	1	3	1		
Whipple, Jonathan	2		2		
Watkins, Jared	1	2	4		
Whipple, Nehemiah	2	2	4		
Whipple, Benjamin	1		1		
Whipple, David	1	1	4		
Whipple, Benja., Junr	1	4	4		
Watkins, Aaron	1		2		
Watkins, Moses	1	1	1		
Wright, Simeon	3	4	5		
Weller, Amos	1	3	6		
White, John	2	1	3		
Wheler, Obadiah	1				
SHREWSBURY TOWN.					
Aldridge, Zeba	2	4	4		
Aldridge, Solomon	1	3	3		
Ashley, Martin	3	1	3		
Allen, Joseph	1				
Barrit, Asa	1		2		
Billings, Joseph	3		2		
Barny, A. Jeffery	3	2	4		
Barny, Joseph	1	3	3		
Buckmaster, Joseph	1	2	3		
Bishop, Bethuel	1	2	4		
Bishop, Samuel	1		2		
Bishop, Robert	1	1	2		
Bishop, Jeremiah	1				
Bishop, George	2		1		
Carr, Emanuel	1	3	5		
Cass, Isaac	1	2	2		
Comstock, Eunice		1	1		
Deasanee, Martin	1	2	2		
Dennis, Samuel	1	1	1		
Dennis, Solomon	2	1	2		
Davis, John	1	2	3		
Finny, Charles	1		1		
Finny, Nathan	2	2	4		
Foster, Abijah	1		2		
Farmer, Simon	1	4	3		
Holden, David	2		1		
Cook, Uriah	1	1	2		
Fords, Charles	1				
Jones, Jonathan	1	2	4		
Jones, Archilaus	1	1	1		
Jennison, Abijah	1	3	2		
SHREWSBURY TOWN—continued.					
Knight, Amos	2	4	2		
Johnson, Elisha	1		2		
Kilburn, John	1				
Lincoln, Daniel	1	1	3		
Laland, Thomas	1	2	6		
Marsh, William	1	2	2		
Niles, David	1	3	3		
Orsburn, Isaac	1	4	3		
Orion, Jonathan	2	1	3		
Perry, David	1	1	1		
Peters, Israel	1		4		
Parker, James	1	1	2		
Parsons, Ebenezer	1	1	4		
Plummer, Asa	2				
Pope, William	1		1		
Rood, Daniel	1	2	4		
Russil, William	2	2	3		
Robertson, Ichabad	2		3		
Rogers, John	1	2	2		
Rawson, Simeon	2	3	5		
Richardson, Richard	1	2	3		
Wilson, Jacob	2		3		
Whiteman, James	1	2	1		
Wood, Joseph	2		2		
Webber, Benedict	2	2	3		
Wyman, Seth	1		1		
Wyman, Israel	1	1	6		
Wilson, Jacob, Jur	1	1	4		
White, John	1				
White, Lemuel	3	4	4		
Sparowhawk, Noah	1	1	5		
Simmons, John	1	1	1		
Smith, Ahial	2		2		
Sanderson, Moses	1	2	5		
Sanderson, Moses, Jr	1	2	2		
Smith, William	2	3	4		
Shirtliff, Heman	2		2		
Swetland, David	1	1	2		
Smith, Nehemiah	1	4	6		
Streeter, Josiah	1		2		
Smith, Elisha	1	3	1		
Zemichiple, P. John	2		2		
SUDBURY TOWN.					
Allen, Reuben	1	1	2		
Allen, Elisha	1	1	2		
Allen, Ebenezer	2		3		
Bratton, David	1	3	1		
Blanchard, Amasa	2	1	5		
Barr, Roger	1	1	1		
Bullen, Samuel	1		6		
Barker, Elisha	1	4	3		
Conker, Jonas	1	2	4		
Farrand, Benoni	1	2	4		
Foster, Zadock	3		2		
Gates, Andrus	1				
Gage, John	4	3	6		
Hall, Abner	3	3	1		
Hall, John	1	3	3		
Huff, Isaac	1	3	3		
Jackson, Aaron	1	2	2		
Jackson, Nathan	1				
Ketchum, Thos	1	5	6		
Ketchum, Platt	1	1	2		
Kingsley, David	1	2	6		
Little, Joseph	3	1	4		
Little, Joseph, 2nd	1	1	2		
Miller, Timothy	2	2	5		
Murray, Stephen	1	2	4		
Parmer, William	1	1	3		
Pond, Paul	1	3	1		
Parmer, Samuel	2		1		
Parmer, Aaron	1	1	1		
Parks, Aaron	1	2	1		
Rice, Eli	1	1	2		
Rainger, Samuel	3	2	3		
Reynolds, Peter	1	2	4		
Smith, Benjamin	1	2	1		
Smith, Danl	1	1	1		
Stone, Jeremiah	1	1	3		
Sanderson, Benja	2	1	1		
Sanders, Ashbel	1	2	2		
Towner, Shalah	1		1		
Townes, Comfort	1		3		
Smith, Phinehas	1		2		
Wood, Joseph	1	1	4		
Wood, Abel	1	3	5		
Warner, Joseph	3	1	1		
Williams, Asa	2		2		
Ricky, John	2		2		
Bush, William	1	2	1		

RUTLAND COUNTY—Continued.

NAME OF HEAD OF FAMILY.	Free white males of 16 years and upward, including heads of families.	Free white males under 16 years.	Free white females, including heads of families.	All other free persons.	Slaves.
TINMOUTH TOWN.					
Ambler, Moses	1	1	1		
Allen, Saml., Junr	1	2	2		
Andrus, Joseph	1	1	5		
Allen, Samuel	1	2	2		
Adjutant, Danl	1		1		
Andrus, Ephraim	2		1		
Adams, Amos	2	2	3		
Alkins, Isaiah	1		2		
Andrus, Moses	1		1		
Bingham, Salmon	2	2	3		
Brewster, Charles	1	1	5		
Bill, Oliver	1	2	4		
Burk, Henry	1	2	2		
Bartholomew, Isaac	1	2	3		
Bingham, Silas	1	2	3		
Blackamoor, Stephen	1	2	4		
Bell, Jonathan	2	2	2		
Ballord, Jelly	3	1	4		
Bass, Jonathan	1		1		
Brown, Isaac	1	3	3		
Babcock, Champlin	1	1	3		
Benom, Samuel	1	5	3		
Britain, Benjn	1	2	1		
Blodget, Artemas	1	5	4		
Barker, Samuel	3		2		
Briton, Thaddeus	1	2	2		
Baldwin, Joel	1		4		
Brewster, Eliphas	2	2	3		
Bingham, Oliver	3	1	4		
Bingham, Asaph	1		1		
Brewer, Jonathan	1	3	4		
Calkins, Levi	1	1	4		
Calkins, Thomas	1	2	1		
Calkins, Joseph	1	1	4		
Crampton, Neri	2	3	4		
Crampton, Augustus	1		1		
Chandler, John	2	4	3		
Chandler, Jesse	5		3		
Curtiss, Zechariah	2		3		
Clark, Elisha	4	3	3		
Campbell, Ebenezer	3	2	5		
Carpenter, Beriah	3	4	3		
Cronkhite, James	2	1	6		
Condon, Benjamin	1		1		
Chipman, Darius	5	1	6		
Chipman, Samuel	1		2		
Castle, David	1	2	4		
Chittenden, Bethuel	2		2		
Dyke, Jonathan	1	3	2		
Doolittle, Luther	1	1	4		
Dootey, Osmond	2	4	3		
Fox, Amos	1	3	2		
Fox, Elijah	1	5	3		
Fargo, Jabez	1	2	4		
Farr, Elias	2	7	5		
Fox, Oliver	1	1	1		
Fargo, Aaron	2	1	2		
Fariman, James	4	3	4		
Fargo, Jason	1	1	2		
Gillet, William	1		3		
Gillet, Abraham	1	1	3		
Gillet, Sylvester	1		2		
Gillet, Jonathan	1	3	2		
Gerrard, John	1		2		
Hooker, Roland	2	3	4		
Hamilton, Elisha	2	2	2		
Hooker, Martin	1		6		
Hamilton, Nathn	1	2	1		
Hamilton, John	2		6		
Hamilton, Aaron	1		1		
Hill, Luke	2	1	3		
Hill, Erastus	2		1		
Hurd, Daniel	2	1	3		
Hill, Zenas	2		3		
Hill, Uri	1	1	1		
Hill, Ira	1	2	2		
Hill, Zenas, Jur	1	1	2		
Hude, Stephen	1	2	2		
Hopkins, John	1	2	2		
Hazelton, Thaddeus	1	3	3		
Hazleton, Royal	1	2	2		
Harkness, John	1		2		
Hutchinson, Thos	3	1	5		
Johnson, Jacob	3	4	1		
Ives, David	1	4	2		
Johnson, Jesse	1	1	1		
Jones, Samuel	2		2		
Johnson, Lawrence	1	2	4		
Johnson, Elihu	1	2	1		
Johnson, John	1		3		
TINMOUTH TOWN—con.					
Lyn, James	1		2		
Leets, Wid Polly		4	3		
Lilly, Elijah	1	1	1		
Lacy, Isaac	1	2	3		
Lawrence, Clarke	2		5		
Loveland, Lawrençe	1	4	2		
Lingham, Robert	1		5		
Livington, James	1	2	3		
Landon, Luther	2	2	4		
Langdon, Heman	1		2		
Marvin, Ebenezer	1	2	4		
Mallocks, Samuel	6		3		
Mahama, John	1	3	2		
McLean, Samuel	1	4	1		
Mann, John	1		1		
Miles, Charles	2	5	2		
Noble, Obadiah	1	3	4		
Newhall, Joseph	1	1	4		
Newhall, Daniel	2	3	3		
Newhall, Saml	1	2	1		
Newhall, Danl., Jur.	1		1		
Nickerson, Henry	2	1	2		
Nickerson, Glon	1		3		
Osburn, Benjamin	1		3		
Pratt, John	1	1	2		
Pratt, Lemuel	2		1		
Pier, Elnathan	1	1	1		
Pier, Chauncey	1		1		
Perry, Eliakim, Jr	1	4	3		
Perry, Eliakim	1		2		
Perry, Ozias	1	1	4		
Paul, Joshua	1	1	1		
Porter, Thomas	1	1	2		
Porter, Thos., Jur	1		1	1	
Parmer, Jared	1	2	2		
Parmer, Juhoniah	1	2	1		
Parmer, Simeon	2	1	1		
Ridley, Samuel	1	1	2		
Rogers, Nehemiah	1	1	4		
Rice, Stephen	2		4		
Rice, Heber	1	1	1		
Riley, Lawrence	1	3	1		
Remington, Uri	2	2	3		
Ross, James	1	1	3		
Rice, Samuel	1	2	4		
Rice, Charles	1				
Smith, Elisha	1		4		
Smith, Cephas	2		2		
Smith, Joseph	1	1	2		
Shepherd, Ralph	1		1		
Shepherd, Jonan., Jur.	1		4		
Spafford, John	3	4	5		
Swift, Barney	3	1	2		
Smith, Abraham	1	3	3		
Sweet, James	2		1		
Sweet, John	2		1		
Southward, Obadiah	1	2	3	1	
Southward, Joshua	1	1	3		
Sheffield, Ichabod	1		1		
Shepherd, Jonathan	1	2	2		
Shuts, Simeon	1	1	1		
Shepherd, David	1	2	3		
Swift, Heman	1	2	4		
Taylor, Eldad	1		1		
Thomson, Jonathan	3		4		
Tift, Royal	1	1	1		
Tift, John	1	1	2		
Train, Orange	1	1	7		
Turner, Samuel	2		1		
Thomas, John	1		2		
Utley, Elisha	1	2	1		
White, Gregory	1	2	3		
Wentworth, Edward	1		3		
Willman, William	1	2	1		
White, Philip	1		1		
White, Nehemiah	1	1	2		
Wheeler, John	2		2		
Willford, Joseph	1	3	3		
White, Zephaniah	1	3	4		
Wills, L. Thomas	1	1	1		
Van, William	4	1	6		
WALLINGFORD TOWN.					
Aeyre, Oziel	2	1	2		
Adams, Alden	1		5		
Button, Stanley	3	1	7		
Bumpus, James	3	2	4		
Benson, Joseph	3	2	4		
Benson, Roland	1		1		
WALLINGFORD TOWN—continued.					
Bradley, Benjamin	2	1	2		
Bumpus, Edward	2	3	5		
Bull, Crispin	1	2	6		
Brawton, John	1	5	4		
Burr, Samuel	1	3	5		
Barber, Hoxy	1		1		
Crary, Elias	2	2	2		
Crary, William	1	4	2		
Crandall, Luke	1	2	4		
Clark, Gardner	3		1		
Clark, Edmund	1	3	4		
Clark, Chauncy	1		3		
Clark, Jonah	1		2		
Clark, Stephen	1	5	3		
Clark, Goodyear	1	3	5		
Clark, John	1	1	2		
Clark, Salmon	1		1		
Davis, James	1	2	2		
Davis, Andrew	1		1		
Dumoon, Ichabod	1	2	3		
Dickerson, Simeon	2		2		
Douglass, Willm	1				
Dolly, Pedigreen	1	5	2		
Fox, William	2	2	4		
Finny, Isaac	1	1	1		
Freeman, Daniel	1		1		
Fish, Isaac	1		1		
Forbs, Charles	2				
Green, Henry	2	2	4		
Hinman, John	1		1		
Hill, John	2	2	5		
Hill, Caleb	1		2		
Hammond, Jedh	1	1	1		
Hull Zephaniah	3		3		
Hale, Abner	2		2		
Harrington, Jacob	1	2	5		
Hale, Jonathan	3		6		
Hammond, Jedh	1	1	1		
Ives, Amos	1	2	7		
Ives, Ebenezer	1				
Ives, Jonah	1				
Ives, Nathaniel	2	2	6		
Ives, Lent	2		3		
Jackson, Joseph	1		2		
Jenny, Aaron	2	2	3		
Jackson, Jethro	1	4	3		
Jackson, Asahel	2	1	4		
Jackson, Jedediah	2	1	5		
Jackson, Abraham	6	5	5	1	
Jones, William	2	4	4		
Jackson, Stephen	3		4		
Kinny, Benoni	1	1	3		
Kinny, Seth	1	2	2		
Kingsley, Sylvanus	1	3	4		
Kent, Charles	1	2	3		
Lamb, Ebenezer	1	2	2		
Loomis, Solomon	1	1	4		
Mighell, Ezekiel	2		1		
Miles, Eleaser	2		5		
Miller, Solomon	2		2		
Mix, Thomas	1	4	4		
Miller, Thomas	1	1	4		
Miller, Thomas, Jr	1	1	1		
Negro, Jim				2	
Preston, Coleburn	2	2	1		
Randall, Joseph	3		2		
Richmond, Gerge	2	1	2		
Richmond, Eliakim	1		1		
Robbins, John	2		5		
Russell, Samuel, Jr	1	1	2		
Russell, John	2	3	3		
Randall, John	1	1	5		
Randall, Joseph	2	2	2		
Sherman, George	1	3	4		
Swift, Phililus	1		2		
Sweet, William	1	2	3		
Swift, Samuel	1	2	3		
Swift, Charles	1	3	3		
Swift, Samuel, 2nd	1		2		
Tift, Samuel	1	3	1		
Wily, John	1	2	1		
Whitehorn, John	2		2		
Wilcox, Jacob	1	3	4		
Wilcox, Thomas	1				
Wilcox, Benjn	1				
Yaw, Joseph	1		3		
Van, George	1	3	3		
Whipple, Jeremiah	2	1	2		
Jenny, George	1		1		
Arnold, John	1	1	3		

RUTLAND COUNTY—Continued.

NAME OF HEAD OF FAMILY.	Free white males of 16 years and upward, including heads of families.	Free white males under 16 years.	Free white females, including heads of families.	All other free persons.	Slaves.
WELLS TOWN.					
Andrus, Richard	1	1	1		
Baker, Seth	4	1	5		
Briggs, Jonathan	1	3	1		
Butlen, Joseph	1	3	3		
Beardsly, Emanuel	1	1	2		
Beardsly, Beverly	1		1		
Birch, Jonathan	1		5		
Bellamy, Lydia			2		
Broyhten, John	2		3		
Blossom, David	1	3	5		
Blossom, Abigail			2		
Blossom, Peter	1	3	4		
Beardsley, Andrew	2	2	5		
Blackman, Elijah	1		1		
Bellamy, Samuel	1	1	2		
Clemons, Michael	2		3		
Clemons, Joel	1	1	2		
Cross, Daniel	2		1		
Condor, William	1	2	1		
Cone, Abner	3	2	4		
Cone, Enoch	1		2		
Cole, Zebulun	3		2		
Cook, Childs	1	4	3		
Carpenter, Woodbery	1	1	1		
Cole, Amos	1	1	2		
Culver, Joshua	2	1	4		
Culver, Samuel	1	4	1		
Clark, Andrew	1	3	6		
Clark, Stephen	3	1	6		
Calkins, Aaron	1		1		
Calkins, Caleb	1	2	6		
Clark, Roswell	2	2	2		
Culver, Daniel	1		5		
Darby, Azariah	1	1	3		
Dolittle, Rueben	1	2	1		
Doud, Seth	1		1		
Doud, Jesse	1	2	3		
Doud, Samuel	1	1	2		
Dewry, Elias	1		2		
WELLS TOWN—con.					
Francis, Simon	2	3	3		
Francis, John	1		4		
Francis, Thankful		2	4		
Francis, Nathan	1	1	5		
Freeman, Gideon	1		2		
Francis, Daniel	1		2		
Francis, Sarah	1		1		
Goodsill, Danl	1		3		
Glass, Rufus	1	2	4		
Glass, Samuel	1	2	2		
Giddings, Benjamin	1	3	4		
Gutridge, Daniel	2	3	4		
Geers, Alba	1	1	1		
Gifford, Gershom	2	3	3		
Hambleton, John	1	1	3		
How, Joshua	2	1	2		
How, Samuel	1	2	1		
Holt, Epiphas	1	2	2		
Hill, James	2	1	5		
Hill, Caleb	1	1	3		
How, David	1	2	6		
Hunt, William	1		1		
Henshaw, Wm., Jur	1		2		
Henshaw, William	2	5	1		
Johnson, Comfort	1	2	2		
Johnson, Israel	1	2	3		
Jones, Nathan	1	2	1		
Ives, Aaron	1	2	3		
Lamb, Joseph	2	1	1		
Lewis, Nathaniel	1	4	3		
Lathrop, Zaccheus	1		1		
Lane, Allen	1	2	2		
Lewis, William	1	2	2		
Lewis, Uriah	1	2	2		
Lewis, David	3	2	2		
Lathrop, Samuel	1	1	1		
Lathrop, Thomas	1	9	5		
Lewis, Jacob	2	2	3		
Lownesbrough, Danl	1	4	2		
WELLS TOWN—con.					
Lovel, Joseph	1	4	4		
Law, John	2	3	3		
Merritt, Halliwell	1	2	2		
McGrith, Thomas	2	2	3		
Merrills, Nathaniel	1	1	2		
Moss, Timothy	1		2		
Merriman, Saml	1	1	2		
Merriman, Abel	1		1		
McIntosh, Danl	1	1	2		
Mallory, Gill	1	2	3		
Paul, James	2		2		
Parker, Elijah	2	2	3		
Parsons, Jesse	1	1	4		
Pember, John	1	4	5		
Pray, John	2				
Preston, Moses	1	1	2		
Pond, Benjamin	1	1	2		
Summer, Persie			1		
Snow, Jonathan	2		3		
Summer, Danl	1		2		
Summer, Shubal	2	2	2		
Smith, Eleazer	1	1	2		
Stephens, Peter	2	4	3		
Stephens, Asa	1	2	3		
Stephens, Abner	1	1	1		
Stephens, James	1		3		
Shumway, John	1	3	4		
Silly, Joseph	1		1		
Woodworth, Roswel	1	2	3		
Ward, David	2	4	3		
Way, John	1		2		
Warren, Nathan	2	3	2		
Wilton, Ebenezer	1		2		
Wyman, Elizabeth	3	3	4		
Wilcox, Saml	1	4	2		
Wyman, Danl	1	1	3		
Williams, John	2	1			

WINDHAM COUNTY.

NAME OF HEAD OF FAMILY.	Free white males of 16 years and upward, including heads of families.	Free white males under 16 years.	Free white females, including heads of families.	All other free persons.	Slaves.
ATHENS TOWN.					
Alexander, Thaddeus	1	1	2		
Atwood, Saml	1		2		
Beale, Wm	3	2	5		
Blanden, Leml	1	1	5		
Blanden, John	1	1	3		
Bunden, John	1	1	1		
Bullen, Joseph	2	3	5		
Bayley, Saml	1	4	3		
Chafee, Alvord	1				
Cobleigh, Danl	1	2	5		
Chafee, Ezra	3	1	8		
Chafee, David	1		2		
Carpenter, Timo	1	2	1		
Chipman, Cyrus	1	2	1		
Chapman, Israel	1	4	2		
Crafferd, John	1	2	4		
Crafferd, John, Junr	1	1	3		
Chase, Henry	1	1	1		
Chapman, Ezekl	1	5	2		
Davis, Simeon	2	1	2		
Darry, Abraham	1	2	3		
Denny, Peter	1	3	5		
Denny, Lucius	1				
Devenport, Wm	1	3	1		
Evans, Simon	2	3	4		
Ellmore, Elijah	1	3	4		
Evelith, David	1		2		
Field, Reuben	1	3	3		
Fuller, Danl	1		3		
Foster, Jona	2		2		
Fisher, Gideon	1	2	3		
Fasset, Jesse	1	1	2		
Fletcher, Benja	2		2		
French, David	1	3	3		
Freeman, John	1	2	2		
Farrington, Stephen	1	2	2		
Gray, Jonas	2		3		
Green, Absulum	1	1	1		
Holden, Ephm	1		7		
Hooker, S. Israel	1	2	4		
Hartwell, John	1	3	3		
Knapp, Widow		1	3		
Keyes, Jonas	1	2	3		
Lovejoy, Benja	2	2	3		
Martin, Sylvanus	1	1	2		
ATHENS TOWN—con.					
Nichols, Widow	2	1	3		
Nichols, James	1	4	2		
Merrit, Joseph	1		1		
Oak, Calvin	1	1	3		
Oak, Nathl	1		1		
Oak, Thos	1				
Oak, Seth	1		1		
Oak, John	1	1	1		
Porter, Joshua	1	1	1		
Porter, George	1	1	1		
Perham, Joel	1	3	1		
Perham, Jona	1		4		
Perham, Leonard	1		1		
Richmond, Amariah	1		2		
Robinson, John	1	2	2		
Roger, John	1	1	3		
Robinson, Elijah	1	4	2		
Shafter, James	1	3	4		
Skinner, Wm	1	1	2		
Skinner, Eliphalet	1	3	2		
Skinner, Zachariah	1	4	2		
Stanhope, Peter	1	4	4		
Tinckham, Jerh	2	2	3		
Thayer, Zephb	1	2	2		
Tarbel, Zachh	1	1	2		
Underwood, Joseph	1	3	2		
Walker, Timo	4	2	2		
Walker, Timo. Junr	1	2	1		
Whipple, Jabez	1		2		
Whitney, Ezra	2		2		
Whitney, Ezra, Junr	1	2	2		
Wright, Thos	2	1	3		
Welman, Timo	2	1	2		
Welman, Isaac	1	3	1		
Welman, Timo., Junr	1	3	3		
Whitcomb, Silas, Junr	2	4	4		
Welman, Ebenr	1	2	2		
Welman, Darius	1		4		
Wheat, Joseph	1	3	2		
BRATTLEBORO TOWN.					
Arms, Josiah	6	4	8		
Allen, Elnathan	4		3		
Avery, Wm	2		1		
BRATTLEBORO TOWN—continued.					
Alexander, John	2	1	8		
Akeley, Thos	1	3	3		
Adams, Nathan	1	1	6		
Avery, Wm., Junr	1				
Blakeley, Nathl	1	2	3		
Blakeley, James	2		1		
Butterfield, Jesse	1	4	3		
Bennet, John	1				
Bennet, Stephen	3	1	2		
Blakeley, Danl	1	1	2		
Bumpus, Isaac	1	4	4		
Burnham, Nathl	1		1		
Bigelow, David	1	3	3	1	
Baker, Benja	1	3	5		
Briggs, Solomon	1	5	3		
Burt Joseph	1		1		
Burnham, John	1	1	3		
Bemis, John	1	5	3		
Butterfield, Benja	2	2	4		
Briggs, Gideon	1	3	4		
Barret, Isaac	1	3	5		
Briggs Saml	1	2	4		
Bennet, Noah	3	2	6		
Blake W. John	3		2		
Briggs, Levi	1				
Basset, Joseph	1	4	2		
Briggs, Elisha	1		2		
Baker, Fredrick	1		2		
Bond, Thos	1		2		
Blair, John	3				
Burnham, Lem'	1	2	3		
Blasdale, Wm	1				
Bayley, Dudley	1	4	2		
Badger, Gideon	2	4	5		
Brush, Solomon	1		1		
Carpenter, John	1	2	4		
Cole, Nathl	1	3	4		
Chase, Benja	1	6	1		
Covell, Peter	1	2	2		
Church, Jona	3	3	5		
Cook, Oliver	3	2	2		
Chamberlain, Joseph	2	2	2		
Clark, Joseph	4	4	5		
Chandler, Henry	1		5		
Church, Malachi	1	1	4		

WINDHAM COUNTY—Continued.

NAME OF HEAD OF FAMILY.	Free white males of 16 years and upward, including heads of families.	Free white males under 16 years.	Free white females, including heads of families.	All other free persons.	Slaves.
BRATTLEBORO TOWN—continued.					
Church, Timo	3	2	4		
Church, Josiah	3	2	3		
Chandler, Nathl	1	3	1		
Chandler, Saml	1	1	3		
Church, Eber	1		3		
Church, Eber, Junr	1				
Crosby, Isaac	3	4	3		
Croswell, Peter	1	2	8		
Church, Reuben	1	2	5		
Cook, Solomon	1		3		
Carter, Benja	2	2	5		
Chandler, Gardiner	4	2	3		
Cune, Wm	2		4		
Cune, Wm., Junr	1	2	4		
Chappel, John	2		4		
Cune, Isaac	1	4	3		
Cook, Joseph	1	4	1		
Carpenter, Saml	2	3	3		
Cranny, Wm	2	2	4		
Castle, Peter	1	3	2	1	
Castle, Joseph	1	2	1		
Croswell, Elias	1	4	1		
Cole, Henry	1	3	2	10	
Dogget, Asa					
Dickerman, Leml	2	2	7		
Dickerman, John	2	1	1		
Dunkley, Jona	1	2	5		
Dunkley, Joseph	1	3	3		
Dudley, Benajah	1	1	1		
Dickerman, John, Junr	1	2	2		
Dickinson, Saml	6	1	5		
Easterbrook, Warren	2	4	4		
Ellis, Benja	1	3	1		
Ellis, John	1	1	3		
Ellis, Simpson	3	3	6		
Eaton, Simeon	1	3	4		
Evans, Wm	1	5	1		
Easterbrook, Benja	3	1	5		
Evans, Widow	2		2		
Earl, Saml	1		1		
Evans, Imry	1		3		
Ferrand, Andrew	1	3	1		
Fisher, Ebenr	2	1	8		
Fox, Ebenr	1	1	4		
Frost, Danl	1	4	2		
Frost, Jesse	1	2	3		
Frost, Jesse, Junr	1	2	5		
Fuller, Joseph	1	5	4		
Frazer, Danl	3		8		
French, Nathl	1		1		
French, John	1		3		
French, Asa	1	4	2		
Fisk, Isaiah	1	1	2		
Frost, Asa	1				
Field, Bennet	1	2	5		
Gale, Isaac	2		4		
Greenleaf, Stephen	1	3	4		
Goodenow, Jona	2	3	4		
Gould, John	1	4	3		
Grout, Abel	1	4	3		
Guernsey, Saml	1	1	2		
Greenleaf, Stephen, Junr	1	1	2		
Gorton, Benja	2	1	1		
Greenleaf, Danl	1	1	1		
Greenleaf, Saml	1				
Goddard, Moses	1	4	3		
Gardiner, Abner	2		2		
Gould, Nathan	2	2	5		
Gould, Benja	1	3	2		
Goodenow, Levi	1	3	1		
Goodale, Joseph	1		1		
How, Artemas	3		4		
Harris, Valentine	1	1	2		
Haws, Ebenr	1	3	6		
Harris, Calvin	1	1	1		
Hadley, Jesse	1	5	2		
Hail, Wm	2	1	2		
Hall, Josiah	1	4	5		
Harris, Oliver	1	1	3		
How, Joseph	1	1	2		
Houghton, Hiram	2	2	2		
Houghton, Philemon	1	1	3		
Harris, Joshua	1	5	2		
Houghton, John	2	2	2		
Hadley, Jacob	1	1	1		
Harris, ——	1	1	2		
Houghton, Peter	1	2	3		
Harris, Wm	1	1	3		
Hadley, Ebenr	2		2		
Hays, Rutherford	1	3	4		
Holton, Wm	3	1	2		
Herrick, Jona	3	3	5		
Hopkins, John	2	2	6		
Hager, Widow		3	3		
Harris, James	1	5	2		
Houghton, James	1				
Hopkins, Jeremiah	1	1	3		
Houghton, Phinehas	1		3		
Houghton, Nehh	1	4	4		
Harris, Welman	1		2		
Haven, Nathl	1		2		
Kelsey, John	1	2	1		
Knap, David	1	2	4		
Knight Saml	3	2	6		
Kendall, Isaac	1	2	3		
Knap, James	2	1	5		
Knap, Ebenr	1		1		
King, Wm	2	1	2		
King, Adonijah	2	1	2		
King, Cushing	1	1	1		
Knight, Seth	1	1	1		
King, Ezra	1	3	1		
Lamb, Peter	1	4	2		
Lawton, James					
Mixer, Saml	1	3	5		
Mixer, Danl	1	1	2		
Munro, Rosbotham	3	2	1		
Morgan, Wm	1				
Morgan, Caleb	2	3	4		
Martin, Mathew	2		3		
May, David	1	2	3		
May, Saml	1				
Mills, Widow		1	2		
Nash, Oliver	1	2	4		
Nash, Moses	1	1	4		
Nash, Aaron	1	4	3		
Nash, Ephm	1	1	3		
Newton, Saml	2		6		
Nobles, Saml	1	1	5		
Nichols, Saml	1		7		
Owin, Saml	1				
Otis, James	1	1	3		
Plummer, John	3	2	5		
Packard, Caleb	2	3	4		
Peabody, Jona	1	2	1		
Prouty, Elijah	2	2	4		
Paddleford, Philip	3	4	4		
Prince, Nathan	1		2		
Prince, Elisha	2	4	4		
Prouty, Francis	3		4		
Putman, Asa	2	4	2		
Pettis, John	1	2	7		
Prince, Nathan, Junr	1		3		
Pratt, Benja	1	2	5		
Redfield, Levi	2	3	2		
Rice, James	1	1	2		
Root, Saml	3	1	5		
Rice, Ephm	1		3		
Rice, Widow		1	1		
Reaves, Abner	2	2	3		
Smith, Jona	2		2		
Salsbury, Barnard	2	4	3		
Salsbury, Oliver	2	1	3		
Simonds, Abel	1	1	5		
Scovel, Abner	2		2		
Stoddard, Jona	1		3		
Stoddard, Jona, Junr	1	1	3		
Stoddard, Jacob	1	1	1		
Salsbury, Hale	1		3		
Steward, Danl., Junr	1		6		
Sharns, Reuben	1	3	4		
Steward, John	2	3	5		
Stockwell, Jesse	1	3	2		
Smith, Levi	3	4	1		
Salsbury, Widow		4	3		
Steward, Benja	3		2		
Stebbins, Zebediah	1		3		
Stebbins, Levi	1	1	2		
Sawyer, Joshua	1		3		
Salsbury, Hezh	1	4	3		
Sargeant, Thos	4	1	3		
Sargeant, John	4	1	5		
Sargeant, Eli	1	2	3	1	
Spalding, Jacob	1		2		
Shelden, Elijah	1		3		
Smith, Noah	3	1	2		
Scovil, Abner, Junr	1		1		
Smith, Josiah	1				
Sawtwell, Sylvanus	1		6		
Shelden, Solomon	1	1	4		
Salsbury, Jon	2	3	2		
Snow, Danl	1	3	3		
Thurber, Warden	1				
Toogood, Danl	1	2	1		
Townsend, Micah	3	4	7		
Tute, Moses	1		3		
Tubbs, Ezra	2	3	5		
Tute, Ziba	1		2		
Wells, David	1	1	3		
Wilder, Charles	1	3	2		
Wilder, Abiel	1		2		
Walkup, Thos	1		1		
Wells, John	1	1	3		
Woods, Jabez	1	5	2		
Woods, Philip	1	2	4		
Wells, Oliver	1	3	2		
Warner, Saml	2	2	6	1	
Wilder, Joshua	3	1	7		
Wilder, Peter	3	3	3		
Whipple, Wm	2		2		
Wells, Saml	1	2	3		
Welman, Saml	1	2	3		
Warner, Adreal	1	1	3		
Ware, Jesse	1				
Wood, Jabez	1		1		
Whipple, Danl	1	3	4		
Wells, Robert	1		1		
Wright, Sawyer	1	1	4		
Wilder, Tilly	1		6		
Wilder, Elias	1		1		
Williams, Widow	2		2		
Whitney, Leml	1	3	3		
DUMMERSTON TOWN.					
Aldrich, Eleazar	1				
Alvord, Benja	2	2	5		
Allen, Josiah	1	1	4		
Aldrich, Moses	1		1		
Allen, Josiah, Junr	1		1		
Black, John	1	3	3		
Burnham, Gideon	2	2	3		
Bigelow, Isaac	1	1	2		
Brown, Elijah	1	1	3		
Baker, Thos	1	2	5		
Ballard, Sylvanus	1		1		
Boyden, Josiah	1	1	2		
Brooks, Aaron, Junr	2	4	3		
Boyden, Isaac	2	2	2		
Boyden, Jona	1	1	1		
Bemis, Philip	1		1		
Butler, Jabez	1	1	2		
Butler, Abel	1	1	3		
Baldwin, John	1	2	5		
Bartlett, John	1	2	3		
Bennet, John	1	1	3		
Boyden, Wm	2	1	3		
Butler, Calvin	2	1	3		
Bemis, Joseph	1	1	4		
Bemis, David	3	2	2		
Bemis, Joshua	1	1	4		
Burrows, Jona	1	3	2		
Beale, Stephen	1				
Briggs, Seth	1		3		
Bennet, Saml	1	3	3		
Bennet, Joseph	1	1	3		
Butterfield, Luke	1	1	2		
Butterfield, Ezra	1	5	3		
Baits, Cornelius	1		3		
Burnet, Isaac	1	2	3		
Baker, Jonas	1	2	3		
Blodget, Josiah	1	2	2		
Belknap, Calvin	2	1	2		
Bennet, Stephen	1	1	1		
Belknap, Asa	1				
Black, John	2	2	4		
Ball, Moses	1	4	3		
Ball, Nathan	1	3	3		
Burbank, Elias	1		3		
Burnham, Thos	1	1	5		
Bemis, Elias	1	1	2		
Bigelow, Paul	1	1	3		
Bryant, Micah	1				
Cole, John	1	1	3		
Cutler, Zachh	2	1	4		
Cook, Nathan	1		2		
Cresey, Henry	1	1	2		
Cook, Solo	2		2		
Clark, Thos	1	5	4		
Crofford, Wm	1	1	3		
Childs, Jona	1	1	2		
Cutler, Moses	1	1	2		
Carrol, Joseph	3	3	4		

WINDHAM COUNTY—Continued.

NAME OF HEAD OF FAMILY.	Free white males of 16 years and upward, including heads of families.	Free white males under 16 years.	Free white females, including heads of families.	All other free persons.	Slaves.
DUMMERSTON TOWN—continued.					
Crosby, Aaron	1	1	3		
Childs, Isaac	1	2	5		
Childs, Moses	1		3		
Cook, Enoch, Junr	2		2		
Crofford, John	1				
Carrol, Asa	2	2	3		
Devenport, Asa	1		2		
Devenport, Danl	1	1	3		
Davis, Danl	1	2	1		
Dutton, Stephen	1	3	2		
Duncan, Jason	2	4	2		
Duncan, Saml	2	2	7		
Dutton, David	1	3	2		
Dutton, Saml, Junr	2		6		
Dutton, Asa	2	1	6		
Devenport, Leml	2		1		
Devenport, Charles, Junr	1	2	3		
Duncan, Seth	1	3	4		
Devenport, Amos	1	1	2		
Duncan, Widow			3		
Easterbrook, Benja	1	3	4		
Evans, Oliver	2		2		
French, Micah	2	2	3		
Fitts, Abraham	2		6		
Fuller, Job	3	2	2		
Fairchild, Silas	1	2	3		
French, Nathl	1	4	4		
French, Micah, Junr	2	1	1		
Flarette, ——		4	3		
Fisher, Ichabod	1	1	6		
Freeman, Adam	1	1	1		
Gibbs, Edmond	1	1	1		
Glazier, Benja	1	1	3		
Graham, Leml	1	1	2		
Graham, Caleb	1	1	2		
Goddard, Levi	1				
Gates, Danl	1	5	4		
Gates, S. John	2	4	4		
Gowen, Saml	1	1	3		
Graham, Andrew	1	1	1		
Griffith, Ellis	1		3		
Gleason, Joseph	1	2	5		
Gibb, Saml	1		1		
Goss, Danl	1				
Gould, Ebenr	1	1	2		
Graham, John	1		1		
Higgins, Peletiah	1	1	1		
Haven, Abel	2	2	4		
Hudson, Seth	3	1	8		
Hall, Ephm	2	1	3		
How, Benja	1	3	4		
Hildreth, Joseph	3	1	5		
Haskell, Andrew	1	1	2		
Haven, Ebenr	2		3		
Hildreth, Jesse	1	2	1		
Hildreth, Joseph, Junr	1	1	3		
Holton, Arad	1	3	2		
Hartwell, Oliver	1	4	2		
Hilliard, Joseph	1		2		
Holmes, Nathl	1	1	3		
Haven, Joseph	1		2		
Hadley, Benja	1				
How, Saml	1		1		
Hazen, Edwd	1	2	2		
Hibbard, Danl	1	5	4		
Holden, Joseph	1	1	2		
Hazen, Silas	1	2	1		
Healy, James	1	1	2		
Hazen, Edwd	3	3	3		
Hill, Isaac	1		2		
How, Widow			3		
Hill, John	1	1	1		
Higgins, Uriah	2	3	2		
Hildreth, Wilson	1		1		
Higgins, Joseph	1	1	2		
Johnson, Simeon	1	1	2		
Johnson, Ashbel	2	3	5		
Jones, Cornelius	1	1	6		
Jones, Aaron	1	4	1		
Jones, Benja., Junr	1	1	8		
Jones, Benja	1		1		
Johns, Abel	1		4		
Johnson, Solomon	3		1		
Knap, Ichabod	2	3	4		
Knight, Joel	1		3		
Kathan, Alexr	3	1	3		
Knight, Saml	1	3	3		
Knight, Jesse	1	2	4		
Kelly, Alexr	1	1	4		
Kelly, Richd	1		2		
Kelly, Saml	2	2	3		
DUMMERSTON TOWN—continued.					
Kathan, Danl	3	1	5		
Kathan, John	4	2	4		
Kathan, Charles	1	2	2		
Kilsbury, John	3		1		
Kathan, Danl., Junr	1	2	2		
Kathan, John, Junr	1	1			
Kelly, Wm	2	4	4		
Knight, Jona	2		2		
Kellogg, Josiah	1	2	3		
Kingsbury, Eleazar	1	3	1		
Knight, Levi	1		2		
Knap, ——	1	1	2		
Kendrick, Heth	1	2	2		
Leonard, Wm	1		1		
Livermore, Jonas, Junr	1	3	2		
Lawton, Thos	2	1	4		
Lawton, Saml., Junr	2		5		
Lawton, Jacob	1	3	2		
Lawton, Jacob, Junr	1	1	2		
Larrabee, John	3		2		
Lawton, James	1				
Lindsey, Peter	1	2	2		
Livermore, Jonas	1		1		
Luster, Wm	1	1	3		
Lamb, Widow		2	2		
Miller, Vespalian, 2nd	1		1		
Miller, Hozea	4	1	5		
Miller, Wm	2	3	5		
Miller, Isaac	1	2	4		
McWain, John	2	1	2		
Middleditch, Wm	1	2	5		
Miller, Marshal	1	6	4		
Manley, Jesse	1	3	5		
Miller, Joseph	1	3	3		
Metcalf, John	1				
Manley, James	2	2	5		
McManes, Patrick	1	1	4		
Miller, Vespn	1	3	3		
Merick, Ebenr	1	1	3		
Marsh, John	1	1	1		
Manley, John	1		1		
Mann, James	1	1	1		
Mann, Timo	2	2	1		
Mann, Nathl	1		1		
Nichols, Saml	1		2		
Nichols, James	2	2	2		
Negus, Wm	2	1	5		
Nichols, John	1	1	2		
Negus, Saml., Junr	1		1		
Nurse, Solomon	1	2	5		
Newton, Charles	3		3		
Nurse, Wm	1	2	5		
Newton, Thaddeus	2		3		
Presson, Lemuel	1	3	3		
Presson, Benja	2	1	1		
Pierce, Wm	2	2	3		
Powers, Elijah	1		4		
Page, Jona	2	2	2		
Philips, Enos	2	2	2		
Philips, John	1				
Peters, Danl	1	1	3		
Rice, Ephm	1	1	2		
Rice, Amos	3	1	4		
Rider, David	1	2	1		
Richardson, Ephm	1	3	5		
Rhoads, Eleazar	1		1		
Rhoads, Ebenr	1	1	3		
Rhoads, John	2	4	2		
Rice, Ezekl	1	2	3		
Rice, Abraham	1	2	3		
Rice, Asa	1		1		
Randal, Robert	1	1	2		
Ramsdel, Robt	1		3		
Spaldin, Reuben	1				
Sargeant, Elihu, 2nd	1				
Sargeant, Elihu	1	4	3		
Stroud, Wm	1	3	4		
Spaldin, John	1				
Sargeant, Rufus	1	4	3		
Shaw, Joseph	1	3	2		
Shaw, Benja	1	1	1		
Stevens, Henry	1	1	2		
Sargeant, Wm	3	4	4		
Simpson, Amos	3	5	1		
Smith, Seth	2	2	4		
Stockwell, Joel	1		4		
Stockwell, Jonas	1	3	2		
Sargeant, Caleb	1		1		
Swear, Danl	1	4	3		
Stroud, John	2	1	2	10	
Stratton, Jona	1	3	3		
DUMMERSTON TOWN—continued.					
Spaldin, Widow	1		2		
Sargeart, Danl	1				
Shaw, Bala	1	3	1		
Town, D. David	1	1	3		
Temple, Joseph	2	1	3		
Town, Abner	2		2		
Town, Elijah, Junr	3	1	5		
Taft, Silas	3	1	3		
Taylor, Isaac	1		2		
Taylor, Ebenr	1	1	3		
Thompson, Saml	1	2	5		
Thompson, Beaman	1	1	2		
Thompson, Wm	1		4		
Taft, Asahel	1	1	6		
Taylor, Danl	2	1	3		
Tarbel, Eleazar	1		3		
Twitchel, Joshua	1	1	4		
Whitney, Benja	1		6		
Wyman, Wm	1	3	4		
Wilder, Saml	1	3	2		
Walker, Jonas	1	5	2		
Wood, Archibald	1	1	3		
Willard, Andrew	1	1	2		
Wilder, Elias	1	5	3		
Willard, Henry	1	1	2		
Wyman, John, Junr	1	2	3		
Wyman, John	1	1	2		
Wait, Ebenr	2	2	2		
Wakefield, Saml	1	3	2		
Wood, Jotham	2	1	1		
Whiting, Adam	1	1	6		
Whipple, John	1	1	2		
Wood, Jona	1	4	4		
Woodbury, Stephen	1				
GUILFORD TOWN.					
Armsbee, Caleb	1				
Ayers, Danl	2	3	5		
Ashcraft, Danl	3	2	3		
Akeley, John	1	1	2		
Aldrich, Jona	2	5	8		
Ayers, Levi	1				
Avery, Nathan	1		5		
Aldrich, Peter	1	3	6		
Allen, Saml	2	2	6	1	
Aldrich, Jona	1		1		
Aylesworth, Robert	3		2		
Aylesworth, Job	1				
Andrews, Nehh	1	5	2		
Ayers, Solomon	1		2		
Aldrich, Joseph	2	2	3		
Alvord, Seth	1	2	2		
Belden, Augustus	1	1	4		
Bennet, Aaron	1		1		
Ballard, Benja	2	1	6		
Bucklin, Benja	1	3	4		
Boyden, Danl	3	1	7		
Boyden, Danl., Junr	1	1	1		
Blanchard, Elisha	1	3	3		
Brown, Ebenr	1	3	3		
Barney, Edward	3	4	6		
Bemis, Edmond	1	3	5		
Bullock, Elkanah	1	1	6		
Bowker, Gideon	1	2	3		
Bowker, Isaac, Junr	1	1	2		
Bowker, Isaac	1	1	1		
Brown, Isaac	1	3	4		
Barney, John	2		3		
Barrey, James	1	5	4		
Barney, John, Junr	2	3	6		
Bond, Jonas	1	1	1		
Bigelow, Josiah	1	3	2		
Battle, John	1	3	5		
Bullock, Joseph	1	2	3		
Blanchard, Leml	2	2	6		
Boyden, Joseph	1	1	2		
Burrows, James	2	1	1		
Bigelow, Joel	3	6	4		
Boyden, James	2	2	1		
Balster, John	2	1	2		
Bullock, Widow	1	2	5		
Bixby, Manassah	1	1	3		
Bixby, Manassah, Junr	1	3	4		
Barron, Nathan	1	1	2		
Briggs, Peter	2	4	4		
Bayley, Richd	1	1	3		
Balch, Saml	2	4	4		
Balch, Saml., Junr	1		3		
Barnard, Saml	1	3	2		
Barney, Sylvanus	1	1	2		

WINDHAM COUNTY—Continued.

NAME OF HEAD OF FAMILY.	Free white males of 16 years and upward, including heads of families.	Free white males under 16 years.	Free white females, including heads of families.	All other free persons.	Slaves.
GUILFORD TOWN—con.					
Barrows, Solomon	1	1	2		
Baker, Saml., Junr	1	5	3		
Bigelow, Wm	2	3	3		
Bixby, Younglove	1				
Brooks, Widow		1	1		
Bradford, Noah	1	3	3		
Bixby, David	1	2	2		
Blanchard, Jona	2	3	2		
Brooks, Ephm	1		3		
Bennet, Moses	1	1	6		
Brooks, Jona	1		1		
Bullock, Lovell	5	3	6		
Cutler, Abner	1				
Carpenter, Asaph	2		5		
Cole, Amos	1	4	3		
Cook, Benja	1	2	1		
Chamberlin, Benja	2		2		
Carpenter, Benja	3	2	4		
Coats, Charles	1	3	6		
Cole, Caleb, Junr	1		4		
Crowningshield, David	1		1		
Culver, David	1		1		
Chase, Dean	1	4	4		
Carpenter, Edwd	2		6		
Carpenter, Joseph	2	1	5		
Cutting, Jonah	1	1	1		
Culver, Joshua	1	1	3		
Crowningshield, James	1	1	5		
Chapen, Joel	1				
Cutler, James	1	2	4		
Chase, James	1	2	3		
Camp, John	2	2	3		
Cutler, Joel	5	3	3		
Crouch, James	2	1	4		
Culver, Nathan	2	1	4		
Chase, Paul	1	5	5		
Colegrove, Reuben	2	2	3		
Culver, Sanderman	1	1	1		
Curtis, Saml	2	2	6		
Chase, Seth	1	2	1		
Chase, Stephen	2	3	4		
Cudworth, Saml	1	2	2		
Chickering, Timo	1	3	4		
Cutler, Thos	2	3	7		
Culver, Wm	2	1	2		
Camp, James	1		2		
Cole, Caleb	2		1		
Cummins, Wm	1		3		
Cole, Danl	1		4		
Curtis, Abijah	1	2	1		
Collins, John	1	3	3		
Crandall, Sylvester	1	3	5		
Carpenter, Rufus	1		1		
Carpenter, Caleb	2	6	3		
Cudworth, James	1		3		
Culver, John	1		2		
Cutler, Silas	1	1	6		
Chase, Rufus	2	2	5		
Crouch, Wm	3	3	4		
Dean, Benja	5	5	7		
Davis, David	4		6		
Denison, Edward	1				
Demander, James	1	1	1		
Denison, Jabez	1				
Densmore, Joseph	2	2	9		
Dennis, James	1		1		
Dennis, John	1				
Densmore, Oliver	1				
Devenport, Paul	1		3		
Dean, Perdy	1	1	2		
Denison, Saml	1	2	1		
Davis, Joseph	1	2	3		
Denison, David	3	1	3		
Dean, Saml	1	2	1		
Dyer, John	2	2	4		
Ellis, Caleb	1	4	3		
Evans, Henry	1	1	6		
Edwards, Joseph	1		3		
Elliot, Joseph	1		1		
Easterbrook, Thos	1	1	1		
Eddy, Wm	2		2		
Edward, Wm	2	1	2		
Evans, Henry, Junr	1	1	1		
Eddy, Joel	1		1		
Eddy, Benja	1	1	1		
Fish, Amos	2	1	4		
Franklin, Aaron	4		1		
Franklin, Aaron, Junr	1	2	1		
Farrist, David	1	3	4		
Field, Elihu	2	3	6		
Fitch, Ebenr	3	1	2		

NAME OF HEAD OF FAMILY.	Free white males of 16 years and upward, including heads of families.	Free white males under 16 years.	Free white females, including heads of families.	All other free persons.	Slaves.
GUILFORD TOWN—con.					
Ferril, Isaac	2	2	4		
Fisher, Isaac	1				
Fox, John	2	2	4		
Franklin, Jabez	1	2	3		
Farnesworth, Joseph	1		1		
Ferril, Widow	1	1	1		
Franklin, Philip	4	3	2		
Fisk, Rufus	2	3	5		
Ferril, Wm	1	1	2		
Farnesworth, Zachh	5	1	1		
Fisher, Edmond	1		1		
Fisher, Nehemiah	1		5		
Goodenow, Isaac	1	1	2		
Gains, David	2		7		
Goodenow, David	1	5	2		
Gilson, David	1		2		
Gale, Ephm	2	4	1		
Grover, Eleazar	1	3	3		
Goodenow, Ebenr	1	2	6		
Goodspeed, Gideon	1	1	2		
Gallop, Joseph	1	1	3		
Goodwin, Joseph	1	1	3		
Gallop, Joseph, Junr	3	1	2		
Gould, John	1	1	4		
Gains, Joseph	1	3	3		
Goodenow, Levi	1	2	2		
Gould, Stephen	2	3	6		
Goodenow, Saml	1	1	3		
Grice, Saml	1	1	2		
Grover, Jacob	1	3	5		
Goodspeed, Joseph	1	4	2		
Goodenow, Ithamer	1		1		
Hill, Asahel	1	2	3		
Healy, Comfort	1				
Hide, Denny	3	1	3		
Horton, Hezh	1	1	3		
Hammond, John	2	1	3		
Harrington, Jona	1	2	3		
Healy, John	1	1	4		
Houghton, Edwd	3		2		
Houghton, James	5	1	2		
Hayward, Nathl	1	1	2		
Horton, Nathan	1	2	4		
Hager, Simeon	1		1		
Hager, Simeon, Junr	1	1	3		
Horton, Stafford	1	2	4		
Hinds, Wm	1	3	3		
Hoit, Wm	1	3	5		
Hanes, Vene	1	2	5		
Hanes, Vene, Junr	1	1	2		
Healy, Ithamer	1	1	2		
Hix, Ezra	1	1	2		
Hix, Henry	1		5		
Harris, Uriah	2	1	1		
Harris, Stephen	1	2	2		
Hix, Peleg	1	2	3		
Hix, Peleg, Junr	1		1		
Hinster, Elisha	1		3		
Hayward, Ebenr	1	1	2		
Joy, Abel	1	2	4		
Johnson, Asa	1				
Joy, Abiather	3	1	6		
Joy, David, Junr	1	3	4		
Jones, Eliakim	1				
Johnson, Jona	1	3	4		
Johnson, Jedediah	1				
Jacobs, Joseph	1	3	4		
Jacobs, Nathl	1	1	2		
Jacobs, Nathan	1	1	2		
Jacobs, Peter	1	2	2		
Jacobs, Stephen	2	1	4		
Joy, Jesse	1	2	3		
Jackson, Widow			2		
Knight, Danl	3	3	4		
Kimball, Ebenr	1	3	5		
King, James	2	2	3		
Kimpton, Saml	1		6		
Kingley, Jona	1	3	2		
Lynde, Danl., Junr	2	3	4		
Leonard, David	1	4	5		
Littlefield, Asa	1	1	3		
Lynde, Joshua	4	1	6		
Lynde, Leml	1	1	2		
Latherbee, Saml	1		2		
Littlefield, Thos	1	1	1		
Latherbee, Timo	2		1		
Lamphier, Isaac	1		2		
Lynde, Saml	2	5	3		
Morton, Abraham	1	2	3		
Morgan, Henry	3	4	4		
Marsh, Orsburn	1		3		

NAME OF HEAD OF FAMILY.	Free white males of 16 years and upward, including heads of families.	Free white males under 16 years.	Free white females, including heads of families.	All other free persons.	Slaves.
GUILFORD TOWN—con.					
Maxwell, Philip	1	1	3		
Mellendy, Saml	2	4	6		
Maxwell, Squire	1	2	2		
Melvin, Saml	1	3	1		
Marsh, Wm	3	1	2		
Marsh, Wm., Junr	1		2		
Morton, Benja	2	1	3		
Miles, Jehiel	1	1	2		
Martin, Cyrus	1	3	1		
Nichols, Asa	1				
Nichols, Ephm	1	1	7		
Noyes, John	3	5	5		
Nichols, James	2	2	4		
Nichols, Paul	2	1	3		
Newel, John	1	3	5		
Newel, Joshua	1	1	2		
Olden, Joseph, Junr	1	3	1		
Olden, Joseph	1	1	4		
Palmer, Charles	1	1	5		
Putman, Adonijah	3	4	3		
Porter, Elisha	1	2	4		
Peck, Elisha	1	2	2		
Paul, Henry	1	2	3		
Palmer, Henry	1	3	4		
Parker, Jerh	1	2	3		
Parker, James	1	2	4		
Parker, James	2	1	3		
Penny, Jona	1	6	4		
Partridge, Jaster	3	1	2	2	
Powers, Manassah	1	1	5		
Pullen, Mathew	2	1	2		
Peck, Seth	3		7		
Parker, Wm	1	2	2		
Pierce, Ichabod	1		1		
Partridge, David	1		2		
Putman, Jesse	1	1	6		
Paine, Miller	1	2	4		
Prentis, Saml	1	1	1		
Packard, Ichabod	2		3		
Rice, Asa	3		1		
Rogers, Abijah	1		7		
Roxby, Danl	1	2	4		
Root, Elisha	1	4	5		
Rice, Ezekl	1	2	5		
Roberts, Ebenr	1				
Reed, George	1	4	4		
Roberts, Giles	3	1	4		
Roberts, Giles, Junr	1	2	2		
Rice, Josiah	2	4	3		
Roberts, John	1				
Rice, Micah	1		6		
Rice, Nathan	1	1	1		
Rice, Phinehas	1				
Reed, Saml	1	1	4		
Root, Timo	3	2	2		
Ramsdel, Wm	3	2	4		
Ramsdel, Wm., Junr	1				
Richardson, Wm	1	1	2		
Rogers, Josiah	1		2	2	
Rice, Jasper	1		1		
Russel Amasa	1	3	3		
Russel , Jona	1	2	1		
Russel, Widow			3		
Reed, Ithamer	3		2		
Rice, Phinehas, Junr	1	4	4		
Shadwick, Wm	1				
Stark, Abijah	1	3	2		
Shepardson, Alfred	1				
Smith, Amos	3	1	3		
Smith, Amos, Junr	1	1	1		
Starr, Comfort	2	1	4		
Smalley, David	2	1	4		
Stowel, David	1	2	8		
Smith, Danl	1	4	3		
Shepardson, Danl	2		2		
Stafford, Isaac	1	1	3		
Slater, John	3	2	6		
Slater, Joseph	2	5	5		
Shepardson, John	1		1		
Salsbury, James	1	3	4		
Shepardson, Jerard	1				
Stanton, Joseph	2	3	3		
Stanhope, Joseph	2	3	3		
Salsbury, Job	1	3	2		
Severance, John	1	2	2		
Stark, Nathan	2	4	4		
Shepardson, Noah	1	2	3		
Stafford, Obediah	1		2		
Streeter, Rufus	1	1	2		
Stafford, Stukeley	1	3	2		
Stevens, Simon	3	2	2	1	

WINDHAM COUNTY—Continued.

NAME OF HEAD OF FAMILY.	Free white males of 16 years and upward, including heads of families.	Free white males under 16 years.	Free white females, including heads of families.	All other free persons.	Slaves.
GUILFORD TOWN—con.					
Smith, Simeon	1	1	1		
Smith, Solomon	1	3	4		
Shepardson, Stephen	1		4		
Slater, Stephen	1	3	4		
Shepardson, Saml	2	2	3		
Stafford, Thos	1	1	3		
Shepardson, Zephh	2	2	4		
Shepardson, Zephh., Junr	1	3	5		
Smith, Isaac	1	2	3		
Sawyer, Leml	1	2	4		
Spears, John	2	1	1		
Smith, Cornelius	1	1	2		
Stanton, Benja	1		2		
Spelman, John	2	1	1		
Stafford, Job	2		1		
Smith, Jona	1	1	3		
Slate, ——	1	1	2		
Stanton, Moses	1	1	5	3	
Smith, Widow		1	2		
Shepardson, Stephen, Junr	1	3	2		
Shepardson, Seth	1	1	2		
Salsbury, Edwd	1	2	2		
Stebbins, Abner	2	3	3		
Streeter, Joseph	3	2	3		
Smith, Amos, Junr	1	1	1		
Torry, Abel	2		3		
Torry, Abel, Junr	1		2		
Torry, Abner	1	4	1		
Thompson, Charles	1	2	4		
Thurber, David	1		5		
Toby, Eleazar	2	3	4		
Tubbs, Isaac	1	6	4		
Tyler, John	1	2	3	1	
Tyler, Jerh	1	1	1		
Torry, James	1				
Tisdel, Seth	2	4	2		
Taylor, Elias	1	1	1		
Travatt, Benja	1	4	3		
Thurber, Squire	1		1		
Thayer, Esick	1	1	3		
Thurber, Edwd	1		2		
Welman, Abiel	1				
Wilder, Aaron	1	2	6		
Wilkins, Andrew	1		3		
Whitney, Abel	1	5	3		
Weld, Calvin	1	1	3		
Weld, Danl	1	3	4		
Williams, Davis	5	1	2		
Wilkins, Danl	2		1		
Wells, Ezra	1	2	1		
Whitney, Ephm	2	1	2		
Ward, Henry	1	3	2		
Weld, Isaac	1	2	3		
Williams, Israel	1				
Wright, John	1				
Whiting, Jona	1				
Wallace, John	1	1	3		
Woolly, Jona	1	1	4	3	
Woodward, Joseph	1	1	2		
Witherhead, Joseph	1	2	3		
Whitney, Job	1	1	6		
Welman, Jedediah	2	1	4		
Weld, Luther	1				
Whiting, Michal	2		3		
Weld, Noah	2	1	2		
Waterhouse, Nathan	1	4	3		
Witherhead, Widow		2	2		
Whitcomb, Saml	1	2	1		
Willis, Slaughter	1				
Wells, Thos	2	1	3		
Wells, Thos., Junr	1	1	2		
Woolly, Theophilus	1	1	6		
White, Wm	3	4	2		
Willis, Beriah	1		3		
Wilson, John	1	1	5		
Wilson, James	2	3	5		
Woolly, Thos	1		1		
Wheeler, Danl	2	2	3		
Williams, Davis, Junr	1		3		
Williams, Richd	1	2	3		
Yaw, Amos	1		3		
Yaw, Moses	1	1	2		
Yaw, Widow	2		1		
Yaw, Wm	1	4	3		
Younglove, John	2	3	3		
HALLIFAX TOWN.					
Alexander, David	1	5	2		
Alexander, John	1	1	1		
Alverson, David	4	3	2		

NAME OF HEAD OF FAMILY.	Free white males of 16 years and upward, including heads of families.	Free white males under 16 years.	Free white females, including heads of families.	All other free persons.	Slaves.
HALLIFAX TOWN—con.					
Alverson, Widow	1	3	1		
Artin, Jona	1		1		
Allen, David, 2nd	1	3	3		
Allen, David, 3rd	1		1		
Allen, David	1	1	3		
Akeley, Francis	2	8	1		
Bennet, Banks	1	1			
Bush, Moses	1	3	4		
Bell, Joseph	2	2	5	1	
Bullock, Darius	2		4		
Barber, Benja	1	5	4		
Bennet, Nathl	1	1	4		
Baldwin, Jeremiah	1	1	2		
Baldwin, Isaac, Junr	1	1	2		
Brooks, Leml	1	3	5		
Brooks, Asa	1	3	2		
Bemis, Israel	1		1		
Baldwin, Isaac	4		3		
Clark, Thos	1	2	3		
Clark, Josiah	3	2	4		
Crozier, Arthur	2	2	4		
Calf, Stephen	1	2	1		
Colefax, Saml	1	1	2		
Conart, Amos	2	4	4		
Clark, Saml., 2nd	1	1	1		
Clark, Ebenr	1		4		
Clark, James	4	2	7		
Clark, Nathan	1		4		
Clark, Asa	1	4	5		
Clark, Elisha	1	3	4		
Crozier, John	2	1	4		
Crozier, Robert	2		4		
Coleman, Joshua	1	4	3		
Crane, Isaac	3	3	3		
Clark, Saml	1	1	3		
Crosby, Israel	1		1		
Canady, Hugh	3	1	4		
Dalrymple, Edwd	1		2		
Darling, Peter	2		5		
Dalrymple, Wm	1	2	4		
Dunnagon, Edwd	1	3	2		
Everett, Jeremiah	2	3	4		
Ellis, Mathew	1	5	3		
Fish, Edmond	1	2	5		
Fish, Saml	1	2	6		
Fish, Nathan	2	3	7		
Farnsworth, Thos	1	3	4		
Forbes, Wm	2				
Fowler, Curtis	2		1		
Feszenden, Solomon	1	3	1		
French, Jesse	1		3		
Fowler, Thos	3	2	3		
Fisher, David	1	5	1		
Fisher, Timo	1	1	3		
Garret, Wm	2		1		
Grover, Aaron	2		2		
Guild, Jesse	1	3	2		
Garret, Wm., 2nd	1	1			
Garret, Widow	1	1	1		
Gore, Elijah	2	1	8		
Gore, Amos	1	1	5		
Gates, Stephen	1	4	3		
Goodale, David	1	3	5		
Hale, Israel	1	4	3		
Harris, John	1	1	1		
Harris, Job	1		2		
Hall, John	2	3	6		
Hall, Joel	2	4	4	1	
Hall, Azariah	2	1	5		
Hotchkiss, Elihu	2	1	2		
Hunt, Jasper	2	2	4		
Henery, Benja	4	2	4		
Henderson, Henry	1	5	2		
Holmes, Saml	1	1	2		
Hambleton, Reuben	1		1		
Harrington, Widow	1		1		
Henderson, Wm	2		1		
Hatch, James	2	1	6		
Hanes, Abel	1	3	4		
Harrington, Danl	1	2	2		
Harris, Joshua	1		1		
Henderson, Wm., Junr	3		1		
Jenks, Benja	1	5	1		
Johnson, Seth	2	1	2		
Jones, Israel	1	2	2		
Joyner, John	1	3	4		
Kirkley, John	2		5		
Kellogg, Jona	1	2	4		
Kingsbury, John	2	3	3		
Little, John	2	4	5		
Lamb, David	1	3	3		
Lamb, Martin	1		3		

NAME OF HEAD OF FAMILY.	Free white males of 16 years and upward, including heads of families.	Free white males under 16 years.	Free white females, including heads of families.	All other free persons.	Slaves.
HALLIFAX TOWN—con.					
Lizieur, Abner	1	1	3		
Littlefield, Edmond	2		2		
Leonard, Moses	1	1	3		
Leonard, Josiah	1	1	4		
Littlefield, Jesse	1		1		
Lamb, Aaron	1				
Murdock, Saml	4	5	5		
Marble, Jona	2	1	3		
Muzzy, Amos	2	1	5		
McClieur, Joseph	1	4	5		
Metcalf, Reuben	1	1	2		
Mathews, Benja	1	4	1		
Mullet, ——	2	4	2		
Morrel, John	1	2	1		
McCloister, ——	1	2	5		
Newton, Shadrach	1	2	2		
Nichols, Saml	1	2	4		
Nemms, Ebenr	1	2	4		
Newton, Zaphon	1				
Niles, Ichabod	1	1	2		
Owen, Caleb	1	1	4	1	
Owen, Joel	1	2	1		
Orr, Isaac	3	1	7		
Orvis, Gersham	1	3	3		
Pannel, John	1		2		
Pannel, James	2	2	2		
Pratt, James	1	2	2		
Philips, Ezekl	1		1		
Pannel, John, Junr	2	3	2		
Pierce, Reuben	1		3		
Pannel, Andrew	1	2	2		
Patterson, Robt	4	1	6		
Paul, Hugh	1	1	2		
Putman, John	1	1	1		
Pratt, Elisha	1	1	2		
Pierce, Saml	2	3	3		
Pierce, Joseph	4		3		
Pierce, Allen	1		1		
Pierce, Benja	1	1	2		
Pratt, Darius	1	1	2		
Perry, Joseph	2		4		
Rich, Thaddeus	2	2	2		
Rich, Jathenial	1	1	2		
Rich, John	1	2	2		
Rider, Joseph	1	1	3		
Stacy, Wm	1	1	1		
Scott, Thos	4	4	3		
Sanders, Aaron	2	3	3		
Sumner, Danl	2	2	3		
Safford, Danl	1		2		
Sumner, Danl., Junr	1	1	2		
Sumner, Joel	1	1	2		
Stow, David	2		5		
Shepard, Jonas	4		2		
Streeter, Nathl	1	1	2		
Shepardson, Wm	2	4	4		
Smith, Hezh	2	1	3		
Swain, Joseph	2	1	4		
Saunders, Jonas	1	2	1		
Safford, Saml	1	2	3		
Slaid, Aaron	2	1	6		
Sawyer, Darius	1		1		
Scott, Josiah	1	2	2		
Stacy, Nymphas	1	3	4		
Scott, Philip	1	1	3		
Stanley, Josiah	2		1		
Stanley, Solomon	1		1		
Tucker, Joseph	1	2	3		
Tilder, Benja	1	3	3		
Thomas, Benja	2	3	5		
Thomas, John, Junr	1	2	2		
Thomas, John	2	1	3		
Tredaway, Benja	2	3	4		
Taggort, James, Junr	1		4		
Taggort, James	1				
Taggort, Thos	3	2	7		
Thomas, Wm	3	3	3		
Tucker, James	2	1	2		
Underwood, Saml	1	3	4		
Underwood, Saml., Junr.	1	2	2		
Woodward, Timo	1	1	3		
Warden, Sylvanus	3	2	4		
Washburn, Eliab	1	2	3		
Wood, Saml	1	2	3		
Wilcox, Burden	2	1	2		
Warden, Peter	1	1	1		
Weeks, Benja	3	4	4	1	
Wilcox, Benja	1	2	3		
Wilcox, Stephen	2	3	3		
Woodward, Saml	2		2		
Warden, Elisha	1	2	3		
White, Giles	1	4	1		

WINDHAM COUNTY—Continued.

NAME OF HEAD OF FAMILY.	Free white males of 16 years and upward, including heads of families.	Free white males under 16 years.	Free white females, including heads of families.	All other free persons.	Slaves.
HALLIFAX TOWN—con.					
Whipple, Joseph	1		3		
Woodward, Art	1	1	3		
Wilcox, Tabor	1		5		
Woodward, James	2	2	3		
Wilcox, Wm., Junr	3	2	3		
Wills, Jona	2	3	2		
Wills, Hubbel	2		1		
Warden, Joseph	1	4	3		
Wills, Hubbel, Junr	1		1		
Woolly, Thos	1	1	1		
Wilcox, Nathan	2	4	4		
Whitney, Ebenr	1	3	1		
HINSDALE TOWN.					
Alexander, Jonathan	2	5	2		
Bandwell, Moses	1		3		
Brown, C. Jude	1	4	4		
Bridgman, John	4	2	5		
Barret, Moses	3	3	4		
Brooks, Nathl	2	1	4		
Bascom, Timothy	3	1	3		
Belden, Saml	3		3		
Brooks, Cephas	1	2	2		
Bullock, Wm	1	1	1		
Clark, Jabez	1	1	1		
Clark, Noah	1	1	2		
Chamberlain, Ebenr	1	1	4		
Clark, Saml	1	3	3		
Dickinson, Moses	2	1	1		
Davidson, James	1	2	2		
Ellmore, Jacob	4		3		
Ellmore, Reuben	1	3	3		
Ellmore, Elisha	1	5	3		
Farmer, John	1	2	2		
Foster, Nathl	3	2	6		
Thirzel, Benja	2	5	3		
Goss, Danl	1	2	1		
Goss, Jonas	2	4	2		
Goss, Wm	2		1		
How, Squire	1	3	3		
How, Moses	2	3	6		
Hunt, Jona	3	3	5	1	
Houghton, Nathl	1	1	2		
Houghton, Danl	1	2	2		
Hall, Simeon	1	2	2		
Houghton, Edwd	3	4	5		
Hide, Joseph	1		3		
Joy, John	1	2	4		
Johnson, Stephen	1	3	5		
Linkfield, Benja	1	1	1		
Lee, Benja	1	1	4		
Lee, Jesse	3	4	6		
Newel, Joshua	1	3	2		
Orvis, Oliver	1	3	5		
Orvis, Waitstill	1	7	2		
Orvis, Ambrose	1	1	3		
Pratt, Isaac	1		2		
Pratt, Isaac, Junr	1	1	3		
Parsons, Andrew	1	2	1		
Patterson, Eleazar	1		1		
Patterson, Jona	3	3	2		
Palmer, Jonah	1		5		
Palmer, John	3	5	5		
Patterson, Widow		1	2		
Pelton, Moses	1	1	5		
Rowley, Israel	1		1		
Rowley, Widow			1		
Smith, James	4		3		
Stebbins, Joseph	1	1			
Streeter, Saml	3	1	5		
Smith, Simeon	1	1	1		
Streeter, Enoch	2	1	3		
Streeter, James	2	2	4		
Streeter, Joel	1	1	1		
Streeter, Jona	1	1	1		
Scott, Ebenr	1	3	4		
Streeter, Nathl	1	3	5		
Tate, Widow	1	1	3		
Thayer, Zephh	2		3		
Thayer, Jerijah	1	3	2		
Thayer, Frederick	1		2		
Stebbins, Elijah	3	3	5		
Thomas, Israel	1	3	3		
Tubbs, Saml	1	2	2		
Stebbins, Eliakim	2	2	1		
Wood, Wm	1		2		
Wright, Jona	1		3		
Wright, Gad	2	3	8		
Wentworth, Charles	1	4	2		
Wright, Amasa	2		2		

NAME OF HEAD OF FAMILY.	Free white males of 16 years and upward, including heads of families.	Free white males under 16 years.	Free white females, including heads of families.	All other free persons.	Slaves.
JAMAICA TOWN.					
Adams, Seth	2		6		
Averdon, John	2	3	3		
Berry, Saml	1	1	6		
Brown, James	1		2		
Brooks, David	1		2		
Blanchard, Joseph	1	4	3		
Burnap, John	2		1		
Butler, Widow	2	1	2		
Chase, Elisha	1		4		
Chase, Stephen	1				
Crapoo, Francis	1	2	2		
Cushing, Solomon	1	2	4		
Crapoo, Jona	1		3		
Davidson, Nathl	1	4	2		
Danolds, Joshua	2	1	6		
Glazier, Benja	1	2	2		
Glazier, Elisha	1				
Gleason, Josiah	1				
Gage, Asa	2	4	4		
Goff, Ezra	1	1	1		
Grover, Joseph	1	2	1		
Taft, Oliver	1	2	2		
Higgins, Joseph	1	1	2		
How, John	3	3	4		
Hayward, Paul	3	2	1		
Hayward, Oliver	2		3		
Hayward, Nathan	1		7		
Hayward, Silas	4	3	4		
Hayward, Caleb	3	5	3		
Hayward, Dependd	2	1	4		
Hayward, Seth	3	5	3		
How, Peter	1	2	2		
Higgins, Ephm	1				
Sabin, Stephen	1		6		
Lawton, David	1	3	2		
Livermore, Saml	1	1	2		
Livermore, Ezra	1		2		
Livermore, Elijah	1	1	2		
Livermore, Lott	1				
Stone, Isaac	1	2	2		
Muzzy, Benja	1	1	3		
McGarr, James	1	1	2		
Moson, Lemuel	1		2		
Vialls, Saml & Nathl	2	4	5		
Whitney, Aaron	2		2		
Watson, John	1		3		
Williams, John & Reuben	4	2	4		
JOHNSON'S GORE.					
Brooks, Ebenr	1	1	3		
Coovey, Joseph	2	3	4		
Fisher, Noah	2	1	3		
Fisher, Isaac	1		1		
Holden, Philemon	1	3	2		
Jennison, Wm	1	1	3		
Johnson, Wm	1				
Newton, Silas	1				
Scott, John	4	2	2		
Wilder, Danl	1	2	3		
LONDONDERRY TOWN.					
Aiken, Edwd	4	1	2		
Aiken, Danl	3		3		
Aiken, Nathl	1	5	4		
Ayers, Saml	1	1	3		
Arnold, Saml	1				
Andrews, John	1				
Ammidon, Ephm	1	2	4		
Babbit, Ira	2	1	2		
Bickford, Saml	1		3		
Bowen, Francis	1	2	2		
Brintnal, Jona	1	1	2		
Babbit, Danl	2	1	5		
Cox, William	1	5	3		
Cox, Edwd	1	2	4		
Cary, James	1	2	3		
Cook, Ezekl	1				
Cook, Elisha	1	2	2		
Cook, Ebenr	1				
Cox, John	1	3	2		
Chase, Pratt	1	1	4		
Cockran, David	1	4	4		
Cole, Jesse	1	2	2		
Cole, John	1				
Cole, Widow			1		
Cole, Benja	1	3	2		
Center, Parker	1				
Cole, Sabin	1				

NAME OF HEAD OF FAMILY.	Free white males of 16 years and upward, including heads of families.	Free white males under 16 years.	Free white females, including heads of families.	All other free persons.	Slaves.
LONDONDERRY TOWN—continued.					
Cole, Amasa	1	1	1		
Cummins, Stephen	1		4		
Cole, Salmon	1	2	1		
Daggot, Amos	1	1	2		
Derby, Eliah	1	4	5		
Derby, David	2	5	3		
Daggot, Joseph	1		4		
Eastman, James	1		4		
Eddy, Elial	4	1	5		
Fox, John	1	1	2		
Fletcher, Sherebiah	1				
Grimes, Moses	3	1	3		
Grimes, James	1	1	2		
How, Nehemiah	1	1	7		
Hodges, Emerson	1				
Hassa, John	1		3		
Hopkins, James	1	4	3		
How, Darius	1	2	3		
Hopkins, John	1		2		
Jacobs, John	1	1	1		
McMurphy, George	2	1	3		
Marsh, Joseph	2		2		
Marsh, Israel	1	2	3		
Mark, John	1				
McCormick, James	3	1	4		
McCormick, Archibald	1	1	2	1	
Marsh, Archibald	1	1	3		
Montgommery, Hugh	1	4	2		
Oughterson, Joseph	1	3	3		
Patterson, John	1	2	3		
Pierce, Nehemiah	1	2	2		
Pierce, Benja	1	1	2		
Patterson, Ebenr	2	3	4		
Thompson, Saml	2	4	4		
Thayer, Rufus	1				
Taggert, Patrick	1	1	3		
Taylor, John	1	2	1		
Woodburn, John	1	3	5		
Whitman, Abiel	1	1	2		
Warren, Joshua	2	2	5		
Woodward, Nathl	1				
Williams, John	1		2		
Whitman, Noah	1	2	4		
Wait, Barnabas	1		1		
MARLBOROUGH TOWN.					
Allen, Salmon	1	3	4		
Adams, Freegrace	1		3		
Adams, Bildad	1				
Adams, Levi	1	1	1		
Angel, Jona	1	1	3		
Adams, Joel	2		2		
Bellows, Charles	1	4	3		
Bellows, Joseph	1		2		
Bryant, Jacob	1	4	6		
Bartlett, Joseph	1	1	3		
Bartlett, Zarah	1	4	5		
Brown, Lyman	2		2		
Bishop, Sylvester	2		1		
Bryant, Joseph	1	1	3		
Barret, Levi	1		2		
Burbanks, Joel	1		4		
Bartlett, John	1	3	3		
Bartlett, Nathl	1		2		
Ball, Saml	2	5	5		
Chandler, Jehiel	1		1		
Church, Moses	2	2	4		
Cresey, Moses	1		2		
Church, Joseph	1	1	3		
Cresey, Wm	1				
Cutler, Anthony	1		1		
Cutler, Josiah	1	4	2		
Cooley, Enos	1				
Dodge, Wm	1		1		
Dunlap, Saml	1	2	4		
Day, Giles	2	3	4		
Ervin, John	1	2	5		
Farr, Thomas	1	2	2		
Gilbert, Solomon	1				
Gault, Eli	1				
Giles, Widow		2	2		
Gilbert, Saml	1		4		
Higley, Elijah	1	3	3		
Harris, Ebenr, Junr	1	1	1		
Higley, Danl	3	4	4		
Hays, Jeremiah	1	3	4		
Higley, Joel	2	1	2		
Harris, Abner	1	1	1		
Harris, Asa	1	2	2		
Holton, Nahum	1	3	1		

WINDHAM COUNTY—Continued.

NAME OF HEAD OF FAMILY.	Free white males of 16 years and upward, including heads of families.	Free white males under 16 years.	Free white females, including heads of families.	All other free persons.	Slaves.
MARLBOROUGH TOWN—continued.					
Hayward, Jonª	2	1	6	....	....
Holliday, Dan[l], Jun[r]	1	1	2	....	....
Holliday, Dan[l]	1	1	3	....	....
Holliday, Eli	1	2	2	....	....
Ingram, Jon[a]	2	5	4	....	....
Jenks, Jonas	1	3	3	....	....
Isletine, John	2	1	2	....	....
Kelly, Simeon	1	1	2	....	....
King, Ichabod	2	3	2	....	....
Knights, Benj[a]	2	3	5	....	....
Lyman, C. Gersham	2	3	4	....	....
Miller, David	5	1	5	....	....
Mather, Phin. & Sam[l]	6	10	9	....	....
Mather, Erastus	1	2	2	....	....
Mather, Sam[l]	1	......	......	....	....
Miller, Thaddeus	1	1	4	....	....
Miller, David, Jun[r]	1	2	7	....	....
More, Sam[l]	1	3	4	....	....
Mather, Tim[o]	1	......	......	....	....
Manley, John	3	......	2	....	....
Olds, Benj[a]., Jun[r]	1	3	2	....	....
Olds, Benj[a]	2	1	2	....	....
Olds, Thaddeus	1	2	2	....	....
Otis, Hannah	1	......	3	....	....
Pratt, Isaac	2	......	2	....	....
Pratt, Sam[l]	1	1	1	....	....
Pratt, Emerson	1	......	2	....	....
Pratt, Amos	1	3	2	....	....
Pratt, Oliver	1	1	2	....	....
Pratt, Asa	1	......	2	....	....
Perry, Benj[a]	1	2	2	....	....
Phelps, Abel	1	1	3	....	....
Paul, James	1	2	2	....	....
Pratt, Alpheus	3	1	2	....	....
Pratt, Orlin	1	......	......	....	....
Phelps, Francis	1	3	3	....	....
Phelps, Tim[o]	2	2	5	....	....
Parks, Amariah	1	1	4	....	....
Prouty, Amor	1	1	2	....	....
Packard, Josiah	1	2	5	....	....
Parsons, Sam[l]	1	1	2	....	....
Rising, Jon[a]	1	2	5	....	....
Ransom, Luther	1	2	3	....	....
Smith, Isaiah	3	5	4	....	....
Simonds, Dan[l]	1	2	4	....	....
Sawtweel, Levi	1	......	1	....	....
Smith, Joseph	1	1	3	....	....
Stockwell, Abel	1	2	4	....	....
Sumner, Tho[s]	1	......	1	....	....
Smith, John	1	2	3	....	....
Smith, Jonah	1	1	4	....	....
Slaid, Dan[l]	1	3	1	....	....
Tamlin, Tim[o]	1	1	5	....	....
Underwood, Thaddeus	2	1	4	....	....
Underwood, Jon[a]	1	3	5	....	....
Whitney, Jonas	3	......	8	....	....
Winchester, Joseph	2	......	1	....	....
Winchester, Asa	1	1	1	....	....
Winchester, Joshua	1	......	......	....	....
Winchester, Benj[a]	1	3	1	....	....
Whitney, Moses	1	1	1	....	....
Whitney, Sam[l]	2	1	4	....	....
Whitney, Guilford	1	......	......	....	....
Winchester, Joseph, J[r]	1	1	2	....	....
Whitney, Nath[l]	1	3	5	....	....
Warren, Jon[a]	1	2	5	....	....
Warren, Dan[l]	1	2	2	....	....
Whitmond, Abraham	1	4	2	....	....
NEW FANE TOWN.					
Allen, Eben[r]	1	......	2	....	....
Allen, Amos	1	1	1	....	....
Arnold, Gamaliel	1	......	1	....	....
Burnham, Gabriel	1	2	4	....	....
Bruce, Elijah	1	4	3	....	....
Balcom, Isaac	1	2	4	....	....
Bullard, Abel	1	2	3	....	....
Bruce, Artemas	1	......	2	....	....
Bruce, Eph[m]	1	2	2	....	....
Bruce, Asa	1	1	5	....	....
Balcom, Henry	1	......	3	....	....
Bartlett, W[m]	1	1	2	....	....
Bond, Aaron	1	1	3	....	....
Boyden, Hez[h]	1	2	4	....	....
Boyden, Hez[h]., Jun[r]	1	......	......	....	....
Bitterly, Tho[s]	2	2	4	....	....
Cobleigh, Reuben	1	3	2	....	....
Crowle, Andrew	2	3	2	....	....
Cook, Jonas	1	2	5	....	....
Davis, Joshua	1	......	2	....	....
NEW FANE TOWN—con.					
Darren, Ethan	1	4	3	....	....
Dewey, Sylvester	1	......	2	....	....
Dyer, Joseph	2	......	2	....	....
Ellis, Abijah	1	1	1	....	....
Eager, Ward	1	3	6	....	....
Fuller, Ephraim	1	3	1	....	....
Fisher, Dan[l]	1	3	3	....	....
Gale, Paul	1	......	4	....	....
Goodale, Solomon	1	......	3	....	....
Gates, Silas	1	2	4	....	....
Goodenow, Silas	4	......	4	....	....
Gamble, James	1	......	1	....	....
Grimes, Andrew	1	7	1	....	....
Gamble, W[m]	1	1	1	....	....
Green, Tho[s]	1	......	1	....	....
Houghton, Asa	1	......	6	....	....
Hall, Joseph	3	......	2	....	....
How, Talmon	1	......	3	....	....
Holland, Eph[m]	2	1	2	....	....
Holland, Jonah	1	3	2	....	....
Harris, Eben[r]	1	2	7	....	....
Hall, Jon[a]	1	3	3	....	....
Houghton, Jotham	1	2	3	....	....
Houghton, Solomon	1	3	4	....	....
Holland, Paul	1	1	1	....	....
Holland, Joseph	2	3	4	....	....
Hall, Eph[m]	1	1	1	....	....
Holden, Josiah	1	4	4	....	....
Higgins, Tho[s]	2	......	3	....	....
Houghton, James	1	2	5	....	....
Jewel, Jesse	1	3	4	....	....
Jones, Seth	1	3	3	....	....
Kenny, Moses	4	4	7	....	....
Keyes, Ashley	1	......	3	....	....
Knoulton, Silas	1	1	1	....	....
Kimball, Asahel	2	1	2	....	....
Knoulton, Nathan	1	3	3	....	....
Knoulton, Luke	7	......	3	....	....
Lane, Isaac	1	4	3	....	....
Lawrence, Elias	5	1	2	....	....
Mold, Joseph	1	......	1	....	....
Morse, Eben[r]	1	......	3	....	....
Morse, John	2	3	3	....	....
Marble, Sam[l]	3	......	2	....	....
Morse, Jacob	3	2	5	....	....
Morse, Joshua	1	3	4	....	....
M[c]Masters, John	1	2	7	....	....
Merrifield, Aaron	3	3	5	....	....
Marsh, Sam[l]	1	3	3	....	....
M[c]Culler, Joseph	1	3	4	....	....
Morse, Artemas	1	2	3	....	....
Marsh, Zebediah	1	4	4	....	....
Newton, Marshal	2	2	3	....	....
Newton, Sam[l]	1	3	2	....	....
Nelson, Nehemiah	1	2	4	....	....
Ober, Eben[r]	3	1	3	....	....
Perry, Amos	1	......	......	....	....
Perry, Dan[l]	1	1	2	....	....
Pomeroy, Chester	1	1	4	....	....
Park, Jon[a]	2	3	3	....	....
Philips, Paine	1	......	1	....	....
Philips, John	1	......	3	....	....
Perry, Joseph	1	......	2	....	....
Ransom, Ezek[l]	3	......	1	....	....
Richardson, Jeremiah	1	1	2	....	....
Robinson, Jon[a]	1	5	2	....	....
Richardson, Sam[l]	1	......	2	....	....
Rand, Rich[d]	2	1	4	....	....
Rand, Sawyer	1	......	......	....	....
Rutter, Philip	1	3	6	....	....
Randall, Tho[s]	1	......	1	....	....
Stevens, Lem[l]	2	3	3	....	....
Stillman, E. Amos	2	1	2	....	....
Stone, Nathan	2	1	2	....	....
Stevens, Israel	1	......	......	....	....
Stevens, Jacob	2	......	2	....	....
Snow, Benj[a]	1	1	3	....	....
Smith, Phinehas	2	1	2	....	....
Stedman, Nath[l]	1	1	7	....	....
Saddler, Joseph	1	2	2	....	....
Sikes, Nathan	1	......	2	....	....
Tainter, Steven	1	......	......	....	....
Taylor, Dan[l]., Jun[r]	1	2	5	....	....
Thayer, Widow	1	1	4	....	....
Taylor, Hez[h]	1	2	3	....	....
Wilder, Oliver	1	......	......	....	....
Wheeler, John	4	1	3	....	....
Wheeler, Darius	1	1	2	....	....
White, W[m]	1	2	2	....	....
Woods Solomon	3	3	5	....	....
Wilder Joel	1	3	2	....	....
NEW FANE TOWN—con.					
Whitcomb, Jon[a]	1	3	3	....	....
Wilder, Eph[m]	1	......	2	....	....
Williams, Sam[l]	1	4	3	....	....
PUTNEY TOWN.					
Adams, Sam[l]	1	4	3	....	....
Aplin, Tho[s]	1	2	2	....	....
Alexander, Aaron	1	1	6	....	....
Aynesworth, Benj[a]	1	1	2	....	....
Alexander, Philip	1	2	6	....	....
Allen, Josiah	1	6	3	....	....
Austin, Josiah	1	......	......	....	....
Austin, Apollos	2	......	2	....	....
Armsbury, Christopher	2	4	4	....	....
Allen, Lewis	3	......	6	....	....
Allen, John	1	2	4	....	....
Austin, Eben[r]	1	3	2	....	....
Austin, Nath[l]	1	1	2	....	....
Briggs, Asa	1	3	5	....	....
Briggs, Hez[h]	2	1	2	....	....
Black, Asa	1	......	1	....	....
Black, Steward	1	2	5	....	....
Bantwell, Tho[s]	1	1	2	....	....
Butler, Luther	1	......	2	....	....
Bruce, Josiah	1	2	4	....	....
Brown, Dan[l]	3	3	3	....	....
Brown, Jesse	1	1	4	....	....
Benson, Moses	1	......	2	....	....
Black, James	1	1	1	....	....
Bigelow, Eliphez	1	......	2	....	....
Black, W[m]	1	......	8	....	....
Bishop, Oliver	1	2	4	....	....
Blood, Robert	4	3	3	....	....
Bowen, John	1	2	3	....	....
Bennet, Sam[l]	2	1	3	....	....
Briggs, Abiel	2	1	2	....	....
Briggs, Henry	3	4	3	....	....
Brown, Jabez	1	3	1	....	....
Benson, Dan[l]	1	2	2	....	....
Bugby, Eben[r]	1	1	2	....	....
Baldwin, Levi	1	2	4	....	....
Benson, Peter	1	3	3	....	....
Bennet, Sam[l]., Jun[r]	1	1	4	....	....
Campbell, W[m]	2	1	2	....	....
Cushing, Dan[l]	1	3	4	....	....
Carr, Moses	1	2	3	....	....
Church, Nath[l]	1	2	3	....	....
Cudworth, Charles	3	1	3	....	....
Cudworth, Charles, Jun[r]	1	......	......	....	....
Crosby, Tho[s]	1	2	3	....	....
Cheney, Oliver	2	1	1	....	....
Coddine, Francis	2	1	3	....	....
Chandler, Charles	3	......	......	....	....
Campbell, James	1	2	2	....	....
Collins, David	1	1	2	....	....
Campbell, John	3	3	6	....	....
Campbell, Alex[r]	1	......	1	....	....
Cushing, Asaph	1	1	2	....	....
Clay, James, Jun[r]	2	2	7	....	....
Conn, Tho[s]	1	......	6	....	....
Clay, James	2	......	2	....	....
Church, Titus	1	1	3	....	....
Combs, Medad	2	......	2	....	....
Cushing, Noah	1	4	5	....	....
Cushing, Mathew	2	......	3	....	....
Cushing, Joseph	1	4	2	....	....
Cook, Elijah	1	5	2	....	....
Clay, Eph[m]	2	2	6	....	....
Campbell, Tho[s]	1	2	3	....	....
Campbell, Duncan	2	......	1	....	....
Clay, Seth	2	5	1	....	....
Dickinson, Abraham	1	1	3	....	....
Darling, Widow	......	1	4	....	....
Day, Benj[a]	1	1	3	....	....
Davis, Dan[l]	1	2	1	....	....
Easterbrook, Nathan	3	3	2	....	....
Enus, Joseph	1	2	4	....	....
Ellingwood, Jon[a]	1	......	1	....	....
Foster, David	1	1	6	....	....
Fuller, Dan[l]	1	1	3	....	....
Fisher, Abiel	2	4	3	....	....
Fitch, James	4	2	3	....	....
Fletcher, Benj[a]	1	1	3	....	....
Foster, Nath[l]	2	......	3	10	....
Goodhue, Josiah	2	......	2	....	....
Goodhue, Josiah, Jun[r]	2	2	4	....	....
Goodhue, Alex[r]	1	......	1	....	....
Griffin, John	3	3	6	....	....
Goodwin, John	4	......	6	....	....
Green, John	1	2	2	....	....

WINDHAM COUNTY—Continued.

NAME OF HEAD OF FAMILY.	Free white males of 16 years and upward, including heads of families.	Free white males under 16 years.	Free white females, including heads of families.	All other free persons.	Slaves.
PUTNEY TOWN—con.					
Goodhue, Joseph	2	1	4		
Gould, Jedediah	1	4	2		
Green, Absulum	1		2		
Green, John	1	1	2		
Graham, Wm	1		1		
Gilson, Jona., Junr	1	1	1		
Gleason, Moses	4		5		
Gilbert, Joseph	1	4	4		
Gilbert, Moses	1	3	4		
Gilson, David	2		3		
Graves, Reuben	1	3	2		
Holden, Widow		4	3		
Hibbard, Asa	1	1	4		
Harden, Richd	1	1	6		
Houghton, Ebenr	1	4	2		
Houghton, Cyrus	1		1		
Houghton, Aaron	1	2	4		
Holmes, Thos	1				
Hill, Wm	1	3	4		
Huntington, John	1	1	3		
Hide, Joshua	2		3		
Hide, Joshua, Junr	2	1	4		
Hide, Zenas	2	1	2		
Hunt, Joel	1				
Hale, James	3	2	3		
Hubbard, Elisha	2	5	6		
Haskel, Rufus	1		1		
Hartwell, Joseph	1		1		
Hudson, John	2	5	1		
Hartwell, Wm	2	4	2		
Hale, Amos	6		5		
Hoskins, Nathan	1	3	3		
Hartwell, Timo	1	2	3		
Hutchins, Benja	1	4	3		
Harden, Caleb	1	1	2		
Hunt, Danl	1	3	3		
Jones, Oliver	1	1	3		
Johnson, Elisha	1	3	4		
Johnson, Beaman	1	2	5		
Jewel, Danl	3	3	6		
Johnson, Jonah	1	3	3		
Jones, Benson	1		1		
Joy, Obediah	1		2		
Joy, Obediah, Junr	1	1	2		
Joy, Moses	3	4	4		
Joy, Amos	1	3	2	1	
Jones, Charles	1	4	2		
Joy, David	1	2	3		
Johnson, Sibens	1		1		
Keyes, Israel	1	4	4		
Kathan, Charles	2	3	6		
Keyes, Wm	2		3		
Knap, Aaron	1	1	2		
Lowel, Jacob	3		2		
Lowel, Josiah	1	2	1		
Lowel, Moses, Junr	2		2		
Lowel, David	1	4	4		
Lusher, Joseph	2	5	3		
Lockling, Dennis	1		1		
Lockling, Joel	1	1	3		
Lockling, Levi	2	1	4		
Lockling, Jona	1	4	2		
Leonard, John	1	2	4		
Millet, Joseph	1		1		
Martin, Ichabod	1	2	2		
Miles, Abner	2	2	4		
Martin, Danl	2	1	4		
More, Gardiner	1	3	4		
More, Willard	2		3		
Minot, Saml	2	3	6		
Martin, Danl., Junr	2	1	5		
More, Rufus	1				
Morey, Augustus	1	1	2		
Metcalf, George	1		1		
More, Wm	1	3	1		
More, David	1	1	2		
More, John	1	1	2		
More, Abijah, Junr	1		2		
More, Abijah	2		2		
McWain, Andrew	2	3	4		
Martin, Robt	2	1	2		
More, Gideon	1	1	3		
McWain, Wm	1	2	5		
More, Jonah	2		2		
Martin, Aaron	2	1	1		
More, Fairbank	1	1	2		
More, Abijah, 3rd	1	1	3		
More, Hezh	1	2	2		
Norcross, Saml	1	4	4		
Nichols, Thos	1				
Nichols, Josiah	1	1	2		
Newton, James	2	3	5		
Nichols, Ebenr	4	1	5		
Nelson, John	1	6	5		
Nelson, Thos	1	3	7		
Newton, Danl	2	2	4		
Nichols, Francis	1	2	1		
Nichols, Jona	2		5		
Poole, Wm	2	2	2		
Pettingill, Asa	1		2		
Powers, Jonas	2	2	5		
Packard, E. Saml	3	2	5		
Pierce, Roswell	1		2		
Parker, Ebenr	1	4	5		
Parmeter, Jacob	1	2	2		
Pierce, Danl	2	1	1		
Perry, Amos	4	3	5		
Pierce, Rufus	1		4		
Pierce, Reuben	2		2		
Pierce, Joseph, Junr	2	7	3		
Pierce, Thos	2	2	4		
Parker, Roswell	3	1	5		
Palmer, Isaac	1	2	2		
Pierce, Joseph	1	1	5		
Pierce, Ephm	1	3	4		
Pierce, Jona	2	3	5		
Philips, Charles	1	4	[illegible]		
Perry, Joseph	1	1	[illegible]		
Poole, Joseph	2	2	[illegible]		
Perry, Wm., Junr	1	1	5	1	
Perry, Job	1		3		
Pierce, Ezekl	1	4	3		
Pierce, Ezekl., Junr	1	1	2		
Perry, Wm	1	4	2		
Redaway, David	1	1	2		
Reed, John	1	4	3		
Robbins, Wm	1	1	4		
Redaway, Jona	1	2	3		
Remmington, Peleg	1		1		
Remmington, Elisha	1	1	3		
Rian, Derby	3	1	5		
Reynolds, Grindall	1		3		
Roberts, John	2	1	2		
Reynolds, Benja	1	2	2		
Reed, Timo	3		3		
Richards, Danl	1	3	3		
Reed, Timo, Junr	2	2	2		
Rice, Barzaliel	3	3	2		
Rugg, John	1	1	4		
Reynolds, Nathl	1	1	2		
Reed, John, Junr	1	3	3		
Redaway, Timo	1	1	4		
Redaway, Timo., Junr	1	1	3		
Redaway, Wilmath	1	1	5		
Richards, Jona	1		1		
Richardson, John	1		2		
Smead, Reuben	1		2		
Sabin, John	1	3	4		
Sabin, David	1		1		
Smith, Joseph	3	4	6		
Sabin, Noah, Junr	4	2	11		
Stevenson, Wm	1	1	2		
Soper, Amasa	2	1	3		
Sessions, John	1				
Skinner, Saml	1	1	1		
Sabin, Danl	1	1	7		
Snow, John	3	1	4		
Sanderson, Ebenr	1	4	5		
Smith, Elijah	2		4		
Snow, Jonas	1	2	5		
Smith, James	1	2	2		
Steele, James	1	5	4		
Stockwell, Moses	3	2	6		
Shaw, John	3	2	5		
Stebbins, Solomon	2		1		
Stebbins, Jona	1	3	1		
Snow, Joseph	1	2	3		
Townsend, Richd	1	1	1		
Townsend, John	2	2	6		
Thurstin, James	1		3		
Talbert, Wealthy	1	1	4		
Thurber, Barnabas, Junr	1		1		
Thompson, Benja	1	2	3		
Turner, John	1	1	2		
Thurber, Barnabas	2	1	3		
Turner, Thos	1	1	2		
Thayer, Nehh	1	4	2		
Turner, John, Junr	1	3	3		
Urin, James	2	1	4		
Underwood, Russel	1		1		
Underwood, Timo	2	2	3		
Wilder, John	1	3	2		
Woodward, Saml	1	3	6		
Willard, Prentiss	1	1	3		
Washburn, Asa	2	3	4		
Wilson, David	2	1	6		
White, Josiah	3	2	4		
Witt, Benja	1	1	7		
Wright, Ebenr	2	2	4		
Wilson, John	3		5		
Wheat, Saml	1	3	6		
Wilson, Peter	2	2	4		
Wilson, Edwd	3	2	4		
Wilson, Jeremiah	3	5	4		
Wilson, Lucus	2	1	5		
Wilson, David, Junr	1		1		
Winslow, Peleg	2	2	2		
Winslow, Joseph	2	1	3		
Ware, George	1	3	5		
Walker, Thos	3	3	10		
Wilson, Ezekl	2	5	5		
Wilder, Joel	1	3	2		
Wilson, Paul	1	2	6		
Wilson, David, Junr	1	2	5		
Wilson, Levi	2		1		
Wallace, John	1	1	1		
ROCKINGHAM TOWN.					
Adams, Joseph	3	2	6		
Albee, Joseph	1		1		
Adams, Luther	1		2		
Albee, John	1	1	1		
Archur, Benja	2	2	3		
Ayere, Elisha	2	1	8		
Adams, Eli	1	1	3		
Albee, Ebenr	1	2	3		
Albee, Ebenr., Junr	1		1		
Archur, John	2		1		
Blanchard, Wm	1		1		
Bayley, John	1	2	2		
Benton, Jacob	1	1	1		
Bowtwell, Josiah	1		2		
Burke, Eastman	1		1		
Barret, Joel	1		2		
Bixby, Danl	1	3	1		
Barney, Jona	3	2	1		
Brown, Jona	1	4	2		
Blanchard, Wm., Junr	1		2		
Burt, Jona	1	4	1		
Clark, Timo	4	3	5		
Caldwell, Adam	1		5		
Campbell, David	3	1	3		
Chamberlain, Eli	1		1		
Clark, Charles	1	1	1		
Clark, Hezh	1		4		
Chamberlain, Edmond	3	2	3		
Campbell, Alexr	1	3	2		
Cutler & Caldwell	2	2	3		
Clapp, Joshua	1				
Clark, Wm	2		1		
Clawson, Wildboro	1	4	3		
Cooper, Zeb	1	3	1		
Clawson, Ichabod	1	1	1		
Clawson, Roswell	2		2		
Cooper, John	2	1	1		
Cobourn, Amasa	1	3	3		
Clefford, Jacob	1	2	3		
Davis, Cyrus	1	2	3		
Derby, Edmond	2		3		
Davis, Nathl	1	1	5		
Davis, Henry	1	4	2		
Davis, John	1				
Darling, Timo	1	1	4		
Davis, Levi	3	2	4		
Ellis, John	1	4	5		
Emery, Saml	3	3	5		
Edson, Danl	1		6		
Edson, Isaiah	1		2		
Eames, Thos	2	2	3		
Eastman, Saml	1	1	2		
Evans, Asher	3	3	3		
Evans, Peter, Junr	4	2	3		
Evans, Eli	3	4	4		
Forbes, Saml	1	2	3		
Fletcher, Luke	1		4		
Felt, Eliphalet	1	4	4		
Fuller, Jona	3	3	4		
Fuller, John	2	2	3		
Fish, John	1	5	2		
Fling, Patrick	1		2		
Guslin, Thos	1		4		
Gilmore, John	4	1	3		

WINDHAM COUNTY—Continued.

NAME OF HEAD OF FAMILY.	Free white males of 16 years and upward, including heads of families.	Free white males under 16 years.	Free white females, including heads of families.	All other free persons.	Slaves.
ROCKINGHAM TOWN—continued.					
Goodale, Elijah	2	2	2		
Graves, Phinehas	2		3		
Green, Widow		2	5		
Gilson, Joseph	2	2	2		
Hazelton, Richd	1	1	2		
Hazeltine, Jonas	1	1	2		
Hazeltine, Wm	1	2	2		
Holton, Jona	3	4	1		
Himes, Stephen	1	1	4		
Hall, James	3	1	4		
How, John	1	1	2		
Hale, Joshua	2	3	2		
Hitchcock, Widow			3		
Hall, John	1		1		
Jones, Widow		3	2		
Johnson, Joshua	1	1	3		
Johnson, Isaac	1	3	4		
Johnson, Benja	1		2		
Ingals, Ebenr	2	1	4		
Jennins, Salmon	1		1		
Johnson, A. Robert	1	1	2		
Jewet, Abel	1	3	2		
Kendal, Wm	2	1	2		
Knight, Elijah	1	1	1		
Kendall, Ebenr	1		2		
Kidder, Thos	1	3	4		
Knights, Elisha	1	2	4		
Kendall, Ebenr, Junr	1	2	7		
Knight, Russel	4		2		
King, Danl	2	4	2		
Lovell, Ebenr	1		1		
Lock, Ebenr	1	2	2		
Lane, Obediah	1	2	1		
Lovell, Enos	2	3	4		
Lock, Abraham	1	5	2		
Larkin, Levi	2		1		
Lovell, John	2	5	4		
Lovell, Elijah	3	4	4		
Lovell, Oliver	1	2	7		
Lovell, Timo	2		1		
Larcomb, Job	1	4	6		
Lawson, Ichabod	1	1	2		
McLawland, Thos	1				
McCalvin, Ebenr	1	3	3		
Mellin, John	1				
Marsh, Moses	6	2	7		
Mathews, Asher	2	6	6		
Mathews, John	3	4	7		
Metcalf, Saml	1	2	3		
Minot, Wm	4	3	4		
Miller, Saml	3	1	3		
Muzzy, Joseph	2		3		
McCawly, Saml	1	4	2		
Nurse, Francis	4				
Newton, Silas	2		1		
Olcott, Elias	3	2	5		
Ober, Saml	1	3	4		
Procter, Nathan	1	2	4		
Pulsiford, David & John	4	5	9		
Parker, Abiel	1	1	3		
Pulsiford, Ebenr	1	2	4		
Parker, John	1	2	3		
Pease, Widow	2		4		
Petty, John	2	2	3		
Procter, James	1		3		
Petty, Solomon	1	1	4	2	
Porter, Chandler	1	2	2		
Powers, Timo	1		6		
Pike, David	1	1	1		
Robinson, John	1	3	3		
Roundy, John	1		1		
Ripley, John	1	1	3		
Rose, Edwd	6		4		
Richardson, Jotham	2		1		
Rixford, Saml	1	1	1		
Reed, Isaac	1	3	4		
Reed, Elijah	1	1	3		
Roundy, Uriah	1	3	4		
Ripley, Vespn	1	2	4		
Roundy, John, Junr	2		2		
Reed, Fredrick	1	3	3		
Ripley, Charles	1	1	3		
Richardson, Jona, Junr	1		3		
Stearns, Jabez	1	1	2		
Savage, Ozias	1	1	1		
Savage, John	3	2	1		
Stearns, Isaac	2	3	4		
Sturdavant, Zephh	1	2	1		
Sanderson, Israel	1	2	2		
Stoddard, Josiah	1		2		
Stafford, Philip	3	2	5		
ROCKINGHAM TOWN—continued.					
Stitt, John	2	2	2		
Simonds, Wm	3		3		
Stanley, David	2		1		
Stearns, Wm., Junr	1	3	3		
Stearns, Jona	1	1	1		
Stearns, Wm	2		4		
Shipman, Abraham	1	3	6		
Sabin, Elisha	1	1	3		
Searls, Abijah	1	3	2		
Stearns, John	1		2		
Sanderson, David	5	1	4		
Stocker, Elijah	1	1	2		
Sabin, Levi	1	1	1		
Stowel, John	2	1	4		
Smith, Nye	1	4	2		
Spears, Saml	3	2	2		
Sanderson, Ebenr	1	1	2		
Taylor, Saml	2	1	4		
Thayer, Wm	2	1	1		
Tozzer, Ebenr	1		3		
Thurstin, Nathan	1	1	2		
Whitcomb, Widow		2	3		
Wheelock, Jona	1	1	3		
Wait, John	2	2	6		
Wolfe, C. John	1	3	3		
Wood, William	1	1	4		
Wright, Solomon	1	1	5		
Weaver, Danl	1	1	5		
Wing, Thos	1	2	4		
Wing, Thos., Junr	1	3	1		
Wing, Turner	1		1		
Whiting, John	1	1	4		
Wright, Nathl	1	1	3		
Wright, Moses	1	1	2		
Webb, Charles	1	5	2		
Webb, Joshua	3		3		
Williams, Benja	2		5		
Webb, Calvin	2	2	4		
Webb, Jehiel	3	1	5		
Walker, James	2	1	4		
White, Phinehas	1		3		
White, Abiel	1	1	5		
Wood, Barnabas	2	2	4		
White, Josiah	1		1		
White, Paul	2	3	1		
Whitney, Asa	1				
White, Abijah	1		6		
Wood, David	4	2	1		
Woodbury, Jessee	1	2	6		
Whiting, Saml	2	2	3		
Wilson, Nathan	4	3	1		
SOMERSET TOWN.					
Badcock, David	1	1	2		
Crosby, Silas	1	2	3		
Clark, David	1		1		
Cobb, Nathan	1	1	1		
Hodges, Ephm	1	1	4		
Kempton, Oliver	1		1		
Kelly, John	1	3	5		
Lawton, Wm	2	3	3		
Lawton, John	1		3		
Morris, John	1	2	2		
Parmalee, James	1	2	2		
Parmalee, John	1	2	4		
Palmer, S. Zuri	1	2	2		
Palmer, James	1	2	1		
Rice, Perez	1	2	1		
Rice, Danl	1	3	2		
Richardson, Jona	1	4	2		
Welman, Benoni	1	2	1		
Welman, Silas	1	1	2		
Welman, Jacob	2	1	2		
Waiste, Barzaliel	4	1	6		
STRATTON TOWN.					
Bowtwell, Saml	1	1	1		
Burch, Warren	1	2	2		
Bixby, Sampson	1	2	1		
Chase, Isaac	1	2	1		
Cook, David	1	1	3		
Grout, Joshua	1		3		
Grout, Denison	1				
Greenwood, Jona	1		1		
Gale, Solomon	1	1	1		
Gleason, Saml	1				
Holman, John	1	1	2		
Hale, Joel	2	1	3		
Hobbs, Benja	1	1	2		
STRATTON TOWN—con.					
Kidder, Francis	1		3		
Lamb, Phinehas	1	1	4		
Mann, Wm	2		2		
Morseman, Timo	1	1	5		
Miller, Elkanah	1		1		
Patch, Joseph	1	2	3		
Philips, Asa	1	1	3		
Stone, Clark	2	1	1		
Thayer, Stephen	1	1	1		
Wait, John	1	3	3		
Woodward, Jaras	1				
THOMLINSON TOWN.					
Axtel, Joseph	3	1	2		
Axtel, Alexr	1		2		
Beard, Abijah	3	1	4		
Baker, Danl	1	1	5		
Baker, Cornelius	1				
Burges, Ebenr	4	4	3		
Bixby, Aaron	1	1	3		
Beard, Josiah	1	2	2		
Bond, Henry	1	3	2		
Burdid, Ebenr	1	3	1		
Bennet, Nathl	3	1	2		
Burnham, Peter	1		3		
Burnham, Joshua	1		1		
Cole, Moses	2	2	7		
Challis, Nathl	1	1	3		
Carver, Eleazar	1	2	1		
Chafee, David	2		2		
Dennison, Aaron	1	2	5		
Dwindle, Benja	1	1	3		
Dutton, Thos	2	2	3		
Davis, Oliver	1				
Davis, Thos	1		1		
Dumbleton, Nathl	2	4	4		
Edson, Ezra	1	4	1		
Edson, Nehemiah	1	3	1		
Edson, Robt	1	1	5		
Edson, Rufus	1	3	2		
Edson, John	1	2	2		
Fisher, Asa	2		3		
Fisher, Amos	2	2	2		
Flemons, John	1	2	3		
Fuller, Bartholemew	1	3	3		
French, Wm	1		1		
Farmer, Joseph	1	3	2		
Gibson, Abraham	1	3	3		
Gibson, Nathl	1	2	2		
Gibson, Jona	2	2	4		
Gleason, Job	2	1	3		
Guile, Ephm	1	2	4		
Gray, Moses	1	3	2		
Guttridge, T. Thos	1		1		
Guttridge, John, Junr	1		1		
Guttridge, Moses	1	1	2		
Gibson, Solomon	1	2	1		
Gibson, Zachh	1		2		
Gibson, Uriah	1		2		
Hall, Wm	2	3	1		
Hayward, Stephen	2	4	4		
Hayward, Ziba	1	3	1		
Hayward, Widow		3	2		
Holmes, Robt	3	4	3		
Hadley, Charles	1	4	1		
Harris, Wm	1	2	2		
Heaton, Wm	1	2	2		
Houghton, Manassah	1				
Hooker, Ruel	2	1	4		
Johnson, John	1				
Kenny, Thos	1		1		
Kidder, John	1	1	2		
Kendall, Joseph	1				
Lane, Mathew	1	1	1		
Lane, John	1		2		
Loveland, Israel	2	1	3		
Mastick, Benja	1	1	2		
Mastick, Wm	1	2	2		
Mathews, Ephm	1	2	2		
Martin, Saml	1	1	3		
Perkins, Charles	3	1	3		
Palmer, David	2	4	4		
Palmer, Thos	1	2	4		
Parks, K. Thos	1	1	2		
Parks, John	1	2	3		
Phelps, Elijah	1	2	3		
Putman, Miles	3	1	2		
Putman, Edwd	1	3	3		
Putman, Danl	1	1	1		
Pollard, Jeremiah	1				

WINDHAM COUNTY—Continued.

NAME OF HEAD OF FAMILY.	Free white males of 16 years and upward, including heads of families.	Free white males under 16 years.	Free white females, including heads of families.	All other free persons.	Slaves.
THOMLINSON TOWN—continued.					
Rand, Artemas	1		2		
Rhoads, James	1	1	3		
Rhoads, Joseph	1	3	2		
Rugg, Levi	1	2	5		
Ross, James	2	3	5		
Spring, Sam[l]	3	1	3		
Spaldin, Sam[l]	1	1	2		
Stickney, W[m]	2	3	4		
Stickney, David	2	1	3		
Slack, W[m]	2	2	1		
Smith, John	1	3	2		
Smith, George	1		3		
Smith, George, Jun[r]	1		5		
Smith, Roger	1	3	1		
Shipman, Sam[l]	1	1	2		
Tarbel, Isaac	1	2	1		
Tenny, Eben[r]	2	1	1		
Tenny, David	1		2		
Woolly, John	2		4		
Woolly, Jon[a]	1		5		
Woolly, Tho[s]	2	3	1		
Ware, John	1	1	3		
Walker, Sam[l]	1	3	3		
Wood, W[m]	1	2	2		
Walton, Rufus	1	2	3		
Wyes, Dan[l]	1	2	4		
Witheral, Nath[l]	1	3	4		
Whitcomb, Joseph	3		3		
TOWNSEND TOWN.					
Austin, Asa	2	1	4		
Austin, George	1				
Ames, Lem[l]	2	3	2		
Bemis, Tho[s]	1	2	5		
Burt, Eben[r]	2	1	3		
Brigham, Eben[r]	1	3	3		
Barnes, John	1		1		
Burbee, Jon[a]	3	1	3		
Belknap, Joseph	1	1	1		
Barnes, Sam[l]	2		1		
Barnard, Joshua	3	1	1		
Barnard, Eli	2		2		
Barnard, Joshua, Jun[r]	2	2	2		
Butterfield, Zethan	1				
Cook, Moses	1	1	4		
Clayton, Moses	1	1	1		
Chase, Henry	3	1	3		
Clayton, Jon[a]	2		4		
Chase, Jacob	1	3	4		
Chase, Nath[l]	1	3	4		
Clemonds, Benj[a]	2	2	4		
Chase, Solomon	1				
Chase, Amariah	1		1		
Chase, Tim[o]	1	3	5		
Dyer, John	2	1	3		
Dyer, Widow		2	4		
Dunton, Tho[s]	1	4	3		
Dunton, Joseph	1	4	2		
Doolittle, Amzi	3	3	3		
Drake, Paul	1				
Dunham, Joseph	1	1	2		
Doolittle, Amzi, Jun[r]	2	1	1		
Darling, Caleb	1	3	1		
Ervin, Calvin	1	3	4		
Franklin, Stephen	1	2	2		
Fletcher, Sam[l]	3		9		
Fish, John, Jun[r]	1	1	2		
Fish, John	3	1	2		
Fairbanks, Mourice	2	3	3		
Griggs, Gideon	1		7		
Gray, Jonas	5		5		
Gray, Mathew	1				
Gray, Amos	2	1	2		
Hazeltine, David	1				
Hunt, Isaac, Jun[r]	1				
Hazeltine, ——	3	2	4		
Hayward, Levi	2	2	3		
Hazeltine, Elisha	1				
Holbrook, Tim[o]	1	2	3		
Hazeltine, Paul, Jun[r]	1				
Hazeltine, John	2		3		
How, John, 3rd	1	3	1		
Hayward, Eli	1	2	4		
How, Benj[a]	2	4	5		
How, John	1		2		
Hart, H. Isaac	1	3	3		
Holbrook, Widow			1		
Hazeltine, Paul	2	3	3		
Hazeltine, John, Jun[r]	1	1	1		
Hazeltine, Asa	2	3	4		

NAME OF HEAD OF FAMILY.	Free white males of 16 years and upward, including heads of families.	Free white males under 16 years.	Free white females, including heads of families.	All other free persons.	Slaves.
TOWNSEND TOWN—con.					
Holbrook, Ezra	2	2	4		
Holbrook, Elias	2	2	5		
Holbrook, Eli	2	2	2		
Holbrook, Asa	2		2		
Holbrook, Tho[s]	1	1	3		
Hinds, B. John	1	2	3		
Holbrook, Amos	2	3	1		
Hall, Jon[a]	2		2		
Johnson, Mitchel	1	5	2		
Jennison, Robert	1	1	1		
Johnson, W[m]	1				
Johnson, W[m]., Jun[r]	1		1		
Kimball, Charles	1	2	1		
Kingsbury, John	1	1	1		
Lowel, Solomon	1	3	2		
Lowel, Stephen	2	2	3		
Low, Tho[s]	1	3	4		
Murdock, Benj[a]	1				
Murdock, Jesse	1				
Mitchel, Joshua	1	1	2		
Murdock, Benj[a]	1	1	2		
Mitchel, W[m]	1		2		
More, Jonas	1		1		
Ober, Eben[r]	2	1	2		
Ober, Ezra	1				
Puffer, Amos	1		3		
Puffer, Rich[d]	1	1	3		
Pitts, John	1	1	3		
Parkhurst, Sam[l]	1	4	1		
Rawson, Bala	1		3		
Roberts, Rufus	1	3	1		
Reed, Tho[s]	2	1	6		
Rawson, Gardiner	1		1		
Rawson, Stephen	1	1	6		
Rasey, Asahel	1	4	2		
Reed, Eben[r]	1		1		
Streeter, John	1		2		
Smith, James	1	1	4		
Shaw, W[m]	1		2		
Squire, Charles	1	2	2		
Scott, Robert	1		3		
Smith, David	1	2	2		
Taft, Amariah	3	2	5		
Talbert, Eph[m]	3		1		
Taft, Eben[r]	2	1	2		
Tyler, Joseph	5	1	4		
Taft, Willard	1	1	1		
Town, Wilder	2		2		
Taft, W[m]	1	1	5		
Turtlelow, Abraham	1	1	3		
Watkins, ——			2		
Wood, Joshua	2		2		
Wilkinson, Hez[h]	4		3		
Wiswall, Sam[l]	3	4	8		
Whitcomb, Jonas	1				
White, Edward	1	2	3		
Wheelock, Caleb	1	5	1		
Wheelock, Amasa	1		1		
Walker, Jasoram	1	2	4		
Warren, Jonas	1	2	3		
Wilder, Aaron	1		1		
Wood, Nathan	1	2	2		
Watkins, John	1	2	3		
Wheelock, Eph[m]	2		1		
Wood, Tho[s]	1	2	2		
Wood, Joshua, Jun[r]	1	1	2		
Wood, John	2	3	3		
Wood, Tim[o]	1		2		
Watkins, Dan[l]	1	1	2		
Walding, James	2		1		
Whipple, John	1	2	4		
Wood, Eph[m]	1		1		
WARDSBOROUGH TOWN.					
(North District.)					
Allen, Ithamer	3	3	5		
Allen, Ahaz	1	1	2		
Allen, Sylvester	2	5	2		
Bryant, Lem[l]	1	3	4		
Bill, Eben[r]	1	1	4		
Braley, Lem[l]	1	4	2		
Burnap, Nathan	1	1	3		
Bradley, W[m]	1		1		
Bradley, John	1	1	2		
Beale, John	1		2		
Corben, Stephen	1	1	3		
Chapen, Jesse	1	2	2		
Chapen, Sam[l]	1	3	2		
Chapen, Dan[l]	1	1	2		

NAME OF HEAD OF FAMILY.	Free white males of 16 years and upward, including heads of families.	Free white males under 16 years.	Free white females, including heads of families.	All other free persons.	Slaves.
WARDSBOROUGH TOWN—continued.					
(North District—Con.)					
Cole, Tho[s]	1	2	2		
Crowningshield, Rich[d]	3		3		
Crosset, John	2	2	1		
Chamberlin, Jacob	1		6		
Caldwell, Eph[m]	1	1	1		
Davis, Sam[l]	2	2	5		
Dickerman, W[m]	1	1	2		
Draper, Aaron	2		4		
Davis, Paul	1	3	3		
Dix, Joseph	1	2	4		
Edmonds, Stephen	1		2		
Fisher, Enoch	1	2	3		
Fairbanks, Perley	2	2	2		
Fisher, Simeon	1	1	5		
Glazier, Barzaliel	2	5	4		
Gould, Nath[l]	1	2	1		
Hammond, Hinsdale	1	3	3		
Hammond, Simeon	1		2		
Hammond, Sam[l]	2	3	2		
Harris, Dan[l]	2		3		
Holbrook, Abner	1		2		
Holbrook, John	2	1	3		
Hunt, Richard	1	5	3		
Harvey, Rufus	1		2		
Holbrook, John, Jun[r]	2		3		
Hiscock, Rich[d]	1	2	4		
Hiscock, Sam[l]	1	2	1		
Jewel, Tho[s]	1	1	2		
Johnson, Neh[h]	2	1	1		
Johnson, Tim[o]	1	1	1		
Jones, Asa	1	2	3		
Jones, John	4	4	4		
Kenny, Sam[l]	1	2	1		
Knoulton, Asa	3	1	1		
Kilburn, Dan[l]	1		3		
Keaton, Rich[d]	1	3	2		
Kidder, Sam[l]	2	2	1		
Lizieur, Sam[l]	1	1	3		
Morse, Joseph	1	4	4		
Martin, Abraham	1		1		
Morse, Isaac	1	1	4		
Morse, Abner	1	1	1		
Moffat, Dudley	2	1	2		
Newel, Jerard	1		2		
Newel, Philip	2	1	3		
Newel, Levi	1	1	2		
Newel, Hiram	1		2		
Perry, Stephen	1	1	2		
Philips, Ezek[l]	1	1	1		
Plimpton, Abner	4	1	2		
Perry, Eli	2	1	3		
Ray, Gideon	1	1	3		
Ray, Asa	1	3	2		
Ramsdel, John	2	2	5		
Ramsdel, John, Jun[r]	1	2	2		
Reed, Dan[l]	2	3	1		
Rice, John	1		4		
Sherman, Noah	1		3		
Simpson, Tho[s]	1	1	3		
Stacy, John	2		2		
Smith, John	2		2		
Thayer, David	1		5		
Underwood, Asa	2	1	3		
Underwood, Joseph	2	1	1		
Woodcock, Elkanah	2	1	2		
Woodcock, Asahel	1		1		
Warren, Stephen	1	3	5		
Wallace, James	1	2	3		
Wilder, Joseph	3		3		
Willard, Oliver	1	2	3		
Wakefield, Tim[o]	2	2	3		
Walker, Edw[d]	2	3	2		
Wait, Thaddeus	1		6		
Wait, Silas	1	1	1		
Wheelock, Asa	1	1	1		
WARDSBOROUGH TOWN.					
(South District.)					
Allen, Friday	1		3		
Baxter, Nathan	3	1	6		
Baxter, Uriah	1				
Briggs, Joseph	1	2	3		
Bugby, Willard	1	1	2		
Chittenden, Reuben	1	1	3		
Chamberlain, Joseph	1	3	1		
Converse, Barnard	1	1	3		
Coombs, Jon[a]	1				

WINDHAM COUNTY—Continued.

NAME OF HEAD OF FAMILY.	Free white males of 16 years and upward, including heads of families.	Free white males under 16 years.	Free white females, including heads of families.	All other free persons.	Slaves.
WARDSBOROUGH TOWN—continued.					
(*South District*—Con.)					
Coombs, John	1	2	1		
Cheney, Eben^r	2		3		
Dexter, David	1	4	2		
Dexter, Jon^a	1	1	2		
Ellis, Gamaliel	1	1	1		
Fitts, John	2		1		
Foster, Edwd	1	1	1		
Hall, William	1	3	2		
Hayward, John	1	2	3		
Hazeltine, Danl	1	1	1		
Holbrook, Silas	1				
Hathaway, Edward	1				
Hodges, Abiather	1	1	1		
How, Gardiner	1	1	1		
Jones, Barzaliel	2	2	2		
Jones, Elias	1	1	2		
Jones, Eleazar	1				
Johnson, Luther	1	1	4		
Johnson, Constant	1				
Johnson, Lem^l	1				
Johnson, Zebediah	1		2		
Johnson, Joab	1				
Johnson, David	2		3		
Kendall, Joshua	1	1	4		
Knapp, John	1		3		
Lazdel, Isaac	1	4	2		
Lee, John	1		2		
McDanolds, Thos	1	3	4		
Perry, Abner	1	3	3		
Putman, Ozial	1	2	3		
Rugg, Joseph	2	1	3		
Sears, Eben^r	1	2	4		
Sears, W^m	1	1	2		
Staples, Jon^a	1	2	3		
Staples, Jacob	1	2	3		
Sparks, Eben^r	1	4	4		
Sears, Widow	1		2		
Stanley, W^m	1				
Stearns, Elijah	1		1		
Stearns, Asaph	1				
Strickling, W^m	1		4		
Southard, David	1	1	4		
Thompson, Jon^a	3	1	6		
Wood, Aaron	2		3		
Wood, Tim^o	1	3	3		
Warner, Danl	3	1	3		
Wood, Nathan	1		4		
Wells, Danl	1		1		
Wright, Silas	1	3	2		
Weston, James	1	3	1		
Whitney, John	1	2	2		
WESTMINSTER TOWN.					
Arnold, Seth	3	2	1		
Averal, John	1		1		
Averal, John, Junr	1	3	3		
Abbee, Jacob	3	2	6		
Averal, Thos	1	3	5		
Averal, Asa	7		9		
Averal, Saml	1	1	6		
Abbee, John	3	2	5		
Avery, Saml	1	2	5		
Burt, Benj^a	2		3		
Burke, Saml	2		4		
Bundy, James	1	2	3		
Burke, Silas	3		7		
Brown, Barron	1	2	4		
Baldwin, Thos	1	2	5		
Bragg, Eben^r	1	1	3		
Baldwin, Thos., Junr	2	1	2		
Bradley, R. Stephen	3	2	3		
Bartlett, Moses	1	1	2		
Briggs, Silas	4	1	3		
Baxter, John	2	3	3		
Burke, Jesse	4		3		
Burke, Eliab	1				
Bradley, Thaddeus	1	2	4		
Burke, Joseph	1	1	3		
Baits, Jabez	1	3	3		
Brown, Benj^a	1		4		
Bayley, Clark	1	1	5		
Bayley, Jon^a	2		2		
Baldwin, Jon^a	1		2		
Bemis, John	1	2	4		
Bradley, John	2	3	3		
Bliss, Nathl	1	1	1		
Bragg, Eben^r., Junr	1	2	1		
WESTMINSTER TOWN—continued.					
Carpenter, Abiel	1	3	3		
Carpenter, Abiel Junr	1	2	1		
Clark, Seth	1	2	3		
Chafee, Squire	1	1	2		
Chamberlain, Jedediah	1	1	3		
Chafee, Otis	1	2	2		
Chafee, Clifford	1	4	1		
Chafee, Constant	1	1	1		
Carpenter, Abner	1	3	4		
Cook, William	2		4		
Chamberlain, Isaac	1	1	2		
Cone, Samuel	5	2	3		
Cone, Thos	2	3	1		
Chafee, Widow			1	1	
Clark, David	1		1		
Campbell R. Edwd	3	1	4		
Chafee, Atherton	1	3	1		
Cook, Robert	4	4	6		
Crook, W^m., Junr	1		1		
Carpenter, Abner, Junr	1	1	3		
Carpenter, Amos	1	1	4		
Cook, Eph^m	1	3	2		
Crafford, James	1		2		
Crafford, Theophilus	2	1	2		
Cummins, P. Saml	1		2		
Colten Charles	1		2		
Craige, Thos	2	2	9		
Carpenter, Comfort	3		4		
Cone, Lem^l	2	1	1		
Cone, Joshua	1		1		
Clark, Calvin	1	2	3		
Cary, Ebcn^r	1	2	4		
Dickinson, Azariah	3	1	3		
Doubleday, Widow			2		
Doran, Rich^d	1	2	5		
Downe, Saml	3	1	5		
Dickinson, Job	1	2	4		
Dickinson, Danl	1		1		
Dickinson, John	1				
Day, Elkanah	1	1	1		
Darling, Oliver	1	1	3		
Easton, Bildad	2	2	6		
Eaton, Marvelick	1	1	1		
Edgel, John	3	2	5		
Eaton, Asa	2	3	3		
Eaton, Asa, Junr	3	3	3		
Eaton, David	3	1	2		
Eaton, Marvelick, Junr	1	1	1		
Ervin, Joseph	2	2	7		
Fletcher, Artimus	1	1	2		
Fairbanks, Eph^m	1	3	4		
Fuller, Widow	1		1		
Fuller, Thos	1	3	4		
Farmer, Benj^a	1	2	5		
Gansoy, Amos	2		1		
Gilson, Joel	2	2	4		
Grout, John	1	3	2		
Gilson, Zachariah	3	1	5		
Gilson, Michael	4		3		
Gilson, Simon	1				
Gould, John	4		3		
Gould, John, Junr	1	1	3		
Gates, Dan	1	4	4		
Goodale, Amos	1		1		
Gibbs, Nathan	2		4		
Gould, Danl	2	1	3		
Gould, Nathan	2				
Gould, Seth	2	1	4		
Gransey, Oliver	3	5	4		
Gould, Danl., Junr	1	1	3		
Goodale, Edwd	2	3	6		
Goodale, Moses	2	3	2		
Gilson, Danl	1	1	1		
Goodridge, Levi	2	2	4		
Goodridge, Benj^a	2	2	3		
Gerry, Edwd., Junr	1				
Gerry, Edwd	2		1		
Gerry, Jon^a	1		2		
Goodale, Abiel	1	4	5		
Goodenow, Adino	1	3	5		
Goodhue, Eben^r	1		1		
Goodale, Asahel	3	1	5		
Hildreth, Sheltial	1	2	6		
Hitchcock, Heli	1	2	3		
Holden, Charles	2	2	4		
Hutchins, Buckley	1	2	1		
Houghton, Jon^a	1	4	3		
Holton, Eben^r	2	3	2		
Hatch, Isaiah	3	3	6		
Holten, Joel	4	4	5		
WESTMINSTER TOWN—continued.					
Hall, Lott	2	2	3		
Hall, W^m	1		2		
Holden, Francis	2	5	4		
Hitchcock, Eldad	2	3	3		
Hide, W^m	1	2	5		
Holt, John	2	4	3		
Hooker, Asahel	1	1	3		
Hunt, Jasaniah	1		1		
Heaton, David	2	1	1		
Hitchcock, Elisha	1	6	2		
Hindey, Caleb	1	2	2		
Heaton, W^m	1	3	2		
Harlow, Eleazar	3	3	7		
Ide, Joseph	2	4	6		
Ide, Israel	1	2	4		
Ide, James	1	4	4		
Ide, Jesse	2		5		
Ide, Ichaboo	1	2	5		
Ingram, Gersham	1		1		
Jones, Amos	3	2	6		
Keth, Danl	1	1	2		
Kittridge, Jon^a	3		2		
Kittridge, Nathl	1	3	1		
Lippingwell, Reuben	1		4		
Lippingwell, Reuben, Junr	1	1	2		
Lane, Jon^a	3	1	2		
Lovejoy, John	2		1		
Lovejoy, Peter	1	2	5		
Martin, W^m	2	3	8		
Mason, Oliver	4		2		
Mason, Isaac	1		2		
McNeal, John	1				
McNeal, Neh^h	1		6		
Morse, John	2	3	2		
Miller, Robt	1	2	4		
Miller, John	1		2		
Norton, John	3	2	7		
Norton, Cyrus	1		2		
Noyes, Danl	3	2	4		
Partridge, Lovett	2	2	6		
Paine, Jabez	2		2		
Powers, Asa	1		1		
Page, Thos	2		3		
Phippen, Saml	1		1		
Phippen, Saml., Junr	1	1	5		
Pomeroy, Phenny	2	2	5		
Parker, Tim^o	1	1	5		
Peck, Levi	1	2	1		
Peck, Ariel	1	1	2		
Parmeter, Joseph	1	2	4		
Pierce, Charles	1	2	2		
Perry, W^m	1		2		
Phippen, Joseph	1	3	6		
Pigsley, Robert	1	1	3		
Pigsley, Paul	1	4	2		
Philips, Zebulun	1	4	2		
Paul, John	1	5	3		
Perry, Jabez	2	1	3		
Perkins, Tim^o	1	1	4		
Pratt, Saml	3	2	2		
Phippen, Atwater	2	1	3		
Perkins, Neh^h	1		2		
Pierce, Ezek^l	1	2	1		
Perkins, Elder	1	3	3		
Priest, John	2		2		
Ranny, Jannah	1	1	2		
Ranny, Elijah	2	1	3		
Robinson, Noah	1	3	3		
Ranny, Joel	1		1		
Rand, Robert	2	2	6		
Richardson, James	3	3	4		
Robinson, Solomon	3	3	5		
Ranny, W^m	3	2	5		
Robinson, Reuben	1	3	5		
Robinson, Nathan	2	1	5		
Ranny, Eph^m	3	2	3		
Rice, Charles	1	2	3		
Ranny, Eph^m., Junr	2	1	2		
Robinson, Nathl	2		1		
Sanderson, Hez^h	1				
Shipman, Abraham	2	3	4		
Shipman, Abraham, J^r	1		1		
Spooner, Eliakim	2	3	4		
Sessions, John	4		3		
Spencer, Eph^m	2	2	5		
Stoddard, Danl	1		2		
Stiles, David, Junr	4	1	3		
Stone, Benj^a	1		2		
Smith, Benj^a	1	5	3		

WINDHAM COUNTY—Continued.

NAME OF HEAD OF FAMILY.	Free white males of 16 years and upward, including heads of families.	Free white males under 16 years.	Free white females, including heads of families.	All other free persons.	Slaves.
WESTMINSTER TOWN—continued.					
Shipman, Edwd	3	1	3		
Shipman, Abraham, 3rd.	1		1		
Stoddard, John	1	1	2		
Stoddard, Joshua	3	2	3		
Stoddard, Joshua, Junr.	1				
Sage, Sylvester	2		1		
Temple, Urijah	1	2	3		
Thomas, Joseph	2	1	2		
Turtle, John	2	4	5		
Town, Joseph	1	3	4		
Tower, Lynde	1		2		
Talmon, John	1	1	1		
Talmon, Widow		1	3		
Upham, James	1		2		
Webb, Joseph	1	1	4		
Wright, Medad	5	3	3		
Wright, Joseph	1				
Wheeler, Danl	1		1		
Winter, John	1	1	2		
White, Joel	2	2	4		
Whitney, Elijah	1	1	6		
Wilder, Wm	4		5		
Wilcox, John	1		3		
Whitcomb, Benja	1				
Willis, John	2	1	3		
Wilcox, Ephm	1	3	3		
Wilcox, Waitsill	1		1		
Wales, Aaron	3	2	2		
Woolly, Augustus	1	1	1		
Whitney, Benja	2	4	5		
Wright, Azariah	4		3		
Wall, Patrick	2	3	5		
Woolly, Amasa	1	1	2		
Willard, Abel	1	2	4		
Willard, Lynde	1	4	5		
Willard, Joseph	2	1	3		
Willard, Billy	2	1	5		
Woolly, Nathan	2	1	3		
Wells, Oliver	1	2	1		
Wells, Joshua	1	3	2		
Wales, Saml	1	1	1		
Wilson, Luke	1	1	3		
Wells, John	2	2	5		
Wyman, John	2	1	3		
Wright, Caleb	1		2		
Wright, Salmon	1	1	2		
Willard, Wm	1		1		
Wallace, Ebenr	1	1	2		
WHITINGHAM TOWN.					
Angel, James	3		4		
Anderson, Wm	2	1	3		
Armstrong, Simeon	1				
Bratton, Robert	3	1	2		
Bratton, David	1	3	2		
Barton, Jona	1	3	2		
Barton, Timo	1	3	3		
Barton, Benja	1	1	1		
Bishop, Solomon	1	3	4		
Bradley, Eli	1				
Butler, Saml	1	2	1		
Blodget, Thos	3	3	5		
Blodget, Benja., Junr	1	4	2		
Bond, Solomon	1		2		
Blodget, Benja	2		3		
Barr, Simeon	1		3		
Carnaga, Andrew	2	2	2		
Colman, Joseph	1				
Cooley, Benja	1	3	3		
Carley, Jona	1	2	1		
Clark, Billy	1	2	5		
Day, Saml	3	4	4		
Dodge, Joshua	1	1	2		
Dix, Jona	1	2	3		
Davis, Nathl	1	2	5		
Doubleday, Elisha	1	3	3		
Foster, Jabez	1	5	1		
Frazier, James	1	1	3		
Fuller, Calvin	1		3		
Gustin, Eliphalet	2		2		
Goodenow, Benja	3	1	2		
Graves, Jesse	1	4	2		

NAME OF HEAD OF FAMILY.	Free white males of 16 years and upward, including heads of families.	Free white males under 16 years.	Free white females, including heads of families.	All other free persons.	Slaves.
WHITINGHAM TOWN—continued.					
Gains, James	1	3	4		
Green, Amos	1	2	3		
Green, Nathan	1	1	5		
Glass, James	4	3	5		
Hunt, Thomas	3	2	3		
Hayward, John	5	1	3		
Hayward, John, Junr	1	1	2		
Hambleton, Jona	1				
Lyman, Isaac	3	2	5		
Lyman, Benja	2	2	5		
Lyman, Eleazar	1	1	2		
Lyman, Silas	1				
Lamphier, Banajah	1		2		
Lamphier, Reuben	1				
Lamphier, Chandler	1				
Lyon, Joseph	2		2		
Lovell, Saml	1	1	2		
Mullet, James	2	5	1		
Munn, Calvin	2	1	4		
Morey, John	1	1	2		
Nelson, John	1	2	2		
Nye, Jona	2	1	1		
Nye, Wm	1		5		
Otis, John	1		2		
Otis, John, Junr	1		2		
Pike, Leonard	1	6	7		
Pike, Elisha	1		1		
Pike, Elijah	1		1		
Pike, Nathl	1		3		
Roberts, James	1	3	4		
Rugg, John	4	1	8		
Rider, Caleb	1	2	3		
Reed, James	1	2	2		
Sikes, Francis	1	1	3		
Smith, Jonas	2	1	2		
Streeter, James	1	1	2		
Shumway, Levi	1	4	2		
Shumway, Amasa	1	2	6		
Sprague, Nehemiah	1		8		
Tarr, Simeon	1				
Vicary, Merrifield	1	1	1		
Wilcox, Danl	1	5	4		
Wilcox, James	2	2	6		
Whitney, Aaron	1		2		
Wright, Richard	2	2	3		
Wood, John	1	1	1		
WILMINGTON TOWN.					
Alvord, Gad	2		3		
Austin, Danl	4		2		
Averil, James	2		2		
Axtel, Silas	1	1	7		
Baldwin, Caleb	2	1	4		
Burchard, Roger	1		2		
Basset, Jedediah	2	1	3		
Buel, Saml	1	2	2		
Buel, Saml., Junr	1				
Ball, David	2		1		
Bangs, Abner	2		2		
Ball, David, Junr	1				
Ball, James	1	1	3		
Ball, Lemuel	1				
Ball, B. Gideon	1	1	3		
Badger, Saml	1		2		
Boyd, Abraham	4	2	1		
Bill, Calvin	3	2	5		
Ball, Noah	1	2	5		
Cushman, Barnabas	1	2	4		
Chandler, John	1	1	6		
Chandler, Henry	2		1		
Chandler, Simeon, Junr.	1	1	2		
Chandler, Henry, Junr.	1	1	4		
Cummins, Reuben	1	2	5		
Childs, Jona	1	1	3		
Castle, Timo	1	2	4		
Cook, Widow		5	6		
Coss, James	1	2	4		
Coss, Rufus	1	1	5		
Chandler, Simeon	1		5		
Coss, Reuben	1	1	1		
Doty, Ellis	1		1		
Dix, Ozias	2	3	4		

NAME OF HEAD OF FAMILY.	Free white males of 16 years and upward, including heads of families.	Free white males under 16 years.	Free white females, including heads of families.	All other free persons.	Slaves.
WILMINGTON TOWN—continued.					
Davis, Saml	1	3	2		
Davis, David	2	2	1		
Doty, Ezra	2	2	6		
Edgscom, Roger	1	2	5		
Eason, Elijah, Junr	3	1	3		
Forbes, Stephen	2	2	4		
Forbes, Asa	1		2		
Flagg, Josiah	4	1	3		
Flagg, Nathan	1		2		
Freeman, Watson	5		3		
Fox, Amos	5	1	4		
Fitch, Jesse	1	1	3		
Hastings, Jona	1	2	3		
Griswall, Jerard	1		1		
Hunter, Robert	1	1	6		
Hudson, Nathl	3		4		
Hall, James	1				
Haskell, Thos	3	3	4		
Haskell, Moses	1		3		
Haws, Jabez	1		3		
Haskell, Andrew	1	1	2		
Lock, John	1	1	1		
Livermore, Danl	4	5	5		
Lamb, Jona	1		3		
Lamb, Job	1	1	3		
Lincoln, Jonah	1	1	2		
Lock, Josiah, Junr	1				
Long, Mathew	1	2	4		
Lock, Josiah	1	1	4		
Marks, Jona	1	3	4		
Morgan, Reuben	3		4		
Morgan, Benja	3		2		
More, Judah	2	2	7		
Metcalf, Benja	2	2	4		
More, Judah, Junr	2		1		
Mellen, Richd	1	2	1		
Mellen, Wm	2		1		
Marks, Widow			1		
Mudge, Ezra	1	1	4		
Morgan, Nathl	1	1	2		
More, Walden	1		1		
Winslow, Danl	1	2	2		
Newton, Israel	1		4		
Nye, Joseph	2		2		
Nettleton, George	2	2	1		
Wilder, Oliver	1	4	2		
Pettis, Saml	1	1	3		
Pond, Zebulun	1	2	1		
Packard, Levi	1	1	3		
Packard, Timo	3	3	6		
Pierce, Benja	1		2		
Parmalee, Jeremiah	3	1	3		
Parmalee, Gilbert	1	2	2		
Pierce, Benja., Junr	1		2		
Purlington, Sylvanus	2	1	5		
Pierce, John	1	3	4		
Perry, Benja	2				
Ray, Zalotas	1		5		
Ray, Wm	1	2	3		
Rugg, Joseph	3		1		
Smith, Medad	1	2	3		
Spencer, Thos	5				
Stacy, Abel	1		1		
Swift, Chipman	1	1	5		
Swift, Jesse	1	2	4		
Swift, Perez	1		1		
Stevens, Israel	1	3	3		
Smead, Eli	1	1	1		
Studson, Anthony	1				
Smith, Phinehas	1		1		
Thompson, Saml	2	1	3		
Thompson, Saml., Junr.	1		4		
Titus, Ephm	2	2	3		
Witheral, Lott	2	4	3		
Wheeler, Amos	1	2	4		
Ware, James	1	4	2		
Williams, James	2	1	3		
Witt, Jona	1	1	2		
Ware, Meletiah	1	3	3		
Ware, Asaph	1	3	3		
Waste, Eli	2	3	4		
Wheeler, Isaac	1	2	3		

WINDSOR COUNTY.

NAME OF HEAD OF FAMILY.	Free white males of 16 years and upward, including heads of families.	Free white males under 16 years.	Free white females, including heads of families.	All other free persons.	Slaves.
ANDOVER TOWN.					
Baldwin, Jesse	1	2	1		
Bailey, Nathaniel	1		1		
Manning, Joel	3		2		
Pettingill, Samuel	4	1	4		
Felt, Abner	1	3	3		
Cram, Joseph	1	1	4		
Cummings, Ebenezer	2		3		
Sherwin, Daniel	4	3	2		
Nichols, Aaron	1	1	5		
Smith, Samuel	1		2		
Clark, Bunker	1	3	4		
Adams, Levi	1	3	2		
Balch, Hart	2	4	4		
Warner, Moses	1	3	6		
Nichols, Timothy	2	1	4		
Drury, David	1		2		
Richardson, Josiah	1	1	3		
Lamson, Daniel	1		2		
Dale, Joshua	1	1	1		
Parkherst, Isaac	1		1		
Burt, Gordin	3	4	5		
Brown, Samuel	3	3	5		
Pease, Ezekiel	4	1	4		
Hall, Henry	1	2	3		
Cogswell, Nathaniel P	1				
Simond, John	1	2	1		
Simond, Alven	1		1		
Simond, John, Junr	1	5	1		
Allen, Daniel	2		2		
Perry, Ichabod	1	1	2		
Jackworth, Joshua	2	1	2		
O'Brian, Partrick	1	4	2		
Simonds, Dan	1	2	1		
Rogers, Fradrack	1	3	5		
Dudley, Stephen	2	1	4		
Pease, Ezekiel, Junr	1	3	2		
Pease, Augustus	2	2	4		
Allen, Peter	1	1	1		
Adams, Thomas	1		1		
Johnson, Abel	1	1	3		
French, Thomas	2	2	5		
Howard, David	2	4	3		
French, John, Junr	1	3	3		
Howard, Joseph	1		3		
Howard, Solomon	4	2	1		
French, John	2		2		
Town, Aaron	1		4		
BARNARD TOWN.					
Aikens, James	1		2		
Aikens, Nathaniel	1		3		
Aikens, Solomon	2	1	3		
Aikens, Solomon	2		3		
Ashley, Lemuel	2	3	4		
Babbet, Abel	1		1		
Baniston, Jason	1	2	2		
Barlow, Aaron	1	2	4		
Barlow, Benjamin	1		3		
Barlow, Joseph	1		3		
Barlow, Nathaniel	1	1	1		
Barns, Elijah	1	4	3		
Belding, James	1		3		
Belding, Moses	1	1	4		
Benjamin, John	2		1		
Bennet, Sylvanus	1	2	4		
Bicknel, Amos	1	1	1		
Bicknel, Amos	1	1	2		
Billings, Gideon	1	1	3		
Biram, James	1	3	3		
Blackman, Hollon	1	2	3		
Blackman, Timothy	1		1		
Blackman, William	2		6		
Bowman, Joseph	2		3		
Bowman, Joseph	2	1	2		
Bowman, Nathan	1	1			
Briggs, Ephraim	2	3	3		
Brigham, Asa	1		3		
Brown, Mathew	1	3	1		
Butman, William	2	1	1		
Call, Silas	1		1		
Chamberlin, John	1		3		
Chamberlin, Joseph	2	6	2		
Chamberlin, Thomas	2		4		
Chamberlin, William	1	4	3		
Chedle, Asa	1	2	1		
Chedle, Asa	2	2	3		
Chedle, William	1		2		
Clap, Benjamin	1		3		
Cox, Benjamin	2	1	4		
Cox, George	1	1	1		
BARNARD TOWN—con.					
Crowell, Sheferick	1		4		
Danforth, Isaac	2	1	2		
Davis, Moses	2	1	3		
Dean, Robert	1	3	2		
Dean, Seth	1	4	2		
Eastman, Timothy	1	1	4		
Ellis, Joseph	2		3		
Ellis, Stephen	1				
Emerson, Asa	1	4	3		
Fairbanks, Calvin	1	5	2		
Fay, Aaron	1	2	2		
Fay, Eliakim	1		2		
Fay, Moses	1		2		
Finley, John	2	2	2		
Fisk, John	1	3	2		
Foster, Asa	1	1	4		
Foster, Jacob	1	1	1		
Foster, John	1	1	4		
Foster, Joseph	2		2		
Foster, Joseph	1		1		
Foster, Peter	1	1	2		
Freeman, Elisha	1	1	2		
Freeman, Thomas	1	1	2		
Freeman, Thomas	1		1		
Freeman, William	2	1	1		
Fuller, Thomas	1	3	2		
Gamble, John	1		2		
Gilford, Samuel	1	3	2		
Gray, Samuel	1				
Gray, Thomas	1		2		
Green, Beriah	5	2	4		
Green, Charles	2	1	3		
Harradan, John	2		2		
Haskel, Nathaniel	1		1		
Haskel, Prince	1	2	3		
Howard, Simeon	1	1	2		
Jones, John	3	1	3		
Hinney, Jesse	1	2	3		
Lawton, Jacob	1	4	3		
Luce, Jonathan	1	1	2		
Lurvey, Moses	1	1	4		
Lurvey, Peter	1	1	3		
McCormack, Daniel	1				
Maynord, Stephen	3				
Marrick, Eleazer	1		3		
Mason, Clemont	1				
Morgan, Benjamin	2	2	3		
Newton, Gideon	1	1	2		
Newton, John	1	3	4		
Newton, Timothy	1	3	1		
Page, Asa	2		2		
Page, George	1	3	4		
Page, Nathaniel	1	2	3		
Parmeter, Nathan	1	3	3		
Perkins, Abner	1	2	3		
Perkins, William	1	2	4		
Reed, Job	1	1	3		
Richmond, Amaziah	3	2	2		
Richmond, Amaziah	1	1	5		
Richmond, Ebenezer	4	2	2		
Richmond, Lemuel	2		1		
Sabens, Ebenezer	1	2	3		
Sharp, Daniel	1	2	2		
Smith, Jesse	1	1	4		
Southgate, Steward	2		6		
Steatson, Benjamin	1	2	4		
Stebbins, Benjamin	3	3	6		
Stevens, Andrew	2		2		
Stevens, Andrew	1	1	2		
Steward, Samuel	1		2		
Swift, Heman	1		5		
Swift, Joseph	1				
Swift, Levi	1	1	1		
Swift, Thomas	2	2	5		
Townshend, George	1		2		
Tucker, Robert	1	1	1		
Tupper, Israel	1	3	4		
Tupper, Samuel	1				
Tupper, Silas	2		1		
Walcott, William	2		2		
Wheelock, Peter	2	2	3		
White, David	1				
White, Thomas W	3	3	6		
Wight, Nathaniel	1	1	5		
Wilburr, Aaron	1	2	4		
Wilburr, Benjamin	1	5	4		
Wilson, Elizabeth		2	4		
Wing, Benjamin	1	1	2		
Wood, Paul	1	1	1		
Wright, Thomas M	1	1	4		
BETHEL TOWN.					
Ainsworth, Wyman	1	2	2		
Babbet, Joel	1		1		
Bartlett, Joseph	1	3	5		
Beal, Obediah	1		3		
Bliss, Levi	1	1	3		
Brown, Ebenezer	1	1	1		
Brooks, Simeon	1	2	1		
Buckman, Josiah	2		4		
Buckman, Jeremiah	1	1	2		
Burbanks, Eleazer	1	1	2		
Burnap, Abner	3	1	3		
Burnap, Jonathan	1		4		
Burroughs, Abner	2	1	2		
Chaplin, William	1	1	1		
Chase, Joshua	2		2		
Cleaveland, Stephen	3	1	3		
Copeland, David	3	2	3		
Cotton, Bibye L	1	1	3		
Crane, Amos	1				
Crane, Benjamin	3		3		
Crane, Ebenezer	1	1	4		
Curtis, William	1	1	4		
Day, Ralph	1	2	2		
Dean, Zachariah	3	3	4		
Dike, Daniel	1	1	3		
Dudley, Samuel	1		2		
Dunham, John	1		2		
Dunham, Thomas	1		1		
Eddy, Caleb	1	2	6		
Eddy, John	1	1	3		
Finley, John	1	2	1		
Flyner, Michael	1	2	3		
Gould, Asa	1	4	2		
Green, Amaza	1	3	2		
Green, Uzziah	1	2	4		
Grover, Amaza	2		2		
Hibbard, Timothy	1	4	2		
Hinshaw, Isaac	1		3		
Hinshaw, Isaac	1		1		
Huntington, Abner	2		1		
Huntington, David	1	3	2		
Kellogg, Martin	1	2	3		
Kinney, Daniel	1	1	4		
Kinney, John	2	2	3		
Kinney, John	1	3	2		
Lathrop, John	1	1	1		
Lilley, David	3	5	3		
Lovet, David	2	1	6		
Ludington, Lemuel	1	1	2		
Mackinster, Alexander	1				
Mackinster, Paul	1	1	4		
McGayham, Dennis	1	1	2		
Marsh, Joel	4	3	3		
Moody, John	3	1	3		
Owen, Sylvanus	2	2	4		
Parish, Jeremiah	1	1	2		
Parish, John	1		1		
Parish, Nathaniel	1		3		
Parker, Stephen	2	2	2		
Peck, Samuel	1	2	5		
Perham, David	1		1		
Putnam, Ebenezer	3	2	5		
Putnam, Ezra	1	1	3		
Putnam, Thomas	1	3	2		
Rich, Justus	2	2	3		
Russell, Thomas	2	1	1		
Rogers, Jeduthan	1	1	1		
Sanford, Seth	2	1	3		
Smith, Benjamin	1	3	4		
Smith, George	2	1	2		
Smith, Willard	3	4	3		
Stone, David	1	1	4		
Strong, Benajah	3		3		
Tenney, Ephraim	1	2	4		
Tenney, John	2	1	5		
Thoop, Nathaniel	2	3	4		
Walker, Asaph	1		1		
Wallis, Joseph	1	2	3		
Wallis, John	1	1	5		
Wheeler, Rice	1	2	3		
Wittard, Jonathan	1	3	1		
Wilson, William	3	1	3		
Witchinson, Joseph	1	1	4		
Wood, Joseph	1	1	3		
Woodward, Ezekel	1		1		
Woodworth, Benjn	1	3	2		
BRIDGWATER TOWN.					
Bassett, Howard	2	1	1		
Bassett, Zachariah	1		2		

WINDSOR COUNTY—Continued.

NAME OF HEAD OF FAMILY.	Free white males of 16 years and upward, including heads of families.	Free white males under 16 years.	Free white females, including heads of families.	All other free persons.	Slaves.
BRIDGWATER TOWN—continued.					
Boyse, George	1	2	4		
Bozworth, John	1	2	3		
Davis, Samson	1	1	1		
Fletcher, James	1	3	3		
French, Aaron	1	1	2		
French, Ephriam	1		5		
French, Ezekiel	1	1	2		
French, Joseph	1	1	3		
French, Joshua	1	1	3		
Foster, John	1		2		
Foster, Rufus	1				
Gillett, Elisha	1				
Green, Asa	1	2	2		
Grow, William	1	3	2		
Hawkins, John	3	2	5		
Hawkins, Joseph	1	1	3		
Hoisington, Bliss	2	1	5		
Hoisington, Isaac	2	1	4		
Hoisington, John	1	2	3		
Hoisington, Virlina	1	1	1		
Jones, Ariel	1		1		
Jones, Ariel	1		2		
Knowlton, Stephen	1	3	3		
Mendall, Amos	1		5		
Montague, Selah	1	2	3		
Murdock, John	1	1	1		
Palmer, Robert	1		2		
Palmer, Thomas	1	2	3		
Pierce, Thomas	1	2	3		
Perkins, Benjamin	1		3		
Perkins, Cyrus	1	1	2		
Perkins, Joshua	1		3		
Powers, Abraham	1				
Powers, Thomas	1				
Pratt, Jonathan	1	1	3		
Pratt, Nathan	1	2	2		
Rice, Stephen	1	1	3		
Ripley, Samuel	1	3	3		
Robinson, Eleazer	1	2	3		
Sabins, Clement	1	1	1		
Safford, Chellis	1	1	1		
Shaw, Benoni	1	3	1		
Shaw, Daniel	1	4	4		
Shaw, Isaiah	1	1	3		
Shaw, James	1	1	3		
Shaw, Job	1	1	2		
Simons, Caleb	2	2	6		
Southgate, Richard	2		3		
Southgate, Thomas	1	2	2		
Stevens, Peter R	1	5	1		
Thomas, Zeb	1	5	2		
Topliff, James	1	3	3		
Tora, Caleb	1		2		
Tours, Jonas	1				
Walker, Elijah	1		1		
Walker, John	1	2	2		
White, Sylvanus	2		5		
Woodbury, Joshua	1	1	4		
CAVENDISH TOWN.					
Morse, Joseph	3	2	5		
Cheney, Waldo	1	2	6		
Sherwin, Ahionaas	1	1	5		
Rice, Silas	2	2	2		
Ramsey, Simeon	2		2		
Atherton, Joseph	1	1	2		
Briant, John	2		1		
Taylor, Edmond	1	5	2		
Manning, Levi	1		1		
Kimball, Amos	2	2	5		
Smith, William	1	2	4		
Kendall, James	1		1		
Gordin, James	1	5	1		
Coffin, John	3		1		
Preston, Aner	1	1	2		
Dix, Samuel	1	1	3		
Conant, Nathan	1		1		
Preston, Lemuel	1		3		
Holt, William	1	1	2		
Hutchinson, Samuel, Junr	1	2	2		
Hutchinson, Samuel	2		5		
Kimball, Ebenezer	2		5		
Spaulding, Willard	1	2	3		
Spaulding, Benjamin	1	3	2		
French, Josiah	2	1	3		
Swift, William	1		1		
Gerald, Gamaliel	1	1	2		
White, Samuel	3	4	3		
Adams, Samuel	1	2	3		
CAVENDISH TOWN—con.					
Wright, John	1	1	2		
Chaplin, William	1		1		
Parker, Aaron	3	1	4		
Smith, Moses	1	3	2		
Wheeler, Joel	1	2	3		
Stone, Timothy	1	3	3		
Wheelock, Jonathan	4	1	2		
Dodge, John	1		4		
Joy, Silas	1	1	1		
Searls, Robert	1		1		
Parker, Jemsy	1	2	2		
Powers, Nahum	2	1	2		
Adams, Timothy	1	3	2		
Coffin, Daniel	1	1	3		
Baldwin, Thomas	2	1	2		
Parker, Joshua	1		2		
Baldwin, Abel	1	2	1		
Baldwin, Isaac	2	2	4		
Preston, Abiel	2	1	1		
Jackman, Abner	3		2		
Tarble, Edmond	1	2	4		
Willington, George	2				
Tarble, Whitcomb	1	2	3		
Jackman, Abner, Junr	1	2	3		
Russell, John	1	2	4		
Hardy, Samson	2		5		
Hardy, John	1		4		
Lynd, Benjamin	2	3	2		
Peck, Daniel	1	1	2		
Chapman, Reuben	2	3	3		
Snow, Robert	1		2		
Lovell, Randall	2	1	3		
Chubb, David	1	2	3		
Spaulding, William	4	2	3		
Pelton, Freeman	1	1	3		
Dodge, Shadrack	1	3	3		
Russell, Noadiah	1	2	3		
Atherton, Jonathan	1	2	4		
Spaulding, William, Junr	1	1	3		
Patch, John	1	3	2		
Boyden, Jonathan	1	2	4		
Haven, Hezekiah	1		5		
Proctor, Leonard	3	3	4		
Proctor, Isaac	1	1	5		
Spaulding, Jesse	1	5	2		
Parker, Isaac	1	1	3		
Wyman, Samuel	1	2	6		
Ross, Donald	1	2	6		
Wheeler, Asa	1		2		
Piper, James	1	1	2		
Fletcher, Asaph	1	3	5		
Houghton, Elijah	2		2		
Dutton, Salmon	4	1	4		
Dutton, Ephraim	1	2	4		
Carey, Joseph	1	1	1		
Proctor, Timothy	2	1	2		
Baldwin, Joseph	1	3	2		
Woodbury, Joseph	1				
CHESTER TOWN.					
Blanchard, Isaac	1	4	2		
Chandler, Thomas	2		1		
McCollester, Peter	2	1	1		
Wallis, John	1	2	2		
McCollester, David	1	2	2		
Turner, Ishmael				3	
Drake, Abijah	1		1		
Drake, Seth	1	3	1		
Drake, Abijah, Junr	1	2	3		
Jewitt, Joseph	1	1	2		
Hewlet, Joseph	1	2	3		
Hutchinson, Moses	1		1		
Tarble, Peter	1	1	3		
Robinson, James	3	1	2		
Colborn, Ezekiel	1	4	2		
Case, James	1	1	2		
Hutchins, Simon	3	2	2		
Tucker, Caleb	1	1	3		
Dutton, Stephen	2	1	8		
Sanders, Solomon	1	3	1		
Polly, John	2		4		
Duncan, Abel	4	5	3		
Parker, Elijah	1	3	2		
Lord, Nathaniel	1	1	4		
Church, Joshua	1		2		
Sartwell, Solomon	1	3	3		
Johnson, Phebe	1		3		
Walker, Elisha	2		1		
Warren, Thomas	4		1		
CHESTER TOWN—con.					
Johnson, Hezekiah	1		1		
Johnson, Uriah	1		3		
Stevens, Samuel	2	1	5		
Stevens, John	1		1		
Eaton, Abraham	1	1	3		
Taylor, John	1	4	4		
Gibson, John	1	2	1		
Cook, Joshua	1	1	3		
Bullard, Nathan	1	1	3		
Gowing, Nathaniel	1	1	2		
Mitchel, Thomas	1	4	1		
Johnson, David	3	2	6		
Caryl, Thomas	3	4	4		
Pierce, Joseph	1	1	2		
Snell, Solomon	1	5	5		
Hoit, Francis	1	1	4		
Turner, Joshua	1	2	4		
Leeland, Joshua	1	2	2		
Ellis, John	4	2	3		
Chandler, Willard	2	2	3		
White, John	1	2	4		
Jacobs, John	1	1	3		
Jacobs, Daniel	1	2	1		
Farmer, Henry W	2	5	3		
McCuller, William	2	1	3		
Toby, Paul	1	1	2		
Axtel, Samuel	1	1	1		
Hole, Josiah	1	1	4		
Johnson, Samuel	1	1	1		
Sergeant, Jabez	3	2	5		
Sergeant, Amos	1	2	4		
Caryl, John	3	2	3	1	
Pierce, Eliab	1		2		
Chamberlin, Isaac	1		2		
Caryl, Jonathan	3	1	2		
Rice, Jason	1	1	2		
Caryl, Jonathan, Junr	1	2	1		
Heald, Daniel	3	3	2		
Carpenter, Knight	1		2		
Parker, Obediah	1		1		
Gould, Otis	2		2		
Kimball, Thomas	3	2	5		
Whitmore, Elias	3	1	2		
Gile, Amos	1	2	5		
Ranny, Waitstill	3	2	1		
Stone, John	2		2		
Stone, John, Junr	3	2	7		
Fletcher, Daniel	1	2	3		
Perkins, Charles	1		1		
Marshall, Elijah	1	1	1		
Mann, Charles	2	1	4		
Tarble, Reuben	1	2	6		
Dean, Samuel	1		4		
Edson, Abel	2	1	2		
Horton, Aaron	1	1	4		
Sterns, Solomon	1	1	2		
Mann, Willard	1	1	6		
Williams, Othmel	2	2	3		
Smith, Nicholas	2		3		
Johnson, John	3	1	2		
Houghton, Joshua	4	5	3		
Stratton, Asa	2	2	2		
Bigelow, Elnathan	1				
Riggs, Thomas	2	1	1		
Lane, Gershom F	1	2	5		
Clark, Ephraim	5	2	3		
Earl, Artimus	1	2	1		
Gilkey, William, Junr	1	1	4		
Babcock, Roswell	2		2		
Tarble, Jonathan	2	1	5		
Morris, Uriah	2	2	6		
Olcott, Timothy	4	1	7		
Chandler, Bela	1		2		
Clark, Joseph	1		2		
Clark, Ephraim, Junr	1	1	1		
Grayham, John	1	1	5		
Grayham, Robert	2	3	4		
Atwood, Jeremiah	1		2		
Thirston, John	1		2		
Williams, Anthony	1	1	1		
Brooks, David	2	2	5		
Stone, Thomas	2		7		
Perkins, Rufus	1	6	4		
Barney, Abel	1	1	1		
Sawyer, Abraham	2	2	1		
Robins, Nathan	1	2	1		
Alverson, Simeon	1	1	1		
How, Ezekiel	1	4	5		
Davis, Daniel	1	1	1		
Earl, Fradrick	1		1		
Earl, George	3	1	2		

WINDSOR COUNTY—Continued.

NAME OF HEAD OF FAMILY.	Free white males of 16 years and upward, including heads of families.	Free white males under 16 years.	Free white females, including heads of families.	All other free persons.	Slaves.
CHESTER TOWN—con.					
Gile, Nathan	1	2	4		
Gile, Stephen	1		2		
Gilkey, William	4		5		
Coffin, Michael	1	3	2		
Laland, Aaron	2	2	1		
Atwood, Oliver	1	2	2		
Hodgman, Nathan	1	2	3		
Willard, Jonathan	1	4	3		
Sergeants, Israel	1	2	2		
Thomson, William	2	3	5		
Bowtell, John	1	2	4		
Atwood, William	2	1	3		
Atwood, Anthony	1		1		
Gile, Moses	1	3	1		
Watkins, Elias	1	3	4		
Larabee, John	1		3		
Horton, Adonijah	1	4	6		
Hoar, William	2	3	4		
Earl, Eseck	3	4	1		
Tarble, Nathaniel	1	3	5		
Wilson, Joseph	1	1	2		
Church, Joshua, Junr	1	1	1		
Chandler, John E	1	2	2		
Putnam, John	3	1	4		
Wilson, Abner	2	3	3		
Wilson, Daniel	1	1	1		
Wilson, Solomon	2	1	1		
Rounds, George	2	1	1		
Field, David	3	1	3		
Wyman, Samuel	1	1	3		
Field, Abner	3	3	3		
Dier, Stephen	1	2	3		
Fuller, John	1		3		
Arnold, Ebenezer	1	1	3		
Barton, Josiah	2	3	3		
Green, Jonathan	1		4		
Waterman, Olney	1	2	2		
Stone, Rufus	1		2		
Field, Nehemiah	2	2	2		
Kindall, Jonathan	3	2	5		
Clay, Timothy	1	1	2		
Whitman, George	1		2		
Field, Pardon	2	3	3		
Johnson, Josiah	1	2	5		
Earl, John	1		1		
Johnson, Willard	1		2		
Clark, Samuel	1	1	1		
Johnson, Ebenezer	2	3	3		
Parks, Thadeus	1		3		
Parks, Jonathan	2		1		
HARTFORD TOWN.					
Allyn, William	1	2	7		
Austin, Abiather	1	1	3		
Baldwin, David	1	3	2		
Ball, John	2	1	5		
Barnet, Moses	1	1	4		
Bennet, John	1	2	5		
Bennet, John	1		1		
Bennet, Jonathan	2	3	2		
Bill, Eliphalet	2	2	4		
Billings, Enoch	2	1	3		
Blackman, Jeffry	2		1		
Bliss, David	2	1	5		
Bramble, Abel	1	1	1		
Bramble, William	2	3	4		
Brink, James	1		1		
Bugbee, Benjamin	1	1	3		
Bugbee, Nathaniel	1	1	4		
Bullard, John	1	1	2		
Burch, Benjamin	2	2	2		
Burch, Eddy	2	4	2		
Burch, Ephraim	1		2		
Burch, James	2	3	4		
Burch, Jonathan	1	6	3		
Burch, William	6	2	3		
Butler, Samuel	1	4	4		
Cady, James	2	2	5		
Chapman, Elias	2	3	3		
Chapman, Erastus	2	2	2		
Chapman, Jeriah	1	2	2		
Chapman, Simon	1		1		
Clark, John	4	3	5		
Clark, Michael	1	1	5		
Clark, Paul	1	2	1		
Closton, Simon	2	1	4		
Colburn, David	2	1	2		
Colburn, Laban	1		1		
Colston, William	1	1	3		
Cowser, Asa	1	1	4		
HARTFORD TOWN—con.					
Demmon, Levi	1	3	4		
Demmon, Nathan	1		2		
Demmon, William	1	1	2		
Dewey, Joshua	3	1	2		
Dillino, Zebulon	1		2		
Dimmick, Phillip	2	2	2		
Dunham, Garshom	1	1	1		
Dunham, William	2	3	7		
Drew, Ezra	1	4	5		
Dutton, Jesse	1	1	3		
Dutton, John	5	2	3		
Dutton, Nathaniel	1	2	3		
Eaton, Brigham	1	2	4		
England, Stephen	1	2	2		
Eudall, Oliver	3	5	5		
Eudall, Samuel	3	1	4		
Fellows, Samuel	2	1	3		
Follet, Thankfull		1	2		
Fowler, Elisha	1		4		
Gillet, Israel	3	2	5		
Gillet, John	2	1	5		
Gillet, Roger	1	2	2		
Gould, Benjamin	1	3	3		
Gross, Thomas	1	3	1		
Hager, John	1	1	3		
Hall, Jacob	1	1	3		
Hall, Willis	2	1	2		
Hatchway, John	1		3		
Hazen, Asa	1	4	4		
Hazen, Daniel	1	2	1		
Hazen, Hezekiah	1	4	2		
Hazen, Joshua	2	3	6		
Hazen, Lemuel	1		1		
Hazen, Solomon	1	3	2		
Hazen, Thomas	1	2	6		
Hazen, Reuben	1		1		
Hewit, Daniel	2		2		
Holbrook, Thomas	1	3	2		
Hopkins, Noah	1	1	1		
How, Samson	1		1		
How, Stuard	1	1	3		
Hoyt, Abraham	1	1	1		
Hoyt, Benjamin	1	2	3		
Hunter, John	2		2		
Hutchinson, Zenos	1	1	2		
Janes, David	2	1	5		
Lincoln, Hezekiah	1	3	3		
Marsh, Abel	2	1	3		
Marsh, Abraham	1		2		
Marsh, Elisha	3	1	2		
Marsh, Eliphalet	1	1	5		
Marsh, John	2	1	3		
Marsh, Joseph	5	1	2		
Marsh, Joseph	2	1	2		
Marsh, Milo	1	2	1		
Miller, Peter	1	1	2		
Muncil, Eliakim S	1	1	3		
Murrel, William	1	1	6		
Muxley, Thomas	2		3		
Newel, Zenos	1		2		
Newton, David	1	4	7		
Nobles, Shadrick	2	4	4		
Pease, Christopher	3	4	4		
Pease, Christopher	1		1		
Pease, Samuel	1	2	6		
Petkin, Rhoda	1	1	4		
Persons, Elias	1	3	4		
Pixley, Asa	1		1		
Pixley, William	2		2		
Porter, Ambrose	1		1		
Porter, William	1	3	2		
Powel, Luther	1	1	1		
Powel, Rowland	1	4	5		
Powel, Rowland	1		2		
Powers, William	1	3	6		
Procter, Isaac	1		1		
Pynneo, Daniel	4	2	4		
Ransom, Daniel	1	2	2		
Ransom, Mathew	1	3	2		
Richardson, Amos	3	1	4		
Richardson, John	1	2	1		
Richardson, Thomas	1	2	6		
Richardson, William	1		3		
Rider, Joshua	2	1	2	1	
Rider, Peter	1		1		
Rider, Peter	1	2	5		
Robinson, Amos	3	2	5		
Robinson, Artemus	1	1	3		
Rust, Lemuel	1	1	1		
Rust, Nial	1	1	2		
Rust, Phinehas	1	3	2		
HARTFORD TOWN—con.					
Savage, Francis	1		2		
Savage, Seth	1	3	2		
Savage, Thomas	1		3		
Scott, Luther	1	2	2		
Shalliss, Francis	1	2	3		
Smith, Ashbel	1		3		
Smith, John	2		1		
Sprague, Elkana	1	2	2		
Sprague, Ignatius	1	2	3		
Sprague, Phillip	1	1	3		
Stoddard, Phinehas	1		1		
Strong, Jedediah	2	2	2		
Strong, Solomon	3	1	4		
Tenny, Reuben	2	1	3		
Tilden, Josiah	2		2		
Tilden, Stephen	1	2	3		
Tilden, Stephen	4		4		
Tracy, Andrew	1	3	3		
Tracy, Thomas	3		2		
Warner, Elisha	1	1	3		
Watkins, Amasa	1		2		
Webster, Samuel	2	2	3		
Webster, Israel	1	3	2		
Whitecomb, Joshua	1	2	1		
Whitney, Jonathan	1	2	3		
Whitney, Nathan	1		2		
Whitney, Jonathan	1	2	3		
Williams, Isaac	1	2	5		
Williams, Josiah	1	1	3		
Wilson, Isaac	1	2	5		
Wilson, Josiah	1	1	3		
Wood, Ephraim	1	2	4		
Woodworth, Benjamin	1		1		
Woodworth, Roger	1	2	4		
Wright, Benjamin	2		3		
Wright, David	2	2	3		
Wright, Jonathan	2		5		
Wright, Benjamin	1		1		
Wright, Phinehas	1	1	5		
HARTLAND TOWN.					
Abbot, Samuel	1	1	2		
Ainsworth, Daniel	1	2	3		
Aldrich, Isaiah	1	2	5		
Aldrich, Noah	1		1		
Alexander, Eldad	3	1	5		
Alexander, Quartus	1	1	4		
Allyn, Ebenezer	1	3	1		
Amris, Ebenezer	1		7		
Anderson, Robert	3	2	3		
Ashley, William S	2	2	3		
Ayers, Peter	1	2	4		
Back, George	1	3	6		
Badger, Daniel	3	3	6		
Badger, Daniel	1	1	2		
Badger, Elisha	3		2		
Badger, Gideon	1	4	4		
Bailey, David	1	3	4		
Bagley, Henry	2		2		
Bagley, Orlando	1	3	2		
Bagley, Thomas	1	2	4		
Billings, Christopher	2		1		
Billings, Joseph	1	2	3		
Billings, Joseph	1	2	1		
Billings, John	2	2	5		
Billings, Nathan	3	3	4		
Belding, Moses	1	3	1		
Belding, Moses	1		1		
Bates, Joseph	1	3	2		
Bates, Jacob	1	2	2		
Bishop, Eleazer	2	3	4		
Briant, Amasa	1	4	2		
Briant, Benjamin	2	2	4		
Brick, Daniel	3	1	4		
Bridge, Ebenezer	3	4	3		
Brown, Solomon	1	3	3		
Brigham, Abner	1	6	2		
Buck, Jonathan	1		3		
Bugbee, Daniel	2	2	2		
Burdick, Stanton	1		2		
Burrell, John	1	1	1		
Cady, Runnells	1	2	1		
Cady, Thomas H	1	1	2		
Cabot, Francis	1	1	5		
Cabot, Marston	2	1	2		
Cabot, Sebastian	2		1		
Call, Elias	1	1	4		
Call, Caleb	1		3		
Capin, Samuel	1		3		
Carey, Ephriam	1	2	4		

WINDSOR COUNTY—Continued.

NAME OF HEAD OF FAMILY.	Free white males of 16 years and upward, including heads of families.	Free white males under 16 years.	Free white females, including heads of families.	All other free persons.	Slaves.
HARTLAND TOWN—con.					
Carver, Nathaniel	2				
Chase, Henry	1	3	3		
Child, Herba	1	1	3		
Child, Lyman	1	3	3		
Clark, Thomas	1	1	1		
Clark, Timothy	1	2	2		
Clark, Wesson	1	1	1		
Cobb, William	1	2	5		
Cotten, Milven	2	1	4		
Cotten, Luther	1	1	3		
Cotten, Thomas	2		2		
Cotten, Willard	2	4	5		
Crandal, Adam	1	3	2		
Croseroot, Lewis	1	1	2		
Currier, Aaron	1	2	3		
Dailey, William J	1		2		
Danford, James	1	2	3		
Danford, Francis	1	1	1		
Danford, William	3	1	2		
Danford, William	1	1	5		
Danforth, Nicholas	2	2	3		
Darby, Samuel	1	2	3		
Darling, Seth	1	1	2		
Davison, Dan	3	1	3		
Davison, Paul	1		1		
Denison, George	2	3	6		
Dinsmore, John	1	2	4		
Dunbar, John	2	2	6		
Elsworth, Ezra	1		2		
Edson, Sylvester	1	2	3		
Emmons, Thomas	1	1	1		
Enos, Roger	4		2		
Evans, Elsi	1	3	2		
Evins, Moses	1	3	1		
Evins, Zera	1	2	1		
Fisher, Timothy	1	3	4		
Flower, Elisha	1	1	2		
Flower, John	2		3		
Freeman, Ned				4	
Gallup, Elisha	3	2	2		
Gallup, Joseph	1	2	2		
Gallup, Perez	1	1	4		
Gallup, William	4	2	6	1	
Garey, Benjamin	1	1	4		
Garey, Thomas	1		2		
Gates, Elias	1	1	4		
Garven, James	1	3	4		
Gay, James	1	1	3		
Goss, Abel	1	1	2		
Grow, John	2	4	5		
Grow, Joseph	4	3	5		
Grow, Samuel	2	3	1		
Grow, Timothy	1		6		
Harris, Ishmael	1		3		
Hatch, Heman	1	2	5		
Hatch, Ichabod	1	2	2		
Harding, John	2	1	2		
Harvey, Nathaniel	2	1	2		
Hathwey, Wilber	1	1	4		
Healy, Samuel	1	2	2		
Hendrick, John	4		3		
Hodgeman, Jonathan	3	1	4		
Hodgeman, Lot	1	2	4		
Hodley, Thomas	3	1	1		
Holbrook, Ebenezer	1	1	3		
Holbrook, Ebenezer, Jr.	2	3	4		
Holbrook, Harba	1		3		
Holdridge, Ephraim	1		4		
Holdridge, Thomas	3	3	2		
Holmes, Stilson	5	2	6		
Holmes, Absalom	1		2		
Holmes, William	1		1		
Hosmer, Levi	1	1	1		
Howard, Elisha	1	3	3		
Hopkins, William	2	1	2		
Jaquith, Benjamin	2	3	3		
Jaquith, William	1	3	1		
Jenne, Lot	1	3	2		
Jenne, Samuel	3		1		
Johnson, William	1	1	2		
Jones, Charles	1	1	1		
Jones, William	1		4		
Keith, Azel	2		4		
Kendal, Amos	2	1	5		
Kendal, Samuel	1	1	1		
Kelley, Ebenezer	1	5	5		
Killam, Phinehas	1		2		
Kimball, Phinehas	1	5	4		
King, Asahel	1	1	2		
Kinston, David	4		2		
Laiton, John	2	2	4		

NAME OF HEAD OF FAMILY.	Free white males of 16 years and upward, including heads of families.	Free white males under 16 years.	Free white females, including heads of families.	All other free persons.	Slaves.
HARTLAND TOWN—con.					
Lamphier, John	2	2	5		
Lauton, Thomas	2	2	5		
Law, Robert	1	4	2		
Lee, Zebulon	4	4	5		
Liscomb, Thomas	1	3	2		
Liscomb, Darius	1	2	4		
Little, George	1	3	3		
Livermore, William	1	3	4		
Loomis, Jonas	3	4	5		
Luce, Andrew	1	5	4		
Luce, Ivory	1	4	6		
Luce, Moses	1		3		
Luce, Oliver	3		2		
Lull, Asa	1	2	1		
Lull, Timothy	4		5		
Lull, Timothy	2		2		
Lull, Nathan	2	1	2		
Lull, Zenos	1	3	4		
Main, Isaac	2		4		
Marbel, Benjamin	1		2		
Marey, William	4		1		
Martin, Duty	1	1	1		
Mash, Abel	1	1	5		
Mash, Daniel	1		4		
Mash, Roger	1	1	3		
Mash, Royal	1		3		
Mash, Joseph	2		3		
Morgin, Isaac	2	3	6		
Morey, Joseph	1				
Moses, John	1				
Morrison, Robert	2	3	5		
Miner, Clemont	1	1	2		
Miner, Ephraim	2	5	4		
Munsel, Daniel	2	2	2		
Munsel, Lazel	1	1	2		
Muxley, Seth	1	1	2		
Nichols, John	1	1	3		
Olverd, Simeon	1		2		
Osmore, John	1	1	2		
Paine, Eleazer	1	1	6		
Patterson, Joseph	4	1	1		
Patterson, William	1	2	1		
Pierce, David	1	2	3		
Pike, Ebenezer	1	1	1		
Remington, Joseph	1	2	3		
Rice, Aaron	1		1		
Rice, Eliakim	1	3	4		
Rice, Obediah	1	3	5		
Richardson, James	1	3	1		
Richardson, Jeremiah	1	3	4		
Rider, Daniel	1	1	1		
Roberts, Clark	1		2		
Rogers, Artha	1	3	2		
Rogers, Benjamin	1	1	1		
Rogers, Eliphalet	1	3	1		
Rogers, Nathaniel	1		3		
Rogers, Paul	1	1	2		
Roode, Humphrey	1	3	1		
Roode, Thomas P	1		1		
Rust, Natthias	1		1		
Rust, Oliver	1	3	4		
Richardson, Thomas	2	4	5		
Sawyer, Abel	1	2	2		
Scott, John	1	4	3		
Scott, Lemuel	1	4	3		
Sergents, Moses	1	2	3		
Shaw, Richard	1	2	3		
Shattuck, Silas	1	2	2		
Shattuck, Silas	1		1		
Short, Daniel	4	3	2		
Simmons, Joseph	2	9	4		
Simmons, Simon	2	1	2		
Smith, Samuel	1		5		
Sprague, Elkanah	2		2		
Spooner, Anna	3	1	3		
Spooner, Daniel	3	3	5		
Stanton, Daniel	1		1		
Stanton, James	1	5	2		
Stanton, Phinehas	2	2	5		
Stevens, Isaac	2	2	5		
Stevens, Oliver	1	3	4		
Stevens, Perula	1	3	4		
Stickney, Thomas	1	1	5		
Stone, Abel	1	1	2		
Sturvant, Job	1	2	2		
Sumner, John	2		3		
Sumner, William	2		2		
Sweetser, William	2		2		
Strater, Isaiah	1	2	2		
Taft, Artimus	1	3	2		
Taylor, Asa	6	3	5		

NAME OF HEAD OF FAMILY.	Free white males of 16 years and upward, including heads of families.	Free white males under 16 years.	Free white females, including heads of families.	All other free persons.	Slaves.
HARTLAND TOWN—con.					
Taylor, Elias	1	4	6		
Taylor, Oliver	1	3	8		
Teuxbury, Ephraim	1		1		
Teuxbury, Israel	3	1	5		
Teuxbury, Jacob	1	1			
Twiner, Elisha	1	1	2		
Tylor, Job	1	2	1		
Tylor, Jonathan	2		2		
Voce, Thomas V	1	1	2		
Walden, John	1		4		
Walden, Nathaniel	1	3	3		
Walker, Elnathan	3		3		
Warren, Zenos	1	3	4		
Waters, Timothy	1	2	4		
Webster, Moses	1	3	2		
Webster, Benoni	1	1	1		
Weed, Nathaniel	4	1	6		
Weeden, Samuel	2	1	2		
Weeden, Thomas	1		1		
White, Asa	1	1	2		
White, Francis	1		3		
White, Thomas	2	3	5		
Wild, Elias	3	2	4		
Willard, Aaron	1	2	4		
Willard, Edward	1		2		
Willard, Ely	1	2	2		
Willard, James	5		5		
Willard, Oliver	5	1	3		
Willard, Oliver	3	1	7		
Willard, Oliver	2	2	4		
Williams, Adam	1	2	3	1	
Willard, Wilder	1	1	4		
Williams, James	1	4	2		
Williams, Samuel	3		4		
Williams, Simeon	1	2	3		
Winch, Jason	1	3	3		
Wood, Edward	1	2	4		
Wood, Jonathan	1		1		
Wood, Josiah	1	3	5		
LUDLOW TOWN.					
Dutton, William	1	2	3		
Hadley, Jonas	1	3	5		
Hadley, John	1	1	2		
Pingery, Nathaniel	1	1	1		
Crowley, Royal	1	1	2		
Crowley, Abraham	3	1	5		
Hill, Isaac	1	4	2		
Farwell, Abel	2	2	4		
Powers, Isaac	1	2	2		
Green, Joseph	2	3	5		
Wilcox, Robert	1	1	6		
Parker, Levi	3				
Duncan, John	1	1	5		
Fletcher, Josiah	2	4	1		
Holden, Jonas	1	4	3		
Reed, Simeon	2	2	4		
Fletcher, Jesse	1	4	3		
Bixby, Thomas	2	1	2		
Bixby, David	1	1	1		
Gaffield, Joseph	1	4	4		
Proctor, Silas	1	2	1		
Beals, George	1	1	1		
Lewis, David	2	1	1		
Whitney, James	2	2	2		
Gleazon, Catherine		1	2		
Patch, Benjamin	2	2	5		
Ives, Levi	3		3		
Reed, Stephen	1	5	3		
Bixby, Levi	2	1	1		
NORWICH TOWN.					
Armstrong, John	2	2	4		
Baldwin, Daniel	1	2	5		
Baldwin, Elijah	1	1	3		
Baldwin, Levi	2	2	6		
Ball, Humphrey	1	1	4		
Ball, Jonathan	1	2	1		
Ball, Joseph	3	1	6		
Ball, Roswell	1	1	1		
Barrett, Jonathan	3	1	2		
Bartlett, Elliot	1	3	2		
Bartlett, Garshom	1	3	4		
Bartlett, Garshom	3		2		
Bartlett, George	1	1	1		
Bartlett, Jonathan	1	1	2		
Bartlett, Joseph	1	2	2		
Bartlett, Ithamer	1	2	5		
Bartlett, Moses	1		1		

WINDSOR COUNTY—Continued.

NAME OF HEAD OF FAMILY.	Free white males of 16 years and upward, including heads of families.	Free white males under 16 years.	Free white females, including heads of families.	All other free persons.	Slaves.
NORWICH TOWN—con.					
Bartlett, Samuel	1	......	6	....	....
Baxter, Elihu	1	6	4	....	....
Bell, Samuel	1	......	1	....	....
Benton, Joel	1	2	2	....	....
Benton, Josiah	1	3	2	....	....
Bissel, Jeremiah	2	......	3	....	....
Bissell, Jeremiah	1	......	1	....	....
Bliss, John	2	1	2	....	....
Boardman, Jehiel	1	......	3	....	....
Boardman, Jonas	1	2	3	....	....
Boardman, Nathaniel	2	......	4	....	....
Braman, James	1	1	2	....	....
Brewster, Cyrus	1	......	3	....	....
Brewster, Asa	1	3	2	....	....
Brigham, Paul	2	2	5	....	....
Broughton, Ebenezer	3	1	2	....	....
Brown, Israel	1	2	7	....	....
Brown, Isaac	1	......	1	....	....
Brown, Martin	3	......	5	....	....
Brown, Nathaniel	1	2	3	....	....
Brownson, Elijah	2	1	4	....	....
Brown, Samuel	1	4	5	....	....
Buck, Daniel	3	4	4	....	....
Burnap, John	1	2	2	....	....
Burnap, John	2	......	2	....	....
Burnap, Elijah	1	......	2	....	....
Burton, Benjamin	1	4	4	....	....
Burton, Elisha	5	3	5	....	....
Burton, Henry	1	......	1	....	....
Burton, John	4	2	6	....	....
Burton, Pierce	1	2	4	....	....
Bush, Timothy	6	3	3	....	....
Burwash, Nathan[l]	1	3	1	....	....
Carpenter, Simeon	1	4	6	....	....
Coit, Samuel	1	1	1	....	....
Crary, James	2	......	1	....	....
Crary, John	1	4	1	....	....
Crary, William	1	1	1	....	....
Curtis, Samuel	1	1	3	....	....
Cushman, Job	1	......	4	....	....
Cushman, Joseph	1	......	1	....	....
Dillino, Jonathan	1	1	1	....	....
Freeman, Elijah	1	1	3	....	....
Freeman, Elisha	1	4	4	....	....
Freeman, Experience	1	2	3	....	....
Freeman, Roger	1	3	1	....	....
Gates, Elijah	1	3	3	....	....
Geer, Jesse	1	2	4	....	....
Gilbert, Cornelius	1	......	4	....	....
Goodrich, David	1	5	3	....	....
Goodrich, Hezekiah	3	1	4	....	....
Goodrich, John	1	......	2	....	....
Goodrich, Josiah	1	1	3	....	....
Grow, James	1	2	3	....	....
Hatch, Adam	1	1	4	....	....
Hatch, Joseph	2	4	5	....	....
Hatch, Benjamin	2	3	5	....	....
Hatch, John	4	......	3	....	....
Hatch, Rufus	2	1	1	....	....
Hammon, William	1	......	3	....	....
Hedges, Jeremiah	1	2	3	....	....
Hibbard, David	1	3	4	....	....
Hibbard, John A	1	1	6	....	....
Hitchcock, Nathaniel	2	3	5	....	....
Hovey, Isaac	2	......	3	....	....
Hovey, William	1	1	6	....	....
Hopson, John	3	2	7	....	....
Howard, John	1	1	1	....	....
Howard, Samuel	1	1	2	....	....
Hows, Joseph	1	4	4	....	....
Hunt, Simeon	1	5	3	....	....
Hutchinson, Sam[l]	5	4	4	....	....
Huchinson, Samuel	1	......	2	....	....
Ingram, Jeremiah	1	2	3	....	....
Jaquis, Ebenezer	2	......	1	....	....
Jaquis, Ebenezer	1	1	1	....	....
Jaquis, Samuel	1	1	1	....	....
Johnson, Calvin	1	2	2	....	....
Johnson, David	1	2	1	....	....
Johnson, Hezekiah	3	......	1	....	....
Johnson, James	1	1	3	....	....
Johnson, John	1	......	1	....	....
Johnson, Seth	1	1	5	....	....
Johnson, William	1	3	3	....	....
Lewis, Asahel	1	1	3	....	....
Lewis, Joseph	2	3	4	....	....
Lewis, William	2	2	1	....	....
Lord, David	4	4	3	....	....
Lord, Jonathan	2	2	3	....	....
Loveland, Joseph	3	4	4	....	....
Marshall, Ichabod	1	1	1	....	....
Messinger, Nathaniel	3	......	1	....	....
Morse, Garshom	1	3	3	....	....
Morgin, Cypran	1	3	2	....	....
Morse, Job	1	3	4	....	....
Morse, Seth	2	2	5	....	....
Mosher, Gideon	1	......	1	....	....
Murdock, Asahel	1	2	4	....	....
Murdock, Thomas	3	......	4	....	....
Newton, Elias	1	3	4	....	....
Newton, Israel	4	1	4	....	....
Nye, Daniel	1	1	3	....	....
Olcott, Peter	5	1	5	....	....
Olcott, Roswell	2	......	2	....	....
Parseval, Ebenezer	1	......	1	....	....
Parseval, Jeremiah	1	3	3	....	....
Parseval, Stephen	1	3	5	....	....
Patridge, Isaac	3	2	4	....	....
Patridge, Elias	1	1	2	....	....
Patridge, Elisha	4	2	6	....	....
Patridge, Samuel	2	2	4	....	....
Partril, Joseph	1	......	2	....	....
Pennick, Bezaleel	1	1	1	....	....
Perkins, Barnabas	1	3	4	....	....
Persons, Moses	1	6	2	....	....
Potter, Lyman	2	3	5	....	....
Rice, Isaac	1	3	3	....	....
Richards, Jonas	2	3	2	....	....
Sawyer, Conant	1	2	3	....	....
Sawyer, Jacob	1	4	2	....	....
Sever, Calvin	1	2	2	....	....
Sever, Nathaniel	1	1	4	....	....
Smalley, Justus	1	1	1	....	....
Smalley, Joseph	3	3	2	....	....
Smalley, Sarah	......	2	2	....	....
Smith, Asa	2	3	5	....	....
Smalley, Francis	2	3	6	....	....
Smith, Eleazer	2	2	3	....	....
Smith, Reuben	1	1	1	....	....
Smith, Phillip	1	1	3	....	....
Spear, Joshua	1	2	5	....	....
Stafter, John	2	3	4	....	....
Starkwether, Amos	1	2	3	....	....
Stimson, Joel	1	2	3	....	....
Smith, Sylvanus	1	6	4	....	....
Storrs, Aron	6	2	5	....	....
Stowel, Ira	2	......	2	....	....
Stowel, Ebenezer	1	5	2	....	....
Thatcher, Bliss	1	1	1	....	....
Thatcher, Peter	1	3	2	....	....
Tucker, Joseph	1	2	2	....	....
Vincent, Joseph	2	1	6	....	....
Watton, Oliver	1	2	3	....	....
Waterman, Daniel	2	2	6	....	....
Waterman, Daniel	2	3	2	....	....
Woodworth, Benjamin	1	2	3	....	....
Waterman, Elijah	1	1	4	....	....
Waterman, Elisha	1	2	5	....	....
Waterman, James	1	3	4	....	....
Waterman, Samuel	3	2	3	....	....
West, Caleb	1	3	4	....	....
White, Solomon	1	2	4	....	....
White, Eli	1	2	4	....	....
White, Elisha	1	......	2	....	....
White, Samuel	2	......	1	....	....
White, Solomon	1	1	5	....	....
Whitecomb, Elisha	1	......	......	....	....
Wilder, Abel	1	1	5	....	....
Willis, Nathan	1	4	1	....	....
Wilmot, Timothy	1	1	4	....	....
Woodward, Elihu	1	1	3	....	....
Wright, John	1	2	5	....	....
Yemmons, Elijah	2	......	3	....	....
Yerangton, Ebenezer	1	3	3	....	....
POMFRET TOWN.					
Allyn, Elnathan	1	5	2	....	....
Anesworth, Henry	1	3	3	....	....
Badcock, Josiah	1	3	2	....	....
Baker, Abel	1	1	4	....	....
Bass, Cuff	......	......	......	5	....
Beebee, Eli	2	2	3	....	....
Bennet, Amos	1	3	1	....	....
Boynton, Amos	1	3	1	....	....
Bugbee, Abiel	3	4	4	....	....
Bugbee, Benjamin	2	1	2	....	....
Carpenter, Nathaniel	1	2	3	....	....
Chamberlin, Wire	1	1	3	....	....
Chedle, John	2	2	5	....	....
Child, Abijah	2	4	3	....	....
Child, William	1	1	2	....	....
Conant, Jeremiah	1	3	2	....	....
Culver, Rothmel	1	1	1	....	....
POMFRET TOWN—con.					
Dana, Isaac	2	1	1	....	....
Dana, John	5	3	6	....	....
Dana, Jonathan	1	3	2	....	....
Deane, Nathan	1	1	2	....	....
Dexter, John	1	3	3	....	....
Dotin, Isaac	1	1	3	....	....
Dotin, John	1	1	1	....	....
Drepen, John	1	1	1	....	....
Drew, Ezra	1	4	5	....	....
Durkee, Andrew	1	2	1	....	....
Durkee, Bartholomew	4	2	3	....	....
Durkee, Ransom	2	2	4	....	....
Dwyer, Jeremiah	1	4	4	....	....
Finno, Joseph	1	......	2	....	....
Frasier, John	1	1	3	....	....
Frasier, Nathaniel	2	......	2	....	....
Goff, Oliver	1	3	3	....	....
Green, Barkos	2	1	6	....	....
Harding, Timothy	1	2	7	....	....
Harkins, Dexter	1	......	1	....	....
Hathway, Seth	1	2	1	....	....
Hewit, Increase	3	3	4	....	....
Hoar, John	1	2	1	....	....
Hogges, Asa	1	2	2	....	....
Hogges, Seth	2	......	4	....	....
Hutchinson, Aaron	4	1	4	....	....
Hutchinson, Elisha	1	3	5	....	....
Ingraham, John	1	......	......	....	....
Johnson, Timothy	1	3	2	....	....
Keth, Israel	5	3	5	....	....
Kimball, Richard	4	1	3	....	....
King, Daniel	1	1	3	....	....
Lake, Elij	1	......	4	....	....
Lamb, Samuel	2	1	1	....	....
Lamphier, Thomas	1	......	3	....	....
Lazell, Joshua	1	......	1	....	....
Lazell, William	1	......	2	....	....
Lebaron, Isaac	1	......	4	....	....
Lebaron, Wellman	1	1	3	....	....
Leonard, Enoch	2	1	1	....	....
Leonard, Jonas	1	......	2	....	....
Leonard, Rowland	1	2	1	....	....
Leevel, John	1	3	2	....	....
Marsh, Samuel	1	1	2	....	....
Mason, Elijah	1	2	6	....	....
Mason, Marshall	i	......	4	....	....
Michel, Timothy	2	2	1	....	....
Morris, Asa	1	2	3	....	....
Morse, Abiel	1	4	1	....	....
Newton, Isaac	2	......	2	....	....
Paddock, Zenos	1	2	1	....	....
Paddock, John	2	4	2	....	....
Paine, Asa	1	4	2	....	....
Peak, Ephraim	1	2	4	....	....
Peak, Jonathan	1	......	1	....	....
Peak, Lemuel	3	......	4	....	....
Perkins, John	3	5	2	....	....
Perkins, William	1	3	3	....	....
Perkins, Thomas	1	2	2	....	....
Perrin, Abel	1	3	5	....	....
Perrin, John	1	3	1	....	....
Perrin, Peter	2	2	4	....	....
Perry, William	2	4	1	....	....
Perry, Robert	2	1	5	....	....
Petty, William	1	2	2	....	....
Porter, Ellot	1	2	2	....	....
Porter, Samuel	1	......	2	....	....
Pratt, Benjamin	1	2	1	....	....
Pratt, John	5	2	4	....	....
Raymond, Phinehas	2	......	1	....	....
Ruggles, Nathaniel	1	1	2	....	....
Pratt, Jeremiah	1	1	7	....	....
Runnell, Jonathan	1	1	3	....	....
Sessions, Darius	1	4	5	....	....
Sessions, Simeon	2	......	4	....	....
Simmons, Moses	3	1	5	....	....
Skinner, Benjamin	1	1	3	....	....
Soule, John	2	4	4	....	....
Smith, Abisha	3	1	3	....	....
Smith, Christopher	3	1	3	....	....
Snow, Samuel	1	5	3	....	....
Thompson, Benj[n]	1	4	3	....	....
Throop, John W	1	1	3	....	....
Throop, John	3	1	2	....	....
Tinkham, Josiah	1	2	2	....	....
Vales, Abraham	1	2	3	....	....
Vales, Thos	2	2	5	....	....
Vaughan, Jabez	1	2	3	....	....
Walcott, Charles	1	1	5	....	....
Walcott, William	2	......	2	....	....
Walkins, John	1	4	3	....	....
Washburn, Barnabas	1	2	4	....	....

WINDSOR COUNTY—Continued.

NAME OF HEAD OF FAMILY.	Free white males of 16 years and upward, including heads of families.	Free white males under 16 years.	Free white females, including heads of families.	All other free persons.	Slaves.
POMFRET TOWN—con.					
Washburn, Nathaniel	1		1		
Whore, Elijah	3	1	3		
Wilson, William	1	1	1		
Wire, Frederick	1	2	3		
Winslow, Ebenezer	1	1	2		
Winslow, Samuel	2	2	3		
Woolf, Charles	1	4	2		
READING TOWN.					
Ackley, Joseph	1	2	3		
Allyn, John	1	2	2		
Amsden, Abel	1	3	3		
Amsden, Abraham	1	1	1		
Bailey, Levi	1		2		
Barker, Annaniah	1	1	4		
Bevins, Edward	1		5		
Bevins, Edward	1	1	2		
Bigelow, Elisha	2	2	3		
Bigelow, Noah	1		2		
Bigsbee, Ephraim	1	1	5		
Bigsbee, Jacob	1	2	4		
Bigsbee, John	1		1		
Bowen, Daniel	1	1	2		
Bowtell, Asa	1	4	2		
Brown, Thomas	3		3		
Buck, Benjamin	1		1		
Burdoo, Aaron				3	
Burdoo, Silas				3	
Burnham, David	1		4		
Butterfield, Stephen	2	5	5		
Cady, Baracthial	2	1	4		
Cady, John	2	1	2		
Cady, John	1	2	1		
Cady, Jonathan	1	2	1		
Cady, Nedabiah	1	1	5		
Cady, Pearley	1	2	4		
Call, Asa	1		5		
Call, James	1	2	4		
Carlton, Abraham	1		3		
Carlton, Asa	1	2	3		
Carlton, Gideon	1		2		
Carlton, Henry	2		2		
Carpenter, Joseph	1	1	1		
Chandler, Ebenezer	1	4	2		
Chandler, Isaac	1	1	3		
Chandler, Jonathan	1		3		
Chandler, Zebulon	1		7		
Chaplin, Moses	2	4	2		
Cheevee, Ebenezer G	1	3	4		
Clark, Benjamin	1	1	1		
Clark, George	2	4	6		
Clark, Thomas	2	1	5		
Conant, Jonathan	1	3	3		
Cowley, William	3	1	2		
Davis, John	1	1	2		
Davis, Cornelius	1		1		
Davis, Ezekiel	1		1		
Davis, Ezekiel	2	1	3		
Davis, Thomas	1		3		
Davis, William	1				
Day, Elkanah	1	2	1		
Dinsmore, Abraham	1	5	3		
Easterbrooks, Jonathan	1	2	4		
Edson, Daniel	1	2	2		
Edy, Zachariah	1	1	1		
Emerson, Rindall	2	3	2		
Farmer, John	1		2		
Fay, Ezra	1		1		
Fay, Sherabiah	1	1	2		
Fay, Thomas	1	2	3		
Felch, Nathan	1	4	3		
Fish, Samuel	1	2	2		
French, Jonathan	1		3		
Gilson, Daniel	1		4		
Goose, John	1	2	1		
Grandy, Bezaleel	1	5	3		
Grandy, Robert	1	1	2		
Grandy, Robert	2		1		
Grandy, Samuel	1	4	1		
Habgood, Asa	1	2	2		
Habgood, David	2	2	3		
Hammon, Faunce	1	3	2		
Hatch, Nathan	1	4	3		
Hatheme, Benjamin	1	4	1		
Hayward, William	1	4	3		
Hichcock, Ephraim	1	1	3		
Hichcock, Paul	2	1	3		
Hubbard, Elijah	1		3		
Hubbard, Ephraim	1	1	3		
Jones, Elias	1	2	4		
Kendall, Isaac	2	1	4		
READING TOWN—con.					
Kendell, Zimre	1		2		
Keyes, Solomon	1	2	3		
Kile, William	1	1	2		
Kimball, Aaron	1		1		
Kimball, Isaac	1		2		
Lamfier, Abijah	1	1	1		
Luke, John	1	7	3		
Marks, Adonijah	2	1	2		
Morse, Alpheus	1	3	4		
Morse, Jonathan	1		3		
Nichols, Levi	1	1	3		
Nutting, David	2	2	4		
Orcutt, Elisha	1		2		
Page, John	2	3	2		
Parker, Reuben	1	2	5		
Parker, Samuel	1	1	3		
Peabody, Daniel	1		2		
Philbrooks, James	1	1	1		
Pope, Michael	1	2	1		
Pratt, Nathaniel	2	1	5		
Rice, Abiah	1	1	1		
Rice, Peter	4		3		
Rest, Samuel	1	2	3		
Reed, Aaron	1	2	6		
Robinson, Ebenezer	1				
Robinson, James	1	2	2		
Robinson, John	1	3	2		
Roe, John	1	3	4		
Roe, John	1	1	3		
Salsbury, Jacob	1		3		
Sawyer, Benjamin	1	1	3		
Sawyer, Cornelius	1	4	1		
Sawyer, John	1	3	3		
Seargent, Nahum	1		4		
Shed, Jonathan	1		1		
Sherwin, John	1	1	5		
Sherwin, Nathan	1	2	2		
Sherwin, Samuel	2	1	2		
Smith, Benjamin	1		1		
Spear, Anchier	2	3	3		
Stanly, John	3	3	5		
Stanly, Joseph	1	2	3		
Stone, Abijah	2	2	3		
Swain, Nathaniel	2	2	3		
Taylor, Abraham	1	3	1		
Taylor, Amos	1				
Taylor, William	1	1	1		
Thompson, Seth	1		2		
Townshend, Thomas	2	2	5		
Wild, John	4		2		
Wilkins, Asa	1	4	4		
Wilkens, Joseph	2	2	6		
Wilson, George	1	2	4		
Witherill, Simeon	1	4	2		
Young, Samuel	1	3	1		
ROCHESTER TOWN.					
Antizzle, Perez	1	4	3		
Astins, David	1		2		
Astins, John	1		1		
Astins, John	1	4	2		
Bartlett, Ebenezer	1				
Bliss, Elijah	1	1	2		
Bowman, Isaac	1		4		
Boyse, Joseph	1	2	2		
Carpenter, Nathan	2	2	2		
Chandler, Nathan	1		3		
Chandler, Stephen	1	4	1		
Clements, Isaac	1	1	2		
Clements, Timothy	1	1	1		
Currier, David	2	3	4		
Currier, Moses	1	2	3		
Eastman, Benjamin	3	2	5		
Emerson, Daniel	1	1	7		
Emerson, Enoch	1		1		
Emerson, John	1		2		
Emerson, Thomas	2		2		
Guggins, James	1	2	5		
Harseal, David	2	2	4		
Hoyt, Jacob	1		1		
Jepperson, Ichabod	1		1		
Jepperson, Jacob	2		1		
Knights, Abel	1		2		
Marsh, Clark	1	1	2		
Martin, Samuel	1		3		
Martin, Thomas	1		2		
Morgin, Enos	2	1	4		
Morgin, Timothy	3	3	3		
Packard, Allen	1		1		
Packard, John	1	3	1		
Parker, Jesse	2		2		
ROCHESTER TOWN—con.					
Patridge, Stephen	2	2	6		
Powers, Asahel	1	1	1		
Sangar, John	2	1	1		
Shelding, Cephas	1	2	4		
Smith, Samuel	1		2		
Smith, Samuel	1		3		
Smith, William	1	2	1		
Sparhawk, Ebenezer	3		1		
Stacy, Ebenezer	1				
Whipple, Moses	1		4		
Whitcomb, Charles	1		2		
Wing, Isaac	1				
Wing, Nathaniel	1				
ROYALTON TOWN.					
Allyn, Silas	2	4	3		
Anderson, Thomas	1	1	2		
Anderson, William	1	1	2		
Back, Lyman	1	1	3		
Backus, Stephen	1	1	2		
Banister, Artimus	2		4		
Banister, Timothy	1	2	3		
Bacon, Jerub	1	1	4		
Bacon, Thomas	2		3		
Benton, Medad	2		2		
Billings, John	2	2	6		
Bingham, Thomas	3	5	5		
Bliss, Jonathan	3	3	3		
Bloyes, Reuben	1		2		
Boardman, Joseph	2	4	1		
Bowen, David	2		2		
Brown, Aaron	1	2	1		
Brown, Alexander	1	1	5		
Burbank, Abijah	1	2	3		
Burbank, Abijah	1		2		
Burbank, Henry	1	2	1		
Burroughs, John	1		2		
Burroughs, Stephen	1		2		
Church, Ebenezer	2	1	3		
Clapp, Daniel	1	1	2		
Clapp, Samuel	1	3	2		
Cleaveland, Chester	1		3		
Cleaveland, Jeddediah	1	1	4		
Cleaveland, Samuel	1	1	1		
Cleaveland, William	1		2		
Crane, John	2				
Crandall, Gideon	1	2	3		
Curtis, Samuel	2	2	2		
Curtis, Zabad	2	2	2		
Dame, Ebenezer	1	1	3		
Day, Benjamin	2	2	2		
Day, Benjamin, Junr	1	2	2		
Dewey, Darias	1	1	2		
Dewey, Ebenezer	4		2		
Dewey, Ebenezer	1	1	1		
Dewey, Pollus	1	3	2		
Dunham, Ebenezer	1		3		
Dunham, Jesse	1	2	3		
Durfy, Benjamin	2	1	4		
Durfy, James	1	2	1		
Durkee, Timothy	1	1	3		
Durkee, Hermon	3	2	2		
Durkee, Timothy	2	1	2		
Dutton, Amasa	3	3	3		
Evins, Cotton	2	1	1		
Fairbanks, Luther	1	1	6		
Fitch, Ebenezer	1	1	3		
Fish David	3	5	4		
Freeman, Joshua	2				
Fuller, Daniel	2	1	2		
Gates, Rosimond		1	5		
Gilbert, Nathaniel	1				
Green, Adrijah	1	1	2		
Havens, Daniel	1	1	2		
Havens, Joseph	1	2	4		
Havens, Robert	1	1	1		
Hibbard, James	4		2		
Hibbard, John	1	3	5		
How, Samuel	1	2	1		
How, Squire	1	1	4		
How, Theodore	1	3	5		
Hutchinson, John	2		4		
Kent, Elisha	1	2	2		
Kent, Elisha	1	1	2		
Kimball Jared	1		2		
Kimball John	2	1	3		
Kimball, John	1	2	5		
Kimball, Richard	1		3		
Kingsley, Elias	1		1		
Kinney, Bradford	2		4		
Lion, Zebulon	1	3	2		

WINDSOR COUNTY—Continued.

NAME OF HEAD OF FAMILY.	Free white males of 16 years and upward, including heads of families.	Free white males under 16 years.	Free white females, including heads of families.	All other free persons.	Slaves.
ROYALTON TOWN—con.					
Lyman, Asa	1		2		
Lyman, Eliphalet	1		1		
Lyman, Daniel	1		2		
Lyman, Ezekiel	2		3		
Lyman, Samuel	1	2	1		
Lyman, William	1		2		
Medcalf, Samuel	2		2		
Miles, Ephraim	1	3	2		
Morgin, Isaac	1	3	4		
Morgin, Nathan	1	2	5		
Morse, Nathaniel	1		3		
Munroe, Isaac	1	3	1		
Nobles, Nehemiah	1	4	2		
Page, Nathan	1	2	2		
Palmer, Paul	1	3	1		
Parkhurst, Benjamin	1	3	5		
Parkhurst, Calvin	3	1	5		
Parkhurst, Jabez	2		4		
Parkhurst, Joseph	2	1	5		
Parkhurst, Tilley	1	1	2		
Parks, John	2	1	1		
Paul, Hibbs	1	3	2		
Perrin, Asa	1		3		
Perrin, Asa	1	3	1		
Perrin, Nathaniel	1		2		
Pierce, Jeddediah	3	3	4		
Pierce, Nathaniel	2	1	1		
Pierce, Palmer	1	3	1		
Pierce, Willard	1	2	2		
Pinney, Asa	1	2	3		
Reed, Nathaniel	1	2	2		
Richardson, Godfrey	1	2	3		
Richardson, Jesse	1	2	3		
Richardson, Sanford	1	1	2		
Rix, Daniel	4		3		
Rugg, David	1	1	2		
Rust, Jeremiah	1	1	2		
Safford, Jacob	1		2		
Serls, Samuel	1	2	2		
Serls, John	2		3		
Sever, Comfort	1		1		
Sheppard, Timothy	3	1	1		
Skinner, Isaac	1	1	2		
Skinner, Luther	1	1	1		
Smith, Mary		1	4		
Stevens, Abel	2	1	6		
Stevens, Elias	3	2	8		
Sylvester, Seth	2	2	1		
Taylor, Elnathan	1		2		
Terry, Daniel	1		3		
Stone, Nathan	1	1	2		
Triscott, Experience	1		2		
Triscott, Jeremiah	1	2	4		
Waller, John	1				
Warriner, John	1		3		
Washburn, Asahel	1		1		
Waterman, Abraham	1	4	2		
Waterman, William	1	1	1		
Wells, Ebenezer	1		6		
Wells, Jonathan	1		2		
Williams, Silas	1	4	3		
Wheeler, Josiah	1	5	3		
Woodward, Ebenezer	1	1	4		
Woodworth, Timothy	1	3	4		
Young, Ebenezer	1	3	2		
SALTASH TOWN.					
Adams, Ephraim	1	1			
Brown, Boardman	3	3	5		
Coolidge, John	1	3	3		
Coolidge, Obediah	1	1	2		
Corey, Ebenezer	1	2	2		
Corlile, William	1	4	3		
Jones, Nathaniel	1	1	2		
Merdye, John	3	1	3		
Nichols, Robert	1	3	3		
Page, Samuel	1	2	2		
Priest, James	4		1		
Sawyer, Paul	1		1		
Sawyer, Thomas	2	2	3		
Taylor, John	1	1	1		
Wheeler, Asa	1	2	2		
Wilder, Ebenezer	1	3	3		
Wilder, Jacob	1	2	3		
Wilder, Jacob	1				
Wilder, Jonathan	1	3	2		
Wilder, Reuben W	2	1	1		
SHARON TOWN.					
Ames, David	1	1	1		
Basset, Jared	2	4	5		
Bewel, Abel	2	1	6		
SHARON TOWN—con.					
Benton, Nathan	1	1	3		
Bruce, Jesse	1	2	3		
Bruce, Jonas	1	2	2		
Bruce, Jonathan	1		4		
Brown, James	1	4	4		
Burton, Josiah	1	1	3		
Calkins, Jedediah	1		2		
Carpenter, Alvin	2	1	3		
Carpenter, Asa	4	2	5		
Carpenter, James	2	3	5		
Carpenter, James	1	2	1		
Carpenter, Nathan	1	1	2		
Chiel, David	1	3	2		
Cleaveland, John	2	1	4		
Darbe, Jesse	1	1	1		
Day, Orson	2	1	1		
Doubleday, Jacob	1		3		
Downer, Andrew	4	1	3		
Downer, Jason	2	2	2		
Downer, Zacheus	1	2	2		
Eldridge, Caleb	1		2		
Foster, Aaron	1	1	4		
Foster, Thomas	1		6		
Foster, William	1	1	1		
Frink, Willard	1	1	1		
Gallup, Joseph	1	2	2		
Gilbert, Daniel	2	2	3		
Goodspeed, Elisha	1	2	4		
Hatch, Abner	2	5	1		
Hatch, Isaac	2		1		
Howard, Thomas	2	1	2		
Haze, Philemon	2	3	4		
Herrington, Mathew	1	1	3		
Herrington, Stephen	1		2		
How, Jonathan	4	2	4		
How, Simeon	2	2	4		
Holt, Abiel	1		3		
Holt, Isaac	1	1	1		
Hunter, Lark	1		3		
Ladd, Frederick	1	1	1		
Ladd, Samuel	1	2	5		
Lazel, Zenos	1	1	3		
Leonard, Daniel	1	3	3		
Leonard, Silas	1		3		
Lovejoy, Daniel	1	1	3		
Lovejoy, John	1	1	3		
Lovejoy, Nehemiah	1		2		
Lovejoy, Oliver	1		2		
Lovejoy, William	1		1		
Mann, Benjamin	1	2	3		
Marsh, James	1	3	2		
Marsh, Joel	2	3	5		
May, Elisha	1	1	2		
Morgin, Roswell	1		1		
Morse, Anthony	1	4	4		
Mosher, Aaron	1	1	3		
Mosher, Nichols	3	1	4		
Mosher, Pardon	1		1		
Mosher, Rodman	1		1		
Mosher, Thomas	1	3	2		
Mosher, Eber	1	2	4		
Palmer, Amos	1	2	5		
Parker, Amos	1	1	4		
Parker, James	1	1	2		
Parkhurst, Asahel	1	2	2		
Parkhurst, George	1	2	2		
Parkhurst, Ebenezer	2	5	5		
Parkhurst, Jonathan	1		1		
Parkhurst, Jonathan	1	1	2		
Parkhurst, Lemuel	1	2	3		
Parkhurst, Lydia	2	1	2		
Parkhurst, Noah	1	3	3		
Parkhurst, Reuben	2	1	3		
Pigsley, John	1	2	4		
Plumley, Jonathan	1	1	2		
Plumley, Samuel	1	3	3		
Powel, Stephen	1	1	2		
Powel, Stephen	3	1	1		
Rockwell, Adonijah	1	2	5		
Shepard, Moses	2	1	3		
Shepard, Squire	4	1	3		
Shepard, Willard	1		1		
Shermon, Joseph	1	1	2		
Simons, Joshua	3		2		
Smith, Moses	5				
Spalding, Asahel	1	3	3		
Spalding, Reuben	1	2	3		
Spalding, Royal	2		2		
Spalding, Wright	2	3	2		
Spear, Edward	1	2	5		
Thompson, Lathrop	2		2		
Town, James	1	3	5		
Tucker, John P.	1	2	2		
Walbridge, John	3	2	4		
SHARON TOWN—con.					
Wheeler, Ebenezer	1		1		
Wheeler, Isaac	1	4	2		
Wheeler, Nathaniel	1	1	1		
White, Lemuel	1	1	4		
Williams, Ebenezer	1	1	1		
SPRINGFIELD TOWN.					
Bragg, Nicholas	2		4		
Chapman, Eliphalet	2	2	3		
Bates, Roger	1	3	6		
Hubbard, Calvin	1	2	7		
Martin, Margaret	2	1	1		
Bisbee, John	2	3	4		
Thomson, Peter	1				
Paine, John	1		2		
Paine, Ephraim	1		3		
McRoberts, William	2		4		
Gill, Amos	1		1		
Barrett, John	2		2	2	
Millwain, William	1		1		
Swan, John	2		1		
Swan, Aaron	1	1	1		
Sartwell, Jacob	1	3	1		
Sartwell, Daniel	1		2		
Kemp, Elijah	2	2	2		
Goodenough, Timothy	1		1		
Ward, Nathan	2	5	4		
Ward, Samuel	1	1	2		
Covell, Joseph	2	4	1		
Corlew, Edward	1	1	2		
Wright, Joseph	2		1		
Thomson, John	2	1	6		
Stevens, Solomon	1	1	1		
Bragg, William	1		1		
Holmes, Hezekiah	1		1		
Holmes, Walter	1		2		
Pearl, Phinehas	1	3	3		
Bradford, Asa	1		1		
Burge, Nathaniel	1	3	1		
Bradford, Simeon	4	1	4		
Weston, Nathaniel	3	2	2		
Weston, Jerusha			2		
Clark, Elisha	1		3		
Corlew, Silva			4		
McRoberts, John	1	2	2		
Farrington, Dan	1		1		
Caldwell, Ebenezer	1		1		
Tuttle, Isaac	1	1	2		
Herrick, William	1	2	3		
Haskins, Samuel	1	4	3		
Bragg, Nicholas, Junr	1	2	5		
Powers, Asahel	1	2	4		
Tower, Isaac	2	2	5		
Bates, Theophilus	1		3		
Bates, Phinehas	1		2		
Bisbee, Abner	2	4	2		
Blis, Oliver	4		3		
Holmes, Orsamus	1	3	3		
Wells, Obediah	1	1	2		
Killient, Charity	1	3	3		
Ward, Jabez	2	1	2		
Ward, Jedediah	1	1	3		
Ball, Daniel	1	2	1		
Whitney, Lemuel	4	3	3		
Rugg, Josephas	2	3	3		
Houghton, Abel	2	2	4		
Nye, George	1		2		
Lockwood, Joseph	1		5		
Cobb, Samuel	2	4	4		
Nichols, Levi, Junr	1	1	2		
Barnard, Jonathan	2		2		
Moore, Mary		3	2		
Tolman, Elijah	1				
Nichols, Levi	1	3	5		
Gould, Jonas	1	2	3		
Barrell, John	1		2		
Gell, John	1	2	3		
Bates, Moses	1		2		
McElroy, James	3	2	2		
Kingsley, James	1	2	2		
Parks, David	2	1	1		
Wyman, Jeduthan	1	2	2		
Burr, Jonathan	1		3		
Stevens, Simon	2	1	1		
Stevens, Simon, Junr	1				
Luther, Wido.——			5		
Caldwell, Nathan	2	1	2		
Scott, Samuel	1		3		
Giles, Samuel	1	1	2		
Hall, George	1		1		
Hall, James	1	1	2		
Sartwell, Oliver	3	2	3		
House, Prudence			1		

WINDSOR COUNTY—Continued.

NAME OF HEAD OF FAMILY.	Free white males of 16 years and upward, including heads of families.	Free white males under 16 years.	Free white females, including heads of families.	All other free persons.	Slaves.
SPRINGFIELD TOWN—continued.					
Rogers, Elisha	1	1	2		
House, Simon	1				
House, David	1	3	2		
Sawyer, Josiah	1		1		
Stow, Amos	1	2	3		
Allen, Ebenezer	1				
Griswould, Matthew	1				
Griswould, Daniel	1	1	4		
Griswould, John	2	3	3		
Kirk, William	1	1	3		
Field, Luther	1		2		
Waistcoat, Charles	1		1		
Williams, Timothy	1		2		
Packard, John	1	2	3		
Smith, Thomas	1	1	3		
King, Daniel	1	2	4		
Shirtliff, John	2		5		
Spooner, Benj[a]	1		1		
Lockwood, Abraham	2	1	5		
Pollard, James	1	3	1		
Cook, Thomas	1	4	2		
Rogers, Chester	1		3		
Williams, John	2	4	2		
Scofield, Thomas	3	5	7		
Lockwood, Jacob, 2[d]	1	4	4		
Blue, Stephen	3		3		
Temple, Fraderick	1	2	4		
Williams, Timothy, Jun[r]	1	1	1		
Olney, Abraham	2	1	5		
Olney, William	1	1	2		
Olney, Benony	1	1	1		
Herford, Thomas	1	2	2		
Parker, Robert	1		1		
Parker, Amos	3	1	3		
Parker, Ezra	1	3	2		
Williams, Nicholas	1	4	3		
Redfield, Ezra	2		2		
Stinson, David	1		2		
Haywood, John	1		3		
Haywood, Paul	1	2	1		
Hall, John	1	3	2		
Cass, John	1	1	7		
Sanborn, John	1		1		
Brown, Elisha	1	3	2		
Bemis, John	1	2	5		
Bemis, Isaac	1	2	3		
Sartwell, Oliver, Jun[r]	1	1	1		
Sartwell, Hale	1		2		
Latham, Simeon	1		4		
Aldrich, Benjamin	1	1	2		
Wight, Abner	1	3	2		
Dunphy, James	1	4	3		
Cummings, Joseph	2		2		
Lockwood, Henry	1	2	1		
Lockwood, William	4	1	4		
Lockwood, William, Jun[r]	1	3	1		
Griffith, William	1	3	2		
Phillips, Levi	1	5	5		
Field, Daniel	1	3	6		
Lockwood, Abraham, 2[d]	1	2	3		
Hudson, Benjamin	1	3	4		
Hudson, William	1		2		
Hudson, Benarah	3	1	5		
Taylor, Jacob Lockwood	1	1	2		
Lockwood, Amos	1		2		
M[c]Collester, John	1				
Balch, Timothy	1	1	1		
Dennison, Daniel, Jun[r].	1	2	1		
Lockwood, Benony	1	5	1		
Randall, Elisha	2	1	2		
Hall, James	1				
Maynard, John	1				
Lock, John	2				
Bailey, Jethro	1				
Nott, John	1	3	4		
Bailey, Luther	1	3	4		
Jervis, Robert	1	3	2		
Marks, John	1	1	1		
Sheldin, Anthony	2	1	3		
Spencer, Nehemiah	1		1		
Spencer, Simeon	4	2	2		
Randall, John	2	1	2		
Randall, James	1	3	4		
Sartwell, Reuben	1	1	2		
Sartwell, Ezekiel	1		2		
Sartwell, Daniel	1		2		
Wilson, John	5	1	5		
Corlew, Thomas	3	2	3		
Smith, Isaac	4	2	4		
Randall, Amos	1	7	1		
Reed, Josiah	2	3	4		
Putnam, Thomas	1	3	2		
Clary, Dolly		1	2		

NAME OF HEAD OF FAMILY.	Free white males of 16 years and upward, including heads of families.	Free white males under 16 years.	Free white females, including heads of families.	All other free persons.	Slaves.
SPRINGFIELD TOWN—continued.					
Fletcher, Ebenezer	1				
Parker, Isaac	2	1	7		
Parker, Leonard	1				
Harlow, Levi	2	5	5		
Bellows, Ezra	1	3	4		
Shead, Solomon	5	1	4		
Dennison, Daniel	4	2	4		
White, Jotham	2	3	3		
Graves, Daniel	1	1	6		
Morris, Lewis R	3	2	2	1	
Young, Duncan	1	2	2		
Stafford, Thomas	1	2	2		
Sheldin, Nathaniel	1		2		
Carr, John	1	1	1		
Barrett, William	1				
Gill, Daniel	2	1	5		
Parker, Jeremiah	3	3	5		
Holden, William	1		1		
Holden, Nathaniel	1	4	3		
Barker, Daniel	2	2	3		
Spencer, Taylor	2	1	6		
Wilson, Deliverance	3	1	6		
Stafford, Stakeley	1	1	5		
Hubbard, Lemuel	1	3	5		
Stone, David	1				
STOCKBRIDGE TOWN.					
Abbot, Nathan	2	2	5		
Adams, Joseph	1	1	2		
Carpenter, Aaron	1	1	2		
Cleaveland, Samuel	1	1	3		
Conkey, Joshua	1	2	4		
Durkee, David	2	2	2		
Durkee, Ebenezer	1		1		
Durkee, John	1	2	3		
Durkee, Joseph	3	1	2		
Happer, George	1	2	2		
Holland, Elihu	1		1		
Holland, Reuben	1	3	3		
Keyes, Elias	5		2		
Lyon, Robert	1		1		
Moffit, Heber	1		1		
Parmeter, Isaiah	3	1	2		
Webber, Norman	1		1		
Whitecomb, Asa	1	1	1		
Whitecomb, John	1	2	1		
Whitecomb, Thomas	1		2		
Wiley, Robert	1		1		
Wiley, Samuel	1	4	1		
WEATHERSFIELD TOWN.					
Haskell, John	3	1	4		
Steel, Stephen	2	2	5		
Taylor, David	1	3	3		
Hubbard, George	1	1	3		
Pierce, Ebenezer	1				
Danforth, Joseph	1	3	1		
French, Jacob	2	1	3		
Steel, Samuel	1		5		
Haskell, Roger	1				
Nye, Jonathan	1	2	5		
Robinson, Charles	1	1	2		
Haskell, Jacob	1	1	2		
Gilbert, Elisha	1	1	2		
Babcock, William Smith	1				
Stafford, Caleb	1				
Treet, Thomas				2	
Hill, Richard				3	
Hubbard, Joseph	3	1	6		
Pryer, Jedediah	2		4		
Dike, Samuel	1	1	1		
Harris, Luther	2		2		
Haskell, John, Jun[r]	1	1	3		
Goodwin, Davis	2	1	1		
France, Christopher	1	1	2		
Hart, Ozias	1		1		
Brown, William	1	2	3		
Blakely, Moses	1	2	2		
Finch, Eleazer	1	1	5		
Blakely, Wid[o]. Avis		1	1		
Cook, Reuben	2	1	2		
Whitney, Wid[o]. Barsheba		1	3		
Kidder, Oliver	2	3	4		
Bingham, Reuben	1		1		
Sterns, Asa	2	2	4		
Culver, Oliver	1	1	1		
Lewis, Samuel	1		2		
Nutting, Abel	1	2	4		
Bolder, John	2	1	4		
Richards, Thomas	2		2		

NAME OF HEAD OF FAMILY.	Free white males of 16 years and upward, including heads of families.	Free white males under 16 years.	Free white females, including heads of families.	All other free persons.	Slaves.
WEATHERSFIELD TOWN—continued.					
Dix, Benjamin	1	2	3		
Dean, William	3	4	2		
Boynton, Stewart	2		2		
Beckley, Zebedee	1		2		
Parkhurst, Pearl	1		1		
Field, Levi	1		2		
Bobcock, Lemuel	1	1	1		
Clark, Gershom	1	4	5		
Cary, Richard	1	1	2		
Cady, Elijah	1		1		
Cady, Noah	1	2	3		
Burmingham, Israel	1	3	4		
Allen, Samuel G	1				
Burmingham, John	1	1	1		
Preston, Tivers	2	3	5		
Parkhutt, Timothy	2		3		
Tuttle, Ezra	1	1	2		
Blakely, Hannah	2	4	3		
Jackson, Marvel	1		1		
Upham, William	4	1	2		
Stevens, Lunis	1		2		
Pierce, John	1		3		
Adams, Jacob	2		3		
Foster, Rev[d]. Dan	2	3	5		
Mather, Elihu	2	2	2		
D[e] Wolf, Elias	1	3	2		
Taylor, James	1	1	2		
Warren, Thomas	2				
Hicks, Jonah	1		4		
Gilbert, Jesse	3		1		
Deckins, Oliver	2	1	4		
Humphry, Daniel	1	2	3		
Pettegrue, William	1	1	4		
Upham, Asa	2	2	4		
Clark, Dan	1		2		
Grovenor, John	3		2		
Reed, Thomas	1		2		
Cook, Paul	2		2		
Ingels, Darius	1	1	5		
French, Abner	1	2	2		
Peters, Joseph	1	1	1		
Hicks, Levi	1		3		
Beckley, Josiah	1	3	2		
Chittendon, James	1	1	2		
Toles, Henry	4	3	3		
White, John	1	2	7		
Spencer, Luther	1	1	3		
Thomas, Zebel	1	3	3		
Parkhurst, Jonathan	1		2		
Cole, Amos	2	1	1		
Matthews, Jesse	3	1	5		
Towns, Jacob	2	1	1		
Wetherbe, David	1	1	2	1	
Prentice, Thomas	7	3	3		
Dart, Joshua	2		2		
Dart, Olivet	1		3		
Divoll, James	2	2	1		
Cook, Oliver	1	1	3		
Toles, Clark	2	2	3		
Worcester, Benjamin	1	3	6		
Toles, David	2		1		
Newton, Edward	2	2	3		
Babcock, Daniel	1	3	2		
Lymon, Gideon	1	3	3		
Fellows, Verney	1		2		
Cummings, Amos	1				
Cummings, Benjamin	1				
Bennitt, John	1	1	4		
Lewis, Jabez	2	3	1		
Judd, Ebenezer	2		4		
Norton, Joseph	2	1	5		
Norton, Levi	1	1	2		
Elmore, Daniel	2		3		
Parker, Isaac	1	1	3		
Hatch, Josiah	1	2	6		
Hills, Simeon	1	2	4		
Cutting, Jonas	1	4	1	1	
Dunphy, Thomas	1		3		
Robinson, Elijah	2	1	3		
Downer, Abraham	1	1	5		
Downer, Gaylord	1	2	1		
Robinson, Benjamin	2	2	5		
Newton, Samuel	2	5	4		
Newton, Edward, Jun[r].	1	2	1		
Pierce, Oliver	1	1	1		
Mason, Joseph	4		3		
Wright, Ephraim	1	2	5		
Carter, Asa	2		5		
Dart, Josiah	1	2	3		
Joslin, Joseph	1	7	4		
Thomson, Isaac	1		2		
Hardy, Jacob	1	3	4		
Gitchell, Jacob	1	2	3		

WINDSOR COUNTY—Continued.

NAME OF HEAD OF FAMILY.	Free white males of 16 years and upward, including heads of families.	Free white males under 16 years.	Free white females, including heads of families.	All other free persons.	Slaves.
WEATHERSFIELD TOWN—continued.					
Hatch, Ebenezer	1		1		
Luther, Ellis	3	2	3		
Straw, Reuben	1	1	1		
Hatch, John	1	1	3		
Powers, Jonathan	1	1	4		
Herwood, Archebald	1	2	2		
Chamberlin, Oliver, Junr	1	1	2		
Grout, Asa	2	1	5		
Young, Joseph	1	1	5		
Glazier, Ebenezer	1	3	3		
Chamberlin, Oliver	4	1	5		
Chilson, Waters	1	4	6		
Chilson, Nathan	1		1		
Spafford, Eliphalet	2	1	2		
Sisko, William	2	3	6		
Marsh, John	1	1	2		
Boynton, John	5	2	4		
Bigelow, Silas	1		1		
Winn, Caleb	2	4	3		
Newton, Elijah	1	2	2		
Chapin, Gideon	1	2	2		
Howard, David	1	5	2		
Grout, Hezekiah, Junr	1	1	3		
Jones, Nathaniel	2	1	3		
Boynton, Jewitt	2	1	2		
Boynton, Ephraim	1	1	3		
Larabee, William	1	4	2		
Grout, Seth	1	1	2		
Grout, Hezkiah	5	1	4		
Grout, Elihu	1	2	4		
Sears, Silas	1	2	2		
Hutchins, Serrell	1		2		
Holmes, Joseph	1	1	3		
Williams, John	2	3	4		
Lawrance, John	1	2	5		
Ordway, Nehemiah	1	3	2		
Parmale, John	1	1	1		
Dickey, Joseph	1	3	3		
Farr, Samuel	1	1	2		
Warner, Benjamin	1	3	3		
Bowman, Thadeus	1	1	6		
Bowman, Thadeus, Junr	1	1	2		
Chapin, Joseph	1		3		
Nichols, David	1	3	3		
Nichols, William	1	1	2		
Piper, Noah	1	4	6		
Sherman, Samuel, Junr	1	1	1		
Hall, James	1		2		
Adams, Samuel	1		4		
Crague, William	1	2	2		
Willard, James	1	1	3		
Willard, Longly	1	3	2		
Willis, Meletiah	1	1	3		
Stoughton, Nathaniel	1	3	5		
Belnap, Joseph	1	3	5		
Glazier, Joseph	2		1		
Glazier, Aaron	1	2	3		
Howard, Archebald	1	1	3		
Hutchins, Thomas	2	4	6		
Webb, Joseph	1	2	6		
Young, Ichabod	1	3	5		
Edy, Newberry	2	1	1		
Edy, Allen	1		2		
Whetmore, Jerusha		3	2		
Stoughton, Joseph	3		3		
Spafford, Joseph	1		1		
Spafford, Joseph, Junr	2	1	1		
Hadlock, Thomas	2	2	1		
Hadlock, James	1		2		
Hadlock, John	1		1		
Culver, Andrew	2	3	3		
Potwine, George	1	2	4		
Morgin, Samuel	1	1	1		
Sherman, Samuel	2	2	4		
Allen, Jonathan	1		2		
WINDSOR TOWN.					
Adams, Abel	4	2	4		
Adams, Isaac	1	1	2		
Adams, Thomas	2		3		
Ainesworth, Thomas	1	1	2		
Arkins, Israel	1	4	2		
Bailey, Joshua	2	2	6		
Bailey, Samuel	1	1	3		
Banister, Lazarus	1	5	4		
Banister, Silas	1	4	4		
Bark, Solomon	3	4	3		
Barrett, Joseph	1		1		
Barrett, Oliver	3	2	5		

NAME OF HEAD OF FAMILY.	Free white males of 16 years and upward, including heads of families.	Free white males under 16 years.	Free white females, including heads of families.	All other free persons.	Slaves.
WINDSOR TOWN—con.					
Bean, William	1	3	4		
Beach, Elihu	1	1	2		
Beach, Stephen	1	1	1		
Beach, Elihu	1	1	1		
Bill, Benjamin	1	1	3		
Bishop, Benjamin	1	1	2		
Bishop, Levi	1	2	5		
Blake, William	1	3	4		
Blood, John	1	2	3		
Bradley, William	1		2		
Brown, Briant	7	4	7		
Brown, John	1		2		
Bugbee, Daniel	2	1	2		
Burk, Isaiah	2	2	3		
Burnham, Ebenezer	1	1	4		
Burnham, Frederick	1	4	4		
Burnham, Samuel	1	2	1		
Burt Jonathan	4	5	4		
Cady, Abel	1				
Cady, Manassah	1	1	4		
Cady, Stephen	1	1	8		
Capin, Abijah	2	1	6		
Cady, Benjamin	3	2	3		
Capin, John	4		2		
Capin, Edmond	1	1	2		
Capin, Philip	1		3		
Chapin, Calvin	1	1	5		
Colburn, Nathan	1	4	3		
Coldwell, Ebenezer	1		2		
Conant, Stephen	5	2	3		
Cooledge, Nathan	1	1	1		
Crandall, Joel	4	2	1		
Cooper, Thomas	1	3	5		
Cummings, Jerathmel	2	5	6		
Currier, Peter	1	1	3		
Currier, Samuel	3		1		
Curtis, Silas	1	1	1		
Curtis, Zebina	11	4	10	1	
Dake, Benjamin	1	4	1		
Dake, Susanah		1	5		
Danford, Samuel	1	2	3		
Dean, Reuben	1	2	3		
Dean, William	1		1		
Dean, William	4	2	5		
Dononghue, James	1	1	2		
Ely, Joel	2		1		
Ely, Joel	2		5		
Eastman, Timothy	1		1		
Eastman, Clark	1	3	2		
Edman, Joseph	1	2	3		
Emmons, Solomon	1		2		
Fisk, Nathan	1	1	3		
Fuller, Joseph	1	2	4		
Gill, John	1	1	2		
Green, Benjamin	1		4	3	
Green, Isaac	2		2		
Hall, Jonathan	1	1	3		
Hall, David	1	3	5		
Hale, Benjamin	1	2	4		
Hale, David	1	4	3		
Hale, Israel	1	2	3		
Hale, Silas	1		3		
Harlow, William	1	2	2		
Hawley, Elijah	4	6	5		
Hawley, Ezekiel	1	3	4		
Hawley, Jesse	2	1	5		
Hawley, Josiah	3	3	5		
Hayard, Ebenezer	1	1	1		
Hayard, Ebenezer	1		1		
Hastings, Daniel	1	3	2		
Hedge, Solomon	1	2	3		
Hemingway, Phinehas	1	1	2		
Herrick, Henry	1		1		
Hewit, John	3		1		
Hibbard, Elnathan	3	5	2		
Hoisington, Elias	2	4	1		
Hoisington, Ebenezer	1	2	4		
Hoisington, Ebenezer	4	1	6		
Hoisington, Nathann	1		2		
Hopkins, John	1	2	1		
Houghton, Darius	1	5	1		
Hubbard, Eldad	1	1	2		
Hubbard, Watts	2		2		
Hunter, David	2	4	4		
Hunter, Thomas	1	2	3		
Hunter, William	1	1	3		
Hurd, Abijah	1	1	6		
Jacob, Stephen	5	1	4	2	
Jenny, Noah	1	1	1		
Jewit, William	3		4		

NAME OF HEAD OF FAMILY.	Free white males of 16 years and upward, including heads of families.	Free white males under 16 years.	Free white females, including heads of families.	All other free persons.	Slaves.
WINDSOR TOWN—con.					
Kendall, Amos	4		3		
Kendall, Nathaniel	1		2		
Kendall, Reuben	1		2		
Langdon, Ira	1		2		
Langworthy, James	1	7	5		
Leavins, Charles	1	6	4		
Ledgard, Joseph	2	2	3		
Leonard, Nathaniel	4	2	3		
Leveritt, William	2	1	4	1	
Lincoln, James	1		2		
Lincoln, Nehemiah	2	2	4		
Lumbard, David	1	3	1		
Lumbard, John	1	2	4		
Lumbard, John	2		2		
Lumbarrd, Stephen	1	1	4		
McDaniel, James	1	3	2		
Marey, John	1		3		
Marey, John	1	2	5		
Martindale, Elias	1	3	1		
Mason, Isaac	1	1	7		
Meachum, Elizabeth		2	4		
Meers, Solomon	4	2	3	2	
Minor, Aaron	1	3	3		
Molton, Benjamin	1	2	3		
Moor, John	2	2	7		
Orvis, David	1	4	3		
Paines, Amasa	3	2	5		
Parker, Joseph	1	3	3		
Parmerle, Alexander	6	3	5		
Parmertree, Joseph	3	3	6		
Patrick, Benoni	1		6		
Patrick, Mathew	2	1	2		
Patrick, Samuel	2	2	5		
Peak, John	1	1	3		
Persons, Samuel	2	1	3		
Persons, William	2	2	1		
Persons, William	1	2	3		
Pollard, John	1	1	2		
Porter, William	1	3	3		
Prier, Cloaher	1	1	5		
Prowty, Jacob	1	2	5		
Root, Abel	1		2		
Root, Rufus	1	1	2		
Root, Samuel	1	1	1		
Robinson, Silas	1	3	3		
Ruggles, Samuel	2	3	3		
Rumrill, Henry	3		1		
Russel, Asa	1	2	4		
Russel, Ely	1	5	1		
Russel, John	1	3	2		
Russel, Jonathan	2		2		
Russel, Reuben	1	1	3		
Sabin, Seth	2	2	3		
Savage, Samuel	2	2	5		
Savage, Nathan	1	1	3		
Savage, Samuel	1	1	1		
Sawing, Munnun	2	2	3		
Severance, Ebenezer	1	2	3		
Shepard, Jonathan	1		1		
Smeed, Joel	1	1	4		
Smeed, Elisha	2		5		
Smeed, John	2	3	3		
Sawing, Samuel	2	2	4		
Smith, Asahel	1	3	4		
Smith, Abner	1	1	2		
Smith, Edward	4		2		
Smead, Asa	1	2	6		
Smith, Joseph	1	1	2		
Smith, Reuben	1	1	3		
Smith, Samuel	1	1	2		
Smith, Steel	2		1		
Spalding, Andrew	1	3	3		
Spalding, Leonard	2	1	2		
Spalding, Timothy	2	3	4		
Spafford, John	1	2	3		
Spafford, Taylor	2	3	5		
Stark, Jesse	1	2	3		
Spooner, Alden	5	2	5		
Stark, William	1	3	4		
Stacy, John	4		3		
Stockings, Joseph	1	1	2		
Stoddard, Semion	1	1	3		
Stoel, Joel	1	1	2		
Stoel, Jacob	3	2	4		
Stone, Caleb	2	2	3		
Stone, Daniel	1	2	4		
Stone, Ephraim	1	1	4		
Stone, Hezekiah	1		2		
Stone, Nathan	4	1	2		
Stone, Samuel	1	3	3		

WINDSOR COUNTY—Continued.

NAME OF HEAD OF FAMILY.	Free white males of 16 years and upward, including heads of families.	Free white males under 16 years.	Free white females, including heads of families.	All other free persons.	Slaves.
WINDSOR TOWN—con.					
Story, Zachariah	1	5	5	....	....
Stow, George	1	2	2	....	....
Stricklin, Jonah	1	3	5	....	....
Spicer, Zephaniah	1	....	1	....	....
Tarbox, James	2	4	1	....	....
Taylor, Abraham	1	2	....	....	....
Taylor, Jacob	1	2	2	....	....
Taylor, Joseph	2	2	8	....	....
Taylor, Leonard	1	2	3	....	....
Taylor, Simeon	3	1	4	....	....
Temple, Nicanor	1	....	1	....	....
Thompson, Hezekiah	1	....	1	....	....
Thompson, Joseph	1	1	7	....	....
Thompson, Hezekih	1	2	2	....	....
Tinkham, Amos	1	3	2	....	....
Tinkham, Seth	1	3	3	....	....
Tooley, Josiah	1	5	4	....	....
Town, Edmond	1	....	1	....	....
Trask, Nathan	4	....	2	....	....
Tuttle, Isaac	1	1	1	....	....
Wait, Richard	2	2	4	....	....
Wakefield, Joseph	1	5	2	....	....
Warner, Cyrus	1	2	3	....	....
Washburn, Sylvanus	3	....	2	....	....
Waters, Sylvanus	2	3	3	....	....
Weeks, Nathaniel	1	2	4	....	....
Wheeler, William	1	2	1	....	....
West, Elijah	3	2	5	....	....
White, Archibald	3	2	5	....	....
White, Charles	1	1	2	....	....
White, Thomas	1	....	1	....	....
White, William	1	2	3	....	....
Wilkins, Uriah	2	2	5	....	....
Willard, Oliver	1	2	1	....	....
Willard, Peter	1	....	1	....	....
Willis, Joseph	1	2	2	....	....
Willis, Jonathan	1	....	3	....	....
Willston, Caleb	2	....	1	....	....
Wilson, Ami	2	2	5	....	....
Wilson, Jacob	1	1	3	....	....
Wilson, James	2	2	2	....	....
Wilson, Joshua	2	2	2	....	....
Wilson, Samuel	1	....	2	....	....
Wilson, Thomas	4	....	4	....	....
Wilson, William	1	....	1	....	....
Wood, Daniel	2	....	6	....	....
Woodrough, Joseph	1	2	5	....	....
Woster, Asa	3	1	4	....	....
WOODSTOCK TOWN.					
Allyn, Ephraim	2	2	2	....	....
Alverd, Stephen	1	1	5	....	....
Alverd, Stephen W	1	....	1	....	....
Atwood, Joseph	1	....	1	....	....
Austin, Joshua	1	1	2	....	....
Avery, Nathan	1	3	4	....	....
Avery, Sanford	1	....	1	....	....
Bailey, Elijah	2	....	5	....	....
Bailey, Stephen	1	1	3	....	....
Barns, William	2	3	3	....	....
Barns, Joseph	1	....	1	....	....
Barrow, Samuel	2	1	5	....	....
Barrows, Samuel	1	....	1	....	....
Baker, Artemus	2	....	....	....	....
Barrett, Joseph	4	6	4	....	....
Bennet, Arthur	1	2	1	....	....
Bennet, Jabez	2	2	4	....	....
Bennet, William	1	....	2	....	....
Benjamin, Jonas	1	3	2	....	....
Benjamin, Jonathan	1	3	3	....	....
Bessa, Anthony	1	3	2	....	....
Bessa, Nehemiah	1	3	3	....	....
Besbee, Isaac	1	....	3	....	....
Bevins, Jacob	1	....	1	....	....
Boston, Cato	....	....	....	3	....
Boyse, Daniel	1	....	2	....	....
Brannack, Consider	2	....	1	....	....
Brewster, Ephraim	2	2	3	....	....
Bugbee, Abel	3	3	5	....	....
Burch, Benjamin	2	3	5	....	....
Burk, Ebid	2	1	2	....	....
Call, Ebenezer	1	2	3	....	....
Call, John	1	2	2	....	....
Carpenter, Rufus	1	2	5	....	....
Chapin, Pelatiah	1	....	2	....	....
Church, Edward	1	3	3	....	....
Churchill, Ichabod	3	2	6	....	....
Churchill, Joseph	2	3	5	....	....
Claflin, Ephraim	1	....	2	....	....
WOODSTOCK TOWN—con.					
Claflin, Timothy	2	....	2	....	....
Clark, Josiah	2	3	4	....	....
Cleaveland, Edward	1	3	3	....	....
Cobb, Isaac	1	1	1	....	....
Cobb, Benjamin	1	....	3	....	....
Cobb, Elias	1	1	1	....	....
Cobb, James	1	2	4	....	....
Cobb, Thomas	3	2	4	....	....
Cottle, Jabez	1	4	7	....	....
Cottle, John	1	1	6	....	....
Cottle, Joseph	1	2	3	....	....
Cottle, Nathan	1	....	1	....	....
Cottle, Sylvanus	1	5	4	....	....
Cottle, Warren	1	5	3	....	....
Cox, Daniel	1	2	2	....	....
Cox, Timothy	1	1	4	....	....
Cummins, Israel W	2	1	2	....	....
Damon, George	3	1	6	....	....
Darling, John	1	2	3	....	....
Darling, John	1	3	3	....	....
Darling, Joseph	3	1	5	....	....
Davis, Salmon	1	1	1	....	....
Davis, Simon	1	3	3	....	....
Davis, Simon	2	1	2	....	....
Delano, Amaza	2	2	7	....	....
Delano, Jonathan	1	1	2	....	....
Delano, Stephen	1	4	4	....	....
Dexter, Luning	1	1	6	....	....
Dike, Calvin	1	1	3	....	....
Dike, Ebenezer	1	3	4	....	....
Dimmick, Benjamin	2	1	1	....	....
Dunham, James	1	....	1	....	....
Dunham, Josiah	2	3	4	....	....
Dunham, Simeon	2	....	6	....	....
Dunham, Uriah	....	4	2	....	....
Dutton, Samuel	3	3	3	....	....
Eddy, Ephraim	1	1	4	....	....
Eddy, Thomas	1	2	2	....	....
Ellis, Charles	1	1	1	....	....
Ellis, Charles	2	....	2	....	....
Ellis, Ephraim	1	1	2	....	....
Ellis, John	1	3	2	....	....
Ellis, Samuel	1	1	1	....	....
Ellis, Thomas	2	1	1	....	....
Ellis, Thomas	1	3	5	....	....
Ellis, William	1	2	4	....	....
Emerson, James	1	....	1	....	....
Emerson, James	1	3	4	....	....
Emerson, Abel	2	....	4	....	....
Emmons, Benjamin	2	4	6	....	....
Farnsworth, Jonathan	1	1	3	....	....
Farnsworth, Stephen	2	1	4	....	....
Field, Elijah	2	5	5	....	....
Field, Samuel	1	....	3	....	....
Fletcher, James	1	3	3	....	....
Fletcher, Nathan	3	1	4	....	....
Fowls, Nathan	1	2	3	....	....
Freeman, Samuel	3	1	5	....	....
Fuller, Amasa	1	3	2	....	....
Fuller, Consider	1	3	4	....	....
Fuller, Seth	3	3	3	....	....
Fuller, William	3	2	5	....	....
Goodale, David	1	....	3	....	....
Green, Benjamin	1	....	3	....	....
Hacket, John	1	1	2	....	....
Hammon, Jabez	2	3	6	....	....
Harlon, Lemuel	2	2	3	....	....
Hayes, Abner	1	....	1	....	....
Hayes, John	2	4	3	....	....
Hammon, John	1	....	6	....	....
Hervey, Edmond	1	2	2	....	....
Hervey, Marshall	1	2	2	....	....
Hile, Robert	1	....	4	....	....
Hoisington, Asahel	1	1	2	....	....
Hoisington, Titus V	1	2	1	....	....
Holt, Jacob	1	3	2	....	....
Holt, Uriah	2	....	1	....	....
Houghton, Israel	2	1	5	....	....
Houghton, Taylor I	1	1	2	....	....
Horwood, James	2	....	3	....	....
Howard, Benjamn	1	....	3	....	....
Howland, Nathan	1	1	2	....	....
Howland, Seth	1	....	1	....	....
Hurlbutt, John	2	2	3	....	....
Inglish, Joel	1	2	1	....	....
Killam, Nathaniel	2	6	5	....	....
Kindall, Abraham	2	2	4	....	....
Kindall, Isaac	1	2	1	....	....
Kindall, Jacob	1	....	2	....	....
King, Jabez	1	1	2	....	....
WOODSTOCK TOWN—con.					
Kingsley, Ebenezer	1	4	3	....	....
Kingsley, Jonathan	2	....	1	....	....
Kingsley, Jonathan	1	4	3	....	....
Knoutton, Robert	1	4	2	....	....
Knox, Timothy	2	2	6	....	....
Ladd, Nathaniel	1	3	4	....	....
Lake, George	1	4	5	....	....
Lamb, Josiah	2	1	2	....	....
Lamphire, Luke	1	3	3	....	....
Lord, Elisha	2	....	3	....	....
Lucus, Confidence	1	1	1	....	....
Mack, Benjamin	1	2	4	....	....
Mack, David	1	2	2	....	....
Mack, Nehemiah	1	4	2	....	....
Mack, Nehemiah	4	....	2	....	....
McClay, William	1	1	5	....	....
Mason, Benjamin	1	1	2	....	....
Mathews, Arthur	1	....	3	....	....
Mathews, Joel	1	....	2	....	....
Mathews, Jonas	1	2	3	....	....
Mathews, Samuel	1	2	3	....	....
Meachum, Eleazer	2	....	1	....	....
Meachum, Frederick	1	....	4	....	....
Miner, Christopher	1	2	2	....	....
Murch, Charles	1	1	2	....	....
Myrick, Samuel	2	....	5	....	....
Murdock, James	2	1	3	....	....
Niles, Daniel	1	....	1	....	....
Niles, Eliphalet	2	....	2	....	....
Norlon, Elijah	1	1	5	....	....
Nye, Elisha	1	....	1	....	....
Paddock, Gains	1	....	4	....	....
Paine, Abel	1	2	3	....	....
Paddock, Stephen	1	1	1	....	....
Palmer, Ezekiel	2	2	5	....	....
Palmer, Garshom	2	2	4	....	....
Palmer, John	1	....	2	....	....
Palmer, Oliver	1	....	3	....	....
Parker, Eleazer	1	1	5	....	....
Perry, Daniel	1	....	5	....	....
Perry, Ezra	2	1	5	....	....
Perry, James	1	3	4	....	....
Perry, Joseph	1	....	4	....	....
Perry, Silas	1	1	4	....	....
Perkins, Elisha	1	4	6	....	....
Perkins, Nathan	2	1	6	....	....
Phillips, Asa	1	1	2	....	....
Pool, Nathaniel	1	3	5	....	....
Powers, Andrew	1	....	1	....	....
Powers, Abraham	1	....	3	....	....
Powers, Stephen	2	....	4	....	....
Powers, Stephén	1	1	1	....	....
Pratt, John	1	1	1	....	....
Pratt, Joseph	1	3	3	....	....
Ralph, Daniel	3	3	5	....	....
Randalls, Micall	3	....	2	....	....
Randalls, William	2	....	1	....	....
Ransom, Elisha	1	3	4	....	....
Ransom, George	2	2	6	....	....
Ransom, John	2	2	1	....	....
Ransom, Lynde	1	2	1	....	....
Ransom, Richard	6	1	4	....	....
Raymond, John	2	4	3	....	....
Raymond, John	1	1	3	....	....
Raymond, Samuel	1	1	4	....	....
Raymond, Sylvester	1	3	4	....	....
Raymond, William	4	2	3	....	....
Richardson, Israel	1	4	1	....	....
Richardson, Israel	1	1	1	....	....
Richardson, Jason	3	2	5	....	....
Richardson, Leander	1	....	3	....	....
Rise, Elijah	1	2	1	....	....
Root, Thomas	1	2	4	....	....
Russ, Nathan	1	3	3	....	....
Safford, Jesse	1	2	2	....	....
Safford, Joseph	1	....	1	....	....
Safford, Joseph	1	3	2	....	....
Samson, Abisha	1	3	1	....	....
Samson, George	1	....	3	....	....
Samson, Philemon	1	1	2	....	....
Sanderson, Benjamn	2	....	4	....	....
Sanderson, James	3	3	3	....	....
Sanderson, John	1	3	9	....	....
Sanderson, Phinehas	2	4	6	....	....
Simmons, David	1	1	2	....	....
Simons, George	3	1	3	....	....
Shaw, David	1	....	2	....	....
Shaw, James	1	....	1	....	....
Shaw, Lemuel	1	....	1	....	....
Sears Paul	1	....	1	....	....

WINDSOR COUNTY—Continued.

NAME OF HEAD OF FAMILY.	Free white males of 16 years and upward, including heads of families.	Free white males under 16 years.	Free white females, including heads of families.	All other free persons.	Slaves.
WOODSTOCK TOWN—con.					
Shaw, Chrispas	3	1	3	....	....
Slayton, Amasa	1	......	4	....	....
Slayton, Samuel	1	1	5	....	....
Smith, Andrew	1	2	3	....	....
Smith, Benjamin	1	2	1	....	....
Smith, Bariah	3	2	2	....	....
Smith, Jason	1	3	2	....	....
Smith, Stephen	3	......	3	....	....
Stanton, David	1	......	1	....	....
Sterling, Joseph	4	2	3	....	....
Sterling, Sith	2	1	2	....	....
Spooner, Gardiner	1	5	4	....	....
Streater, Daniel	1	2	4	....	....
Strong, John	2	......	2	....	....
Taylor, Amos	1	......	1	....	....
Taylor, Elisha	2	......	2	....	....
Taylor, Robert	1	2	2	....	....
WOODSTOCK TOWN—con.					
Taylor, Silas	1	......	1	....	....
Thomas, Andrew	2	2	3	....	....
Thomas, David	1	2	3	....	....
Thomas, Elias	1	4	3	....	....
Thomas, George	1	2	4	....	....
Thomas, Jonathan	1	......	2	....	....
Thomas, Nathan	1	......	1	....	....
Thomas, Phinehas	1	2	5	....	....
Thomas, Solomon	2	2	4	....	....
Tinkham, Nathan	2	3	3	....	....
Turner, Adam	1	2	3	....	....
Waldo, Daniel	1	......	5	....	....
Warner, Josiah	1	5	1	....	....
Warner, Samuel	1	1	6	....	....
Washburn, James	1	1	3	....	....
Washburn, Seth	3	4	3	....	....
West, Elisha	1	4	4	....	....
WOODSTOCK TOWN—con.					
West, Thomas	1	1	2	....	....
Williams, Oliver	2	2	4	....	....
Williams, Phinehas	3	1	4	....	....
Williams, Roger	1	......	1	....	....
Willis, Edmond	1	......	3	....	....
Willis, William	1	2	4	....	....
Williams, Jesse	6	1	1	1	....
Winslow, Timothy	1	1	2	....	....
Wood, Benjamin	1	1	1	....	....
Wood, Ezra	2	2	1	....	....
Wood, Joshua	1	1	2	....	....
Wood, Nathaniel	1	......	2	....	....
Wood, Nathaniel	1	3	4	....	....
Wood, Nathan	2	......	4	....	....
Wood, Williams	1	3	1	....	....

INDEX

O